Canyon of Dreams

CANYON OF DREAMS

STORIES FROM GRAND CANYON HISTORY

Don Lago

THE UNIVERSITY OF UTAH PRESS

Salt Lake City

Copyright © 2014 by The University of Utah Press. All rights reserved.

 The Defiance House Man colophon is a registered trademark
of the University of Utah Press. It is based on a four-foot-tall
Ancient Puebloan pictograph (late PIII) near Glen Canyon, Utah.

18 17 16 15 14   1 2 3 4 5

LIBRARY OF CONGRESS CATALOGING-IN-PUBLICATION DATA
Lago, Don, 1956-
  Canyon of dreams : stories from Grand Canyon history / Don Lago.
      ages cm
  Includes bibliographical references and index.
  ISBN 978-1-60781-314-9 (pbk.) — ISBN 978-1-60781-315-6 (ebook)
    1. Grand Canyon (Ariz.)—History—Anecdotes. 2. Grand Canyon National Park
(Ariz.)—History—Anecdotes. I. Title.
  F788.L336 2013
  979.132—dc23   2013026909

Cover photo: "Rainbow over Zoroaster." Photo by Soa Curtis-Conde.

An extension of this copyright page begins on page 351.

Printed and bound by Sheridan Books, Inc., Ann Arbor, Michigan.

CONTENTS

ILLUSTRATIONS

ACKNOWLEDGMENTS

Kim Besom, Mike Quinn, and Colleen Hyde of the Grand Canyon National Park Study Collection, and Betty Upchurch of the park library, are always highly knowledgeable and helpful. Karen Greig made an invaluable contribution with her dedicated and resourceful research at the Bancroft Library. Richard Quartaroli of the Cline Library Special Collections at Northern Arizona University shared not just his broad knowledge but his enthusiasm for Grand Canyon history. Earl Spamer and Mike Anderson applied their deep expertise in Grand Canyon history to reviewing this manuscript, but of course all the mistakes belong to me. Mary Williams, the editor of the *Ol' Pioneer*, the magazine of the Grand Canyon Historical Society, shepherded most of these chapters into their original appearance there. John Alley, my editor at the University of Utah Press, is also a good historian of the Colorado River and the Grand Canyon. Freelance editor Alexis Mills made many appreciated improvements with the final copyediting.

The Grand Canyon history community is filled with wonderful people, and those who contributed their knowledge and enthusiasm to this book include Wayne and Helen Ranney, Keith and Nancy Green, Marker Marshall, Drifter Smith, Richard and Sherry Mangum, Eric Berg, Amy Horn, Tom Myers, Tom and Hazel Martin, Stew Fritts, Virginia Martin, and Michael Ghiglieri. Julie Russell's skillful National Park Service interviews about Grand

Canyon history are an invaluable resource. And thanks to Jessica Cadiente of the Flagstaff Public Library for helping to locate research sources.

The Apollo astronaut chapter benefited greatly from the personal responses of astronauts Neil Armstrong, Eugene Cernan, Paul Weitz, Al Worden, Charlie Duke, Bill Pogue, Jack Lousma, and Jerry Carr; scientists Carolyn Shoemaker, Gordon Swann, Gerald Schaber, Don Wilhelms, and Marie Jackson; and historians Andrew Chaikin, James Hansen, Francis French, and Sherry Mangum. At Lowell Observatory Kevin Schindler and Antoinette Beiser were, as always, a great source of knowledge and enthusiasm. For the observatory chapter, thanks to Ronald Florence, Gale Christianson, Dan Lewis, Carolyn Landes, Jan Balsom, Jessica Moy and NOAO/Kitt Peak, and, worth repeating, Antoinette Beiser. For the Egyptian caves chapter: Keven McQueen, Marshall Trimble, Chris Reid, John Schwegman, and Brian Butler. For the China chapter: Marilyn Sounders and Charlotte Rees. For the Brighty chapter: David Pimental. For the Roger Miller chapter: Glenda West, Mary Miller, Mike Verkamp, Steve Verkamp, Susan Verkamp, Don Cusic, Al Richmond, Mike Anderson, Lyle Style, Al Trammell, Bob Kemp, Eagle Jones, Lowell Fay, Sam Turner, and Mrs. Tram Bowman. For the dog story: David Stratton and Harry Butowsky. For the Hearst chapter: David Nasaw, Peter Runge, Susan Snyder, Mark Renovitch, and especially Karen Greig. For the Henry Miller chapter: Barbara Stuhlmann and Steve Verkamp. For the American writers chapter: Miriam Farris and Christine Colburn. For the British writers chapter: Alison Cullingford, Adam Nicolson, and Juliet Nicolson. For the John Hance chapter: John Bradbury of the Western Historical Manuscript Collection at Missouri University of Science and Technology, Mike Mauer, Glenda Williams Dickman, Mary Taylor, Marguerite Mason, Shirley Brinkman, Joanne Brady, Martha Bennett, Joyce Heiss, Danette Welch, Laura Hinchey, Shane Murphy, and Richard Mangum. For the yellow brick road: Norm and Betty Roller, Amy Horn, and Hank Ottinger. And for the beautiful cover photo, which reflects their decades of exploring the canyon: Alfredo Conde and Sheri Curtis.

INTRODUCTION

Powerful landscapes have always held great power over the human mind.

The geological forces that have pushed and folded and eroded the earth into mountains, volcanoes, rivers, and canyons have also folded the human mind into wonder, into questions and answers about the origins of our lives. Humans have filled mountaintops with the gods who created us. We have filled volcanoes and oceans with monsters that threaten our lives. We have also filled nature with our own human heroes, with Odysseus and Jason, who went on quests that won victories for order over chaos, for life over death.

The Grand Canyon, too, has been a magnet and catalyst for the human imagination, for ultimate questions.

The first humans who encountered the Grand Canyon had seen many other canyons, but they must have recognized that the Grand Canyon was something far beyond all others. For the Hopis and Zunis, who live a long way from the Grand Canyon, it is their place of emergence into this world. One of the Hopis' central hero stories is that of Tiyo, who rode in a hollow log down the Colorado River, through the Grand Canyon, enabling him to meet the Snake People, who gave the Hopis the secrets of bringing rain. The Hopis believe that their dead return to the Grand Canyon to emerge into the afterlife.

For Europeans, even after they had been settling the North American continent for three centuries, the Grand Canyon came as a shock. The nature they were familiar with held mountains and gorges, but not sharp, deep canyons. It held forests and pastures, but not deserts of naked stone, empty of life and greenness. Nature held great rivers that provided humans with water and transportation, but not great rivers that were inaccessible and blockaded with rocks and rapids. The Grand Canyon's shapes and colors were a violation of European ideas of beauty. Among the first tourists, and especially the first writers and poets to see the canyon, there was a vigorous debate about how to react to the Grand Canyon and to the rest of the desert Southwest. Were they beautiful or ugly? Was it an image of heaven or hell? Was it proof of the existence of God, or of the mindlessness of nature?

One of the first Euro-Americans to explore the Grand Canyon region seems to have felt the ancient human impulse to place gods upon prominent landscapes. Clarence Dutton was a secular-minded geologist, but he felt that only mythic names could do justice to the canyon's grandeur. He gave its inner buttes names like Buddha Temple, Zoroaster Temple, Shiva Temple, and Vulcan's Throne. Other geographers followed Dutton's example, and thus today the canyon is full of mythological names, including those with Native American origins. Dutton saved the Grand Canyon from the fate of so many other American landscapes that were named for the first pioneer to arrive at a place, or to die there, or to have his horse stolen there. And Dutton was right: the Grand Canyon is a mythic place that has continued to stir deep human yearnings.

Euro-Americans also filled the canyon with their own hero myths. Some of them were real men, like John Wesley Powell, whose life-and-death struggle down the Colorado River in 1869 offered many of the elements of the quests of Tiyo or Odysseus, a brave triumph over chaos for the sake of human enlightenment. Other heroes were imaginary, born from tall tales like those told by John Hance, the canyon's first white settler.

The stories in this book are diverse, but they share one larger theme: they are about how the Grand Canyon has stirred the human imagination, in many forms. The canyon has stirred scientists to become irrational, and believers in the esoteric to see grand meanings. It has inspired some Americans to pursue the national dream of conquering the wilderness, and others to oppose them with a dream of shared, preserved natural beauty. It has stirred writers and songwriters to create American classics, and both average tourists and famous poets to ponder ultimate realities. It has stirred famous nature writers to discover nature anew, and ordinary people to feel and think deeply, confront themselves, and change their lives.

One of the guiding myths of science is that scientists are supposed to be dispassionate servants of facts, but of course most of them are driven by a passion for the subjects they love. It takes a lot of passion for geologists to climb all over the Grand Canyon looking for rocks. It also took some imagination for geologists to name canyon features after mythological figures and places; there's even a Camelot section in the canyon, featuring King Arthur Castle, Merlin Abyss, and Lancelot Point.

At the start of the twentieth century everyone in the world of astronomy knew that George Ritchey had plenty of imagination, but it was technological imagination: Ritchey had solved some of the toughest problems in building the greatest telescopes of the age. Yet his imagination took an odd turn when he decided that his next telescope, the world's greatest by far, should be located on the rim of the Grand Canyon. It was not just imagination, it was obsession, for there were good scientific reasons why the rim of the Grand Canyon was a terrible place for a telescope. But Ritchey seems to have been captured by the canyon's grandeur, its revelation of the greatest depths of nature and time. Thirty-five years later the Apollo astronauts, who were training for their flights to the moon, took a curious detour by hiking to the bottom of the Grand Canyon, which didn't hold any of the types of rocks they would find on the moon, but did offer plenty of inspiration.

If astronomers and astronauts can do odd things in the grip of the Grand Canyon, then there may be little hope for those who are already living comfortably in the esoteric universe. Today New Age books, websites, and radio shows are constructing a rich lore about how the ancient Egyptians inhabited the Grand Canyon and left a cave full of tombs and treasures and occult secrets. This idea arose from one hoax newspaper article published a century ago, and mostly forgotten since. For those who prefer the esoteric with an oriental flavor, a similar tradition claims that the ancient Chinese discovered the Grand Canyon and used it for occult purposes. Unlike the humble origins of the Egyptian story, the Chinese story was started by some of the greatest scholars of their age. These esoteric visions of the Grand Canyon may be quite different from the visions of astronomers or geologists, but at least the occultists have the right idea, that the Grand Canyon is the perfect place to search for the deepest secrets of reality.

One of the largest dreams that has been played out in Grand Canyon history is the American dream of conquering a vast, wild continent and turning it into personal and national wealth and power. The first Europeans to encounter the Grand Canyon were Spanish conquistadors searching for the seven cities of gold that existed only in their dreams. The first Americans to explore the canyon on foot were prospectors searching for minerals. Today many tourists see the canyon not as geology but as a proud theater for a western saga of explorers and pioneers and cowboys; when looking into the canyon, they are most excited to see human trails and rafts and mule trains.

This national dream has proven to be a major obstacle for those who value the canyon for its geology, wilderness, scenic beauty, and glimpse of the cosmic. It took nearly half a century after Yellowstone became the first national park for the Grand Canyon to earn similar protection, thanks to the staunch opposition of Arizona's political leaders, who viewed the land as a treasure chest for private gain. Two decades later, the National Park Service was still waging epic battles to gain control of private lands inside park boundaries. Two of those battles are detailed in this book. Both of them involved powerful men who invoked the national dream of wilderness conquest to fight against the idea of national parks, of preserving wilderness. Both battles reached into the White House. In one the protagonist was newspaper baron William Randolph Hearst. At the same time that Orson Welles was turning Hearst's Faustian strivings into the movie *Citizen Kane*, Hearst was acting out Kane's story at the Grand Canyon. If there is anywhere on Earth that should be a refuge from human egos and politics, it should be primordial natural wonders like the Grand Canyon and the other national parks. Yet sometimes the canyon only magnified human egos.

The frontier myth has also generated some more innocent expressions in popular culture. One of these was Marguerite Henry's now-classic novel *Brighty of the Grand Canyon*. Brighty's story is a good illustration of how easily history gets forgotten, for Brighty would have been if not for Henry's chance discovery of his story in a small Illinois public library. Like Brighty's story, most of the stories in this book were forgotten or never chronicled. But Brighty's novel also serves as a lesson in how history gets rewritten. The realities behind the novel, both historical and ecological, were considerably less innocent than the fictional story.

One element of the frontier myth that appeals deeply to Americans is the idea of the open road, of moving onward to new horizons, new adventures, and better opportunities. One classic expression of this yearning is the song "King of the Road." When Roger Miller wrote it, he was drawing upon his own experience of the open road the summer he left home and traveled west on Route 66 to the Grand Canyon, where he spent the summer singing cowboy songs and living in a "trailer for rent" that he paid for by "two hours of pushin' broom."

Along with pop culture, the Grand Canyon has generated quite a bit of energy in intellectual and literary circles. The first years of Grand Canyon tourism—which began in earnest in 1901 when the Atchison, Topeka, and Santa Fe Railway reached the rim—were also years of scientific revolution. As the world was still trying to come to terms with Darwin's theory of biological evolution, geologists were adding their vision of deep time and powerful, ancient, inhuman forces; physicists were adding their vision of atomic worlds within worlds; and astronomers were adding their vision of a vast cosmos full of beauty but also violence. Intellectuals were trying to figure out the meanings of this bold new universe, whether it was ruled by order or chaos, benevolence or evil, God or nature—or nothingness. For many visitors the Grand Canyon quickly became a Rorschach test in the midst of uncertainty and debate. In 1901, when the canyon was still clashing with people's cultural expectations about natural beauty, it was far more of an undefined entity than it is today. People looking into its depths often felt great confusion and saw very different things: a generous and powerful God, an orderly nature, or an existential abyss. Even average tourists pondered these questions, as we will see in a chapter devoted to the comments they wrote in the public journals of El Tovar Hotel.

More sophisticated visions came from the poets who visited and pondered the canyon. They were led by Harriet Monroe, who would found *Poetry* magazine and mentor the modernist revolution in poetry. Monroe had a troubling, existential vision of the Grand Canyon, but in spite of that she fell in love with it and returned often. Her circle of poets knew about her interest, and this encouraged them to write Grand Canyon poems. These poets, which included Carl Sandburg and Edgar Lee Masters, used the canyon to test the ultimate nature of reality and to search for God or other meanings.

The Grand Canyon also attracted America's leading nature writers, who were not inclined to feel existential doubt before nature, but to find order and beauty and meaning. Yet even for John Muir and John Burroughs the Grand Canyon brought confusion, as it was very unlike the nature they knew and loved. The Grand Canyon and the rest of the desert Southwest forced writers to look at nature anew, and a few of them, including John C. Van Dyke and Mary Austin, rose to the challenge. The Grand Canyon was also visited by some prominent British novelists and playwrights, who brought their personal and national experience to the canyon.

The American novelist Henry Miller wanted to be a European and, after finding a home in Paris, thought he had rejected America for good. But with the outbreak of World War II, Miller was forced to flee Europe. In his youth he had fallen in love with the American Southwest, and now a visit to the Grand Canyon helped him decide that he could not only make America his home, he could live in a wilderness utterly different from Paris.

The "writer" who knew the canyon best, however, was John Hance, who showed plenty of creativity in taking the American tradition of the tall tale and stretching it to do justice to a very tall landscape. Hance also told quite a few tales about his own life, which has left his origins and personal history obscure until now. Hance also inspired the final coda chapter of this book, a personal inquiry into the mysteries and meanings of history, and how even a very small thing can embody the hopes and motions of a nation.

All of the stories in this book are original, resulting from new research. Grand Canyon history books tend to follow well-trod paths, which do offer plenty of great stories, like those of John Wesley Powell, the Kolb brothers, Mary Colter, and the Harvey Girls. But Grand Canyon history is a rich lode, and many great stories have barely been noticed or have remained entirely unknown. For me, pursuing these stories was another instance in which the Grand Canyon has reached out and stirred the human imagination to come up with answers.

All of these chapters were originally published in slightly different form in *Ol' Pioneer*, the magazine of the Grand Canyon Historical Society, which also sponsors an occasional history symposium at the canyon.

THAT'S ONE SMALL STEP...
IN THE GRAND CANYON

The Apollo Astronauts Hike to the Moon

When Neil Armstrong climbed down the ladder of the *Eagle* and took the first step on the moon, the footprint he made there included the thousands of footsteps he had taken into the Grand Canyon. When he picked up the first moon rock, he saw it with insights he had picked up in the Grand Canyon.

Five years earlier, in March 1964, the crew of Apollo 11—Neil Armstrong, Buzz Aldrin, and Michael Collins—had spent two days hiking to the bottom of the Grand Canyon and back up. They were part of the first of three groups of astronauts to make this hike. All but one of the twenty-four astronauts who journeyed to the moon hiked into the canyon.

The March 1964 hike was the first event in a new NASA program to train the astronauts in geology and, it was hoped, to inspire them in that pursuit. When the astronauts were first told that they would need to study geology, many were openly hostile to the idea.

When President John F. Kennedy stood before a joint session of Congress on May 25, 1961, and committed the nation to going to the moon, he did not say anything about going to the moon to study geology. Everyone understood that Americans were going to the moon as an assertion of national pride, which had been deeply wounded by the Soviet launch of Sputnik in

1957, and again when Soviet cosmonaut Yuri Gargarin became the first human in space on April 12, 1961. A central element of American national identity was belief in American superiority in matters of exploration and technology; this technological superiority was offered as proof of the superiority of the democratic system. By this standard, the Soviets now had the right to claim that their system was superior. Kennedy's speech, delivered only six weeks after Gagarin's flight, placed the moon goal almost entirely within the context of proving national superiority: "If we are to win the battle that is going on around the world between freedom and tyranny, if we are to win the battle for men's minds.... No single space project in this period will be more impressive to mankind...."[1]

Privately, Kennedy had been alarmed by the audacity of the moon goal, and he'd asked his advisors if there were some other—and cheaper—technological goal by which the United States might prove its superiority. No one could assure Kennedy that a moon landing was even possible, but it did appeal to Kennedy's personal taste for adventure and bravado; five years later a similar bravado would lead his brother, Senator Robert Kennedy, to ignore the strong warnings of his raft guide and jump into the Colorado River in the Grand Canyon and swim through a dangerous rapid. President Kennedy did recognize the importance to the American psyche of exploration and the frontier. He called his administration "the New Frontier," which invoked the glamour of the space frontier. But in the American psyche, exploration was more about national destiny than science.

The military pilots who responded to America's call for astronauts felt the importance of national pride, technological superiority, and exploration of new frontiers. They did not necessarily feel the call of geology. The astronauts were the knights of the "Right Stuff," the daring masters of the most roaring, soaring, cutting-edge technology. Collecting rocks was for nerds.

Besides, in the first years of America's space program the astronauts were seriously preoccupied with matters of life and death. They needed to learn how to fly new, complicated, dangerous spacecraft, how to respond to a thousand emergencies that could ruin a mission or result in their death. They had to train for survival in case their capsules crashed in remote deserts or jungles or seas. They helped design and test spacecraft and other equipment. The astronauts didn't have enough time for the necessary life-or-death training.

If they crash landed on the moon, the mineral composition of the rocks wouldn't matter—they would be just as dead.

While the astronauts were preoccupied with the piloting challenge, much of the rest of NASA viewed the Apollo program as an engineering challenge. Tens of thousands of engineers, under pressure from deadlines and budgets, had to come up with new ideas and materials and designs—and test them. Hundreds of thousands of components had to be integrated perfectly, and any one component might mean the difference between success or failure, life or death. For the engineers the whole point of Apollo was to build a successful machine. The astronauts were there to prove that it was a successful machine. It hardly mattered what the astronauts did when they got to the moon. The first designs for the Apollo spacecraft made no allowances for space or weight for taking scientific instruments to the moon or for bringing moon rocks back to Earth. It was nearly a year after President Kennedy's speech that NASA convened a meeting to consider what kind of science the astronauts should do on the moon.

For geologists, the Apollo program would be one of the greatest opportunities in the history of science. Humans had always wondered about the moon, and now they would finally have a chance to examine it. For decades scientists had debated the moon's composition and how it had formed. They had debated what the moon said about the formation of Earth and the solar system. They had debated whether lunar craters were formed by volcanic eruptions or by asteroid impacts. Other scientists felt that the geologists and their moon theories were presumptuous, for the moon did not belong to the realm of geology, it belonged to the realm of astronomy, which couldn't determine much about distant rocks.

Even after President Kennedy propelled humans toward the moon, geologists remained a small and relatively powerless part of the Apollo program. They had to push hard and long to get geology taken seriously, to obtain NASA funding and facilities and astronaut time and engineering planning. At least it seemed obvious to NASA that after all the effort and money spent to get astronauts to the moon, they shouldn't leave without taking a look around. And geology could turn out to be a matter of life or death. Cornell University astronomer Thomas Gold had theorized that the lunar surface consisted of a thick layer of fluffy dust, into which a landing spacecraft might sink and disappear. Other scientists wondered if the lunar dust might prove explosive when exposed to oxygen from the lunar lander. Few geologists took these ideas seriously, but NASA couldn't afford to ignore such possibilities. It was October 1963 before NASA made an official commitment to include geology on Apollo, but still there were no promises about what this would involve.

NASA assigned the U.S. Geological Survey (USGS) the job of training the astronauts. At first this consisted mainly of classroom lectures—fifty-eight hours' worth. The astronauts became restless, partly because they were busy training for the Gemini program, an intermediate step between the Mercury and Apollo programs that would not go to the moon. Yet the geologists had already discovered that the astronauts became much more interested in geology if it was taught in the real world.

In January 1963, geologist Eugene Shoemaker had made a trial run at the training by taking nine astronauts—including Neil Armstrong—to Meteor Crater in northern Arizona. It had been only two years since Shoemaker and his colleagues at Cal Tech had proven that Meteor Crater was indeed the result of a cosmic impact and not volcanic action. Meteor Crater was the best-preserved impact crater on Earth and a natural classroom for showing astronauts the craters they would encounter on the moon. A few dozen miles west of Meteor Crater was a volcanic range that included six hundred dead volcanoes of various kinds, and they offered another natural classroom for learning about the volcanic features on the moon. In the center of this volcanic range was the town of Flagstaff, where astronomers at Lowell Observatory, proud of their discovery of Pluto, had spent decades studying the planets and moons while most other astronomers had been preoccupied with stars and cosmology. An hour north of Flagstaff was the Grand Canyon, the best display of sedimentary strata on Earth. Shoemaker decided to base the Apollo geology program in Flagstaff, mainly because of all the nearby assets for hands-on preparation for the moon. Shoemaker had many other responsibilities, including preparing maps and tools and cameras and surface instruments for the moon landing, and planning and supervising the actual lunar fieldwork, so he turned over most of the astronaut training to other geologists. He placed in charge Dale Jackson, a former U.S. Marine and veteran of the battle of Iwo Jima; Shoemaker hoped he would hit it off with the astronauts, knock the right stuffiness out of them, and cure them of their stereotypes that geologists were nerds.

The geologists decided to kick off astronaut training with a hike into the Grand Canyon. The Grand Canyon could teach some of the basic principles of geology, especially stratigraphy—the idea that older rocks are lower down. The canyon could teach that erosion and faulting could alter original, orderly strata. It contained all the basic types of rocks. The canyon could teach geological map reading, high-altitude photograph recognition, and long-distance descriptive accuracy. This latter skill became more important as the Apollo missions went on, as they went from landing in the blandest landscapes to landing amid mountains and valleys. Apollo 15 landed right next to a deep, sinuous valley called Hadley Rille, which the astronauts needed to look across and along and describe accurately, a skill they had practiced at the canyon of the Little Colorado River near the Grand Canyon.

Yet the Grand Canyon was also an unlikely place to learn about the moon. It was made of sedimentary rocks, and no one was expecting to find sedimentary rocks on the moon. The canyon held ocean-deposited limestone full of fossils, sandstone piled up by winds, and it had been carved by a powerful river. No one expected to find oceans or wind or rivers or limestone or fossils on the moon. To teach the astronauts about stratigraphy, it would have been easier to go to a road cut on the interstate highway than to spend two days hiking in and out of the Grand Canyon.

But the geologists did have other motives for selecting the canyon as their first training event. They wanted grandeur, the most impressive on Earth. They wanted to inspire the astronauts with the power and beauty of geological forces. They wanted to make the point that doing geology was a great adventure worthy of macho astronauts. Elbert King, one of the geologists who went on the canyon hikes, explained: "In addition, the Grand Canyon is such a scenic place that we hoped to get even the most reluctant astronaut students 'hooked' on the charisma of geology and field work."[2] With so much NASA inertia and resistance working against geology, the geologists needed to get the astronauts on their side.

The geologists also wanted to prove that it was indeed possible to do realistic and valuable training for the lunar surface. For the scientists who scoffed at the idea of "astrogeology" (the term the Apollo geologists had chosen for their field), the geologists were glad to show that this was not only a legitimate field but one that now had the power and prestige of NASA behind it.

The geologists planned to spend a day taking the astronauts down the South Kaibab Trail. They would separate into groups of two or three astronauts led by one geologist. They'd spend the night at Phantom Ranch and hike up the Bright Angel Trail to Indian Garden, about halfway up, and from there the astronauts could ride mules the rest of the way. The astronauts were divided into two groups: some would do the trip on March 5–6 and the others on March 12–13, 1964. The first hike included eighteen astronauts, two—Alan Shepard and Scott Carpenter—from the original seven Mercury astronauts, two—Neil Armstrong and Elliot See—from the second group of astronauts, plus all of the third group. The second hike included ten astronauts, four of them Mercury astronauts—Gus Grissom, Wally Schirra, Gordon Cooper, and Deke Slayton—plus the rest of the second group. Two years later, on June 2–3, 1966, eighteen astronauts from the fourth and fifth groups hiked into the canyon.

Some of the geologist-instructors were not sufficiently familiar with the canyon, so they did their own training hike on February 27–28 led by Eddie McKee. Then with the USGS, McKee had been a longtime Grand Canyon National Park ranger-naturalist, had done important geological field research there, and was organizing a major conference on Grand Canyon geology for later that year.

We are fortunate that the 1964 hikes were covered in detail by William Hoyt of the Flagstaff newspaper, the *Arizona Daily Sun.* Hoyt was very enthusiastic about astronomy and space exploration, and he would soon start a career as an astronomy historian, writing important books about Percival Lowell and Mars, the discovery of Pluto, and the long controversies about the origin of Meteor Crater. Hoyt covered the astronaut hikes better than any other newspaper or magazine. The coverage in the Phoenix newspaper, the *Arizona Republic,* was more in the spirit of celebrity gossip. Unfortunately, Hoyt left the Flagstaff newspaper in 1966, and the newspaper offered no coverage of that year's astronaut hike, mainly because NASA did not invite any reporters.

The first hike included six of the twelve astronauts who would later walk on the moon: Neil Armstrong, Buzz Aldrin, Alan Bean, Eugene Cernan, Dave

Scott, and Alan Shepard. It also included three astronauts who would orbit the moon: Michael Collins, William Anders, and Dick Gordon.

The astronauts were supposed to land at Red Butte, the airport nearest to the Grand Canyon, but a snowstorm left its dirt runway too muddy, so they landed in Flagstaff instead. They arrived in two planes, one of them a scheduled Frontier Airlines flight, a precaution against an accident wiping out most of the astronaut corps. About thirty local officials and residents greeted them. The public and press were mainly interested in Alan Shepard and Scott Carpenter, the only astronauts on this hike who had already flown in space. The first Gemini mission was still a year in the future, and the Phoenix newspaper wouldn't even call the others "astronauts," only "new trainees." Most of the astronauts quickly gathered their luggage and climbed onto a bus, but Shepard and Carpenter took twenty minutes to extract themselves from the attention of the local officials, who required greetings and autographs and photo poses.

"All were dressed," William Hoyt reported, "in unmarked jackets and slacks and their luggage consisted of loaded backpacking gear for their hike into the Canyon. Carpenter, the target of more than a dozen young autograph seekers on hand at the airport, was dressed…in blue denim jacket and pants."[3] The astronauts had to provide their own boots, some of which were ill-suited for a Grand Canyon hike. Carpenter wore white tennis shoes on the hike.

The astronauts headed for the South Rim and the Yavapai geology museum, where Eddie McKee greeted them and gave them an hour-long orientation using a large relief map of the Grand Canyon to illustrate his points.

At 11 a.m. the astronauts started down the trail at five-minute intervals. At least they didn't need to worry about heat; the temperature when they started out was a bit above freezing. The Phoenix newspaper reported that "Jay Goza, chief wrangler for the Grand Canyon mules, said 'I hope they aren't afraid of high places.' Shepard assured Goza that they were not."[4]

Each astronaut was provided with an aerial photograph of the canyon so that they could try matching its features with the landscape they saw before them, a skill that might prove useful when trying to recognize a planned landing site on the moon, or if they landed in the wrong place and needed to figure out where they really were—which would indeed happen on Apollo 11.

The hikers stopped frequently so that the geologists could point out types of rocks or large landscape features, or talk about geological principles. They all carried rock hammers and had permission from the National Park Service (NPS) to chip off rocks. The geologists tested their "students" with questions, and they were impressed by how fast and how well the astronauts were learning. The astronauts also practiced taking field notes.

The hike took most of the day, and they arrived at Phantom Ranch fairly late. When the hypercompetitive Alan Shepard got within a hundred yards of the guest cabins, he challenged NASA public affairs officer Paul Haney to a race, and Shepard won by a yard. Ranch manager Ben Clark reported that they arrived "real good, with nobody crippled up from hiking. But they were very hungry, believe me." The hikers feasted on "a hefty amount" of roast beef, mashed potatoes, carrots and peas, cake and coffee. "They were pretty serious young men," reported Clark, "and very nice, and they seemed to enjoy the Canyon very much. Both Astronaut Shepard and Astronaut Carpenter were particularly enthusiastic about the Canyon."[5]

This comment about Alan Shepard didn't reveal that Shepard was and would remain one of the most antigeology astronauts. He may have enjoyed the hike for the adventure of it, but the canyon didn't inspire him about geology. Some geologists would blame Shepard's lack of enthusiasm and preparation for his failure to locate the crater that was the main objective of one of his Apollo 14 moonwalks.

Yet for other astronauts, the Grand Canyon worked its magic. Apollo 11's Buzz Aldrin wrote:

> There was a tendency among most of us, myself included, to regard the training rather disdainfully, like going to camp. It didn't take long, however, before I was a willing convert, especially to the many geology field trips....
>
> Geology opened my eyes to the immensity of time when one day I found myself standing at the bottom of the Grand Canyon paying rapt attention as the instructor talked about things that took place eons before man existed on this earth.[6]

Apollo 11's Michael Collins recalled:

> Our first geology trip was to the Grand Canyon and was one of the most interesting, partly because it was the first trip and partly because

of the natural beauty and awesome grandeur of the place. Of course, the idea was to give us an opportunity to augment our classroom knowledge with field experience, to see not just a half-pound chunk of 801 on a desk top, but miles of it clearly delineated in a horizontal bed…. About a dozen different rock formations have been exposed as the Colorado River cuts ever deeper into the Arizona desert, crashing along nearly a mile below the rim…. As we descended the south rim along the famous Kaibab Trail, we examined and recorded ("hypidiomorphic granular") each succeeding layer of rock, passing from the upstart limestones and sandstones through the older shales and finally, near the bottom, discovering very old rock, the tortured and baked Vishnu schist, over two billion years old. The flaw in all this was that…the rocks we saw were sedimentary types, having been water-deposited, and many contained fossil plants and animals, including shark teeth. Of course in 1964 no one knew what rock types awaited us on the moon, but no reputable scientists believed we would find sedimentary rock there…. In fact, we used to joke about carrying a few fossils to the moon to mix in with the lunar rock samples, and I am surprised that no lunar crew has announced the discovery of a fossil or two on the radio, just to shake up the geologists in Mission Control.

Nevertheless, it was a beautiful trip down in the Grand Canyon…we relaxed and chipped rocks with our hammers, enjoyed the magnificent scenery, and wondered at the changing world we were entering…. I confess that on this trip—indeed all geology trips—I found the flora and fauna much more interesting than the rocks. Some in our group, like Roger Chaffee, were becoming damned good geologists, perhaps because they truly enjoyed it or perhaps simply because they were quick studies. However, I never quite did get into the spirit of the thing, and spent as much time engaging in rock-throwing contests with Gene Cernan as I did filling my field notebook with maps of outcrops and such.

Our trip down into the canyon took nearly the whole day, so we spent the night in a charming inn at the bottom, and the next morning those of us who wanted to rented burros for an expedited ascent. I chose to ride, but picked an animal which stopped walking whenever I stopped kicking, so I got as much exercise as if I had been afoot. I also had plenty of time to contemplate the rapid pace at which I was

speeding toward the moon. From supersonic jets at Edwards, I had pro-
gressed all the way to kicking a burro up out of the Grand Canyon. Just
as the jets had their tricks, so did this creature.... I certainly was willing
to share my burro with a deserving scientist or two, provided they did
their share of kicking and I got to steer.[7]

Ten of the eighteen astronauts on the hike had visited the Grand Canyon
previously, as tourists, but only two of them had hiked into it. One was Neil
Armstrong. In 1952 Armstrong returned to the United States from air combat duty in Korea and had a period of military leave. Earlier that year he had
paid $2,000 cash for his first car, a new two-door Oldsmobile 88, the same
model his father owned. Neil's brother Dean traveled from Ohio to California to join him, and they went on a long road trip that stretched from Canada
to Mexico and included ten national parks. They camped most of the time.
At the Grand Canyon they hiked to the bottom and back out. This hike may
have been the highlight of their adventure. Armstrong probably was remembering that hike during astronaut training. He did feel the charisma of the
canyon and of rocks, and became one of the most eager geology students.
Apollo historian Andrew Chaikin said:

> For years, the geologists had the feeling that Armstrong was genuinely
> interested, and that he was picking up more than most of the other
> pilots; Armstrong turned in an excellent performance on the moon. In
> the postflight briefings he was full of detailed comments on what he
> had seen, and he made clear the potential for a scientific observer on
> the moon.[8]

I was told this again in a conversation with Gordon Swann, one of the
leaders of the geology training. He wasn't on the 1964 hikes but did conduct
briefings with Armstrong. Swann said that Armstrong was more motivated
and perceptive than most of the astronauts, and Swann wished that Apollo
11 had been able to spend more time on the moon so that Armstrong could
have done more geology.

In response to my inquiry, Neil Armstrong responded with an e-mail recollection of his Grand Canyon hike:

Neil Armstrong riding up the Bright Angel Trail, March 6, 1964. *(Courtesy of the U.S. Geological Survey)*

I do remember the trip (it was my second trip to the bottom), staying at the lodge at the bottom, riding out the Bright Angel trail on mules (I walked out the first time), and studying the stratigraphy.... I thought all the "students" in the geology field trips took the opportunity of making it a true learning experience. They recognized that their proficiency in this subject (generally not previously known to them) might have an influence on their Apollo assignments. As for myself, I found the geophysics more akin to my engineering background than the geology. Although I enjoyed the geology, I never had a "passion" for it and, consequently, never considered myself a real geologist.[9]

Armstrong did recognize his mount to be a mule and not a burro. Yet Armstrong may have shared Michael Collins's musings about the dubious trajectory of his career, from super jets to cranky mules. There is a photo of Armstrong riding his mule out of the canyon, and he does not appear to be very inspired.

Armstrong would be inspired by the moon. Shortly after climbing onto the lunar surface he commented, "It has a stark beauty all its own. It's like much of the high desert of the United States. It's different, but it's very pretty out here."[10] Armstrong may have been thinking of his experiences in Arizona.

Also on the hike was Eugene Cernan, who would be the commander of Apollo 17 and the last man on the moon. To my inquiry, Cernan answered:

> The intent was to walk through the millennium of time that was exposed in the walls of the Grand Canyon from top to bottom where the Colorado River now flows to get a better understanding not just about geology or the geologic times that were evident, but as well to get a feeling for the enormous impact of nature.... It was a day-long trip from top to bottom and back up to the top again. What I remember very vividly is that all of us in the group walked down to the River and most of us, but not all, walked all the way up. Those who didn't, chose to ride on the back of a burro. Those who chose to walk up were probably the more competitive of our group. Although I couldn't tell you by name who they were, but yes, I was one of them.[11]

Another astronaut on the hike was Alan Bean, who walked on the moon on Apollo 12 and who later became a full-time painter of scenes from the Apollo missions, including a few of astronauts doing geology on the moon. In 1998 Bean and Andrew Chaikin published a book about Bean's art, and in the introduction John Glenn (who wasn't on the Grand Canyon hike, having retired from the astronaut corps to run for the U.S. Senate) compared Bean with Thomas Moran. Moran's 1870s paintings of Yellowstone and the Grand Canyon had given Americans their first visions of the great landscapes of the West. Alan Bean would inspire Earthlings about the moon.

But Bean needed the Grand Canyon to help inspire him about geology. Chaikin wrote:

> The future lunar explorers were expected to learn geology. That meant hours of difficult lectures and laboratory exercises on subjects such as rock and mineral classification. Strange as it may seem, Bean had never heard of terms like "aphanitic vesicular basalt" or "plagioclase feldspar phenocryst." Now he was expected to make them part of his working

vocabulary. But there was good news, too: field trips to spectacular places like the Grand Canyon, where a billion years of history were written in layers of rock.[12]

The astronaut who became most devoted to geology was Dave Scott; his enthusiasm helped motivate his fellow Apollo 15 crew members, Jim Irwin and Al Worden, to take geology seriously. They needed to do so, for their mission was the first with a multiday stay on the moon, a lunar rover for more extensive travel, and nearly twenty hours for science on the ground. When NASA planners were debating where Apollo 15 should land, Scott argued for a more difficult landing site, Hadley Rille, because it offered the best geology. When the HBO miniseries *From the Earth to the Moon* devoted one episode to lunar geology, it was centered on Dave Scott.

Scott was on the first Grand Canyon hike. Andrew Chaikin wrote:

> Early on, Scott had shown more enthusiasm for geology than most of the pilots. He'd long harbored an interest in archaeology; as a fighter pilot stationed in Tripoli he'd visited the ruins of Roman cities in the Libyan desert. When the astronauts hiked into the Grand Canyon...Scott saw nearly two billion years of history written in twisted metamorphic rocks and perfectly exposed strata of limestone, sandstone, and shale. For the first time he understood what it meant to talk about *geologic* time, in which millennia are reduced to moments. And each outing brought new spectaculars.... At his home in El Lago [Texas], Scott proudly displayed his rock collection in a specially made wooden cabinet.[13]

Scott's wife began taking a college class in geology so she could share his interest. Scott became very frustrated at the lack of interest among NASA managers. He had to argue strenuously to get them to include on his mission a light aluminum geology rake and a telephoto lens for taking high-resolution photos of features too far away to visit. One small tool Scott took to the moon was a hand lens he borrowed from Gordon Swann. Swann told me that a year after Apollo 15 Scott came through Arizona and took his family to see the Grand Canyon, and afterward Scott came through Flagstaff and returned Swann's hand lens, now in a shopping bag from the canyon's Verkamp's Curio Store. Scott had named a lunar mountain range for Swann.

The astronauts left Phantom Ranch at 7:45 a.m. and headed up the Bright Angel Trail in the same groups as the previous day. On the way up, the geology instruction consisted mostly of the geologists quizzing the astronauts to see how much they had learned and could identify. They ate lunch at Indian Garden. From there eight astronauts hiked out and ten rode. William Hoyt reported in the Flagstaff newspaper: "Shepard was the first of the 18 Astronauts...to reach the South Rim...reaching the head of the Bright Angel Trail at 2:05 p.m., a full hour before the first group on muleback. Chomping a cigar, he gleefully greeted his saddle-sore companions as they climbed down off their mounts."[14]

Also hiking out was Scott Carpenter. In the lobby of Bright Angel Lodge someone asked Carpenter why he wanted to go to the moon. According to the Phoenix newspaper, Carpenter "waved his hands and answered 'Because it's there.' You would expect that kind of answer from a mountain climber, and Carpenter got his spurs in that field while attending Boulder, Colorado, High School and the University of Colorado at the foot of the Rockies."[15]

The Phoenix newspaper also reported, "The climb was comparatively easy for one astronaut trainee. Walt Cunningham...once climbed Mt. Fujiyama in Japan."[16] Cunningham was the only other astronaut, with Neil Armstrong, who had hiked into the canyon before. But Cunningham remained a cynic about geology. In his memoir he complained that geology lectures were boring and said that new astronauts attended the optional lectures only because "we were looking desperately for an edge," a way of standing out. But "the professors had zero influence, and there weren't many dramatic possibilities in that situation: no safely bringing down a burning aircraft, no untying little Nell from the railroad tracks."[17] At least hiking out of the Grand Canyon offered a chance to prove something.

Some of the geologists were well-conditioned by years of fieldwork, but according to Elbert King, "The astronauts' better physical condition annoyed the geologists throughout the geology training course. Some of the instructors started running and exercising regularly, but it always seemed the astronauts were far ahead of us.... In the end, it was just a fact of life we had to accept."[18] The truth was that the astronauts suffered quite a bit too on their canyon hike, mainly from using the wrong footwear, but they wouldn't admit it.

Elbert King, whose hike students were Michael Collins and Roger Chaffee, was also impressed by their mental prowess: "They were willing students who had no trouble grasping the concepts we wanted them to understand…. The astronauts much preferred this form of instruction to formal lectures and classes. The geologist instructors agreed that a lot of teaching and learning had been accomplished in the field with relative ease."[19]

In the lobby of Bright Angel Lodge the astronauts held a press conference, though Alan Shepard did almost all the talking. "I'm just a little old farm boy from New Hampshire," he said, "but to me the Grand Canyon was very impressive indeed." His mention of New Hampshire prompted reporters to ask Shepard if he were going to vote in the upcoming New Hampshire primary where Arizona's Senator Barry Goldwater was launching his presidential candidacy, and Shepard said no, though he'd vote in November. Another reporter asked Shepard if he, like John Glenn, had any plans to run for office, and Shepard admitted that he'd been asked to run, but he wasn't interested. The Phoenix newspaper's story was mostly about Shepard's political comments. At least William Hoyt was interested in the purpose of the trip:

> Dr. Jackson and other geologists explained briefly at the press conference that the Astronauts were studying the geology of the Grand Canyon "to make them more competent as scientific observers and sample collectors when they reach the surface of the moon."
>
> The Astronauts will take the samples they collected on the trip back to Houston where they will study them in laboratories.
>
> "This will give the Astronauts a representative geological collection," Dr. Jackson noted. "We're interested of course in training them to be good geological samplers so they'll know what to look for and bring back from the surface of the moon. We will be able to learn a great deal from such geologic samples…."
>
> All have flown over the Canyon and Carpenter said he went over it during his triple-orbit flight "but I didn't get much of a look as it was covered with clouds."
>
> Following yesterday's press conference, the astronauts watched briefly as the Canyon's Hopi Indian dancers performed in front of Hopi House and then ate dinner at Bright Angel Lodge….[20]

The newspaper article included photos of Alan Shepard mobbed by local Boy Scouts, Elliot See signing his autograph on a girl's forehead, and an older lady tourist in Hopi House warning Scott Carpenter, "Please don't go up there again, and the rest of you should stay down here too." There was no report of why she was worried. Perhaps she was reading the Dick Tracy comic strip—which abutted Hoyt's articles—that detailed Dick Tracy's adventures flying in a "moon coup" and meeting a sexy moon maiden with forehead antennas. Moon fever was in the air.

A week later the rest of the astronaut corps arrived. Once again the center of attention was the Mercury astronauts—Gus Grissom, Gordon Cooper, and Wally Schirra—who had already flown in space, plus Deke Slayton, who had been grounded due to a heart condition. It was Schirra's forty-first birthday, and at the Flagstaff airport city officials presented him with "a chocolate birthday cake suitably inscribed and contained in a bright pink cake carton...."[21] Schirra, wearing a cowboy hat and a camera, happily showed off his cake to his fellow astronauts.

The second hike included two astronauts who would walk on the moon, Pete Conrad and John Young, and three who would orbit the moon, Frank Borman, Jim Lovell, and Thomas Stafford.

This group of astronauts repeated the schedule of the first group, starting with an orientation lecture at the Yavapai geology museum, though this time USGS geologist Al Chidester substituted for Eddie McKee. They took six and a half hours to reach Phantom Ranch. After dinner they sat in the dining hall for awhile and talked. "But they went to bed early," according to ranch manager Ben Clark. "They were all in by 8:30 p.m. and they sacked right out."[22]

During the night, snow began falling on the rim and it continued into the morning, five inches of it by the time the astronauts started their hike at 8 a.m. Lower in the canyon, it was rain. There was also lots of fog. The astronauts were warned that the trail ahead was a muddy and slippery mess, and this time all of them chose to ride mules from Indian Garden to the rim. "It was a bit chilly," commented Frank Borman. An *Arizona Daily Sun* photograph of Borman and Pete Conrad on mules was captioned that they "looked more like a couple of veteran mule skinners than spacemen as they ride out of the Grand Canyon."[23] The Phoenix newspaper captioned its photo "Orbit Canyon on Mules: Some members of the astronaut space team orbit the spaces of the Grand Canyon."[24] At the rim the mule wranglers gave the astronauts certificates declaring them to be Genuine Grand Canyon Mule Skinners.

William Hoyt asked Deke Slayton whether the heart fibrillation that had grounded him was an issue on the hike, and Slayton replied that, on the contrary, vigorous exercise made his heart fibrillation go away. Slayton also said that the geology training was a success: "We really learn something when we actually see the rocks and formations. They say the best geologist is the one who has seen the most rocks and we've seen a lot of rocks in the last two days."[25]

Unlike the astronauts on the first hike, the participants on the second hike have left few comments about it. In his memoir Gordon Cooper didn't say anything about the hike, but he did mention that when he was hosting some Soviet cosmonauts on a goodwill tour of the United States, he took them to the Grand Canyon, and Disneyland too. Frank Borman said of the overall training:

> Some of it was valuable; some I judged to be a waste of time. They gave us about fifty hours of geology, which included trips to such fun places as the Grand Canyon and Meteor Crater in Arizona. The idea was to prepare those astronauts who would be assigned moon landings and subsequent exploration of the lunar surface, but fifty hours? I didn't think that much was necessary.[26]

It probably wasn't necessary for Borman, who never landed on the moon. But the geologists considered the canyon hikes a great success. In a 1965 *National Geographic* article about all aspects of astronaut training, which included photos of the astronauts working in the canyon, geologist Uel Clanton was quoted, saying, "Grand Canyon makes a magnificent classroom."[27] Thus when two newly selected groups of astronauts needed to start geology training, the geologists brought them to the Grand Canyon, on June 2–3, 1966.

This hike included eighteen astronauts, with three future moonwalkers—Charlie Duke, Jim Irwin, and Edgar Mitchell—plus six astronauts who would see the moon from above: Ron Evans, Fred Haise, Thomas Mattingly, Stuart Roosa, Jack Swigert, and Al Worden.

It's not clear why no reporters were invited to cover the hike, but for NASA, 1966 was a very busy year. Five Gemini missions were planned, and many astronauts felt that reporters and public relations duties were a huge distraction. This hike followed the same schedule as the first two, beginning with a talk at the Yavapai geology museum, again with Eddie McKee. The main difference was that it was now summer and very hot at the canyon bottom. This time the astronauts would camp out.

Future Apollo 16 astronaut Charlie Duke knew what the canyon was like in summer: he had been there in July 1964. He and his wife, Dotty, were driving from Boston to Edwards Air Force Base in southern California, where Duke was to begin his career as a test pilot. They'd had time to spare, so they went camping in the Rockies and spent a few days at the Grand Canyon, even riding mules. Duke recalled his 1966 hike:

> At first we thought of our field trips in terms of, "Ho hum let's go out and look at some rocks." We soon learned that such trips can be demanding exercises....
>
> Our first trip...was a hike to the bottom of the Grand Canyon. When Dotty and I had visited the canyon several years earlier, we had ridden mules from the north rim. This walk was to start from the south rim....
>
> It took us all day to reach the bottom, and by the time we got there most of us had feet that were just one big blister. My flying boots really didn't double as hiking boots.
>
> Blisters and all, it was great to have arrived. I was surprised to find a virtual oasis of cottonwood trees and a grassy meadow in the bottom of the canyon....
>
> We were all ready to jump into the river to cool off, then were delighted to find that someone had been foresighted enough to bring some beer down for us to have a cool one. Once cleaned up and cooled down by a few beers, we enjoyed a hearty meal that had been prepared by the ranch staff.
>
> It was a beautiful night—so we threw our sleeping bags on the ground and settled down to get some rest.... The moon was out and the walls of the canyon were silhouetted in its light. Lying in my sleeping bag, I was transfixed by this magnificent sight above me. I couldn't help wondering if one day I might actually set foot on that moon.

I was sleeping soundly when suddenly I awoke with a start! *Something ran over my sleeping bag!*

I sat up quietly and looked around. I don't know whether it was a male chasing a female or two males, but a pair of skunks were engaging in a big fight, running wildly about among our party of ten guys.

We're really in trouble now, I told myself. *If one skunk catches the other on top of our sleeping bags, we're going to get wiped out!* I stayed very still so that they wouldn't know I was awake. If I frightened them, they surely would have gassed us all. Eventually they ran off into the night.[28]

Most of the other astronauts never learned what nearly hit them. NASA was spared from having to explain why America's bravest men went fleeing from a cute little animal.

While Apollo 15's Dave Scott and Jim Irwin were doing geology on the moon, Al Worden was circling miles above them in the command module. Worden, too, had become captivated with geology, partly from the influence of Dave Scott and partly from the Grand Canyon:

> The dry training style our teachers used in the classroom never really gripped me, but my attention picked up when we started to make geology field trips. To be out in the wild landscape made a huge difference.... I loved the feeling of being out in the field and so, it turned out, did my fellow Apollo crew mates....
>
> If I hadn't already been awed by natural wonders, the long trek down to the floor of the Grand Canyon would have done the trick.... Hiking down from the canyon rim, we examined the layers of rock all the way down to the primeval crust. The experience taught us little about the moon. Nevertheless, it exposed us to more geological processes and examples. We were better prepared, because we were seeing things in context, a whole awe-inspiring mile of context.
>
> This sense of context was particularly important for me. I already knew I wouldn't be walking on the lunar surface. Instead, when I made my flight, I would have an incredible view of the grand sweep of lunar features from only a few miles up. I would be looking at the big picture, and that could often tell us much more than standing on the ground in one place.[29]

Unfortunately, American politicians didn't share this interest in science. They cancelled three planned Apollo missions, though the hardware for them had already been built, the training done. The long frontier experience that had given Americans all the practical skills to reach the moon had failed to instill in them the values required to justify going there: the values of wonder and exploration for its own sake.

Half of the men on the 1966 hike would never fly on an Apollo mission, but some would fly on Skylab and the space shuttles. Among these was Paul Weitz, who was so impressed with northern Arizona that he moved there after his NASA career. Thus I was able to have breakfast with him one morning in downtown Flagstaff.

Weitz was on the first Skylab mission and the first launch of the space shuttle *Challenger* (the sixth flight for any shuttle), and later he became the deputy director of the Johnson Space Center. He was selected in April 1966 as part of the fifth group of astronauts. By then NASA was looking for stronger science credentials, not just piloting skills. Only a few weeks after being selected, the new astronauts found themselves hiking into the Grand Canyon. Weitz had never been to the canyon before. He was paired with Jack Swigert, who would be the command module pilot on the ill-fated Apollo 13 mission, and for an instructor they had Aaron Waters, a UC-Santa Barbara volcanologist who was on Eugene Shoemaker's team for planning the actual lunar fieldwork. Waters had been in charge of one of the first astronaut training trips, to the volcanic fields near Bend, Oregon, in October 1964. Weitz would also go to Meteor Crater with Eugene Shoemaker. He told me that he recalled Eddie McKee's orientation talk, and he found the instructors to be very capable and personable. The trip was well organized, except for NASA's continued neglect of proper boots for a Grand Canyon hike. NASA left it to the astronauts to guess their own footwear. Like other astronauts, Weitz got bad blisters. But at least someone brought along moleskin. That night Weitz slept outside. I asked him about Charlie Duke's encounter with the skunks, and Weitz said he must have slept right through it. But on one of his later geology field trips in Alaska, Weitz was chased by a bear.

As on the first two canyon hikes, the astronauts were met by mules at Indian Garden on the way out, but the mules too caused blisters, another subject on which the astronauts kept quiet. Weitz wasn't sure which type of blisters was worse. The geology training was done on the way down the trail and included many stops. Weitz found the training to be quite valuable, and the canyon inspiring. Weitz wasn't aware of the behind-the-scenes political struggles that had prompted the geologists to use the Grand Canyon to inspire the astronauts and impress NASA managers. In later years Weitz came back to the Grand Canyon just to see more of it. He did find his geology training useful on Skylab, much of which was devoted to studying Earth landscapes.

I also heard from three other astronauts who were on the third hike.

Jack Lousma was on the second Skylab mission and commanded the third space shuttle flight. His memories of the Grand Canyon hike included the same highlights as the other astronauts: the drone of classroom lectures, the drama of the hike, the vivid rock layers. Lousma added, "We were equipped with standard geology tools and equipment; just enough to be dangerous!... It was hot. We came across a few visitors who were stalled out and without water, so we got help for them. We slept under the stars at Phantom Ranch."[30]

Bill Pogue was on the third Skylab mission. In 1955, as a gunnery instructor at Luke Air Force Base in Phoenix, Pogue led one training flight over the Grand Canyon and was awed by the view from close above the rim. Now he got to see that view from the inside. Pogue sent me an excerpt from the autobiography he was writing:

> The one I'll never forget was the first one, a two-day field trip to the Grand Canyon.... After we reached the bottom we walked to Phantom Ranch. They didn't have rooms for us but did provide the evening meal. Sleeping bags had been transported down on donkeys and we unrolled them and slept on the ground. It was a beautiful starlit night and we practiced a little of our star and constellation identification. The muscles in the front of my thighs were quite sore from the downhill walk so I was a bit uncomfortable and had difficulty going to sleep. However, that was the least of my worries.
>
> I heard a disturbance and raised my head to see what was going on. Two skunks were leaping over and around our sleeping bags: one was chasing the other, which I assumed was a mating ritual. I kept very quiet and didn't move. Suddenly Charlie Duke who had already fallen

asleep rose up out of his sleeping bag and I said, "Charlie, don't make any noise; there are skunks among us!" He lay back down and I pulled my bag over my head for protection in case they hosed down the area. Soon they left and the rest of the night was peaceful....

It was really a quite interesting and enjoyable field trip.[31]

Gerald Carr was the commander of the third Skylab mission. He illustrated the astronauts' sense of humor:

> The next morning we began the hike up Bright Angel Trail and got to a rest stop part way up where mules were waiting for us for the rest of the hike. We had a television camera man with us who documented the training exercise, and by the time we got to the rest stop he was exhausted. He laid down his large, heavy camera on a table and went to sleep next to it. Astronaut Jack Swigert sneaked over, stole his camera, and while someone held up a mule's tail Jack took extensive footage of the south end of the animal. Then he quietly placed the camera next to the sleeping camera man, and not another word was said.
>
> We all enjoyed the mental picture of the video people reviewing the tapes, but they never gave us the satisfaction of acknowledging the camera work.[32]

One astronaut told me a story about an unnamed astronaut who wanted to collect a fossil trilobite from the Bright Angel Shale. His instructor warned him that he would probably break the fossil, but he tried anyway. He broke the fossil.

Of the twenty-four men who flew to the moon, the only one who missed going on a Grand Canyon hike was the only astronaut who was also a geologist. Harrison "Jack" Schmitt studied geology at Cal Tech, earned a Ph.D. in geology from Harvard, and walked on the moon on Apollo 17, the final mission. There's no record of why Schmitt wasn't included on the 1966 canyon hike, but clearly Schmitt didn't require an introduction to geology.

By 1967 NASA had expanded its standard geology training to one hundred hours in the classroom and ten field trips, but for the last three, science-rich missions, there were about twenty field trips designed to fit each mission. In all NASA conducted about two hundred geology field trips. Many of these occurred in northern Arizona, which offered Meteor Crater, many volcanoes and lava flows, and even an artificial moonscape where technicians had blasted dozens of craters into a volcanic cinder field and set up a mockup of the lunar lander. Other field trips included Hawaii, Iceland, Alaska, Big Bend, the Mojave Desert, and Craters of the Moon National Monument in Idaho. Yet when the astronauts came to write their memoirs, it was the Grand Canyon hike they remembered best.

Somewhere along the South Kaibab Trail there are dozens of boulders and cliff faces with pieces missing, chipped off by the astronauts whose same hands chipped off moon rocks and brought them back to Earth. Grand Canyon rocks held the same primordial mystery as moon rocks. The South Kaibab Trail was, for the astronauts, the pathway to the moon.

ON THE RIM OF CREATION

The World's Greatest Telescope

People come to the Grand Canyon not just to see a visual spectacle, but with a sense that here they are seeing the forces of creation. They are looking deep into time, time made manifest in rock. They are seeing the power of nature to create a mile of rock and then to carve and carry that rock away. They are seeing a record of life's evolution. British author J. B. Priestley called the canyon "Our nearest approach to fourth-dimensional scenery.... You feel that some elements of Time have been conjured into the immensities of Space."[1]

This encounter with the forces of creation seems to have inspired one man with the idea that the Grand Canyon was the best place for an even greater encounter with time and space and creation. In the 1920s the world's foremost designer of telescopes, George Ritchey, decided that the world's greatest astronomical observatory should be built on the rim of the Grand Canyon. At sunset astronomers could gaze into the depths of the Earth, then walk into the observatory and gaze into the even greater depths of the sky: strata of light, fossil stars, rivers of galaxies. Ritchey took a photograph of the canyon from Desert View and imposed onto the rim a drawing of his planned observatory, about 250 feet tall. In 1928 Edwin Hubble, already the world's most famous astronomer, drove from Pasadena to the Grand Canyon to test out the viewing conditions from the canyon rim.

George Ritchey's composite photo and drawing of the proposed observatory at Desert View, 1928. *(Courtesy of the Carnegie Institution of Washington)*

The observatory was never built. Indeed, it was a downright foolish idea. There was no scientific advantage to building an observatory right on the rim of the canyon, and there was a compelling reason not to build it there. George Ritchey should have known this. His persistence in dreaming of a Grand Canyon observatory can only be called an obsession. Ritchey seems to have fallen under the canyon's spell, and not the scientific spell it casts on geologists, but the spell that made Romantic poets and artists see "the Sublime" in the canyon's depths.

Ritchey was the answer to an era that actually required a few obsessive astronomers. Not just eccentric, absent-minded professors like Einstein, but men with a touch of the mad scientists who in Hollywood movies harnessed lightning to energize time machines or Frankensteins they'd invented in the basement. It was an era—the late 1800s and early 1900s—when technology was rushing ahead much faster than scientific institutions. The era of the gentleman naturalist was giving way to the era of Big Science, meaning big institutions, big technology, and very big money. In astronomy, new technologies were opening up powerful new possibilities for probing the universe.

The glass lens refracting telescopes astronomers had used since Galileo had evolved as far as possible, and now astronomy needed to develop reflecting telescopes using large mirrors. New instruments like the spectrograph meant that astronomers could read all sorts of new information in starlight. Photography meant that astronomers could record details far beyond the capabilities of the human eye.

Yet there were enormous obstacles. Many astronomers failed to see the new possibilities, and even among the most visionary, no one really knew how to build large reflecting telescopes, and no one had the money to do so. Into this impasse strode two men, George Hale and George Ritchey, who often had little besides obsession to sustain them. Hale's obsession resulted in his building, over four decades, three cutting-edge observatories—Yerkes, Mount Wilson, and Palomar—the leaders of astronomy for nearly a century. Ritchey was Hale's master optician and telescope designer, the man who figured out how to build great reflecting telescopes. Yet with two obsessive, neurotic men working together in high-pressure circumstances, there was bound to be trouble.

Hale and Ritchey met in Chicago in 1890, when both were in their twenties and aiming for careers in astronomy. Hale had the advantage of a wealthy father, which allowed him to build a private observatory. Ritchey had inherited only his father's mechanical aptitude, and soon Ritchey was machining lenses and instruments for Hale's observatory.

Soon after Hale and Ritchey began their partnership, Hale got the notion that the best place for astronomy, or at least one aspect of it, was the Grand Canyon. Hale was mainly interested in the sun, including the solar corona. To observe the corona, astronomers had to wait for an eclipse to cover the sun and allow the corona to emerge from the sun's glare. Astronomers had tried a few strategies for viewing the corona in the daylight, including climbing mountains where, they supposed, the thinner air would hold less glare. All of these had failed. Hale realized that with the spectroheliograph he had invented for studying the sun, he might have a new way for viewing the corona in daylight. Hale tried this method in Chicago, but the glare was still too great. Somehow he got the idea that at the bottom of the Grand Canyon, so much sunlight was blocked by the cliffs that the sky was "nearly black."[2] Perhaps Hale had seen F. W. von Egloffstein's highly exaggerated illustrations of the Grand Canyon, with their overly gloomy depths. More likely, Hale simply picked up an idea that was fairly common at that time, and sometimes found in books, that the bottom of the Grand Canyon was so dark that you could see the stars in the daytime. In the 1920s the Zion National Park publication *Nature Notes* reported that some people believed that in the Zion Narrows you should be able to see the stars in the daytime. Hale was ready to travel to the Grand Canyon and to hire John Hance, the canyon's first white settler, miner, and trail builder, to guide him to the bottom with a burro carrying his spectroheliograph. On February 16, 1893, Hale wrote letters to John Hance and John Wesley Powell, who had explored the canyon by river in 1869, inquiring about the "nearly black" canyon depths. It appears that, for once, Hance refrained from encouraging a tall tale. At least, Hale soon headed for Pike's Peak instead.

Hale's private observatory was absorbed by the young and very ambitious University of Chicago. Hale started dreaming big, of building the world's largest telescope. Though Hale and Ritchey knew that the future of astronomy belonged to reflectors, they also knew that the technology wasn't ready yet, so Hale settled for a refractor with a 40-inch lens, a 4-inch advancement over Lick Observatory's 36-inch. Hale and Ritchey also knew that Lick's location, atop a California mountain, was also the future of astronomy. But Hale had to settle for Lake Geneva, Wisconsin, the playground of the Chicago rich; Hale had to satisfy the vanity of Chicago Gilded Age robber baron Charles Yerkes, who was paying for the telescope strictly as a monument to himself. At least Hale persuaded Yerkes not to build the observatory in downtown Chicago, where the observing conditions would have been miserable. Hale was a frail, sickly, high-strung man, and dealing with people like Yerkes, along with all the technical uncertainties and setbacks of building observatories, would frustrate him into repeated nervous breakdowns.

As feared, Lake Geneva proved to be too cloudy and muggy for the best astronomy. This was also the era when astronomers were realizing the advantages of locating observatories at high altitudes and in dry climates. Most observatories had been built on college campuses, inside cities, often near sea level, or in the muggy Midwest, leaving star images blurred by a thick, wet blanket of air. Higher and drier locations made star images much sharper and steadier. When Lick Observatory was built on a 4,200-foot mountain in the 1880s, this was a radical idea, but it still stopped well short of the possibilities. Lick was only twenty-five miles from the southern tip of San Francisco Bay. George Hale recognized that Southern California was much drier, and he picked out a 5,900-foot peak, Mount Wilson, for his next world's-best observatory. Yet Hale may have wondered if Percival Lowell, who a decade previously had built his own observatory at over 7,000 feet in Arizona, both higher and drier than Mount Wilson, might just know something he didn't.

It was in the building of Mount Wilson Observatory that Ritchey's genius came forth. He built a 60-inch telescope, then the mirror for a 100-inch telescope, overcoming numerous, major technical challenges. In only twenty years these telescopes transformed our understanding of the universe, revealing it to be much vaster and much more complex and dynamic than humans had ever imagined, an expanding universe with billions of galaxies.

Ritchey's obsession for building telescopes, however, soon began to alienate Hale. In May 1906, during a pause in the building of the 60-inch telescope, Ritchey went to Flagstaff, Arizona, to consult with Percival Lowell, who wanted to outdo Hale and build an 84-inch telescope. Ritchey decided that Lowell's telescope design was fatally ambitious, and nothing came of it. Soon Ritchey conceived of a new, more elaborate design for reflecting telescopes, the Ritchey-Chrétien system. Ritchey insisted that Hale's planned 100-inch telescope had to be a Ritchey-Chrétien design, but Hale refused to take a chance on an untried and very tricky new technology. The Ritchey-Chrétien design was indeed the future of astronomy, used in most of the great telescopes of the latter half of the twentieth century, including the Hubble Space Telescope. Ritchey went to the financial patron of the 100-inch telescope, John Hooker, and tried to persuade him, telling him that Hale's plans were foolish. Hale was enraged by such disloyalty, and he had been tired of Ritchey's egotism for a long time. As soon as the 100-inch telescope was finished in 1919, Hale fired Ritchey and used his salary to hire a young man named Edwin Hubble. Ritchey retired to his lemon ranch and fantasized about building telescopes bigger and better than the 200-inch that Hale was planning next. In 1924 Ritchey was hired by the Paris Observatory, and he began drawing up plans for the world's greatest observatory—to be placed on the rim of the Grand Canyon.

It's not clear when Ritchey became obsessed with the Grand Canyon. It could have started on his 1906 visit to northern Arizona to visit Percival

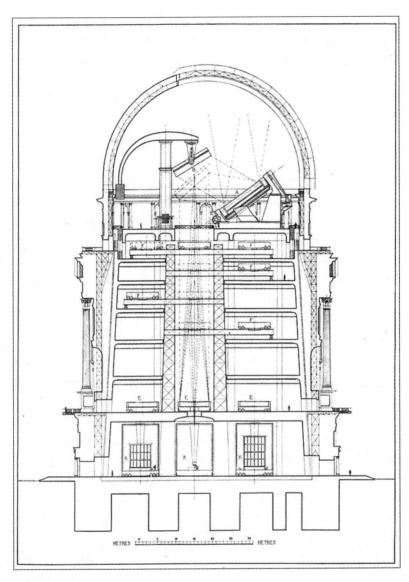

Architectural drawing of Ritchey observatory. *(Courtesy of the Carnegie Institution of Washington)*

Lowell. Lowell had always insisted that his observatory had better viewing conditions than any other. Ritchey surely looked through Lowell's 24-inch telescope, and he may have been quietly shocked to see that Mount Wilson didn't have the best viewing conditions after all. Ritchey surely noticed how easy it was to drive right up to Lowell Observatory. At Mount Wilson, construction supplies had to be carried on the backs of mules up a long, torturous trail; Ritchey had been in charge of improving this trail into a road, but it was still treacherous. But much of northern Arizona consisted of a flat plateau, higher than Mount Wilson, that reached right to the rim of the Grand Canyon.

The following summer, immediately after completing the 60-inch mirror, Ritchey made his first visit to the Grand Canyon. He wrote to the manager of the Grandview Hotel, saying he was planning a "stay of 10 days, or more probably 2 weeks."[3] It's interesting that Ritchey chose the Grandview Hotel, since this was two years after the Atchison, Topeka and Santa Fe Railway had opened its luxurious El Tovar Hotel with great fanfare, and now the Grandview, a dozen miles from the train station, was not only antiquated, it was largely abandoned. Perhaps Ritchey was more interested in grand views for his camera—and a telescope.

Ritchey was quite serious about photography, and he did pioneering astrophotography through the sixty-inch telescope. According to Ritchey biographer Donald Osterbrock, at the Grand Canyon "he had taken numerous black-and-white photographs, and he hoped to return in the coming summer and try the color plates as well."[4] With his connections Ritchey had obtained some of the first plates for color photography. If he did return to the canyon the next summer, he may have been the first person to take color photographs of the canyon; historians of Grand Canyon photography don't know of anyone else who had done so by 1908. In 1908 Ritchey gave John Hooker an elegant mahogany display case showing off his astronomical and Grand Canyon photos. Nearly twenty years later in Paris, at a gala event at the Saint Gobrain glassworks, which had made the glass blanks that Ritchey had cut and polished into the Mount Wilson mirrors, Ritchey displayed fifty or so of his astronomical photos, plus some of the Grand Canyon. It's likely that he also took the Desert View photo onto which he etched a drawing of his Grand Canyon observatory.

Ritchey announced his plans for the Grand Canyon Observatory in Paris in June 1928. Technically it was quite extravagant, far beyond anything ever attempted or even imagined. It was a "fixed vertical telescope" with ten mirrors. The primary mirror would be 235 inches; Hale's planned telescope was "only" 200 inches. It also had nine other mirrors, each nearly 200 inches, mounted on wheels so they could be moved about and adjusted to change the telescope's focal length.

The observatory's look was also grandiose. It was a dome approximately twenty-five stories tall, with the columns and statues of a Greek or Roman temple. In the French magazine *L'Astronomie* Ritchey published his illustration of the observatory, perched on the South Rim of the Grand Canyon, overlooking the Tanner Rapid S-curve of the Colorado River.

To locate the exact site of this photo-illustration, I consulted with Mike Quinn, longtime archivist for Grand Canyon National Park, who often has to identify the locations in old Grand Canyon photos. Mike compared Ritchey's photo with photos taken from Desert View Point, and he concluded that Ritchey's photo was taken from a bit east of there. Mike observed that in Ritchey's photo the Colorado River was just barely showing between the cliffs and shorelines of the *S* curve above Tanner Rapid, while in Desert View Point photos the river was just pinched off from visibility. I visited Desert View and found that, sure enough, Ritchey's photo appeared to have been taken from a promontory about a quarter mile east of Desert View. When you walk any further east along the rim, this promontory blocks any further view of the Tanner Rapid zone. The surprise was that the cliff face on which Ritchey pictured his observatory doesn't exist. The depicted spot is actually just thin air, inside Tanner Canyon.

This raises the question of exactly where Ritchey intended to build his observatory. I corresponded with Ritchey biographer and prominent astronomy historian Donald Osterbrock, but Osterbrock was not sufficiently familiar with the Grand Canyon to make sense of Ritchey's intentions. It also appears that Ritchey himself had not made up his mind between Desert View Point and Comanche Point, which is further east of Desert View. Ritchey appears to have used both names at different times. Ritchey mentioned an observatory altitude of 7,500 feet: Desert View is 7,438 feet, Comanche Point 7,073 feet. Ritchey's illustration places the observatory pretty close to Desert View but about three miles from Comanche Point. The cliff face in the illustration has some of the upsweep of Comanche Point, but otherwise it is a stair-step cliff full of pine trees, quite unlike Comanche Point's steep, naked rock. It's likely that this illustration was done by the architect—apparently

French—who designed the observatory building, and who was unfamiliar with the real canyon. From a practical viewpoint, Desert View offers a generous flat platform on which to build a complex of buildings, while Comanche Point is a narrow, sharp point that falls off steeply on its back side. On the other hand, when Ritchey wrote to the National Park Service (NPS) on July 5, 1928, requesting use of the site, he named Comanche Point. Ritchey's official proposal, now in the National Archives, also names Comanche Point and an elevation of 7,100 feet. Ritchey's proposal proclaims: "The view from this point is one of the most sublime to be found on Earth. This observatory would be a noble monument, a majestic cathedral, to Science, to Education, to international peace and good-will."[5] Ritchey needed to include "international peace and good-will" because he was hoping the Paris Observatory would sponsor the canyon observatory.

The proposal's rationale for a Grand Canyon location concluded: "Its extraordinary transparency, required for the most exacting and accurate astronomical photography, have [sic] been demonstrated by many years' tests by Professor Ritchey."[6] I suspect it would have been more accurate to say: tests over many years of vacations.

"Transparency" is one measure of astronomical viewing conditions. Good astronomical viewing is determined by a number of factors, especially elevation, dryness, absence of clouds, remoteness from city lights, and the "seeing"— the calmness or turbulence of the air. On the first four points the Grand Canyon is excellent. But it's the final point that turns Ritchey's noble vision into a foolish scheme. Even the casual tourist soon notices that on the rim of the canyon the air is not calm. It can be quite turbulent. The bottom of the canyon is usually at least twenty degrees Fahrenheit hotter than the rim. The canyon bottom can be over one-hundred degrees as early as April and as late as October, and much hotter in between. The hot air rises, confined by the canyon cliffs, and as soon as it hits the rim it rushes outward, mixing energetically with the cooler air on the rim. This turbulence also stirs up lots of dust. This turbulence is visible in many ways: in all the lost hats just below the rim; in aircraft pilots struggling for control and sometimes crashing; in ravens and condors coasting for hours on warm updrafts; in clerks constantly dusting gift-shop shelves; and in ponderosa pine trees that refuse to grow close to the rim because the hot wind dries them out too much.

The Desert View area is especially bad for hot updrafts, turbulence, and dust. Hot air rises not only out of the canyon, but out of the lower-elevation Painted Desert just to the east. Desert View gets hit by the prevailing up-canyon winds that have had a long west-east racetrack but now run into cliffs as the canyon bends north. The canyon bottom is more wide-open below Desert View than anywhere else in the canyon's first half, leaving little shade, prompting river runners to call it "Furnace Flats" and to dread camping there. Geologically the canyon bottom here consists of the Supergroup, meaning lots of sandstone, meaning lots of sand, meaning sandstorms. The conditions on the Desert View rim can best be measured by the absence of ponderosa trees. Grandview Point, at 7,400 feet, is one of the few places on the South Rim that is high enough and cool enough for ponderosas to grow right along the rim. Desert View is thirty-eight feet higher than Grandview, yet the ponderosas stay far away.

For astronomy, turbulent air means blurry images. This turbulence can lessen at night, but in Grand Canyon summers there are heat waves climbing the canyon walls all night. While today there are lots of observatories atop desert mountains, the heat rising around them is diffused, not aimed straight at one abrupt rim intersection between heat and coolness. The canyon's abundant dust would be bad for astronomy too.

Ritchey would have done much better to locate his observatory a few miles behind the rim, even one mile. There was no scientific benefit to being right on the rim. Desert View was an especially poor choice, Comanche Point even worse. Was Ritchey oblivious to the drawbacks? Did he happen to visit Desert View on an unusually calm day? Or perhaps he was looking not at the sky but downward, hypnotized by the Sublime, the grandeur which at Desert View is especially grand. Or perhaps Ritchey had learned from George Hale that if you wanted to find funding, an observatory needed to inspire awe. Even the French loved the Grand Canyon.

The Grand Canyon observatory did inspire the *New York Times* to cover it in three articles over the next weeks. On June 17, 1928, on the top center of the front page of its Sunday editorial section, the *Times* announced: "Secrets of Planet Mars to Be Revealed By a Huge Telescope At Grand Canyon":

PARIS, June 14—The world will know within eight years whether or not there are cities on the planet Mars if the plans of Professor N. W.

Ritchey, American astronomer, who superintended the construction of Mount Wilson Observatory, materialize.

During an exhibition of glass transparencies as applied to astronomical photography, which he gave in Paris today, Professor Ritchey disclosed that efforts are being made in the United States, France and England for the construction of a huge new observatory, one unit of which will be situated beside the Grand Canyon of Arizona.

With the aid of the giant telescope which it is planned to erect there, Professor Ritchey says that if there are any densely populated sections on Mars they will be readily discernible.

The telescope itself is entirely different from anything designed heretofore and is said to be ten times more powerful than any now being used.

The rest of the article gave technical details. On July 23, as preface to reprinting a famous 1835 hoax article about the moon being inhabited, the *Times* reported:

Professor Ritchey's latest reflector is expected to give ten times the optical power of the most successful modern telescope. He expects to set it up somewhere in the Arizona desert on the edge of the Grand Canyon. Will the scientists, trekking to their desert watchtower seven years hence, appreciate the significance of the anniversary? If not, the newspapers may remind them, for Aug. 21, 1835, was a date famous in local journalistic history....

Notice the *Times'* name for a majestic tower at Desert View: the "desert watchtower."

On September 30 the *New York Times* published a nearly full-page article discussing the genius and technical details of Ritchey's telescope: "A Super Telescope To Peer Into The Cosmos". This article included three illustrations, including a drawing of the observatory, though with no canyon behind it.

In the same weeks that Ritchey's telescope was making headlines, George Hale was almost ready to announce his plans for his new observatory and its 200-inch telescope. The technology and funding were ready, and all that was lacking was a site. By some accounts, Hale had decided early on that the best site was Mount Palomar, north of San Diego. Some historians have suggested that Hale's site selection process was all for show, to impress his fellow astronomers with how careful he was. Yet Hale had genuine reasons to feel insecure about selecting a site. Hale had devoted two decades, millions of dollars, and his sanity to building Mount Wilson Observatory, yet even as Mount Wilson Observatory was becoming world famous, it was being rendered obsolete by light pollution from booming Los Angeles. When Hale first arrived in Los Angeles it had a population of only 100,000. Boosters were promising that Los Angeles would soon be a city of millions and bright lights, but Hale had his head in the clouds, or maybe in the lack of clouds above Mount Wilson. Now Hale had to admit that he had made a disastrous mistake. Maybe Percival Lowell had been right all along about Arizona being a smarter choice. Now the *New York Times* was trumpeting George Ritchey's claim that the world's best site for an observatory was the Grand Canyon. Hale had already been disconcerted when tests atop Mount Palomar suggested that its seeing wasn't as good as Mount Wilson's. The hyper-insecure Hale must have been unnerved by the possibility that his rival Ritchey might be right about the Grand Canyon. Hale had been ridiculously wrong about the Grand Canyon a third of a century before, when he had believed its depths would be almost night-dark. The last straw was probably the *New York Times* article of September 30, hailing Ritchey's genius for a telescope that was much more ambitious than Hale's 200-inch.

A few days later George Hale ordered Edwin Hubble to drop everything and rush to the Grand Canyon. Hubble was already the world's most famous astronomer. Now Hubble was right in the middle of one of the most important projects in the history of astronomy, only weeks away from proving that the universe is expanding. The fact that Hale would interrupt Hubble's work and send him to the Grand Canyon was a measure of how seriously Hale took Ritchey's claims about the canyon.

Edwin Hubble had become the world's most famous astronomer three years before, for proving that there were many other galaxies outside our Milky Way galaxy. Astronomers had long debated the nature of nebulae, little smudges of light, often spiral shaped. In the 1920s most astronomers believed that nebulae were merely clouds of gas inside our Milky Way. A few daring astronomers suggested that nebulae were other galaxies, entire systems of stars, but this remained an outrageous idea, requiring a universe unbelievably large. Edwin Hubble took a new method for measuring the distances to stars and applied it to the nebulae and found that the nebulae were indeed far distant galaxies.

In the summer of 1928 Hubble began intense research into the motions of galaxies. In 1914 V. M. Slipher of Lowell Observatory had announced his spectrographic discovery that the nebulae were moving through space, moving very fast, mostly redshifted—moving away from us. Hubble took Slipher's measurements of galactic motions and tried to correlate them with his own measurements of galactic distances. Hubble soon found a very strong pattern: the farther away a galaxy was, the faster it was moving. The galaxies were flying outward from some common beginning; the universe was expanding. On January 17, 1929, Hubble submitted his findings to the *Proceedings of the National Academy of Sciences.* Three months previously, when Hubble rushed off to the Grand Canyon, he surely already knew that he was transforming the universe.

This circumstance makes it remarkable that when, on October 5, 1928, Hubble wrote to V. M. Slipher at Lowell Observatory to plan his Arizona trip, Hubble made no mention at all that he was right in the middle of using Slipher's data to transform the universe. Nor, it seems, did Hubble mention it when he saw Slipher in Flagstaff. In the weeks after Hubble's visit Slipher wrote two letters detailing Hubble's activities, including one letter to Lowell Observatory trustee Roger Lowell Putnam, with whom Slipher was always ready to share good news about Lowell Observatory achievements, but Slipher gave no hint that Hubble was making the most important discovery ever connected with Lowell Observatory.

Hubble's letter was also secretive about the purpose of his visit:

> Dear Mr. Slipher,
>
> Mr. Hale and Mr. Adams have requested me to make a preliminary investigation of conditions in Arizona in connection with a proposed plan for another observing station in the Southwest. The subject is in a rather confidential stage at present so I will explain more fully when I see you.

Mr. Anderson has devised a simple scheme for rating seeing numerically with a small telescope and I propose to take the instrument with me. We all agreed that the first step was to run over to Flagstaff for a talk with you and while there, to request permission to calibrate the small telescope to your scale of seeing. Among other things I would like to go to El Tovar and interest one of the Park Service men in watching the seeing with their exhibition telescope while I go back 1, 3, and 10 miles or 1, 5, and 20, for comparison. The direction of further investigations would depend largely on a conference with you. Arizona is a large field but I suppose that certain areas can be eliminated at once on ground of accessibility, water, vegetation and altitude.

If the scheme meets with your approval, I would probably drive over, reaching Flagstaff sometime next Friday afternoon, October 12th, and planning to stop a couple of days before going to the Canyon. Then we can discuss the further possibilities and I will have a chance to see what you all are doing.

Mr. Hale is rather anxious for me to start as soon as possible—I am writing within a few hours of his communication—so I shall take the liberty of asking you to wire me as to whether the visit will be convenient and agreeable to you.

Sincerely, Edwin Hubble[7]

In a hand-written postscript Hubble said he was bringing his wife and "a neighbor couple who have so much leisure and other things that I am quietly trying to interest them in astronomy," making it sound like a jolly vacation.

Edwin Hubble's activities at the Grand Canyon have to be surmised from this and three other letters in the Lowell Observatory archives. The Mount Wilson Observatory archives contain no obvious documentation about Hubble's trip to Arizona; Hale was probably communicating with Hubble verbally and not in letters. Hubble's trip has been unnoticed by historians, except for a few sentences in Donald Osterbrock's Ritchey biography, an account derived entirely from these four Lowell Observatory archives letters.

After Hubble got home he wrote to Slipher:

Dear Mr. Slipher,

My trip came to an unexpected end in Southern Arizona and I had to get home as soon as possible. The best results are the series of observations to be expected from the Grand Canyon and from Cameron which can be compared with your seeing at Flagstaff. I will send copies of the results as they come in if Tillotson and Hollis do not send copies direct to you. Douglass had a great deal to say about the effects of local conditions, which will be of value when the general location is decided....

You doubtless saw the announcement of the proposition last Monday. The confidential stage is past now and a 200-inch for the California Institute of Technology is definitely assured....

I am sorry to have missed the stop-over at Flagstaff on my return but we had to drive direct from Tucson, two days to Pasadena.

Sincerely, Edwin Hubble[8]

"Tillotson" was Miner Tillotson, the superintendent of Grand Canyon National Park, which indicates that Hubble did receive the highest cooperation from the NPS. "Douglass" was Andrew Douglass, who thirty-four years before had searched Arizona for the best site to establish Lowell Observatory; Hubble traveled to the University of Arizona just to meet with Douglass.

The strangest news in this letter is that Hubble conducted seeing tests at Cameron, an even more implausible observatory site than Desert View. Cameron is located at 4,200 feet, and on the edge of a large zone of hot, Painted Desert badlands that are prone to dust storms. But this does indicate that Hubble came out the east end of the park, where he may have taken a look at Desert View and Comanche Point. In Cameron perhaps Hubble and his wife and friends were enjoying an expenses-paid vacation in Navajoland, where the Hubble name was famous, not for astronomy, but for the Hubbell Trading Post, run by Edwin's distant relatives.

In December V. M. Slipher wrote to W. A. Cogshall, his former astronomy professor at Indiana University:

Hubble was over here in October for a day or two and then went over to the Canyon to make some seeing tests. He returned by way of

Cameron and stopped there for a couple of nights and then was here again for one evening. From here he went to Tucson to see Douglass and talk seeing conditions etc. This was just before the publication of the announcement of the 200" reflector. He was making tests with a 2-inch telescope!! It was quite apparent that the new big Bertha had already been located definitely at no very great distance from Mt. Wilson.... Hale is the man behind the undertaking and it is sure to [be] placed within sight of Mt. Wilson....[9]

Slipher was underestimating Hubble's two-inch telescope. George Hale had taken pains to devise a reliable test telescope and a test comparison system. The test telescopes were designed by Russell Porter, a now-legendary telescope designer, and had several unusual features. Most of the test telescopes were four-inch, but in the hands of a skilled observer, a two-inch would suffice. We can suspect that Slipher also discounted Hubble's efforts because Slipher knew how implausible the Grand Canyon rim was for an observatory.

In January Slipher wrote to Roger Lowell Putnam:

Dr. Hubble was over this fall making some tests evidently for publicity material. He had only a two inch aperture telescope for the work! And he thought he was getting worth while tests.[10]

Slipher was no doubt correct that Hale preferred staying close to Mount Wilson with its other, still-valuable facilities; Palomar, a two-hour drive from Mount Wilson, was still much closer than Arizona. Yet Slipher didn't know that his own universe-changing redshift data was laying abandoned on Edwin Hubble's desk for the sake of the Grand Canyon, and Slipher underestimated Hale's neurotic insecurity, which nearly two years later prompted Hale to order Hubble's assistant, Milton Humason, to make another trip to the Grand Canyon to make further tests, to make sure George Ritchey was wrong.

An aside: both of Slipher's letters include a premonition of another great astronomical discovery. To Cogshall, Slipher wrote:

A young man has been writing us from west Kansas about employment in the Observatory. He is a farmer boy, with high school training, good health, much interested in astronomy, planetary work particularly.... He sent us some drawings of Jupiter that look fairly good for such a chap working all alone.... We have not as yet given him any particular encouragement, but his last letter makes us think he might make a good assistant in spite of his deficient training.[11]

To Putnam, a month later, Slipher wrote:

> The young man from Kansas is expected to come on next week. I hope he proves to be good help around the Observatory and that after a time he will be able to make exposures with the 13-inch photographic.[12]

The young farmer boy was Clyde Tombaugh, who within barely a year used the thirteen-inch photographic telescope to discover Pluto.

George Ritchey hoped to get the Carnegie Institute to fund his Grand Canyon observatory, but the Carnegie Institute was already George Hale's patron and didn't want to get embroiled in the Hale-Ritchey feud, especially when Hale was assuring them that Ritchey was a scoundrel and a lunatic. Ritchey's plan did stir up some enthusiasm within Grand Canyon National Park, but apparently not at the highest levels of the National Park Service. The agency was embroiled in numerous conflicts with the holders of private lands inside national park boundaries, and one of the worst battlegrounds was the Grand Canyon. It was not a good time for any private interest to be asking NPS leaders to give away part of Grand Canyon National Park.

George Ritchey eventually got to build a forty-inch Ritchey-Chrétien telescope at his last job at the U.S. Naval Observatory in Washington, DC. When other astronomers got a look at the telescope, it changed astronomy. When light pollution in Washington, DC, got bad, the U.S. Naval Observatory moved the telescope to its new site in Flagstaff, Arizona, not far from—but not too close to—the Grand Canyon. This was in 1955, ten years after Ritchey's death. In his retirement Ritchey began writing a book (never published) called "Our Kindly Mother Earth, with a supplementary volume The Grand Canyon and The Great American Plateau."

Though neither Ritchey nor Hale built a "desert watchtower" on the rim of the Grand Canyon, someone else did. Soon after Edwin Hubble's visit to the canyon, Santa Fe railway architect Mary Colter began designing the seventy-foot-tall Desert View Watchtower. Colter thought of it as a Native American astronomical observatory.

We know quite a bit about Mary Colter's thinking about the Watchtower, for she wrote a one-hundred-page book detailing its archaeological inspirations, architectural features, and mythological motifs. In the first chapter Colter discusses the Ancestral Puebloan towers of the Four Corners region, which had not yet been thoroughly studied by archaeologists. Colter spent over six months studying the towers, even chartering a small plane to locate towers, then driving to them to photograph and sketch them.

Colter discusses the purpose of the towers, a subject still being debated today. She dismisses the idea that they were built as granaries or habitations. She admits that many towers, given their strategic locations, were built for defensive purposes: "However, this does not account for all towers. Some are so located in the bottom of canyons that they evidently were not intended for observation or defense."[13] Colter is drawn to the idea that the towers had astronomical and ceremonial purposes:

> Another very interesting theory of the function of the towers is that they were designed for ASTRONOMICAL OBSERVATIONS, as were the towers of the Aztecs, Mayas and Toltecs in Mexico, Yucatan and Peru. In support of this theory, J. Walter Fewkes, one of the few archaeologists who writes upon the Towers of the Southwest, says: "There are indications that they (towers) were built by an agricultural people, one of the prime necessities of whom is to determine the time for planting. This can be obtained by observations of the sun's rising and setting, and a tower affords the elevation necessary for that purpose, hence the theory that southwestern towers were in part used for SUN HOUSES or OBSERVATORIES. A building from which the aboriginal priests determined calendric events by solar observations very naturally became a room for *Sun Worship* or for the worship of the *Power of the Sky*. The presence of circular subterranean rooms, or kivas, which almost always occur with towers, also indicate religious rites."[14]

By now Colter had done a more thorough survey of the towers than Fewkes did, and she adds:

> While towers frequently stood alone and less frequently were a part of communal villages, there are a number of instances where *towers*, otherwise isolated, were *built* in *conjunction with kivas*. These have been referred to by Dr. Fewkes in reference to the purpose of towers. In these instances there is a PASSAGEWAY—sometimes a tunnel of considerable length—constructed from the subterranean kiva to a flight of STONE STAIRS leading to the first floor of the tower. The best known examples of this construction are at Mesa Verde where several have been excavated.[15]

Today at Mesa Verde, the National Park Servce interpretation suggests that a combined tower-tunnel-kiva allowed a priest or kachina to emerge dramatically into a kiva ceremony from a conduit to the sky.

Mary Colter designed her Watchtower as a connected tower and kiva, though the kiva has lost its dignity by being turned into a gift shop. Colter also intended the top floor to include telescopes, just like her Lookout Studio.

While the Desert View Watchtower offers a good view of the canyon, its larger purpose is to serve as a shrine to Native American culture, especially the Hopis, whose ancestors lived inside the canyon, and for whom the canyon remains their sacred place of emergence. To create the murals on the first floor of the watchtower, Colter hired Hopi artist Fred Kabotie. The murals depict the Hopi cosmos, and are rich in astronomical themes, especially on the ceiling. Colter's book includes fifteen entries devoted to these astronomical motifs, including:

> THE STARS: In the sky realm above, the Hopi have names for the prominent STARS. Each star, or group of stars, means something. The stories of the stars as depicted on the ceiling panels...were taught to Kabotie by his grandmother when he was a very little boy sleeping on the housetop where the bright desert stars were always reminders of the old stories.

MILKY WAY: To the right of the Morning Star comes the MILKY WAY, the PATHS OF GOOD and BAD PEOPLE. The long and continuous line is the path of the good; its branch, which is short, is the path of the evil.

SHOOTING STARS: When a shooting star is seen, it is taken for granted that the star is off to officiate at a wedding, spilling some of its sacred cornmeal from its brilliant tail over the bride. Shooting stars are lucky—a sign of plenty and prosperity.

THE PLEIADES: Kabotie writes: "There is a group of stars that always cling together like mud and they are called by that name— "CHCOHOOKAM."(We call them the Pleiades.)[16]

Was Mary Colter's Desert View Watchtower inspired, at least in part, by George Ritchey's "desert watchtower"? For a couple of reasons, it seems a safe assumption that Colter was aware of Ritchey's plans.

First, in 1916 Mary Colter bought a house in Altadena, California, the town directly below Mount Wilson Observatory. Next-door Pasadena, which held the observatory's headquarters and laboratories, was a national center of Arts and Crafts architecture and design, a style very important to Colter. It's likely that Colter was drawn to the Pasadena arts and social scene, where she would have been mingling with Mount Wilson astronomers and their wives. Colter's Altadena house was a home-away-from-home, primarily occupied by Mary's sister Harriet, but according to Colter biographer Virginia L. Grattan: "Although Mary maintained an apartment in Kansas City, she traveled a great deal up and down the Santa Fe line working on new building projects. She was frequently in California to buy furnishings for hotels she was decorating and to spend time with Harriet."[17]

Second, Colter was close friends with Grand Canyon National Park superintendent Miner Tillotson, with whom she worked on some of her Grand Canyon projects. After her retirement Colter bought a Santa Fe house next door to the Tillotsons. Miner Tillotson assisted Edwin Hubble at the canyon, and he would have already known about the observatory idea from Ritchey's inquiries and publicity. The prospect of a major building on the canyon rim would have been major news for Colter.

All we know for sure is that Mary Colter appreciated astronomy and built her tower nearly on the site George Ritchey had planned for his observatory. Her architectural drawings of her watchtower are dated June 16, 1931, less than three years after Edwin Hubble had probably stood at Desert View, on the rim of creation.

3

"LOOKS LIKE A MULHATTON STORY"

The Origins of the Egyptian Cave Myth

In the years since 1992 some dramatic new Grand Canyon lore has emerged, mutated rapidly, taken on elaborate forms, and won a large, loyal following. This story appears on thousands of websites and has been presented many times on a national radio show. It is now showing up in books and movies, and is well on its way to becoming a standard part of the Grand Canyon landscape—at least the paranormal landscape. This story has the momentum to take a firmly rooted place alongside Roswell, the Sedona vortexes, and Atlantis.

It seems that in 1909 a Smithsonian explorer named G. E. Kinkaid was making a solo boat trip down the length of the Colorado River and discovered a giant cave in a cliff of the Grand Canyon. This cave was located forty-two miles upstream from "El Tovar Crystal Canyon" (wherever that is). Although perched 2,000 feet above the level of today's river, the cave had a set of steps extending 30 yards down from the entrance, suggesting that the river had been 2,000 feet higher—or the canyon 2,000 feet shallower—at the time it was inhabited. Kinkaid reported that it held an elaborate system of tunnels and chambers, and hundreds of rooms with straight walls, obviously cut by humans. The chambers were full of artifacts, hieroglyphs, and mummies, evidently Egyptian in origin. There was also a statue that looked like Buddha. The artifacts included inscribed tablets, gold urns and cups, pottery, weapons, and sophisticated copper tools and instruments. There were granaries made out of cement. A 700-foot-long dining hall still held cooking utensils. These chambers had been home to an estimated 50,000 people.

One thing about this story is absolutely true: it was published on the front page of Phoenix's *Arizona Gazette* on April 5, 1909, under the headlines: "EXPLORATIONS IN GRAND CANYON/ Mysteries of Immense Rich Cavern Being Brought to Light/ JORDAN IS ENTHUSED/ Remarkable Finds Indicate Ancient People Migrated From Orient." The article explained that Professor S. A. Jordan of the Smithsonian Institution had arrived to begin scientific examination of the cavern. He was stringing up electric lights through the passageways. Jordan seemed pretty sure that the cavern was the work of Egyptians. The article said:

> If their theories are born out by the translation of the tablets engraved with hieroglyphics, the mystery of the prehistoric peoples of North America, their ancient arts, who they were and whence they came, will be solved. Egypt and the Nile, and Arizona and the Colorado will be linked by a historical chain running back to ages which will stagger the wildest fancy of the fictionist.

The *Gazette* story was soon forgotten, but in 1962 it was rescued from obscurity by being included in *Arizona Cavalcade*, one of a series of five books of newspaper articles from early Arizona history. From there it eventually came to the attention of David Hatcher Childress, who included it in his 1992 book *Lost Cities of North and Central America*, a personal exploration of the occult secrets of and Old World influences on American archaeological sites. Childress related how, upon discovering the Egyptian cave story, he got out a map of the Grand Canyon and was "shocked" to see that a whole section of formations in the canyon had Egyptian names, such as Isis Temple and the Tower of Ra. Surely this had to be the location of the Egyptian cave. When Childress contacted the Smithsonian and Grand Canyon National Park, he discovered that they were conspiring in a diabolical cover-up of the truth. The Smithsonian tried to deny the existence of Kinkaid and Jordan, and at Grand Canyon National Park, "This entire area with the Egyptian and Hindu place names is a forbidden zone, [and] no one is allowed into this large area."[1]

Childress's presentation of the Egyptian cave story struck a chord—a mystic chord—with seekers of the esoteric. The ancient Egyptians were the masters of spiritual knowledge, their pyramids loaded with cosmic secrets. The Grand Canyon was nature's deepest revelation of primordial power and time. The combination of ancient Egypt and the Grand Canyon was too rich to resist.

A quick Internet search yields highly elaborate theories about the Grand Canyon's supposed Egyptian cave. There are contending schools of thought about its location: some say that it must be in the Egyptian names section, while others insist that it has to be forty-two miles upstream from Kinkaid's "El Tovar Crystal Canyon." Websites show photos of various cave entrances, including that of Stanton's Cave. Stanton's Cave has indeed produced important archaeological artifacts, and today its entrance is caged off to protect endangered bats, but paranormal websites claim this is really because of its Egyptian secrets.

Several groups have traveled to the canyon to search for the Egyptian cave. Theories try to relate the Egyptian cave to Ancestral Puebloan artifacts, Hopi legends, Atlantis, Area 51, and even "The Thing," the Arizona tourist-trap mummy on Interstate 10 east of Tucson—which came from the Grand Canyon cave! People spin new geological theories to explain why the Colorado River was recently 2,000 feet deeper—or maybe the canyon was 2,000 feet shallower. In a cover story in the May 2009 issue of the paranormal magazine *Atlantis Rising*, David Hatcher Childress proposed that the prehistoric settlement on the canyon's Unkar delta was actually built by the Egyptians, and that its name was a corruption of the Egyptian name "Ankh-Ra," a reference to the Egyptian sun god Ra.

To take one example of Egyptian cave research, websites offer long calculations of how sacred geometry connects the cave with the rest of the esoteric world. The Egyptian pyramids are considered the ultimate masterpieces of sacred geometry, their locations and proportions and alignments embodying all the secrets of the cosmos. It thus stands to reason that there should be a sacred geometry connection between the Great Pyramid at Giza and the Grand Canyon, and it turns out that the canyon's Isis Temple fits perfectly into the Egyptian cosmic matrix code. The location, dimensions, and angles of Isis Temple correlate with the Great Pyramid of Giza with fantastic mathematical accuracy, to seven or eight decimal places. Isis Temple also shows amazing mathematical correlations with the Sphinx, Stonehenge, the star Sirius, and the Face on Mars. All of this implies that Isis Temple must be the location of the Egyptian cave and that Isis Temple was actually human-made. But when one expedition to Isis Temple climbed eight hundred feet up to the most promising cave entrance, they discovered that it was clearly human-made and had been dynamited shut.

As theories have become more elaborate, so have claims of a cover-up by the Smithsonian and the National Park Service. David Hatcher Childress now claims that the Smithsonian has been destroying evidence of the Egyptians in America, even towing a barge full of artifacts into the Atlantic and dumping them overboard. Others say that the National Park Service has closed the airspace in the canyon, hiking entry to the Egyptian zone, and entry into all caves in order to hide Egyptian artifacts. Within a few weeks in early 2008, listeners to *Coast to Coast*, the national paranormal radio show, heard David Hatcher Childress say that the Hopis had thrown acid into the eyes of Grand Canyon miner Seth Tanner to blind him and prevent him from finding the Egyptian cave; and they heard giant-expert Steve Quayle say that the occupants of the cave were twelve to fourteen feet tall, and that Quayle had met someone who swore he participated in removing the giants' mummies from the cave and taking them to Area 51.

Does it ever occur to Egyptian cave believers that the *Arizona Gazette* story could have been a hoax? In fact, it does. Even Childress, in *Lost Cities of North and Central America*, admitted that when he first saw the story in *Arizona Cavalcade*, he "bet it was fabricated by the author of that book. It sounds phony."[2] Then Childress looked up the original *Gazette* article, and "There it was in black and white." This verdict is often stated by Egyptian cave believers: if a story appears on the front page of a newspaper, it must be true.

This conclusion would have come as a surprise to American newspaper readers in 1909—and even more so to newspaper editors. Journalism was not yet an honest and honorable profession. Only that year did an American college open the world's first school of journalism. There were no Pulitzer Prizes to reward professionalism. This was the era of yellow journalism, which recently had helped spark the Spanish-American War. Newspapers were often the shameless tools of political parties, town boosters, or businessmen—including swindlers. Arizona was in the midst of a golden age of mining, and nearly every day the newspapers shouted about new mineral discoveries, many of which were merely swindles designed to attract stock money from investors back east. On March 29, only a week before the Egyptian cave article appeared, the *Gazette's* Phoenix rival, the *Arizona Republican*, ran an editorial titled "A Little Essay About Mines and Faking," defending itself from complaints that it was publishing articles that legitimized swindles. The *Republican* denied it, but added that, anyway, all that East Coast money was great for the Arizona economy.

The Egyptian cave story should have been big news for Arizona, eagerly repeated by other newspapers: Another Colorado River expedition! A major Smithsonian expedition to Arizona! Egyptians in Arizona! Yet the *Gazette* story was almost totally ignored by other Arizona newspapers. Of over a dozen newspapers checked for this article, only two reprinted it: the *Jerome Mining News*, without comment, and Flagstaff's *Coconino Sun*, whose editors thought it was necessary to comment. It ran a brief front-page article with the headline: "Looks Like a Mulhatton Story." For American newspaper readers in 1909, this said everything that needed to be said.

By 1909 Joe Mulhatton (his last name gets spelled in various ways, often "Mulhattan") had been famous for thirty years for his hobby of tricking newspapers into publishing hoax stories. According to the Museum of Hoaxes, "During the 1870s and 1880s Joseph Mulhattan was perhaps the most famous hoaxer in America."[3] He was especially fond of—and famous for—inventing outlandish stories about discoveries of caves full of amazing artifacts from ancient civilizations.

In 1883, when Mulhatton was just getting started, the *American Antiquarian and Oriental Journal* thought it prudent to issue a warning to archaeologists:

> Joe Mulhattan is a character of some interest to archaeologists—his residence is in Kentucky, and his business is to invent marvelous stories or lies. He has invented seven stories about finding big caves, Masonic emblems, and other ridiculous things.... Another just sent to us from Eureka Springs, Arkansas, about an iron box and a skeleton chained, in a cave, shows that he is still at work.[4]

In 1888 Mulhatton was included in the book *Prominent Men and Women of the Day*, alongside Mark Twain, Walt Whitman, and Oscar Wilde. The book warned:

When the readers meet with a circumstantial account of hidden rivers being found here or there, of vast bodies of water deep under ground...he is exhorted to think of Mulhattan; and the ethnologist and geologist are warned against believing all they see in newspapers about newly discovered works by prehistoric man. How many persuasively written and circumstantial fabrics of lies Mr. Mulhattan has written probably only their author knows.[5]

On November 12, 1891, the *New York Times* declared:

Joe Mulhattan is known in every city in the United States and has probably caused more trouble in newspaper offices than any other man in the country. His wild stories, written in the most plausible style, have more than once caused the special correspondents of the progressive journals of the United States to hurry from coast to coast to investigate some wonderful occurrence which only existed in the imagination of the great liar.

Mulhatton's first hoax was about discovering "Grand Crystal Cave" beneath Glasgow Junction, Kentucky, a cave which was "wonderful beyond description, and far surpasses in grandeur" nearby Mammoth Cave. On June 22, 1878, the *Cincinnati Commercial* published Mulhatton's article about the cave's discovery, and even though the next day's Louisville *Courier-Journal* exposed it as a hoax, the article was soon reprinted all over the country. "Grand Crystal Cave" was said to be at least twenty-three miles long: "A span of horses can easily be driven through for a distance of eleven miles." There were "three rivers, wide and very deep," one of which "is navigable for fourteen miles, until the passages become too narrow to admit a boat.... Several mummified remains have been discovered in one of the large rooms. They were reposing in stone coffins, rudely constructed, and from appearances, they may have been in this cave for centuries. They present every appearance of the Egyptian mummies." An entrepreneur was planning to offer steamboat rides inside the cave.

A year later, on June 7, 1879, Mulhatton placed his most embellished version of the Grand Crystal Cave story in *Frank Leslie's Illustrated Newspaper*:

they discovered an immense room, in dimensions about one hundred yards in width by about one hundred feet in height.... The beauties of this chamber are simply indescribable. It is called the Crystal Chamber, and is well named.... At a distance of about three miles, in a very picturesque spot, six mummies were found on a ledge of rocks. They were reposing in stone coffins rudely constructed, and presented every appearance of the Egyptian mummies. Three of the mummies were male and three female. [The female mummies had] a fine, intelligent, refined cast, beautiful even thousands of years after the visit of the destroying angel.

On December 12, 1881, the *Chicago Inter-Ocean* reported the discovery at Litchfield, Kentucky, of a new cave that included an Egyptian pyramid and hieroglyphs:

There are evidences on all sides that the cave was the abode of a prehistoric race, and that that race was identified with the ancient Egyptian races.... Joseph Mulhattan, geologist and scientist, from Louisville, Ky., has visited the cave, and secured several mummies and other specimens—but the pyramid and remaining wonders will remain untouched to be gazed upon by a wondering world.

In truth, Mulhatton was a traveling salesman, usually for hardware companies. A salesman needs to tell whoppers with a straight face, and Joe's wide travels provided him with plenty of raw material for stories and access to many newspapers. In 1884 a national convention of traveling salesmen was so proud of Joe's storytelling talents that they nominated him for president of the United States.

Yet another Mulhatton cave hoax was still remembered decades later, as shown by a 1908 story in an Arizona newspaper, the Globe *Silver Belt*.

Joe Mulhatton's story of a wonderful cave in Pike County, Kentucky, was a highly decorated piece of art. It appeared in a Louisville paper, and set people on two continents talking of the rooms full of magnificent jewels, of long halls lined with great blocks of virgin gold and of subterranean rivers rippling over beds of diamonds.... Even P. T. Barnum, the wily old showman, was caught in the trap and hastened to Pike County to see if he might be able to pick up a few rare skeletons of strange cave-dwellers that the excited discoverer had overlooked.[6]

In 1883 Mulhatton got wide circulation for a story about how Birmingham, Alabama, had been built atop a thin crust of stone over a cave with a huge river flowing through it. The construction of a new building had punctured the crust, and several buildings had fallen into the cave.

According to the Museum of Hoaxes:

> Mulhattan apparently concocted his hoaxes purely for the thrill of deceiving the media. He would send his stories to newspaper offices, and editors would usually accept them without question. Many editors probably realized the stories were false, but printed them anyway, knowing that they were amusing and would boost circulation.[7]

Mulhatton did lots of non-cave hoaxes too. His first big hit was his 1877 story about how George Washington's body had become petrified. For April Fool's Day in 1880 Mulhatton placed a story about a little girl who was given a batch of helium-filled balloons at a party. When she tied the balloons around her waist, they lifted her into the air, but luckily an expert hunter was present and shot the balloons one by one to bring the girl to a gentle landing. In 1883 Mulhatton passed off a story about a giant meteor hitting a Texas ranch and killing lots of cattle. In 1887 his story about a Kentucky farmer who was training monkeys to pick hemp brought a strong rebuke from the *New York Times*, which feared that the "scab monkeys" would take the jobs of former slaves. Mulhatton also may have had a hand in the story of David Lang, a Tennessee farmer who was walking across his field and simply vanished, in sight of many witnesses, a story that was given wide circulation by paranormal journalist Frank Edwards in the 1950s and is still alive today.

But Mulhatton enjoyed his cave hoaxes the most. In 1883 he told an interviewer, "I am prouder of my Glasgow Cave story than any of the others. It showed more invention and more imagination."[8] These hoaxes made such an imprint that when the Louisville *Courier-Journal* announced a legitimate cave discovery in 1887, it felt obligated to use the headline: "Not a Mulhattan Story."

In 1893 Mulhatton gave up his salesman's life for the life of a prospector—in Arizona. The details of his time in Arizona are sketchy, and he left the state periodically, partly to sell Arizona mining stocks. We do know that he spent a few months in 1900 at an asylum in Phoenix. Mulhatton was plagued by alcoholism, which reduced him to committing petty crimes and looking like a tramp. But this didn't stop him from inventing new hoaxes, using Arizona as raw material. The state's newspapers were proud to cite him as the source of his tall tales; it was an honor for Joe Mulhatton to walk into your small-town newspaper office and give you a scoop.

In 1899 the *Florence Tribune* reported:

> Joe Mulhatton was in Florence this week from the Ripsey country, where he has recently discovered a magnetic cactus.... Its attractive powers are so great that it draws birds and animals to it and impales them on its thorny spikes. Mr. Mulhatton approached no nearer than one hundred feet to the cactus, which is of the saguaro variety, yet at that distance it was all he could do to resist its influence to draw him to it. While in town he purchased a long rope, which he will tie around his body, and four of his friends will take hold of it and allow him to approach near enough to minutely examine the wonder without danger.... After and just before a great storm the...power of the cactus is indescribable. Calves, birds, and young colts are attracted, impaled, drawn in and quickly converted by the digestive juices of the cactus....[9]

Mulhatton's magnetic cactus became a staple of Arizona folklore, repeated today in books such as state historian Marshall Trimble's *In Old Arizona*.

Also in 1899 the *Tombstone Prospector* reported:

> Joe Mulhatton, the truthful, has made another great discovery. He writes of his latest in the Florence Tribune and describes experiments on Compressed Heat, saying he has invented a very simple apparatus whereby the surplus heat of an Arizona summer may be stored away for use in winter or utilized for generating power for machinery, electric plants, and other uses by compressing 382 degrees above zero into a cake of heat that has dwindled down to 281 degrees Fahrenheit below zero. The expansive power of this compressed heat is enormous, also slightly

dangerous.... A stock company with a capitalization of $500,000,000
is proposed to perfect the new discovery and place it within reach of
the masses, so it might become of practical benefit in the uplifting of
mankind.[10]

Already by 1899 Joe Mulhatton's tales were common currency in Arizona.
In 1910, the year after the *Arizona Gazette* published the Egyptian cave story,
the *Gazette* published a fond tribute to Mulhatton and his talents. In 1952 this
story, and the other Arizona newspaper stories cited above, were reprinted in
The Arizona Story, another in the series of five books of early Arizona newspaper articles that also included *Arizona Cavalcade*, from which the Egyptian
cave story came to the attention of David Hatcher Childress.

Among the miners who wandered into Kelvin the past week from the
surrounding camps was one with a knapsack strapped on his shoulders. The sack was stuffed with food, blank location notices, mail and
miscellany until it would hold no more. The bearer was short of stat-
ure, quick of speech and wore a short, black beard and genial smile. His
name, Joe Mulhatton....

Joe Mulhatton was once a widely known man. He is now known
of throughout the United States, especially in the east and south, but
in his seclusion in the Dagger Wells country, is actually known by few.

Joe Mulhatton formerly gained his livelihood as a traveling salesman. He was a hardware drummer. That vocation gave Joe the opportunity to capitalize affability, suavity and rapidity of speech, all of which
he possesses to a marked degree. He was a successful salesman, and it
was while traveling over the country selling his wares, that Mulhatton
acquired fame as a literary prodigy in the art of prevarication. He is a
burlesquer of facts. His friends, for convenience sake, use the adjective
"liar." Joe never protested then, nor does he object now to reading in
cold type that he was the most artistic, beautiful and consistent liar ever
turned loose on a nation....

The rules of logic nor laws of consistency were never violated by
Mulhatton, and his writings were always embellished with a literary
touch that made them readable, entertaining and almost believable.

He never touched on a scientific matter, but his published story was followed by a flood of letters of inquiry from college professors and other scientific men.... There is nothing disproportionate or contradictory, one part to another, in any of Mulhatton's stories. Every sentence bears a consistent relation to every other sentence.... As a narrator of events that never happened, Baron Münchhausen was much farther away from the people than Mulhatton. Mulhatton's writings catch the interest of the average reader much quicker than Münchhausen's....

Joe Mulhatton, the miner, is the Joe Mulhatton of other days in disguise. Garbed as a miner, living as a miner, and with miners, with attention directed to leads, lodes and ledges, dips and spurs, to the earth's formations and ascertainment of mineral values, suits Joe better than the routine of the drummer's life. He has seen the world, had his experience, and of his own volition chosen the Dagger Wells country, Arizona, as his abode. "It's a place of rest, a kind of retreat, for us who have had our troubles," remarked Mr. Mulhatton. His line of thought is now directed along psychic lines. "I am a spiritualist," he added. "Say that you saw me well and not 'broke.' I believe in spiritualism. I lay in my cabin and commune with the higher powers. Omnipotence directs me, and directs you. All believe in it who understand it." Joe Mulhatton has fifty claims and they are reported as having excellent showing. The vicissitudes of life have not dried up the fountain of milk of human kindness in Joe Mulhatton. Nothing but kindness gleams from his eyes, and the friendly handshake is extended to all. Greed, gain and graft have left no marks on him. If only one meal in his cabin, that would be given to the hungry beggar before he would eat it himself. He has entertained with his stories and spread good cheer and sunshine by his presence, from one coast of the United States to the other.[11]

This 1910 *Gazette* article made no mention of the Egyptian cave story of the previous year.

In the weeks after running the story in 1909, the *Gazette* made no further comment on it. There was really no reason for newspapers to do so. Everyone understood where this type of story was coming from. These were the years when John Hance, a master of tall tales, was a tourist attraction at the

Grand Canyon. Tall tales had long been an American tradition, especially on the frontier. Newspaper hoaxes were also a long tradition: early in the nineteenth century a Boston newspaper ran a hoax story about a treasure-filled cave discovered under Boston Common. Readers didn't even bother to call such stories hoaxes, for their truthfulness was irrelevant. Readers were supposed to admire the authors' talent of imagination.

That's also what the *Coconino Sun* did in its April 16, 1909, article headlined "Looks Like a Mulhatton Story":

> The reported discovery of a mammoth underground city of an ancient race in the Grand Canyon, seems to be a splendid piece of imagination sent out by some Mulhattonized individual.... it would be just possible that some one at the Grand Canyon would have been informed of it if an actual discovery had been made. The man who wrote up the find certainly had to dig for the details and was wise in locating the entrance at a point on a sheer wall where no one but a person with a great imagination could reach it.

It is possible that the Egyptian cave story was hatched not by Mulhatton himself, but by someone inspired by him. If so, the imitator was an excellent student, for the story bore all the subtle fingerprints of Mulhatton's "classic" cave discovery stories. For starters, Mulhatton's cave mummies and artifacts were usually Egyptian, but he also loved to maintain an air of mystery, stopping short of declaring for sure that they were Egyptian. In the Grand Crystal Cave story the mummies "give every appearance of the Egyptian mummies," and in the 1909 *Gazette* story the builders of the Grand Canyon cave are "possibly from Egypt." In both Kentucky and the Grand Canyon, the Egyptians left mysterious hieroglyphs. The mummies are found in large, special chambers deep inside the caves. In Grand Crystal Cave the mummies were said to be arranged "on a ledge of rocks," and in the Grand Canyon cave there were "tiers of mummies, each one occupying a separate hewn shelf." The list of artifacts found with the mummies is similar, such as copper vessels. At Grand Crystal Cave "ladders and bridges are being constructed," and in the Grand Canyon cave, this now being the age of electricity, "wires are being strung from the entrance to all passageways." Mulhatton named his favorite cave "Grand Crystal Cave," and at the Grand Canyon we find "El Tovar Crystal

Canyon." Looks like a genuine Mulhatton story, perhaps the last hurrah of an aging, alcoholic man who had failed as a prospector but sadly remembered his glory days as a celebrated writer.

The *Arizona Gazette* was a good fit for the Egyptian cave story. It had a flair for humor and sensationalism, and on most days its editorial page included jokes and brief tall tales. On April 8, 1909, the *Gazette* announced, "Astronomers on Mars reported at a recent meeting of the society that observations of the earth showed large patches of the lake region of the United States in the western hemisphere as going dry."

The *Gazette* may have been having some extra fun with the Egyptian cave story by placing it right next to an advertisement from a local candy store. The advertisement ran for one week, offering a Phoenix-style Easter gift that could be shipped to friends back east. The gift was orange blossoms, waxed to preserve them. In large letters the ad was headlined: "ORANGE BLOSSOMS." According to the Museum of Hoaxes entry on Joe Mulhatton: "He was also widely known by his pseudonym, 'Orange Blossom.'"[12]

Since the Egyptian cave story appeared on April 5, close to April Fool's Day, was it supposed to be an April Fool's joke? But if so, why didn't it actually appear on April 1? The *Gazette* does not seem to have had an annual tradition of an April Fool's Day story. In 1909, the April 1 paper was packed with news of the closing and dedication of Laguna Dam on the Colorado River, a major event for Arizona, and there were leftover Laguna Dam stories for the next few days. The *Gazette* didn't publish on Sundays, so there was no April 4 edition. We do know that the Egyptian cave story was planned well in advance, for on March 12 the *Gazette* published a short teaser about explorer G. E. Kinkaid's arrival in Yuma.

The *Gazette* also practiced tabloid style sensationalism, in contrast with the *Arizona Republican*, whose front page headlines were serious news stories. In the weeks around the publication of the Egyptian cave story, *Gazette* readers saw headlines about murders, suicides, crazy people, and freak accidents from around the world: VILLIAN STABS WOMAN TO DEATH. DAUGHTER IS KILLED BY FATHER. WOMAN DIES BY ELECTRIC CHAIR. DENVER SUICIDE BELIEVED INSANE. NEFARIOUS WORK OF A DOG POISONER. NITROGLYCERINE PLANT BLOWS UP, TWO KILLED. INSANE NAVAJO ON RAMPAGE. WHITE GIRL TO MARRY JAP.

The *Gazette* was the smaller Phoenix newspaper, in both circulation and number of pages, and it was trying hard to boost circulation. The Egyptian cave story was published in the middle of the "Young Ladies Popular Contest," in which readers could send in printed ballots to vote for their favorite young lady. The candidates could earn extra points by selling subscriptions.

Where did Mulhatton come up with the details of the Egyptian cave story, such as the names Kinkaid and Jordan? In the case of "Professor S. A. Jordan, the Smithsonian Institute," there's a source that would have been obvious in 1909. One of the most famous naturalists of the era was David Starr Jordan, who had been affiliated with the Smithsonian for thirty years, the length of time that the *Arizona Gazette* listed for Kinkaid's affiliation with the Smithsonian. In 1909 David Star Jordan was the president of Stanford University. He was a leading figure in the worlds of education and science, and even better known for his political activities as an antiwar advocate. Jordan made front-page headlines in the Prescott *Weekly Journal Miner* on May 5, 1909: "Dr. Jordan Addresses the Peace Avocation in Chicago." His views often made him controversial. In a national magazine in 1909 Jordan denounced Christian fundamentalist fervor as "simply a form of drunkenness no more worthy of respect than the drunkenness that lies in the gutter."[13] In 1925 Jordan would be one of the star witnesses in the Scopes trial, defending the teaching of evolution. In 1906 he was offered the directorship of the Smithsonian, and he was ready to accept, but then the San Francisco earthquake wrecked the Stanford campus, and Jordan felt obligated to remain there. A decade before he had been offered the directorship of the Smithsonian's National Museum of Natural History, but Jordan was only five years into his presidency at Stanford and felt that too many of his initiatives remained unfinished.

Jordan began his affiliation with the Smithsonian in the mid-1870s, when he began collecting fish for the museum. The founder of American ichthyology, he named 2,500 species, and more than 25 species were named for him. He published hundreds of scientific papers, a large portion of them in the Smithsonian's journals. He made collecting trips all over the country, trips that automatically made him an explorer of rivers. His adventures often made it into newspapers.

In 1898 Jordan visited the Grand Canyon in the company of Charles Lummis and wrote an article about it for Lummis's magazine, *Out West*. In 1902 this article was reprinted in the Atchison, Topeka, and Santa Fe Railway's promotional book *Grand Canyon of Arizona*. Naturally Jordan was interested in the Colorado River, and his article emphasized how the river, not earthquakes or any other force (unspoken, including God), had carved the Grand Canyon: "the river had done all this alone."[14]

Another connection between Jordan and the Grand Canyon was that in 1903–4 David Rust was enrolled at Stanford. Rust was the developer of Rust's Camp, the tourist facility at the bottom of the canyon (soon to be Phantom Ranch); the trail from the North Rim; and a cable tramway over the Colorado River. While Rust was at Stanford, his wife, Ruth, had a baby whom they named David Jordan Rust in honor of David Starr Jordan.

The name "Professor Jordan" had another connotation. In 1896 David Starr Jordan had perpetrated a famous scientific hoax, though in the end the joke was on him. Jordan was contemptuous of the flourishing belief in psychic powers, and with the complicity of the editor of *Popular Science Monthly* Jordan published an article in which he claimed he had invented a device that could photograph telepathic images. "The satirical nature of my story I had supposed sufficiently clear," wrote Jordan in his autobiography. "But the scientific minuteness of detail proved to be fatally complete, and a surprising number of people took the thing seriously."[15] Joe Mulhatton could have told him that one of the keys to a successful hoax was lots of details. In the words of Professor Keven McQueen of Eastern Kentucky University, who was writing a biography of Mulhatton and who helped with some of the details of this chapter, "Mulhattan's attention to detail is so convincing and diabolically deadpan that it is easy to understand how his hoaxes fooled jaded newspaper editors and their readers."[16] One reason why David Hatcher Childress accepted the *Gazette* story as true was because it "gave a highly descriptive and detailed story that went on for several pages."[17]

The name *Kinkaid* doesn't have such an obvious source. There were no famous American explorers or Egyptologists named Kinkaid or Kincaid. The only possibility is University of Washington zoologist Trevor Kincaid, who was a friend of David Starr Jordan. Jordan once offered Kincaid a job at Stanford, and Kincaid accompanied Jordan on one of his expeditions to Alaska. Kincaid also went on an Alaska expedition that included John Muir and John Burroughs.

There is a promising archaeological connection with the name *Kincaid*. One of the largest and most significant sites of the Mississippian culture is the Kincaid Mounds, near the Ohio River in southern Illinois. Like the most famous Mississippian site, Cahokia, the Kincaid site holds a large cluster of mounds, the tallest ten feet tall, arranged around a plaza, all once enclosed by a wooden palisade. The Kincaid Mounds are located in the tip of southern Illinois, which European settlers named "Little Egypt" for its main city of Cairo and for the Nile-like grandeur and fertility of the Mississippi and Ohio Rivers. Little Egypt also includes towns named Thebes and Karnak, and it includes Southern Illinois University, whose mascot is the saluki, an Egyptian hunting dog, sometimes called "the royal dog of Egypt," for salukis have been found mummified in the tombs of the pharaohs. Today Southern Illinois University is excavating the Kincaid Mounds, named for James Kincaid, who settled there in 1835, and for his son Thomas Kincaid, who built his house atop the highest mound in 1875.

The problem with this Kincaid connection is that the Kincaid Mounds didn't become well-known until the University of Chicago first excavated them in 1934. In 1909 they seem to have been quite obscure, even within the world of archaeology. It's not clear that the Kincaid Mounds were even known by that name in 1909. The only plausible way to connect the Kincaid Mounds with the *Gazette* story is to suppose that the story's author happened to be from southern Illinois. But then, Joe Mulhatton lived in Louisville, Kentucky, about 150 miles up the Ohio River from the Kincaid Mounds, and Joe did get around; a farmhouse perched atop a mysterious mound was the sort of thing that would have caught his fancy.

In the same year that Mulhatton was a guest of the state asylum in Phoenix, the city's most prominent resident would have made a perfect model for G. E. Kinkaid, and his name even had the right ring to it—Clarence King. King-kaid. King was the epitome of the romantic naturalist-adventurer, having roamed the West, especially the Sierra Nevada, climbing mountains, crossing deserts, descending rivers, discovering the first known glacier in the United States, and writing popular books and articles about his adventures. Jealous of John Wesley Powell, King wanted to do his own expedition down the Green and Colorado Rivers but never did. He did explore a few caves and many mines. King's adventures were all for the sake of science: he was a geologist and the first director of the U.S. Geological Survey. Like David Starr Jordan, King was associated with a famous hoax, the Great Diamond Hoax, in which swindlers were salting Colorado ground with bogus diamonds; King was the one who exposed the hoax. Though he died in Phoenix in 1901, he remained a legend.

Another right-sounding possibility for the origins of the name *Kinkaid* is the then-prominent archaeologist J. O. Kinnaman. Kinnaman studied archaeology at the University of Chicago and the University of Rome, and a few years after 1909 he became the editor of the leading archaeology journal of the time, *American Antiquarian and Oriental Journal,* which had sounded a warning about Mulhatton's hoaxes three decades before. Yet Kinnaman was also an enthusiast for the esoteric; he sometimes wrote articles for *The Theosophical Path.* He endorsed a 1913 book called *Ancient Chinese Account of the Grand Canyon,* by Alexander McAllan, who claimed that the ancient Chinese knew all about it. Today writers on the esoteric claim that Kinnaman discovered a secret entrance to the Great Pyramid of Giza, as well as secret passageways and chambers that held documents from Atlantis and antigravitational machines that the Atlanteans had used to build the pyramids 35,000 years ago. Kinnaman is said to have believed that a giant crystal inside the Great Pyramid turned the pyramid into a giant telepathic radio system, allowing Egyptian priests to send messages all over the world, including into the Grand Canyon.

Like David Starr Jordan and Clarence King, J. O. Kinnaman became associated with a famous hoax, but in his case he was taken in by it. Starting in 1890, near Detroit, artifacts were discovered that depicted Noah's flood and God handing Moses the Ten Commandments. Prominent archaeologists examined the artifacts and declared them to be hoaxes, but J. O. Kinnaman endorsed them and declared that they changed the entire story of human civilization. Then the head of the archaeology department at the University of Chicago, Frederic Starr, had a talk with Kinnaman, who admitted that he'd been duped.

The *Gazette* article listed few details about Kinkaid's life, but one of them seemed meant to invoke another famous river explorer. Kinkaid was said to have been born in Lewiston, Idaho, a river town named for Meriwether Lewis.

Kinkaid was also said to be a longtime hunter and explorer. A few newspaper articles in early March of 1909 might have set Joe Mulhatton thinking about Colorado River expeditions, big game hunters, and Smithsonian expeditions. On March 3 Congress appropriated money to build a memorial to

John Wesley Powell on the South Rim of the Grand Canyon (it would take the form of a Central American pyramid). The next day, Teddy Roosevelt retired from the presidency and headed off on an African safari; when the public protested his killing beautiful animals, Teddy claimed that he was just gathering specimens for the Smithsonian.

The Egyptian cave article seems to bear the imprint of some of the cultural trends of the time, especially a widespread enthusiasm for ancient Egypt. Europe and America had been smitten ever since Napoleon landed in Egypt in 1798. Egyptian-style architecture flourished in America, most notably with the Washington Monument. Ancient Egypt inspired *Aida* in 1871 and plenty of lower culture, such as the mummy's curse story, a genre invented by Louisa May Alcott in 1869. The years between 1880 and World War I have been called the golden age of Egyptian archaeology, which was finally well organized and had plenty of easy discoveries to make. American newspapers were full of stories of exotic Egyptian discoveries: tombs, secret tunnels, buried statues, mysterious papyri, golden coffins. Americans flocked to museums and world's fairs to see Egyptian artifacts.

Three days before the Egyptian cave article appeared, the people of Phoenix—another town whose name derived from Egyptian mythology—flocked to the auditorium at the Normal College in Tempe to see the opera *The Egyptian Princess*. It seems to have been inspired by *Aida*, which was playing at the Met in New York City that same weekend, starring Enrico Caruso. On April 5, the same day that the *Gazette* published the Egyptian cave story, the *Arizona Republican* reviewed *The Egyptian Princess*: "Through clever arrangements of lights and paintings, the rear of the stage showed…a characteristic Egyptian scene with the pyramids in the back ground and the river Nile. The pillar and lintel were also attractively painted with typical Egyptian figures."

Americans of that era also indulged in the idea that the ancient Egyptians had visited America. It was natural enough to wonder if the pyramids in Central America might have been inspired by the Egyptian pyramids, but Americans were perhaps too eager to attribute ancient American structures to anyone but the Indians; Manifest Destiny was easier on the conscience if Indians were only subhuman savages. Mississippian mounds—such as the Kincaid Mounds—were among the structures attributed to the Egyptians, the lost tribes of Israel, the Celts, the Vikings. Rock art was regularly taken for

Egyptian hieroglyphs. Even in the Southwest, where descendants of Ancestral Puebloans were living in smaller versions of cities like Chaco and Mesa Verde, people preferred to believe that the prehistoric inhabitants had simply vanished. The *Gazette*'s Egyptian cave article supposed that "the present Indian tribes found in Arizona are descendants of the serfs or slaves of the people which inhabited the cave," a people who, like white Americans, considered that the proper place of Indians.

Only eight months before the *Gazette* story, Egyptians were being reported nearby. On August 1, 1908, the *Bullfrog Miner* in Rhyolite, Nevada, just outside of Death Valley, reported that Charles Glastonbury, supposedly a former Egyptologist from Cambridge, England, and a fellow of the Royal Society, had conducted an archaeological study of Death Valley and concluded that it once held an ancient, sophisticated civilization. His main evidence was a huge masonry dam, originally twenty feet high, that Glastonbury said must have been built "for furnishing water power for some mining or manufacturing enterprise.... In other parts of the valley I found hieroglyphic inscriptions on the rocks, very closely resembling the inscriptions found in the Valley of the Nile. I am led to the belief that the ancient inhabitants of Death Valley were closely related to the builders of the pyramids."

Ancient Egypt was especially attractive for seekers into the esoteric, who projected onto Egypt all sorts of spiritual needs and schemes. They were enthralled by reports of tombs and tunnels and chambers inside and under the Sphinx and pyramids, secret chambers that readily symbolized their belief that the world held a hidden spiritual design. American psychic Edgar Cayce, who believed that ancient Egypt was built by refugees from Atlantis, declared that the Atlanteans had stored their spiritual wisdom in a hidden Hall of Records beneath the Sphinx. H. Spencer Lewis, who drew upon Egyptian lore in founding the Rosicrucian order in 1909, declared that he had secret knowledge about chambers and tunnels beneath the Sphinx and pyramids. Today New Age writers claim that pyramid tunnels are aligned with the stars and reveal the spiritual secrets of the universe, while others posit that extraterrestrials built the Sphinx and pyramids.

The golden age of Egyptology coincided with the golden age of enthusiasm for the world underground. Americans were discovering caves full of fantastic formations, including Carlsbad Caverns, which was being explored and publicized in the decade before 1909. On March 17, two weeks before the Egyptian cave story, the *Arizona Republican* reprinted an article from the *New York Times* with the headline "Great Cave in Adirondacks: Explorer Penetrates it 1,000 Feet and Thinks it Rivals Mammoth Caves." (It didn't.) Anthropologists were popularizing the idea of cave dwellers, and popular novels depicted caves as places of adventure, as in *Tom Sawyer;* of lost treasure, as in *The Count of Monte Cristo*; and of fantastic hidden worlds, as in *A Journey to the Center of the Earth.* The latter Jules Verne novel launched a thriving genre focused on journeys into the underworld—sometimes huge cave systems, sometimes a hollow Earth inhabited by strange civilizations. In his book *The Hollow Earth* David Standish counted thirty-four novels published between 1880 and 1908 that involved journeys into a hollow Earth. Many were utopian tales about encountering inner-Earth societies that had lessons to teach foolish humans.

Three of these "hollow-Earth" novels were published in 1908. *The Smoky God* was written by Willis George Emerson while he was digging a gold mine in Death Valley, a place that seemed to legitimize fantastic ideas about the Earth. Or perhaps Emerson's novel was the fantasy of a man suffering from too much Death Valley, for his underworld is full of water, trees a thousand feet tall, and a civilization with choirs of 25,000 voices. It's also full of gold, which Emerson's mine wasn't; he was mainly mining the pockets of his investors.

Eight years after L. Frank Baum published *The Wizard of Oz*, he followed it with *Dorothy and the Wizard in Oz*, in which Dorothy and her kitten Eureka (where's Toto?) are caught in a California earthquake and fall into the earth. Dorothy lands in the Land of the Mangaboos, with its evil sorcerer, but fortunately the Wizard of Oz, in his hot air balloon, has also been sucked into the earth and slays the sorcerer. After the Mangaboos drive them into a cave and seal it up, Dorothy and the Wizard follow the inner passages to the Valley of Voe, whose inhabitants eat a magic fruit that keeps them invisible from bears. Dorothy and the Wizard then go on to Pyramid Mountain, the Land of Gargoyles, and a cave full of dragons before they escape to Oz.

After writing the first thirty-five Tom Swift novels, Howard Garis wrote *5,000 Miles Underground*, in which an eccentric inventor, a big game hunter, and two orphan boys ride a flying ship into the hole at the South Pole, find a world of giant plants and animals and people made of mud; escape many close calls; find a temple full of diamonds; and ride a waterspout back to the surface, where their diamonds make them rich.

Among these tellers of tall tales were those—including those who knew better—who portrayed the Grand Canyon as an exotic underworld. On March 26, 1908, the *Arizona Republican* reprinted a highly overwrought article from the *Providence (RI) Journal* headlined: "Death Toll of Grand Canyon: Venturesome Ones Swept Away by River or Starve on Precipices." The article consisted mainly of quotes from Frederick Dellenbaugh, a member of the second Powell expedition down the Colorado River, who is claimed to have said that in the Grand Canyon:

> It is never fully daylight, except for a few brief minutes at midday....No one knows what immeasurable mineral wealth is hidden in the canyon's walls and every year venturesome prospectors go into those gloomy depths seeking the treasures that they guard. These men, through some sudden rise of water, or for some other reason, infrequently lose their lives in trying to escape from the canyon. Most of them, I fancy, go mad with hunger or die in trying to scale the precipices.

This, then, was the milieu that inspired the Egyptian cave story.

From a harmless beginning in the world of tall tales, the Egyptian cave story had been abducted into a realm where it served as an urgent spiritual revelation. It didn't help that true believers were usually unfamiliar with the Grand Canyon and made all sorts of misconnections, failing to recognize apparent jokes such as "El Tovar Crystal Canyon," which was likely inspired by the Santa Fe Railway's super hyped advertising for its new El Tovar Hotel.

Nevertheless, the vehemence of true believers tells us that there is more than simple misunderstanding going on here. Especially remarkable is their hostility toward the Smithsonian and the National Park Service, agencies that seldom make anyone's list of governmental bad guys, even on *The X-Files*. On the surface this hostility is said to be a response to an "archaeological establishment" that is blindly committed to an "isolationist dogma" in which Native American cultures developed on their own, without any contact from the Old World; some believe this so-called establishment will even destroy all evidence to the contrary. But below the surface, true believers are hungry for the world to be a spiritual realm. The ancient Egyptians have become icons of a universe loaded with hidden spiritual connections. True believers in the esoteric have always been hostile to a secular world view. When the Smithsonian and the National Park Service denied the reality of the Egyptian cave, they denied the existence of the spiritual world, becoming symbols of the secular world view and targets for long-standing hostility against it.

The Egyptian cave story has taken on such momentum that it seems likely to become a permanent part of the esoteric universe and is rapidly mutating into more exotic forms. For example, one website chronicles the channeled wisdom of Archangel Metatron, Lord of Light. Metatron tells us that the Grand Canyon cave is not Egyptian but was built by the people of Atlantis and is part of a planet wide network of tunnels built by the Atlanteans with technology from the star Sirius B (for the Atlanteans are really extraterrestrials). The Atlanteans recognized that the Grand Canyon holds many of Earth's strongest vortexes of spiritual energy, and so they built temples there to focus this energy for healing and rejuvenation. These facilities could also transport people through time. Tragically, Metatron tells us, G. E. Kinkaid and five other Smithsonian researchers, on a later entry into the cave, encountered this highly magnetic technology and were zapped by it and died. (Joe Mulhatton died a bit less dramatically in 1913, trying to cross the flooded Gila River.) This, he says, is why the government has sealed off the cave and covered up its existence. Canyon formations have Egyptian and Buddhist names because canyon vortexes are connected to energy nodes at Giza and Tibet. The vortex in Blacktail Canyon (a side canyon within Grand Canyon) is a star gate to the Pleiades. The Redwall Cavern vortex is especially conducive to astral travel, and Havasu is home to the Faerie Kingdom.

The 1909 Mulhatton story may have inspired a novel that was published the next year: *Prince Izon: A Romance of the Grand Canyon*, by James Paul Kelly. It tells the tale of explorers who discover a lost civilization of Aztecs living in a remote part of the Grand Canyon, after which great adventures ensue. Or perhaps Kelly was inspired by an idea that was "in the air" at a time when humans had finally explored much of the globe: the idea that there might be remote areas with "lost" wildlife or peoples. In 1912 Arthur Conan Doyle published his version of this idea, *The Lost World,* and in 1915 Edgar Rice Burroughs published *The Land That Time Forgot.*

The recent resurrection of the Mulhatton story has begun inspiring works of fiction. In December 2008 the SciFi Channel broadcast its original movie *Lost Treasure of the Grand Canyon*. It was filmed in the deep valley of Cache Creek in British Columbia, which is one of the few places in Canada with a desert environment, but otherwise a poor substitute for the Grand Canyon. The movie itself was a poor impersonation of an Indiana Jones movie, almost a parody, with bad acting, bad dialogue, a melodramatic plot, and cheap special effects, including a laughable quicksand scene. The movie starts with a *Arizona Gazette* reporter showing up at a Hopi ruin where archaeologist Susan Jordan is conducting an excavation. Jordan is the daughter of Dr. Samuel Jordan, who had led a Smithsonian expedition into the Grand Canyon to prove his theories that the ancient Egyptians had explored America. The *Phoenix Gazette* reporter had recently published a story on Dr. Jordan's discoveries and was supposed to meet him there, but he has disappeared. The reporter shows Susan some Egyptian artifacts that Dr. Jordan found in a Grand Canyon cave, which the Hopis say "come from a great pyramid hidden behind the canyon wall." Another archaeologist looks at these artifacts and declares that they are really Aztecan.

The group then sets out in search of Dr. Jordan, and they find his dead horse and his diary, which includes an account of him trying to scale a canyon cliff. They find a secret doorway in this cliff, revealing a cave full of Aztecan symbols. From the cave they emerge into a hidden canyon with an Aztec temple—and living Aztecs! Unfortunately, they are in the process of sacrificing members of Dr. Jordan's team. They cut out one man's heart and offer it to Aztec god Quetzalcoatl, who is depicted as a flying, dragon-type monster. Susan and her friends come to the rescue and then flee and fight their way through a labyrinth of tunnels, where a booby-trap axe falls and cuts off one man's head, and the roof collapses. The *Arizona Gazette* reporter is devoured by Quetzalcoatl, but Dr. Jordan and Susan escape. Dr. Jordan never explains how he could have mistaken Aztecan artifacts for Egyptian artifacts, and it's unclear why the movie's producers didn't choose to fill the hidden canyon with evil Egyptian priests and mummies.

In 2009 a novel by popular kid's novelist Dan Gutman appeared. *The Return of the Homework Machine* was a sequel to Gutman's successful novel *The Homework Machine*, about fifth-grade kids at the Grand Canyon school.

In the sequel the kids run across the 1909 *Arizona Gazette* article in the school library. With their teacher Mr. Murphy, they decide to find the cave. But a bad kid discovers their plan and goes to claim the treasure for himself and an adult accomplice, Richard Milner. The kids and Mr. Murphy hike to Phantom Ranch and borrow a raft and head downstream to the Egyptian temples zone. They climb the cliffs and find the cave, which is full of Egyptian treasures and mummies—and the body of G. E. Kinkaid, who must have returned and died there, perhaps from an Egyptian curse. They also find that their rivals have beaten them to the cave. Richard Milner grabs a golden Egyptian sword and attacks Mr. Murphy, but Milner trips over Kinkaid's body and falls from the cave to his death. The kids decide to leave the Egyptian cave a secret, especially since it seems to be cursed.

Also published in 2009 was the science fiction novel *Secrets of El Tovar Canyon*, by Michael Cole, about rafters who discover a golden tablet buried in the sand along the Colorado River at the bottom of the Grand Canyon. An archaeologist, Cheryl, reads its hieroglyphs and map and realizes the tablet depicts the Great Pyramid of Giza and the Sphinx—and secret underground passageways. Cheryl travels to Egypt and discovers, in a secret chamber in the paw of the Sphinx, a similar golden tablet. It turns out that the pyramids were not built by the Egyptians but by superior, giant beings ten thousand years ago. The pyramids hid a powerful energy source that had allowed its creators to transport themselves between the pyramids and a Grand Canyon cave. Cheryl travels, more conventionally, to the Grand Canyon, pursued by both the U.S. Air Force and a ruthless, Mafia-like collector of ancient artifacts. She rides a mule to Phantom Ranch and then hikes six miles to the Egyptian cave. The cave holds time travel technology with which future humans had tried to come back to the twentieth century to warn people about the dangers of fossil fuels and global warming. But the time travelers had miscalculated and transported themselves back an extra ten thousand years. They then built the pyramids to hide their advanced technologies, which one day would provide humans with clean, abundant energy.

In 2012 the novel *The Shadow of Isis*, by Joel Zarley, appeared. Zarley has a poor grasp of Grand Canyon geography or possibilities, so he has his hero, Mark, who has been inspired by the 1909 *Gazette* story, kayak down the Little Colorado River and then up Bright Angel Creek, where he finds a cave hidden by an illusion projection device. After Mark disappears, his sister Molly, an FBI agent, comes searching for him by rafting down the Little Colorado and up Bright Angel Creek, with the obligatory corny quicksand scene. It turns out that the cave had been home to a mysterious race of superior beings who had filled it with artifacts from all over the world, including ancient Egypt. This superior race finally died off from a mysterious illness that also infected humans and caused the 1918 global influenza pandemic. The technology left behind by this race was the source of all the technological progress of the twentieth century. Now the U.S. government guards the cave as a top-secret base.

Now that a new generation is growing up knowing all about the Grand Canyon's Egyptian cave, the story is sure to continue mutating into new forms and showing up in popular culture.

PANDA TRACKS IN THE GRAND CANYON

Tales of the Ancient Chinese

In 1913, four years after the *Arizona Gazette* announced that ancient Egyptians had inhabited the Grand Canyon, author Alexander McAllan declared that ancient Chinese texts contained elaborate knowledge of the Grand Canyon. McAllan's *Ancient Chinese Account of the Grand Canyon* was an eccentric book, even by the relaxed standards of the literature of the esoteric. It's unlikely that McAllan, who lived in Brooklyn, was inspired by the *Arizona Gazette*, which had little readership outside of Arizona. Besides, he was already immersed in his research: in 1910 he had published another book, *America's Place in Mythology*, claiming that ancient Asian texts held accounts of the American West, mainly the Yellowstone region, though McAllan included some mentions of the upper Colorado River.

McAllan's Grand Canyon book was the first of three that claimed the ancient Chinese knew about the Grand Canyon. All three books were inspired by a long intellectual tradition claiming that the Chinese had discovered America well before Columbus. This tradition had been going strong for 150 years by the time McAllan finally applied it to the Grand Canyon.

This tradition began in France in 1761, when Europeans were still discovering, translating, and trying to figure out the millennia-deep trove of Chinese literature. One of the first European scholars of Chinese literature and history was Joseph de Guignes, who did translations for the French Royal Library and whose accomplishments had earned him admission to the British Royal Society in 1752. In 1761 de Guignes published a book that revealed an official Chinese government record from AD 499 describing how a Buddhist monk named Hui Shen (also spelled "Hwui Shan") had traveled to a land far east of China, called *Fusang* for a tree that grew there. De Guignes claimed that Fusang could only be America, and his book caused a sensation in Europe, launching a vigorous debate among leading scholars that went on for more than a century.

The debate over Fusang had a great deal of initial energy because it took place in a vacuum of geographical and anthropological knowledge about America. De Guignes's book was published seven years before Captain Cook's first Pacific Ocean voyage and forty years before the Lewis and Clark expedition. The French had a great deal of curiosity about America, and not just because they had claimed the center of the North American continent as their own. French intellectuals were eagerly trying to make sense of the flood of new knowledge about world geography, nature, humans, and human societies. Significant misconceptions were common: under the influence of the naturalist Buffon, the French had decided that America was an underevolved continent where the animals, humans, and civilizations were far inferior to those of Europe. Only the Spanish had made significant contact with the Pacific coast and the societies of Central America, but their reports were often vague. When de Guignes took some translated tales from Chinese literature and tried to match them with some vague descriptions of America, there weren't too many facts to stand in his way. Among those impressed by the Fusang idea was Alexander von Humboldt, who noted the similarities between the astrological lore of Asia and Central America.

Despite his scholarly accomplishments, de Guignes was prone to making overenthusiastic connections. He theorized that the Chinese people were a colony and a racial offshoot of the ancient Egyptians, and that there was a strong resemblance between Egyptian hieroglyphics and ancient Chinese characters. He asserted that the hordes of barbarians who had sacked the Roman Empire were the same hordes that had bedeviled China. In his book on Fusang, de Guignes published elaborate maps showing where Hui Shen and four fellow Buddhist monks had reached Alaska, California, and even

Mexico. De Guignes asserted that the monks had impressed the spirit of Buddhism upon the residents of Mexico, which explains why the Aztecs were so much gentler, more polite, and civilized than other American societies. Joseph Needham, a twentieth-century scholar, summarized the situation in his encyclopedic *Science and Civilisation in China*: "The alleged discovery of the American continent by Buddhist monks from China in the +5th century is one of those youthful indiscretions at which modern sinology is accustomed to blush. As usual, Joseph de Guignes was the *enfant terrible....* "[1]

In 1761 very few Europeans had heard about the Grand Canyon, but de Guignes planted the Fusang debate into the canyon's neighborhood. He had decided that the most civilized North American Indians were the tribes on the northern California coast and the Puebloan tribes of the Southwest. The California tribes were civilized because they lived in the area closest to China, and that's where the Chinese first landed and had their greatest influence. De Guignes offered no explanation of how the Chinese could have influenced the Puebloans, but perhaps he thought they too lived near the coast:

> of all the American tribes, the most civilized are situated near the coast which faces China. In the region of New Mexico there are found tribes that have houses of several stories, with halls, chambers, and bathrooms. They are clothed in robes of cotton and of skin; but what is most unusual among savages is, that they have leather shoes and boots. Each village has its public criers, who announce the orders of the king, and idols and temples are seen everywhere.[2]

Of course, the "New Mexico" de Guignes refers to was not the far-future U.S. state but the whole southwestern region north of present-day Mexico. De Guignes cites some sources who claimed that the Puebloans were a remnant of Mexican tribes who had fled north after the conquistadors arrived, but he prefers to believe that the Puebloans were the progenitors of Mexican civilization. The Puebloan tribes would play a large role in future claims that the Chinese knew about the Grand Canyon.

Hui Shen's account of Fusang, which was fairly short, offered lots of specific details, but only vague conclusions. For example, he reported that Fusang was about 20,000 Chinese miles to the east of China, or about 7,000 English miles. The land was thick with Fusang trees, a mulberry with pear-like fruit; wood that made good houses; and bark that the native people turned into clothing and paper for writing. Fusang had lots of copper but no iron, and while it held gold and silver, the native people had no interest in them. The people of Fusang had horses and oxen, and raised deer for meat and milk. They were very civilized: they had no armies, no war, no walled cities or fortifications. There was so little crime that only two jails existed in the entire land. Fusang had no taxes and was ruled by an emperor who wore different colored clothes in different years. When a young man wanted to marry, he had to build a cabin beside the house of his beloved and live there for one year, waiting to see if she would accept or refuse him. When people died, they were cremated. Fusang had no religion until the monks arrived and converted its people to Buddhism. About 1,000 Chinese miles (350 English miles) east of Fusang was a Kingdom of Women, with no men. The women were entirely covered with hair. When they wished to become pregnant, they immersed themselves in a special river. The women had no breasts, but used tufts of hair on the back of the neck to suckle a baby.

In addition to Hui Shen's account, another old Chinese text would play a central role in theories about the Chinese and the Grand Canyon. *The Classic of Mountains and Seas* is a compilation of Chinese fables written over the course of five hundred years, beginning in the third century BCE. It describes hundreds of mountains and the rivers flowing from them, as well as the gods and stories associated with each. The collection has a solid foundation of natural history, with geology and plants and wildlife that are true to China, but its mountains and rivers have mythopoetic names. This tempted Chinese scholars into a long, sprawling, dispute-ridden effort to match these places with real places in China. Now European and American scholars have joined this old game, but trying to match the descriptions with sites in America. The *Classic* invited such an effort for—unknown to de Guignes—it contained some mentions of Fusang, indicating that the idea existed well before the Hui Shen account, as well as several chapters devoted to lands beyond the seas. One entry in particular would be claimed to be about the Grand Canyon:

> Beyond the East Sea is the Big Chasm. It is the country of the great god Young Brightsky. Young Brightsky nurtured the great god Fond Care

when he was a child. Here it was that Fond Care threw away his five-stringed lute and his twenty-five-stringed lute. Mount Sweet is here. The River Sweet rises on it and flows on to create Sweet Deeps.[3]

Both the *Classic* and the Hui Shen account of Fusang inspired many subsequent Chinese poets and writers, who spun many more details and versions, including many fantastic tales with mulberry trees a thousand feet tall and silkworms six feet long.

Along with the *Classic* and the Hui Shen account, one other major Chinese legend got mixed into claims about the Grand Canyon. The story of the god Yi the Archer tells of how ten suns rose into the sky one morning, and Yi shot down nine of them, saving the world from burning up.

When de Guignes was writing in 1761, who could say that ancient America didn't have horses, utopian societies, and Buddhists? Europeans long had been tempted to project utopian wishes onto Native Americans, and now the Chinese were encouraging this impulse.

As more knowledge of China and the Americas emerged, more scholars criticized de Guignes for his dubious claims. Maybe Fusang wasn't America at all. How could the ancient Chinese have counted the miles to America, or navigated so far? Maybe Fusang was Japan or somewhere else nearby, and maybe those natives were really the Japanese or the Ainu tribe. Maybe the whole thing was just a fable, like the six-foot-long silkworms.

In 1831 the distinguished scholar Julius Heinrich von Klaproth of Prussia weighed in with a major attack on de Guignes, refuting him point by point, at length. It was Klaproth who introduced *The Classic of Mountains and Seas* into the discussion, but he did so to point out the abundant fantasies in Chinese literature. Many scholars felt that Klaproth had ended the debate, but a few scholars remained true believers, and Joseph Needham would choose a much later date at which the debate was over: "...by the time of the First World War...the Fu-Sang thesis was stone dead."[4] But the idea had already taken on a new life among Americans, who would apply it in new ways, including to the Grand Canyon.

Initially, it seemed that only Europeans were interested in hearing that the Chinese discovered America. Americans might be willing to hear that Columbus had been beaten by the Vikings or the Welsh or the Irish, but not the Chinese. The Chinese were a problem. With the start of the California gold rush, the Chinese were invading the western United States, where many people felt they had no right to be: America had been set aside for the manifest destiny of the white race, not inferior Asians. Americans enacted numerous laws to restrict Chinese rights, activities, and immigration. There wasn't much of an audience for claims that the Chinese were a brilliant people who, more than a thousand years before the Pilgrims landed at Plymouth Rock, were building mighty ships, navigating the Pacific, and exploring and civilizing America.

It's not surprising, then, that the Fusang idea was introduced in the United States by an American intellectual who encountered the idea in Europe. Charles Godfrey Leland was born in Philadelphia in 1824 and studied languages, literature, and philosophy at Princeton, then at the Sorbonne in Paris and at Heidelberg and the University of Munich in Germany. At Munich Leland studied with Carl Friedrich Neumann, a professor of Oriental languages and history. Neumann had spent two years in China and collected ten thousand Chinese books. In 1841, only a few years before Leland's arrival in Munich, Neumann had published a German translation of Hui Shen's story of his trip to Fusang. Neumann added his own commentary, which was not only sympathetic to de Guignes's interpretation, but pushed it further. Professor Neumann drafted Leland to make an English translation of this work.

When Leland finished college, he returned to America and began a journalism career that lasted twenty years. In 1850, soon after returning home, Leland placed Neumann's Hui Shen account in the *New York Knickerbocker Magazine*. A dozen years later Leland placed a longer version, with his own commentary, in *Continental Magazine*, which he edited. These articles helped stir up further newspaper stories. In 1869 two American ministers who had done missionary work in Asia each published an article agreeing with the Fusang idea. That same year Leland returned to Europe, settled in London, and began a career as a writer. Fascinated by European folklore and paganism, he wrote twenty books about them, most notably *Aradia, or the Gospel of the Witches*, a study of Italian witchcraft that became a major resource for students of paganism. One of Leland's first books, published in 1875, was a fuller treatment of Neumann's ideas: *Fusang: The Discovery of America by Chinese Buddhist Monks in the Fifth Century*. Leland incorporated much of

Neumann's commentary into his book and then added more of his own. He brought to the subject a wider and more up-to-date knowledge of American geography and history than had European scholars. Leland suggested many matches between places and people mentioned in Hui Shen's account and those found in America, including southwestern places and tribes, but he didn't mention the Grand Canyon.

Following de Guignes and Neumann, Leland said that Hui Shen's account referred mainly to ancient Mexico, but also revealed knowledge of other parts of the Americas, including the American Southwest. Mexico had "images resembling the ordinary Buddha,"[5] and "The pyramidic-symbolic form of many of the Mexican monuments appears, indeed, to have a resemblance with the religious edifices of the Buddhists for places of interment."[6] "But if Buddhism ever flourished in Central America, it certainly was not the pure religion...but a new religion, built upon its foundations."[7] Leland agreed with de Guignes that "at one time certainly, the most civilized tribes in North America were those nearest China."[8] The Sioux language, he said, had Asian roots. Leland almost quoted Neumann in trying to evade one difficulty: "We may assume that the Fusang-tree was formerly found in America, and afterwards, through neglect, became extinct.... It is, however, much more probable that the traveler described a plant hitherto unknown to him, which supplies as many wants in Mexico as the original Fusang is said to do in Eastern Asia—I mean the great American aloe."[9]

Leland asserted that American explorations of the Southwest offered "not only indubitable proof of the former highly advanced civilization of New Mexico, but remarkable indications of apparent affinity with Chinese culture."[10] And their differences also proved Hui Shen's account: "The manner in which marriage was contracted in Fusang, according to his description, is not at all Chinese—I doubt if it be Asiatic—but it exists in more than one North American tribe, and something very like it was observed by a recent traveler in New Mexico."[11] Leland introduced another Chinese text that described how in the year AD 607 a ship was blown off course and landed on an unknown island where the natives ate small beans and built circular-shaped earthen houses. The women wore dresses made of cloth, and the men were said to have faces and voices like dogs. This "description applies with marvelous exactness to those New Mexican Indians.... The enormous consumption of beans (frijoles), the cloth (which was very beautifully made by the Pueblo-Aztecs, from early ages), and especially the circular walls of earth, all identify these Indians with those of New Mexico. These people…had a curious habit of howling and roaring terribly to express respect and admiration, and this may account for the voices like dogs spoken of by the Chinese."[12] The Puebloan tribes probably used bison as draft animals, which Hui Shen mistook for oxen. Even Hui Shen's report of a Kingdom of Women had plausible explanations in southwestern realities.

Leland tried to maintain a tone of caution and scholarship, but his enthusiasm for the idea often took control. Joseph Needham reported that when he took Leland's book off the shelf at the Cambridge University Library around 1960, many of the pages were still uncut, meaning that no one there had ever read the entire book.

Yet if the Fusang idea was dropping out of the scholarly world, Leland's book stirred up a lot of interest in the idea in America. A few years after its publication, the book drew a response from Samuel Wells Williams, who had served as interpreter for Admiral Perry when Perry landed in Japan in 1853, and who in 1877 became Yale's first professor of Chinese language and literature. In his *Notices of Fusang* Williams offered a fresh translation of the text that included Hui Shen's account. Williams was not impressed by the Fusang idea: "Some have combined many scattered facts so as to uphold their crude fancies; while others have formed a theory, and then hunted over the continent for facts to prove it."[13] Williams said that Hui Shen's account didn't have the ring of the epochal announcement of the discovery of a new continent: instead, "this account reads more like the description of a land having many things in common with countries well known to the speaker and his hearers, but whose few peculiarities were otherwise worth recording."[14] Or worse: "*Fu-sang* and *Päng-lai* are still used among the Chinese for fairy land, and are referred to by the common people very much as the Garden of the Hesperides and Atlantis were among the ancient Greeks."[15]

Leland's book inspired far more enthusiasm in Edward Payson Vining, who worked far outside of academia. In the 1870s Vining was living in Omaha, Nebraska, where he was the general freight manager for the Union Pacific Railroad. Like other Gilded Age rail companies, Union Pacific was loathed for its predatory shipping rates, and Vining himself seems to have been a much-loathed villain. But somewhere, perhaps from his teacher father, he had also picked up a bookish personality.

In 1881 Vining got a major publisher to publish *The Mystery of Hamlet,* in which Vining proposed that Hamlet was really a woman pretending to be a man so as to preserve his/her family's claim to the Danish crown. Hamlet's weak and indecisive actions were obviously not those of a man, and his evasions and stratagems were just like those of a woman. Vining's theory impressed America's leading Shakespearean actor, Edwin Booth, the brother of John Wilkes Booth. In 1921 Vining's book was the basis for the German silent movie *Hamlet,* starring the Danish actress Asta Nielsen. It may have been this movie that brought the book to the attention of James Joyce, for when Joyce published *Ulysses* the next year, it included a discussion of Vining's book.

During the same years that Vining was turning Hamlet into a woman, he was laboring on an eight-hundred-page book intended to prove that Fusang was America: *An Inglorious Columbus,* published in 1885. The book included a detailed comparison between eight different translations of the Hui Shen story, including Vining's own. Vining also translated portions of *The Classic of Mountains and Seas* and various works by other Chinese authors, which he wove into his texts of the Hui Shen story and the *Classic.*

It was Vining who first introduced the Grand Canyon into the Fusang debate. It's not surprising that the canyon didn't appear earlier. The same year—1869—that Charles Godfrey Leland left America for his writing career in Europe, John Wesley Powell was launching his Colorado River expedition, so the Grand Canyon was still *terra incognita.*

As Vining was going through the Hui Shen account line by line, he came to a line stating that north of the Kingdom of Women was a "black gorge." Vining commented, "North of Mexico is found the Cañon of the Colorado River, the most wonderful chasm in the world, with walls so steep, high, and close together, that, as I once heard General Crook express it, 'it is necessary to lie down upon one's back in order to see the sky.' Into much of this deep gorge no ray of sunshine ever falls, and it well deserves the name of the 'Dark Cañon.'"[16]

Vining had a good chance to hear General Crook's accounts of his western adventures, for Crook's home, like Vining's, was in Omaha. It's even possible that Vining heard about the Grand Canyon from John Wesley Powell himself, for Powell used the Union Pacific Railroad to ship his boats and himself west.

Yet when Vining came to the mention in *The Classic of Mountains and Seas* of the "Great Cañon beyond the Eastern Sea," he did not declare this to be the Grand Canyon. He suggested that the geographical descriptions in the *Classic* referred to places in Asia.

Vining did make plenty of other claims about Chinese imprints in the Americas, especially Mexico. He claimed that Buddha was honored in many Mexican place-names, and that the name *Guatemala* means "the place of Gautama." He found similarities between Buddhist temples and Mexican pyramids, even claiming to have found images of elephants and a meditating Buddha on the pyramids. Mexican legends of Quetzalcoatl and Kukulcan, he said, were really garbled versions of the coming of Hui Shen, who did indeed bring civilization to Mexico, though the Aztecs had lapsed. The report of rounded earthen homes referred to Puebloan kivas, and the odoriferous salt-plant eaten in Fusang is the sage-brush: "in the uplands of the valley of the Colorado River, in Arizona, most of the plants...are smeared with a resinous varnish, which gives out a pleasant, stimulating aroma, noticed by nearly all desert travelers."[17] All of the fantastic elements of the Hui Shen story, he said, resulted from the faulty copying of scribes or had logical explanations. The six-foot silkworms were really agave plants that produced threads as strong as silk; the rabbits "as large as horses" were jackrabbits. The Kingdom of Women was just an insult against the manliness of some enemy tribe, or it recalled a raid when all the men were away from a village and the women were the only defenders, or it referred to Mexican monkeys, which were hairy and dog-faced and carried their young on their backs.

Vining's book would be the primary source for the three later authors who made larger claims about the Grand Canyon.

Little is known about Alexander McAllan beyond basic biographical facts: he was born in Ireland in 1848 but had Scottish ancestry; he immigrated to America in 1871; he settled in Brooklyn. In the 1920 census he identified his occupation as "archaeology writer." In 1910, at age sixty-three, he published his first book, *America's Place in Mythology: Disclosing the Nature of Hindoo and Buddhist Beliefs*. McAllan's books are sloppily written, and the connections he makes between Chinese texts and American realities are also sloppy.

McAllan begins *America's Place in Mythology* by announcing that previous books on Fusang have gotten it all backwards:

> The present writer...does not for a moment imagine that Asiatic priests visited America and then returned to China or India—with descriptions of our continent. On the contrary he holds that a superior, intelligent tribe (about 20,000 in all, men, women, and children) of mound-builders succeeded in escaping from the Valleys of the Ohio and the Mississippi, and even from America itself, across into Asia— where an extraordinary destiny awaited them. The fugitive host was led by a princess, born in Mexico, and also by her son, born in Arizona.[18]

McAllan offers no further explanation of this theory, but in his Grand Canyon book he goes into it in more detail. The prince who led this tribe to China had, as a baby, lived within the Grand Canyon. McAllan states that this tribe took with them to Asia strong memories of America's great landscapes, which showed up in Asian literature and even helped to inspire Asia's religions. McAllan concludes *America's Place in Mythology* by asserting that "To an extraordinary degree the religious systems of the Orient are based upon our continent...."[19]

McAllan devotes most of *America's Place in Mythology* to matching places described in Asian texts with American landscapes. Sometimes he berates scholars for misidentifying these landscapes as being in Asia, and he even criticizes the authors of the original texts for garbling their descriptions of American landscapes.

At the center of McAllan's case is a lake called Anavatapta, which he insists is Lake Yellowstone. He claims many matches between them, and between other Asian and American landscapes. For example, the stone trees reported in Asian texts are Arizona's Petrified Forest; a mountaintop Garden of the Gods is the one at Colorado Springs; a land called Mo-kieis that of the Moki, or Hopi, Indians—and so on.

McAllan brings in the Colorado River in connection with Lake Anavatapta having four major rivers flowing from it. McAllan has to do some conjuring to get away with claiming that the Colorado River has the same source as the Yellowstone and the Missouri Rivers: "there are subterranean currents of boiling water which doubtless connect the Colorado with steaming founts of the Yellowstone."[20] And at South Pass, Wyoming, on the Continental Divide, some headwaters of the Colorado and the Platte-Missouri are pretty close together.

McAllan says that the mouth of the Colorado River is described in an Indian text that refers to the Sindhu River flowing to a southwestern sea. The word *sindhu*, he says, "is also applied to a sea-river."

> Undoubtedly the Colorado, widening out gradually until it becomes a wedge-shaped gulf, is a sea-river and deserving of the title "sindhu." It is impossible to tell where the river ends and the sea begins. The Gulf of California—the continuation of the Colorado—is shaped like an enormous river, a "sea-river." The entire arrangement is quite unlike the condition presented at, say, the mouth of the Mississippi. Truly the Colorado is a sindhu or sea-river.[21]

Toward the end of *America's Place in Mythology* McAllan says that this subject would require much more exploration but that he is "so advanced in years that it is improbable anything further will appear from his pen."[22] Yet it seems that McAllan then became enthralled by the Grand Canyon connection. Three years later he self-published a smaller book about it, really a pamphlet, forty-four pages long. McAllan drew upon Vining's book and compared Chinese texts with descriptions of the Grand Canyon that he found in the works of authors such as John Wesley Powell, Frederick Dellenbaugh, and George Wharton James.

In the pamphlet McAllan insists that the "Great Canyon" in the *Classic of Mountains and Seas* is the Grand Canyon: "It is the greatest and grandest on the planet."[23] In Vining's blending of the original *Classic* with subsequent Chinese texts, the stream in the canyon flows to "a charming gulf," which McAllan says must be the Colorado River flowing to the Gulf of California. The "River Sweet" in the *Classic* must be Wyoming's Sweetwater River, which arises at South Pass, near one source of the Green-Colorado River. The *Classic's* claim that the Colorado River is bottomless must refer to Grand Lake, the official source of the Colorado River and said to be bottomless. Then again, maybe the bottomless place is Middle Park in Colorado, where the Colorado River is surrounded by mountains.

McAllan often tries to summon comparisons between ancient and modern reactions: "So impressed were the ancients with the beauty and grandeur of this region that they…declared that here was the Canyon of Almighty God. And those who enter it today, come reeling back from its portals—declaring that…it is the Grand Canyon of Almighty God."[24]

McAllan devotes significant space to the story of the baby suckled in the Grand Canyon who leaves his lute and lyre there. This was no god but a great king. McAllan admits it is silly to imagine a baby playing a lute or lyre, so he says this was just a metaphor for the musical sounds of the canyon's springs and streams. He quotes John Wesley Powell about those sounds, which inspired Powell to name one place Music Temple. In the type of couplet-summary McAllan uses dozens of times in the book, he concludes: "Lutes and lyres are there, say the Ancients. A Temple of Music is there, say the Moderns."[25]

McAllan ties the canyon's baby king to the mystery of the mound builders. As Euro-Americans had pioneered the Ohio and Mississippi river valleys, they encountered elaborate earthworks. There was a genuine mystery about them, but also a racist reluctance to admit that midwestern Indians had once built an elaborate civilization. Euro-Americans theorized that the mound builders were a superior race that had been conquered by the savages who lived there now. Another theory proposed that the mound builders had migrated to the Southwest, where they became the Puebloan tribes. McAllan's version is that the Grand Canyon residents were remnants of the Toltecs, who had built a superior civilization in Mexico before being driven to the north. In Arizona, he said, the Toltecs built impressive structures like Montezuma's Castle, but once again they were besieged by more savage tribes, which is why they were hiding in the Grand Canyon. McAllan believed that from Arizona the Toltecs migrated to the Midwest, where they became the mound builders. Then they were forced to migrate to Asia, where they helped create Chinese civilization, and where their undying memories of the Grand Canyon showed up in Chinese literature. Arizona tribes preserved memories of the Grand Canyon's great baby king, who became a god in their legends.

The ancient residents of the Grand Canyon would have needed houses, and McAllan cites archaeology reports that the canyon does indeed contain ruins. Those governing on behalf of the baby king might have written

proclamations on the canyon walls, and sure enough, McAllan reports hieroglyphs, "Not painted on the cliffs, but cut into the stone! Beyond the reach
or malice of savage tribes, they doubtless furnished directions to friendly
clans, telling where certain companies had moved, and so forth."[26] Chinese
texts mentioned cave dwellings in the canyon, and the Grand Canyon had
those too.

McAllan runs through a list of Chinese descriptions and finds in the
Grand Canyon the matching colorful cliffs, storms, deserts, beauty, and the
sindhu of the Gulf of California. He concludes the pamphlet—seemingly for-
getting that he had explained the baby's lute as a poetic metaphor—by saying: "Have we not found everything except perhaps the abandoned imperial
lute? And even it may yet be recovered. Let it be dug for at the Cliff of the
Harp."[27]

McAllan took out an ad for his Grand Canyon book in the leading American archaeology journal of the time, *American Antiquarian and Oriental
Journal.* The next year, the journal published a favorable review of both of
McAllan's books. There was no byline, but the review very likely was written
by the journal's editor, J. O. Kinnaman, who five years later published similar
comments about McAllan's books in *The Theosophical Path.* Kinnaman had
solid scholarly credentials, having studied archaeology at the University of
Chicago and the University of Rome, but he also entertained some unortho-
dox theories. Yet even Kinnaman had to admit:

> This little book is one of the most peculiar that has come from any
> press to date. We usually consider that the American continents were
> discovered by Columbus, but Mr. McAllan turns to Asiatic literature
> to establish the America's place in the ancient world.... Following this
> pamphlet is its sequel entitled "Ancient Chinese Account of the Grand
> Canyon, or Course of the Colorado," the greater portion of which is
> devoted to the account of the cave dwellings in the Grand Canyon
> and the development of the theory of the flight of the mother of Mu
> or Mo or Mok.... Mr. McAllan substantially makes other interesting
> and unique discoveries, which to thoroughly understand necessitates
> not a reading but a careful study of his works. No library of American
> Archaeology is complete without the works of Mr. McAllan.[28]

In his *Theosophical Path* article, discussing the mound builders of Ohio, Kinnaman endorsed McAllan's theories:

> The writer, in full accord with Mr. Alexander McAllan of New York City, is not going to contend that any Chinese or Hindu priest or traveler ever visited America in the dim past ages, and then returning home wrote an account of his journeys; but rather that a tribe, who afterwards became what we know as Mound Builders of the Mississippi valley, being driven from their homes in Mexico, found their way to Arizona, the Grand Canyon....The Chinese account describes the Grand Canyon with such degree of accuracy that a modern traveler, using the account as a guide book, could easily find his way about and identify the different spots of beauty and interest.[29]

Yet by this time the myths about the mound builders were nearly dead. McAllan's books soon fell into obscurity. In 1926, two years before his death, he was promoting his theories in letters published in the *New York Evening Post*.

Forty years later the Chinese returned to the Grand Canyon, but in the safer guise of the traveling Buddhist priest Hui Shen. Yet for more than two hundred years after Hui Shen was first debated by Europe's leading scholars, he continued falling into less skilled and careful hands.

Henriette Mertz, a Chicago attorney specializing in international patent law, had a passion for exploring Latin America; she once descended the Amazon River by balsa raft and dugout canoe. She also had a passion for the idea that ancient tales of exploration had actually occurred in America and wrote three books about her ideas. *The Wine Dark Sea* discussed classic Greek tales. Odysseus, she believed, had actually sailed past Gibraltar and across the Atlantic, and his encounter with Scylla and Charybdis was an account of the tidal bores in the Bay of Fundy in Nova Scotia. Jason and the Argonauts had also crossed the Atlantic, sailed south along the coast to South America, and journeyed into the Andes, where they found the Golden Fleece. In her book *Atlantis: Dwelling Place of the Gods*, Mertz argued that Atlantis was actually the eastern United States.

Mertz's book *Pale Ink* took its title from a saying of Confucius that "pale ink is better than the most retentive memory." Mertz couldn't find a publisher, so she self-published it in 1953. In 1972 *Pale Ink* was resurrected by

Swallow Press, a respected publisher of literature and American history that was trying to fend off bankruptcy by publishing some potboilers. The huge success of Erich von Däniken's *Chariots of the Gods?*, which offered archaeological proof that extraterrestrials had visited Earth, had created a huge audience for alternative archaeology, so Swallow Press was soon able to sell *Pale Ink* to Ballantine Books for a mass-market paperback. Ballantine retitled it *Gods from the Far East* and gave it a cover with the same bold typeface as *Chariots of the Gods?*.

There aren't any aliens in *Pale Ink*, but there are plenty of bold claims, including the claim that Hui Shen had transformed the Americas:

> He introduced there a new culture and raised it, single-handed, to such a high degree that the world today still stands in amazement of it—even the calendar that he taught was more perfect than is our own. Perhaps no other in the world's history has ever done so much for so many people in such varied fields of activity and yet remains unknown....
>
> Converting an entire country as he did, should rank him with the world's great religious teachers. In addition to a better life, he brought advanced methods of agriculture; of weaving and ceramics; he taught astronomy and the calendar; he taught metallurgy and the art of fine feather-work. His dynamic personality was so strong he was revered as a god, even in his own time—Quetzalcoatl, Kukulcan.... That he was well-beloved by all those with whom he had contact, is evident by the number of towns and villages from one end of Mexico to the other, named in his honor. It is my belief that his journey can be traced by those places.[30]

Mertz repeats many of Vining's correlations between places in Chinese texts and those in America, and she adds more of her own: the dog-faced men were just men wearing kachina masks; the Kingdom of Women was just a Native American matriarchal tribe; the baby suckling from the hair on the back of a woman's neck was just a garbled reference to a papoose, where the baby was sucking on a ribbon; and the "black gorge" to the north of the Kingdom of Women wasn't the Grand Canyon but the Black Canyon of the Gunnison.

Mertz first mentions the Grand Canyon when trying to explain the Kingdom of Women. One Chinese text said that the women there took snakes for husbands. Mertz cited the Hopi legend of Tiyo, who rode down the Colorado River through the Grand Canyon and met the Snake people, who became a central part of Hopi life and gave rise to the Snake Clan and the Snake Dance. The Hopis were matriarchal, and their women could be said to marry snakes.

Mertz quotes Vining's translation of the *Classic of Mountains and Seas,* which often mentions a place where the sun is born. Mertz is especially impressed by the legend of Yi, the archer who shot nine of ten suns out of the sky. She takes this as a poetic metaphor of how the Grand Canyon got its brilliant colors:

> Nature's most magnificent display of her handiwork—the Great Luminous Canyon with the little stream flowing in a bottomless ravine—out spectacles every other natural extravaganza on this earth with its brilliant yellows, vibrant oranges, deep subtle reds and in its shadows pale lavenders toning into rich, velvet blues—like a glorious sunrise or sunset. Nothing but the sun itself could have imparted such rich color—and nowhere else does it exist. To an ancient Chinese, traveling east, this great fissure must be the place where the sun was born.
>
> Hundreds of Chinese apparently saw the Canyon—it was a "must" on their travel-adventure schedule. "I saw the place where the sun was born"—Chinese poetry and literature fairly bulges with cantos of glowing reminiscence. They called it the "Great Canyon," 4000 years ago; we call it the "Grand Canyon," today. No one could stand on the rim of the canyon and be unmoved by it. The Indians could not; the Chinese could not, and we can not....
>
> The "archer story" in the Ninth Book, locates, without a shadow of a doubt, the place where the Chinese legend originated. It is my belief that someday it will be found that the story of the archer came from one of the Indian tribes and was told to the Chinese. They took it home as a legend of the Canyon—the Indian legend of how the Canyon was formed—a legend like that of the origin of the Snake Clan.... In this instance, we have the Indian trying to explain to himself how the Canyon came about and why it was so rich in the colors of the sun. It sounded plausible to the poetic soul of the Chinese and they "borrowed" it and took it home. The legend, in China, has never been

understood—it has just been there always as a part of their folklore with no known beginning. This, it is submitted, is its foundation—here at our Grand Canyon.[31]

Mertz also claims that the *Classic* held descriptions of landscapes near the Grand Canyon, such as a "quaking mountain," referring to the quaking aspen forests on the North Rim.

Even when *Pale Ink* was an obscure book, Mertz won an important supporter in southwestern author Frank Waters, who was an enthusiast for the mystic East. Waters was working on his *Book of the Hopi,* and he was determined to turn the Hopis into Eastern sages whether they liked it or not—which they did not. Waters cited Mertz as his authority in saying that the Chinese had reached the Southwest: "Long regarded as a book of myth [the *Classic of Mountains and Seas*] is now asserted to be an accurate geographic description of various landmarks in America, including the 'Great Luminous Canyon' now known as the Grand Canyon."[32]

Two years before Mertz's book came out as a paperback, a book published in Taiwan made even greater claims about the Grand Canyon. *The Asiatic Fathers of America* was, like Vining's book, about eight hundred pages long. Its author was Hendon Harris, Jr., who was born in China in 1916, the son of Baptist missionaries, and became a missionary in Taiwan and Hong Kong. Harris devoted an entire chapter to the Grand Canyon, and it shows up frequently throughout the book. He claimed that the canyon was well-known to the ancient Chinese and that every ancient Chinese longed to see it, though the canyon's distance made it seem like a legend.

Harris's enthusiasm for the Grand Canyon was fueled by a hike on the Bright Angel Trail in 1961, when he was forty-five. Although it was midsummer, he decided to hike to the river and back in one day. A mule wrangler warned him he would have trouble hiking out, but Harris ignored him. He did indeed struggle getting out—he apparently wasn't carrying enough water—and for three days afterward he could barely walk.

Harris's theories were just as reckless as his hiking. While he gave the Grand Canyon a larger role than other authors, he also dragged it and the once-reputable idea of Fusang further into the realm of crackpots.

Harris was a believer in the theories of Immanuel Velikovsky, whose 1956

bestseller *Worlds in Collision* held that unusual astronomical events had triggered worldwide cataclysms that are recorded in human texts and legends,
including Noah's flood. Harris proposed that the flood had caused Earth's
axis to be thrown out of line and changed Earth's orbit around the sun, after
which the Chinese Emperor Yao sent Prince Yi (Or "Y" as Harris spells it) to
the Grand Canyon to reestablish the world's four directions. Unlike Henriette
Mertz, who took the story of Yi the archer to be a poetic metaphor of how the
canyon became so colorful, Harris makes it a real event. Yi's bow was some
sort of crossbow-shaped astronomical instrument, made of jade, with which
he shoots, or takes the measurements of, the sun. To take these measurements
Yi had to sail across the Pacific Ocean and go to the Grand Canyon.

Yet in trying to make this story real, Harris has trouble explaining those
nine extra suns. Maybe they were just reflections on the waters of the flood,
causing confusion and panic. As Harris considers it further, he becomes dis-
satisfied with his naturalistic explanation. He thinks of Joshua, and God making the sun stand still. Harris decides that maybe the Yi story was miraculous
after all: God really did intervene and melt nine extra suns out of the sky.

Yi needed to go to the Grand Canyon because it was a natural observatory, the best in the world, whose darkness allowed a better view of the heav-
ens. Harris said it was like the Cheops Pyramid, which held a tunnel from
which ancient Egyptian priests observed the pole star. Near Havasupai Point
Harris came upon a large, round ruin with many pottery fragments scattered about. Harris imagined that this was an ancient observatory built by
the Chinese.

Harris also brought Hui Shen into the story. About 2,500 years after Prince
Yi, Hui Shen came to the canyon to make astronomical measurements to
revise the Chinese calendar. For centuries teams of Chinese astronomers continued coming to the canyon to observe the movements of the sun and stars.
These visits were recorded in Chinese texts and in Native American legends.
Paiute shamans still kept watch at the canyon's Angels Gate for their gods
to return and lead them to a more abundant land—a garbled memory of
the Chinese astronomers coming there. The Hopis, too, eagerly awaited the
return of the Chinese. Indeed, Harris claimed that the Hopis *are* Chinese and
that their name derives from the Chinese word *ho-ping-kuo*, which means
"country of peace." Hopi hairstyles are obviously Chinese, Harris said, and

Hopi culture is very Buddhist. Harris agreed with Mertz, whom he cited as a high authority, that Chinese texts contained the tale of Hopis marrying snakes, but Harris goes further and suggests that the Hopis meant to say dragons—Chinese dragons. The Kingdom of Women, which was near the Hopis, did not refer to monkeys but to another Indian tribe descended from the Chinese. The Hopis shared the Chinese recognition that the Grand Canyon was the center of the spiritual cosmos.

Like true believers in the Egyptian cave, Harris pointed to the names of canyon landmarks—Buddha Temple, Confucius Temple—as proof that Asians were there. The Asians who built the Mexican pyramids, he said, were copying Grand Canyon structures, and it was Asians who founded the great civilizations of Mexico; Hui Shen continued visiting America for forty years and built a force of 100,000 missionaries working for the Buddhist cause; the pyramid of Teotihuacan was built to honor Hui Shen; and the four Buddhist priests who accompanied Hui Shen became priests at other great Mexican temples. For Hendon Harris the Grand Canyon offered great spiritual revelation; it was ordained by heaven to show humans their secret connections with the cosmos.

Harris's book was barely noticed, but in 2006 his daughter Charlotte Harris Rees brought out a shortened version in the wake of renewed interest in the possible Chinese discovery of America. This interest was stirred up by the 2002 bestseller *1421: The Year China Discovered America*, by Gavin Menzies. Menzies made little acknowledgment that he was playing a 240-year-old game, perhaps because he was determined to make the Chinese discover America in 1421 and not a thousand years previously. But Menzies played the game with the same recklessness as his predecessors. He didn't bring in the Grand Canyon, but among other things he claimed that Navajo elders can understand the Chinese language. Among the many expressions of renewed interest in the subject was a novel by Thomas Steinbeck (son of John Steinbeck) about the Chinese discovering America, *In the Shadow of the Cypress*.

Of course, it was really the Grand Canyon that discovered Native Americans, the Chinese, and the Europeans staring into it quite late in its long history. It was the Colorado River that served as a mirror of evolving animal faces and continually changing rock faces, until there appeared an animal whose head swarmed with obsessive questions and ideas about the origins of itself.

THE TAIL THAT WAGGED THE PRESIDENT

Or, President Harding's Dogged Secretary of the Interior

Paddy the puppy ran after his red ball as it bounced toward the trees. Paddy loved playing with his red ball, more than chasing squirrels, bunnies, or birds. Paddy couldn't catch any of those, but he always caught—or caught up with—his ball. And playing with his ball meant that he was playing with his human, the one who fed and petted him. Paddy wished that his human played with him more often. It was so sad and boring that his human went away almost every morning and didn't come home until the end of the day, and then sat staring at strange squiggles on papers. Humans were so strange.

Paddy couldn't imagine that at the other side of a vast continent, in a white house with columns and a big green yard, men were sitting at a big table discussing him. The president of the United States was discussing Paddy the Grand Canyon puppy. Two members of the cabinet were arguing about what to do about Paddy. Humans were so strange.

On January 13, 1923, in the pages of the *New York Times*, the controversy over Paddy the Grand Canyon puppy became national news. The *Times* article was headlined: "DOG IN GRAND CANYON DEBATED BY CABINET: Harding Must Decide If Lone Postmaster May Keep His Pet Despite the Law."

WASHINGTON, Jan 12.—A deadlock resulting from a long controversy between the Post Office and Interior Department occupied the larger share of this morning's meeting of the Cabinet. No agreement was reached, and the matter is now before President Harding for final settlement.

The Grand Canyon National Park is under the jurisdiction of the Interior Department, which has a strict regulation against all dogs in national reservations, an order designed to protect wild life. There is a postmaster on this reservation. He is a lonely soul who prefers pets more domesticated than coyotes. He brought a dog with him and thus came into conflict with Interior Department authorities and appealed to the Post Office Department for support.

Voluminous correspondence was exchanged between the two departments. "The dog must stay," announced the Post Office Department. "The dog must go: there is the law," said the Interior Department. The matter passed upward from one official to another until it reached the heads of the departments. Today Secretary Fall and Postmaster General Work brought their controversy to the Cabinet.

The Postmaster General argued at length for his subordinate. Recalling the many editorials Editor Harding wrote for The Marion Daily Star about a dog's love for his master, he appealed to the sympathy of his hearers and described the lonely plight of the postmaster of Grand Canyon without his dog.

Then Secretary Fall spoke for the Interior Department. He is a lawyer and he based his case solely upon the law. He is fond of dogs, he said, but this is a Government of laws and there is a law against dogs in national parks.

President Harding, whose editorial on the death of his bull terrier Jumbo is posted in scrap books of many dog lovers, decided in favor of the postmaster retaining his dog, but an exception was taken to this ruling. The President withdrew his decision and announced that he would not settle the dispute until further information about the dog reaches Washington.

Warren Harding was not the most decisive of presidents. According to historians Eugene P. Trani and David L. Wilson, "Harding relied on his cabinet appointments more than most presidents, depending upon them for the operation of the government.... Cabinet discussions played an important role in determining governmental policy, and Harding allowed each cabinet officer relative autonomy in his particular sphere, seldom interfering.... When they disagreed, Harding was often slow to intervene, because such disputes made him intensely uncomfortable."[1] At this cabinet meeting Harding was also uncomfortable because he was coming down with an acute case of influenza that would leave him bedridden for weeks.

Two days later the *New York Times* came out strongly in favor of the Grand Canyon dog in an editorial titled "The Postmaster's Dog":

> The dog of the Postmaster of Grand Canyon National Park, which has raised such a rumpus in the Federal Government and set the Post Office and the Interior Department by the ears, must be like the Old Prospector's dog:
>
> Well, I don't want no better pard
>   When I tramp up the Great Divide.
>
> President Harding, beset by numerous and knotty problems, has had the fate of the Grand Canyon dog added to his burden. To a man who has a soft spot in his heart for dogs of all degrees, and whose pen as an editor has been used in behalf of the four-footed friend, this is no light matter. One can imagine Mr. Harding saying to the obdurate Fall, who points to his regulations: "In these nice quillets of the law, good faith, I am 'no wider than a daw': let the man have his dog!" There must be some kind of case for the Postmaster, else why the "voluminous correspondence" between the departments and the discussion in the Cabinet? The rule was evidently made only to protect wild life. There are dogs that worry nothing but a bone—well-behaved, meditative, self-respecting dogs, such as a hermit Postmaster might train to share his isolation. The controversy seems to have reached the point of the character of this particular dog. Shall he be saved by a genial interpretation of the rule? There must be room enough for the Postmaster's companion. Are there not something like 2,000,000 acres in the reservation?

John Muir says of this sublime depression in the desert that it is about six thousand feet deep and from rim to rim ten to fifteen miles wide. After all, what is a little thing like a wilderness park regulation between a postmaster and his dog? Would the occasional antelope and the prowling mountain lion care? Does anybody hold a brief for the coyote?

Perhaps if Robert Frothingham's "Songs of Dogs" were read to Secretary Fall he would yield. He must be familiar with Senator Vest's address to a jury in behalf of a dog. No one but a dog hater, who is often a misanthrope, can read it without a lump in the throat. And there is Baudelaire's song to "the poor dog, the homeless dog, the stroller dog, the dog buffoon." Let it be tried on Mr. Fall.... If this question were referred to the boys of America, who after all are the best judges of dogs, does any one doubt what the decision would be? "Near this spot," says the inscription on Boatswain's monument in the garden of Newstead Abbey, "are deposited the remains of one who possessed Beauty without Vanity, Strength without Insolence, Courage without Ferocity, and all the Virtues of Man without his Vices." If that is the kind of dog the Postmaster has, some way should be found to keep them united.

Robert Frothingham was a New York City writer whose recently published *Songs of Dogs* was a popular anthology of dog poetry, from which the editorial had drawn. Frothingham's "Forward" started: "Has the dog a soul and does it obtain immortality?" Frothingham seemed to think so. Two days later, on January 17, the *New York Times* published a letter to the editor from Frothingham, headlined "THE POSTMASTER'S DOG. Plenty of Room in the Grand Canyon Without Menace to the Natives":

In regard to your very interesting editorial in THE TIMES for Monday, "The Postmaster's Dog," any one who is in the slightest degree familiar with the wild animal life of the Grand Canyon knows that it is confined to the vast forests of the Kaibab Plateau, on the northern rim. Here are found innumerable deer, hundreds of mountain lion, or cougar, not to mention that arch-thief and scavenger, the coyote. There is no animal life worthy of the name on the southern rim of the Canyon. In view of the fact, therefore, that in the vicinity of the Grand Canyon Post Office the Canyon itself is from twelve to sixteen miles wide by a mile deep, it is just a trifle difficult for anybody but Mr. Fall to understand wherein the Postmaster's dog is a menace.

Furthermore—when one considers that the very department over which Secretary Fall presides pays a bounty for the extermination of the cougar, which is the greatest menace to the wild animal life in the Grand Canyon Park, and that he is always hunted by hounds in packs— it would be interesting to know how Mr. Fall reconciles his opposi- tion to the Postmaster's dog with his approval of the transportation of hounds in packs through the depths of the Canyon for the purpose of lion hunting on the other side.

ROBERT FROTHINGHAM, New York, Jan 15, 1923

President Harding's discomfort over the Grand Canyon dog debate was partly due to who was making the appeal. Albert Fall was one of Harding's closest friends and most trusted advisers. When Warren Harding had arrived in the U.S. Senate in 1915, his desk happened to be next to the desk of Sen- ator Fall of New Mexico. While Harding's life experience consisted mainly of being a small-town Ohio newspaper editor, Fall was the embodiment of the romantic Wild West. He had been a cowboy, a prospector, a hard rock miner, a rancher, and a roamer of southwestern open spaces that still bore the tracks of Apache warriors. According to one story, Fall had confronted a gun- drawn John Wesley Hardin in an El Paso bar and disarmed him. At the least, as a lawyer Fall had defended Hardin's killer—whose nephew then twice tried to shoot Fall—and the accused killer of Sheriff Pat Garrett. In his legal career Fall had defended fifty-one men accused of murder and had lost only one case. He also claimed that he had defended five hundred men accused of cattle rustling and never lost a case. Such were the powers of argument that were now being aimed against the Grand Canyon dog. In New Mexico Fall had usually carried a gun, even while serving in the state senate, or car- ried a cane that he could wield as a sword. With the outbreak of the Spanish- American War, Fall became a captain of the Rough Riders, though the war ended before he could make it into combat. Eugene Manlove Rhodes, a famous author of western dime novels, used Fall as a character in one novel. Fall's genuine Wild West persona was irresistible to Teddy Roosevelt, and the two became friends and allies despite deep differences over conservation issues. Fall could tell tales of the Wild West with gusto; he wore a black Stetson hat and had a bushy mustache; and in his poker playing and drinking he could compete with any man.

Warren Harding was also fascinated by Fall, who adopted Harding as a protégé. Later they served together on the Senate Foreign Relations Committee, where Fall, who had acquired and read his own small library of Spanish-language books, was an expert on Latin America and a hardliner against revolutionaries who were threatening American interests. Fall and Harding became drinking and poker buddies, and when Harding moved into the White House, so did their poker parties.

When Harding unexpectedly received the Republican nomination for president in 1920 and was feeling out of his depth on the national stage, he urgently summoned Fall to help plan his campaign, advise him on foreign policy, and write his speeches: "Really, I very much need to be surrounded by some of the friends whom I trust most fully.... I would like exceedingly much to have you here so that I may avail myself of your counsel and advice."[2] Elected president, Harding was eager for Fall to serve in his cabinet. Since the Department of the Interior dealt mostly with western lands, it was important to appoint a western man who understood public lands issues, and someone Harding trusted. When Harding offered Fall the Interior post, Fall wrote to his wife: "He thinks that the Interior Department is second only to the State Department in importance and that there is more opportunity for graft and scandal connected with the disposition of public lands &c, than there could be in any other Department and he wants a man who is thoroughly familiar with the business and one he can rely upon as thoroughly honest, etc etc."[3] Harding relied thoroughly on Fall. For example, when Fall asked Harding to sign something-or-other about someplace-or-other called Teapot Dome, Harding never hesitated. The idea of doubting or challenging Fall over one little dog at the Grand Canyon would indeed have made Harding uncomfortable.

It wasn't that Fall's opponent in the Grand Canyon dog debate carried much weight with Harding. Until recently, Postmaster General Hubert Work had been an obscure doctor in Colorado. He had dabbled in local Republican politics, and in 1913 he'd become a member of the Republican

National Committee. For the 1920 election, Republican Party national chair-
man Will Hays asked Work to help organize farmers for Harding, and Hays
was impressed enough by Work's managerial abilities that when Hays was
appointed postmaster general, he selected Work as his deputy. When Hays
resigned after one year, Harding appointed Work as postmaster general. He
was an effective bureaucrat, but no match for Albert Fall.

In arguments, Fall combined a skillful marshaling of facts, personal charm,
and ferocious aggression. In 1923 the bulletin of the National Parks Association reported on the negative encounter that one parks advocate had had
with Fall in the Interior Department:

> His forceful, picturesque personality carries far, and he uses it to the
> limit in gaining his objectives. His speech is fast, his manner is impetu-
> ous, and he becomes instantly aggressive at opposition. At these times
> his powerful face clouds to sternness, he sits forward in his chair, and
> pounds his statements home with gesticulation; or he throws his head
> back till he faces the ceiling while roaring with laughter at his oppo-
> nent's replies. He does not argue, because he does not listen. He con-
> trols absolutely the attention of all hearers, and deeply impresses many
> with his impetuous advocacy and assertion.[4]

Back in New Mexico, Fall had not been content to pound his opponents
with gesticulations. On two occasions, once on the floor of the state senate
and once at the state constitutional convention, Fall became so angered in
debates that he physically struck his opponents. In debates in the U.S. Senate,
Fall would point his finger at opponents as if it were a pistol. It was a nota-
ble event, then, that the humble Hubert Work would challenge Fall and that
President Harding would rule against Fall—at least for a moment.

Fall's real opponent in the Grand Canyon dog debate wasn't Hubert Work,
but someone else who often attended Cabinet meetings, sitting in a wooden
chair carved just for him. This person wasn't a member of the cabinet, and in
fact he wasn't even a person. He was Laddie Boy, Warren Harding's Airedale.

Harding and his wife, Florence, had always been dog lovers, but their history with dogs had been scarred by tragedy. When Harding was a child, he'd
had a black-and-tan mongrel, and one day his great-uncle Perry arrived in the

Harding's barn and announced that Warren's dog was mangling his sheep; Perry picked up Warren's dog by the legs, whirled it about, and smashed its head against a post. The bloody horror of that moment left Harding with a lifelong tender heart for mistreated animals. One time when Warren saw a man with a crate crowded with doves, Warren bought the crate, carried it to the roof of his newspaper office, and released the doves. When a homeless, scruffy Newfoundland dog wandered into the office, Harding let him live there for years. The famous Harding dog editorial referred to by the *New York Times* was written upon the death of the Harding's Boston terrier, Hub, who followed Harding to the office every day. Then someone poisoned Hub, and Harding was convinced it was motivated by dislike of his editorial stands. This was the second time Harding had lost a dog to poisoning, the first being his mastiff, Jumbo. Harding wrote an editorial eulogizing Hub in which he contrasted a dog's trusting friendship with the dishonesty and cruelty of humans: "One honest look from Hub's trusting eyes was worth a hundred lying greetings from such inhuman beings, though they wore the habiliment of men."[5] The murder of Hub was so upsetting to Florence that she swore she'd never get another dog, and she became deeply involved in the rising movement against cruelty to animals. One time Florence saw a man whipping his fallen horse and she rushed out and grabbed the whip away from the man and declared it should be used against him. The fight against cruelty to animals would become Florence's cause as First Lady.

Upon Harding's inauguration, someone gave the Hardings a well bred but scruffy six-month-old Airedale, and they decided to keep him. They had no children, so Laddie Boy received a great deal of affection. He also became the Harding administration's mascot. Just as he had taken his dog to the newspaper office every day, President Harding took Laddie Boy to the Oval Office and to cabinet meetings, and the dog was given his own chair in the cabinet room. Photographs of Harding at work and at play often showed him with Laddie Boy, and the public took notice. Previous presidents had enjoyed their pets more privately, but this was the age of movie newsreels, glossy photo magazines, and celebrity gossip reporters, and soon Laddie Boy became the first presidential pet to achieve national celebrity. Reporters were invited to Laddie Boy's birthday party, which featured a huge cake made out of dog biscuits. Visitors to the White House were happy to shake hands with Laddie

Laddie Boy with President and Mrs. Harding on the White House porch. *(Courtesy of Library of Congress)*

Boy and to pose for photos with him. The dog even started receiving fan mail and being invited to public events. Before long, Laddie Boy was answering his mail, and granting newspaper "interviews," actually written by Harding. In one missive, Laddie Boy talked candidly about the president:

> Sometimes the Chief acts as though he would like to sit down when he and I can be alone, and I can look at him with sympathetic eyes, and he fixes his gaze on me in a grateful sort of way, as much as to say, "Well, Laddie Boy, you and I are real friends, and we will never cheat each other." When the Chief looks at me this way, I know that he feels that I will never find fault with him, no matter what he does, and that I will never be ungrateful or unfaithful.[6]

Albert Fall, President Harding's secretary of the interior. *(Courtesy of Library of Congress)*

Laddie Boy's celebrity made him a valuable symbol in Florence Harding's campaign against animal cruelty, and he led the Humane Society's "Be Kind to Animals" parade through the streets of Washington, D.C. But celebrity has its drawbacks. When a Denver dog was dragged into court for killing chickens, and when a New York dog was accused of street fighting, the dog owners claimed immunity on the grounds that their dog was the secret son or brother of Laddie Boy. After Harding's death, 19,314 newspaper boys donated pennies that were made into a copper statue of Laddie Boy, now in the Smithsonian.

The *New York Times* article didn't mention whether Laddie Boy was present at the cabinet meeting that debated the Grand Canyon dog. If he was, it's likely that Warren Harding glanced in his direction, and with Harding being accustomed to imagining Laddie Boy's thoughts and feelings, it's quite possible that he sensed the dog's answer to Albert Fall: "Surely you would never break the heart of a dog who is so loyal to his lonely human. Surely you would never value wicked, food-stealing squirrels and crows over an innocent, noble dog. The Grand Canyon may be deep, but it's not as deep as a dog's love." Even if Laddie Boy wasn't present, Harding would have thought of him, and of his wife, Florence, and of what Florence and her small army of animal cruelty activists would say if Harding committed such cruelty against a dog. The president did appreciate the national parks; in fact, he and Florence had honeymooned at Yellowstone National Park, where he'd been awed by Old Faithful. But dogs were even more faithful than geysers. Yet it seems that Albert Fall refused to accept Harding's decision and made such "an exception" to it that the president retreated into befuddled indecision.

Fall knew how much Harding loved dogs, and knew that he was making the president uncomfortable and himself unwelcome. So what was Fall's motivation? It wasn't love of wildlife; Fall was no conservationist.

Albert Fall embodied the Manifest Destiny vision of the American continent as a vast treasure chest, a gift to a chosen people. America's natural resources—its forests, waters, soils, minerals, coal, oil, and wildlife—were meant to be exploited to enrich the nation and to make America the dominant world power. There was no need to worry about tomorrow because, as Fall declared, "Man can not exhaust the resources of nature and never will."[7] The men who were bold enough to find and develop America's natural resources were considered national heroes who deserved to become rich as a reward.

But only if they were white men. Fall favored abolishing Indian reservations and opening them to white settlement and resource extraction. When oil was discovered on Navajo lands, Interior Secretary Fall stripped the tribe of any rights to it. He believed that Hispanics, too, should get out of the way of Manifest Destiny, whether they were New Mexico peasants hanging on to the old Spanish notion that water was a communal resource, or Mexican politicians interfering with American mining and oil projects—for which Senator Fall advocated war against Mexico.

As a lawyer, Fall had become rich representing mining and railroad corporations, enabling him to buy a 750,000 acre ranch, the same size as Yosemite National Park. Fall favored abolishing national forests and other federal lands and turning them over to the states for development. As a rancher Fall had used subterfuge to exceed his grazing allotment in a national forest, and when he was caught, he fired off an angry letter to Forest Service director Gifford Pinchot saying that the agency would "rue the day" it had crossed him. The idea of conservation was, for Fall, an irrational betrayal of three centuries of American progress. Conservation "would convert the Western settlers into a lot of peasants."[8] Nearly a decade before becoming secretary of the interior, Fall had called for abolishing the department. On the subject of wildlife, Fall was proud of having killed a mountain lion by clubbing it with his rifle butt and then shooting it with his pistol. In his first speech as a U.S. senator, Fall declared, "The conservation of the natural resources in New Mexico means a restriction upon the individual; means that he must not acquire a homestead in the most habitable portion of the State; and means that upon such forest reserves and Indian reserves the gentle bear, the mountain lion, and the timber wolf are conserved, so that they may attack [ranchers'] herds, his cattle, and his sheep."[9] Twenty years of conservation and progressive politics led by Teddy Roosevelt and Woodrow Wilson seemed lost on Fall. He was the right man for Warren Harding's "Return to Normalcy," a normalcy in which old national myths still worked, and the endless frontier and individual initiative would reward the worthy, solve all problems, and bring national greatness.

When Harding appointed Fall as secretary of the interior, conservationists were horrified. Pinchot, former director of the U.S. Forest Service, declared, "It would have been possible to pick a worse man for Secretary of the Interior, but not altogether easy."[10] Pinchot began a vigorous campaign opposing Fall's policies, but he was rowing against a conservative tide. At the National Park Service, which had been established only five years previously and was still struggling to establish its authority, director Stephen Mather feared that Fall's appointment would mean the annihilation of everything he had worked for. Assistant director Horace Albright said, "When [Harding] announced as his nominee his old Senate crony Albert Fall, gloom settled over all of us in the National Park Service.... [Fall] was known to have personal interests in mining, stock-raising, and ranching and, as far as we knew, had no leanings toward protection of national parks. It looked like very bad news indeed."[11]

Mather and Albright were greatly relieved when their new boss told them he had no intention of firing them or of interfering with the National Park Service. But Mather decided to take the offensive and try to win Fall's support. That summer he escorted Fall on a grand tour of Yellowstone, Yosemite,

National Park Service director Stephen Mather at the entrance of the Ralph Cameron mine at Indian Garden. *(Grand Canyon National Park Study Collection)*

Rocky Mountain, Mesa Verde, and Zion. Mather showed Fall the grandeur of the parks, bombarded him with his considerable powers of persuasion, and introduced him to prominent businessmen who were strong supporters of the parks and could recite their economic benefits. Mather also pointed out threats to the parks, such as how proposed reclamation projects would flood part of Yellowstone.

Fall spent a whole week in Yellowstone, where he enjoyed riding a horse and camping out in the mountains with Mather and Albright. "Secretary Fall must have felt he was among friends," wrote Albright in his memoirs, "for over the campfire one night he poured out his troubles to us." One of

Ralph Cameron. *(Grand Canyon National Park Study Collection)*

those troubles was a place in Wyoming called Teapot Dome, which held vast oil reserves controlled by the U.S. Navy. "He believed they belonged under Interior, and he was going to try to get them back and open some of them to exploration and development." Albright continued:

> I summoned the courage to argue that even if the oil reserves were turned back to the Interior Department, they should be kept "locked up." Secretary Fall replied: "Albright, I'm surprised at you taking that position. You are a western man; you know how important oil is. We must be sure we have enough of it going into production to prevent any slowing up in our industrial growth."
>
> I couldn't let that pass. "Oh, but you see, I'm a confirmed conservationist," I said, "and I want to see our resources protected for the future."[12]

If only Albert Fall had listened to Horace Albright about Teapot Dome that night, the ensuing scandal would have been avoided.

Fall's tour of the national parks did make an impression on him. Albright recalled, "I don't know how much the Secretary knew about conservation when the tour started, but by the time he headed back to Washington, he had become a parks enthusiast."[13] Fall soon put a stop to the reclamation projects that were threatening Yellowstone. And to the delight of Stephen Mather, Fall publicly denounced Arizona senator Ralph Cameron, whom Mather had spent years fighting over private landholdings, development schemes, and political interference at Grand Canyon National Park.

This didn't necessarily mean that Fall had been converted to the idea of conservation. In everything he did, he loved to build empires and to fight and win turf wars. As a New Mexico politician Fall had built a political machine that included squads of armed men at polling places and open violence; when Fall's arch rival, Albert Fountain, mysteriously disappeared, many people assumed that Fall had arranged an assassination. Fall was determined to build a ranching empire, even if he couldn't afford it and had to use dishonest tactics. As a lawyer he had helped mining and railroad corporations build monopoly empires, and he had acquired many mining claims for himself. Fall had campaigned relentlessly to achieve statehood for his home turf, New Mexico. As a U.S. senator, Fall was most proud of helping the United States seize its destiny as a world empire. In the Harding cabinet Fall sought to enhance his Interior Department by seizing assets from other agencies. He tried to transfer the Forest Service from the Department of Agriculture to Interior, infuriating agriculture secretary Henry C. Wallace and starting an intense conflict that led to divisive cabinet debates; in response, Pinchot sent letters to six thousand newspapers to mobilize conservationists against Fall's plan. The senator also wanted to have the vast natural resources on Alaska public lands placed under Interior Department authority. And yes, he did succeed in having the oil at Teapot Dome transferred from the navy into his control. When he secretly signed an exclusive, no-competitive-bid deal with oil man Harry Sinclair to drill at Teapot Dome, but a small oil company refused to give up its existing claims there, Fall sent in the U.S. Marines to squash the leech on the Sinclair dinosaur. Albert Fall was no conservationist, but no matter what else it was, the National Park Service was now part of his empire.

Mather and Albright may have done too good a job at selling Fall on the economic benefits of national parks. Soon after returning from his national parks tour, Fall sprung on Mather a plan for a national park in New Mexico, shaped like a horseshoe and wrapping around Fall's Three Rivers Ranch. A few sections of Fall's proposed park had genuine value, such as White Sands, but most of it was average western scenery, and one section, Elephant Butte Reservoir, was mainly for recreation. Fall would call it the "All-Year National Park" to emphasize its winter resort qualities. He also proposed sanctioning mining, timber cutting, grazing, hunting, and water reclamation projects. Mather and Albright were horrified. They had worked for years to set high standards for the national parks, and now Fall was undermining everything. Yet how could they oppose their boss? Fall held the fate of the National Park Service in his hands, and it seemed like suicide to oppose him. Albright recalled:

> Mather, in a gloomy mood, poured out his feelings about how grotesque Fall's park scheme was, and showed me a penciled draft of the memorandum he had been writing to the Secretary, reporting negatively on the project. But he had been agonizing over whether to send it. He had spent many months trying to educate Fall on the national park concept, and had carefully built a good relationship that had benefited the parks despite this crazy scheme. Now, if he sent the negative report, he would put all that in jeopardy. Yet he could not let this travesty of a park go unchallenged.[14]

Mather was prone to severe depressions and nervous breakdowns, requiring long stays in sanitariums. Now, trapped in a no-win disaster, his spirits failed him again, and he checked himself into a sanitarium and disappeared for six months, which at least had the advantage of freeing him from publicly opposing Fall's plan. Fall then turned to Albright and told him to come to New Mexico to write a report approving his park, but Albright was serving as superintendent of Yellowstone, so he too had a good excuse for not showing up. Undeterred, Fall wrote his own report approving the park, and he raced a bill through the Senate with little scrutiny. But then it had to get through the House of Representatives. A House committee scheduled its hearing on Fall's bill for January 11, 1923. Albright described the drama:

> No representative of the Park Service was present.... Mather was by this time in Chicago, completely recovered and ready to return to work, but

I had advised him to stay away from Washington until after the hearings. We did not want him to come back and face the choice of resigning or writing the report on the all-year park. We also believed that Fall's days as Secretary were numbered. There were indications that his rumored participation in the Teapot Dome and Elk Hills oil leases, being investigated by Senator Tom Walsh, was about to explode into a scandal.

The hearings opened with the big guns of the conservation movement loaded for action....

After lunch, Secretary Fall arrived to testify, having been summoned hastily by a despairing park advocate who perceived that the entire committee appeared to be against it.... All of the committee members asked Fall tough questions, and he was driven during three hours of testimony to abandon point after point in the bill...until nothing was left except New Mexico gaining the status of having a national park. The committee seemed ready to compromise by making it a recreational area under the Indian Bureau, but Secretary Fall stuck to his original concept, and would not accept anything less than a national park.

The opposition by conservationists and the lack of a report by the National Park Service kept the bill from being reported out by the committee so it could come to a vote in the House.[15]

When Secretary Fall walked into the cabinet meeting the next morning, he was probably feeling defeated, humiliated, and angry. He loved to fight and win turf wars, and this one had been in the heart of his own turf: his department, his National Park Service, his New Mexico, his ranch. But at least there was one turf war that Secretary Fall could win today, so he launched into an attack on some stupid little dog who was trespassing at the Grand Canyon.

So what if President Harding was squirming with discomfort. Back in 1909, when President Taft had stopped in New Mexico and attended a VIP banquet, Fall had stood at the podium and lambasted the president for not giving enough support for New Mexico's bid for statehood. The crowd was shocked; President Taft was shocked and angry. Taft wrote to his wife: "He seemed to be a man who likes to cultivate notoriety by saying something rude and out of the ordinary rules of courtesy, and I had to take him and spank him, which I think I did pretty successfully.... He has had aspirations for the Senate, upon the inauguration of statehood, but I don't think those aspirations are likely to be gratified."[16] On the contrary, Fall's boldness had made him a hero to New Mexicans. Warren Harding was too weak a man to spank Albert Fall. Harding was no Taft, and certainly no Teddy Roosevelt. Besides, Fall was resigning from the cabinet, getting out while the going was good. He had nothing to lose now.

When the *New York Times* published its article on the Grand Canyon dog debate, its rival, the *New York World,* sent a telegram to the newspaper in Flagstaff, Arizona, requesting more information. In its next issue, January 19, 1923, the *Coconino Sun* ran the front-page headline: "GRAND CANYON BULL PUP CLAIMS ATTENTION [of] PRESIDENT'S CABINET." The phrase "bull pup" may not mean a bulldog: a few days later in a brief follow-up article, the *Coconino Sun* identified the dog as an "Airdale bull pup." Perhaps *bull* was used for *male*. The January 19 article included three locally drawn cartoons about the Grand Canyon dog, and the dog in the cartoons is not a bulldog but a generic mutt. The captions include: "Well, I'll be dog-gonned. Them fellers in Washington are talking 'bout me." If the Flagstaff newspaper was correct that Paddy was an Airedale, he was the same breed as Laddie Boy, though there's no sign that "them fellers in Washington" knew this.

Whereas the *New York Times* treated the whole story as a curiosity, the Flagstaff newspaper suggested that a long-standing political rivalry was behind the controversy:

> "Paddy," bull pup belonging to Charles M. Donahue [actually Donohoe], postmaster at Grand Canyon, has suddenly become famous....
>
> The story seems to be this:
>
> A female dog brought to Grand Canyon National Park a few months ago by a tourist selected the park as an ideal place to raise a family. Her owner gave the family to a resident of the park. The latter still has part of the family carefully locked up at his home, but one of the pups he gave to Mr. Donahue.
>
> The latter was recently made postmaster following the resignation of L. L. Ferrall.
>
> The park regulations prohibit dogs. That is so that the rabbits, squirrels and other small game will become tame.

Mr. Donahue's ownership of "Paddy" seems to have caused some comment and to have been reported at Washington. Just how it got to the attention of the cabinet is uncertain.

But there is no love lost between U.S. Senator Ralph H. Cameron of Arizona and Director of National Park[s] Stephen Mather. Mr. Donahue is a protégé of the senator—in fact, before becoming postmaster at Mr. Cameron's recommendation, was working for Mr. Cameron and Mr. Stetson at their mining property at the Canyon. Also, the post office building belongs to and sets on land belonging to Senator Cameron.

Possibly Mr. Mather stirred up the tempest that assumed sufficient proportions to be the subject of discussion at a cabinet meeting. It isn't hard to believe he would take a crack at the senator, even over some one else's shoulders, if opportunity offered.

Of course, "Paddy" is a poor dog.

There is another dog at Grand Canyon that is allowed to stay there by special permit granted by Mr. Mather. That is "Razzle Dazzle," the Airedale to whom the late Charles A. Brant, former manager of El Tovar hotel at Grand Canyon, left $5,000. "Razzle Dazzle" has a colored groom, and Mr. Mather granted him domiciliary rights in the national park.

"Paddy" has no inheritance. He's a darned nice dog, but he made the mistake of being born poor and then of picking his friends from among those who are not loved by the big boss of all the parks.

Charles Brant, the longtime manager of El Tovar Hotel, had died in 1921, a year after his wife, Olga. They were buried in a private, rock-rimmed graveyard with a good view of El Tovar. Razzle Dazzle lived until 1928, when he joined his masters in their graveyard and even got his own tombstone that said, "Faithful and Beloved Pet," a measure of how popular Razzle Dazzle was with Grand Canyon residents. Stephen Mather would have made himself unpopular with canyon residents if he had banished Razzle Dazzle from the park. By the time Brant died, Laddie Boy was becoming a national celebrity, and Mather probably wouldn't have risked Harding's displeasure by evicting Razzle Dazzle the Airedale from his home.

Mather was no hater of animals or pets. He not only allowed one Grand Canyon ranger to keep a pet fawn named Chummy, but had the deer sent to Washington to serve as a Park Service mascot at a VIP banquet at the Willard Hotel. The Willard was famous for its cuisine, but someone forgot to feed Chummy, who headed for the salad of secretary of commerce Herbert Hoover and gobbled it down. Mather then sent Chummy to Philadelphia for a banquet that George Horace Lorimer, publisher of the *Saturday Evening Post,* was giving for Park Service leaders. Mather kept Chummy corralled in a bathroom, but as soon as he was brought out, he headed straight for Lorimer's salad. Before Mather could send him back to the Grand Canyon, Chummy came down with a spinal ailment. Mather called in the best veterinarians, even a chiropractor, but Chummy died. Mather felt deeply guilty that someone's pet had died while in his charge. Also, this was the decade when the North Rim of the Grand Canyon was grossly overpopulated with deer, yet Mather couldn't bring himself to support proposals to cull the population. When the Forest Service began transferring North Rim deer to other places, Mather adopted two fawns, shipped them to his home, and kept them as pets.

Mather's persecution of Paddy contained a logic and a motive that even the Flagstaff newspaper didn't glimpse. For twenty years Ralph Cameron had used the Grand Canyon post office as a weapon in his war against threats to his Grand Canyon interests, including threats from Mather.

Cameron had arrived at the canyon in the 1880s, long before it became a national monument and then a national park. It was wide open to private land claims, and Cameron filed extensive claims on the rim and inside the canyon. For years he operated the Bright Angel Trail as a private toll trail. Cameron fought the creation of Grand Canyon National Park, and when it was established, he strongly resisted Mather's efforts to incorporate private in-holdings. The mining laws by which Cameron had made his claims gave him substantial legal clout. By 1926 Mather would be so exasperated with Cameron that he was considering resigning as Park Service director to devote himself and his money to defeating Cameron in his bid for reelection to the Senate. Cameron's clout was also enhanced by all his allies in the park, including in the post office.

From 1907 to 1916 the Grand Canyon postmaster was Louisa Ferrall, wife of L. L. Ferrall, who was Cameron's chief henchman. Louisa was the sister of Grand Canyon pioneer Martin Buggeln, another private landholder who tried to fight off the National Park Service. From 1916 to 1922, L. L. Ferrall was postmaster. At a time when there were few community centers at the canyon, the post office was a meeting place and gossip place—perfect for gathering intelligence for Ralph Cameron. After the election of 1908, when Cameron was first elected to the U.S. House of Representatives as Arizona's territorial delegate, Louisa wrote to Cameron scoping out the "7 votes against you in this precinct.... I am quite sure I have four of the others spotted."[17] Cameron's papers contain many letters on stationery that says "Louisa Ferrall, Postmistress, Grand Canyon, Arizona Territory," but most of these are from L. L. Ferrall and Niles Cameron, Ralph's brother, and are about protecting Cameron land claims and evicting rivals. Ralph Cameron was so confident of his power that he tried to stop the Santa Fe Railway from building the Hermit Road and trail since they would cross Cameron land claims.

When Mather became the first director of the National Park Service in 1916—the same year L. L. Ferrall became postmaster—and set out to evict Cameron from his land claims, he found that his letters to the superintendent of Grand Canyon National Park were not being delivered. In an interview with park ranger Julie Russell, Horace Albright stated that he and Mather were positive that L. L. Ferrall was intercepting and opening Mather's letters. Mather resorted to sending his letters in plain envelopes addressed to the wives of park officials or to school teachers and then to sending telegrams in code.[18] This continued for years, including under Charles Donohoe and his successor, James Kintner, also a Cameron man. Here's one telegram that Superintendent Tillotson sent to Mather in 1927: "Person mentioned last paragraph my letter November sixteenth entirely satisfactory but SASAP-JOB ILBOYHUM in DYBACK TENCODADAEM with ITIFFEGY who indicates he will SASBYEED ILBOYHUM if held stop Personally NYADIFAB to DYBACK VAMDMOL and feel that his GHANTJUG in OACINIZE will not be HUMPYELM interests of RYNKIHUM your previous information to contrary notwithstanding."[19]

Stephen Mather's biographer somehow got the idea that L. L. Ferrall was Ralph Cameron's brother-in-law, and this claim was repeated by Ken Burns in his PBS documentary *The National Parks*, which highlighted the fight between Mather and Cameron. However, Ralph Cameron's papers contain dozens of letters between the Ferralls and Cameron, and they contain no sign of their having any family connection. In his letters to L. L. Ferrall, Cameron addresses him as "Dear Sir," and never mentions Louisa; and in Ferrall's letters to Cameron, he barely mentions "your wife," and not by name. Grand Canyon historian Bill Suran looked into the claim that L. L. Ferrall and Cameron were related and decided it was a case of confusion.[20] But if Mather had gotten the mistaken idea that L. L. Ferrall was Cameron's brother-in-law, this would have only magnified his loathing of the Grand Canyon post office.

Charles Donohoe succeeded L. L. Ferrall as postmaster in 1922. The turf war between Donohoe and the National Park Service included a lot more than just a dog. In 1920 the U.S. Supreme Court had ruled that Ralph Cameron's land claims were invalid and declared his land to be U.S. government property. This included the old Cameron Hotel, now the post office, and the land around it, which held the postmaster's residence. Park superintendents repeatedly asked postmasters to obtain a park permit for living there, but Ferrall, Donohoe, and Kintner adamantly refused. In September 1922 Donohoe told superintendent W. W. Crosby to "go to hell," and Crosby wrote to the postmaster general, care of the National Park Service director, to complain about it.[21] In November Donohoe distributed a leaflet to eight hundred Grand Canyon tourists, representing himself as the "Friends of the National Parks," but as Superintendent Crosby told his boss in Washington, "the matter in it is anything but friendly to the present administration of the Park.... This Donohoe...is extremely hostile to the local organization of the Park Service at Grand Canyon."[22] On December 5 a ranger caught Donohoe cutting firewood inside the park without a permit; when the ranger told him to get a permit, Donohoe refused and said he would "take this up with Washington by cable."[23] Superintendent Crosby also complained to Washington:

> In this particular case of Donohoe's, it is absolutely for the interests and future of the Park Service here to have him recognize the authority of the Park Service in this Park.... So long as the Post Office Department shall continue as its representative here, an individual who persists in exhibiting contempt for the Park Service and the Department of the Interior, and who is actively hostile to both, and who takes advantage of his connection with the Post Office Department to add weight to his words and actions as an individual it is apparently necessary that we

should afford him no advantage in his course by our failing to protect the Service and our own position here by proper action.[24]

It was five weeks later that the dog controversy reached Harding's cabinet meeting. Poor Paddy was just another pawn in the battle to make Donohoe "recognize the authority of the Park Service." Mather wouldn't have imagined that his move to deprive Donohoe of his dog would end up being decided by the president of the United States.

As far as we know, President Harding never did make a decision about Paddy or pet policies in the national parks. Right after that cabinet meeting, Harding was hit so hard by the flu that he was knocked out of action for weeks. By the time he was out of bed, Albert Fall was on his way out of the cabinet. The fate of Paddy and all future dogs in the national parks would be decided by a larger fate, by the turns of history, by events that were larger than even a president of the United States.

When word got out that Secretary Fall had taken control of navy oil reserves at Teapot Dome, Wyoming, and Elk Hills, California—reserves deemed essential to national defense—and had opened them to oil companies for private profits, there were objections from conservationists, admirals, and everyone in between. A Senate committee started hearings, but they dragged on slowly and seemed to be hitting a dead end: Fall had good explanations for everything. But then one of his old enemies in New Mexico happened to see Fall's ranch, which only a few years before had been dilapidated but was now booming with expensive improvement projects. Where had Fall suddenly gotten so much money? Not from his modest government salary. The Senate hearings continued twisting and turning through a maze of leads and disclosures until it turned out that Fall had accepted over $400,000 in bribes from two oil men, Harry Sinclair and Edward Doheny—money delivered in cash in a black suitcase—not to mention many thousands of dollars Sinclair had deliberately lost to Fall in poker games. In return, Sinclair and Doheny had received exclusive, no-bid rights to extremely profitable oil supplies.

Albert Fall became the first cabinet member in U.S. history to go to prison for a crime committed in office. Harry Sinclair also went to prison. Attorney general and old Harding crony Harry Daugherty was forced to resign for obstructing justice. Navy secretary Edwin Denby, who went along with Fall's transfer of the oil, was forced to resign. The Teapot Dome scandal became the greatest in American history to that time. It permanently branded the Harding administration as a failure, one of the worst in American history, which might be a bit unfair to Warren Harding himself, since apparently his only crime was that of trusting his buddies. Harding never had a chance to react to the scandal; on a long summer trip around the western United States and Alaska, he suffered a heart attack and died. Eight years later, when then-president Herbert Hoover spoke at the dedication of the Harding Memorial in Ohio, he declared that Harding had also died of a broken heart, that he was "a man whose soul was being seared by a great disillusionment," by the betrayal and corruption of his best friends.[25] Historians are still debating how much Harding knew at the time of his death, but Hoover's scenario has become the prevailing interpretation of events: that the Teapot Dome scandal killed Warren Harding.

It's not clear to what degree Albert Fall's resignation from the cabinet was motivated by fear of the doom that was unfolding every day in the newspaper headlines. On the same day that the *New York Times* ran the letter from Robert Frothingham denouncing Fall over the Grand Canyon dog, it also carried the headline SINCLAIR EXPECTED FEDERAL OIL LEASE, and described Harry Sinclair's first, defiant testimony before the senate investigative committee. The subheadline read: "Adjournment Comes Just as the Listeners' Expectations of a Sensation Are Highest." The drumbeat of scandal would torment Albert Fall. "I saw a man crumble right before my eyes," wrote his friend Evalyn Walsh McLean. "Drinking had changed him from a virile, sharp-witted man into a trembling wreck."[26] At the time he resigned, Fall claimed he was leaving to make some good money as a private consultant to Harry Sinclair and Edward Doheny, which he did, for awhile.

With Albert Fall leaving, Harding needed a new secretary of the interior. Several men began openly campaigning for the post. The state legislatures of Nevada and New Mexico passed resolutions recommending former Arizona governor Thomas Campbell. Maybe it was true that Harding needed a western man, but Harding was sick of the ferocious controversies that Fall had stirred up over western resources. Harding wanted a man who, while probusiness, was ready to join the conservation movement. He wanted a plodding bureaucrat, not an arrogant, flamboyant, power-grabbing turf fighter. He wanted someone with a heart. Just maybe, someone who wouldn't dream of taking away a man's dog. Harding looked across the cabinet table and saw the right man: a doctor, a man from Colorado, a humble bureaucrat: Hubert Work, the postmaster general.

Work, the man who had argued that dogs should be allowed in national parks, was now in charge of all the national parks. Was he going to suddenly reverse his position and do Fall's corrupt work for him? No way. That rule was a dead letter. There was no Laddie-tude on that one. As long as Work was secretary of the interior, which would be another five years, there seemed to be little danger of dogs being evicted from national parks. Stephen Mather wasn't fussing about it anymore either, for not long after the Paddy controversy blew up in the newspapers, Charles Donohoe resigned as postmaster. For the next five years dogs proliferated at Grand Canyon National Park.

At about the time that Work retired as secretary of the interior, Grand Canyon National Park got a new superintendent, Miner Tillotson. Tillotson decided that the dog situation had gotten out of hand and that he was going to enforce the regulation—still on the books—that banned dogs from the park. He issued an order giving residents thirty days to remove their dogs. Before long, Arizona's senator Henry Ashurst came calling at park headquarters. He was accompanied by Dick Gilliland, caretaker of another large inholding of private land inside the park owned by newspaper baron William Randolph Hearst. Like Ralph Cameron, Hearst was another longtime problem for the National Park Service. Senator Ashurst was a friend of Hearst's, and Gilliland had stirred him up about the dog ban, telling Ashurst that rangers were planning to go around shooting dogs. The senator told acting superintendent Preston Patraw, who was in charge while Tillotson was away for a month, that the park's plans were outrageous and should be stopped. Patraw assured Ashurst that no dogs were going to be shot; the only punishment for those defying the ban might be losing their job. Ashurst was placated, and the dog ban went through without further trouble. But Tillotson and other park managers didn't forget the machinations of Dick Gilliland, whom Patraw referred to as a "dirt house lawyer." This incident was yet another reason why the National Park Service wanted to expel Hearst from the park.

By 1932, if not earlier, the official rules of Grand Canyon National Park allowed residents to own dogs, but this was "subject to such further conditions…as may be determined by the superintendent."[27] Superintendents would choose to maintain a dog ban for decades to come. Was this a legacy of the great Grand Canyon dog debate?

In any case, today there are numerous backyard pens in Grand Canyon Village, full of happy dogs playing with bouncing balls. Today Razzle Dazzle looks down from his grave at all the happy dogs going for walks on rim trails—on leashes, of course—and the ghost of Airedales past smiles.

CITIZEN KANE-YON

William Randolph Hearst's Grand Canyon Estate

When the movie *Citizen Kane* came out in 1941, the officials of Grand Canyon National Park would have had a keen interest in seeing it. It was a story they knew all too well.

Citizen Kane was the thinly disguised story of William Randolph Hearst, the most powerful media mogul in American history. At his peak Hearst owned twenty-eight newspapers in most of the major cities, a syndicated news service, a newsreel company, and some of America's leading magazines. His power was not due to his high journalistic standards. Hearst invented some of the worst practices of tabloid journalism; his papers were full of sensationalized stories of murder and mayhem. For his political journalism, which included fabricating stories that aroused Americans to go to war with Spain, the phrase "yellow journalism" was invented. Hearst was ruthless at pursuing his goals, the foremost of which was his own power. He ran for political office repeatedly, including for president of the United States.

Hearst did have genuine and strong political beliefs, which he had absorbed from his father. George Hearst had remained a struggling working man until about age forty. Then he struck it rich, and soon owned some of the richest mines in America—the Comstock, the Homestake, the Anaconda. Yet George Hearst retained his sympathies for the common man. In his newspapers William Randolph Hearst battled for the common man against the power of monopoly corporations like the railroads, becoming a voice of the rising progressive movement. But as the years passed and Hearst amassed more and more wealth, he became more and more conservative, until in the 1930s he became the fiercest critic of Franklin Roosevelt's New Deal.

William Randolph Hearst also had something to conserve at the Grand Canyon. In 1913, six years before the establishment of the national park, Hearst bought some beautifully forested land on the rim at Grandview. For the next quarter of a century he fended off the National Park Service (NPS), which wanted to acquire Hearst's land but lacked the political muscle to take it away from him. Then in 1939 the Roosevelt administration threw its full weight into the effort to take Hearst's land, resulting in an epic struggle. It would be the only time in the history of Grand Canyon National Park that the NPS seized land through a condemnation lawsuit. During the time that Orson Welles was filming *Citizen Kane*, depicting Hearst's Faustian lust for power and property, Hearst was acting out this story at the Grand Canyon.

William Randolph Hearst first traveled through Arizona in 1886 at age twenty-three. His first known visit to the Grand Canyon was October 16, 1903. Hearst was now a U.S. congressman from New York, and he was seeking the Democratic nomination for president in 1904. In the fall of 1903 Hearst took a train trip through the Southwest with twenty congressional supporters of his candidacy. He was following the example of President Theodore Roosevelt, his would-be opponent in the 1904 election, who had made a train trip through the West earlier that year, including a stop at the Grand Canyon, where Roosevelt made his famous "leave it as it is" speech. If Hearst said anything about the Grand Canyon, the newspapers didn't deem it worth printing. The Flagstaff newspaper, the *Coconino Sun*, commented on October 24, 1903: "The Hearst party stopped here Friday morning—for the engine to take water. They did not take anything else that we have heard of, but we probably owe our escape to the early (7 a.m.) hour of their passing." One of those accompanying Hearst was Arizona senator Henry Ashurst, who would be an important ally in defending Hearst's Grandview lands against the NPS; years later, on the front page of Hearst's *New York American*, Ashurst would credit Hearst's support for his reelection victory. In Prescott and Phoenix, Hearst was given a warm welcome, mainly because he was in favor of Arizona statehood. He was, however, far behind Teddy Roosevelt in knowledge about wildlife: the Phoenix newspaper, the *Arizona Republican,* reported on October 18 that Hearst wanted to see "the wild Arizona ostrich on his native heath."[1] Hearst failed to win the Democratic nomination.

Over the next ten years Hearst "visited this section repeatedly," according to the *Coconino Sun* on December 19, 1913. In the fall of 1911 Grand Canyon pioneer Pete Berry contacted Hearst with an offer to sell him some land at Grandview, which had been the first hub of canyon tourism, with a hotel served by a stagecoach from Flagstaff. But in 1901 the Atchison, Topeka, and Santa Fe Railway arrived a dozen miles to the west and built its far more modern and luxurious El Tovar Hotel, and the Grandview Hotel gradually went out of business. In the canyon about 2,500 feet below Grandview, on Horseshoe Mesa, was a rich copper mine, but a large drop in prices had forced the mine to close. Berry had developed both the hotel and mine, and now he was a bitter man, feeling that not only fate had conspired against him, but so had the Santa Fe Railway and the U.S. Forest Service. The Forest Service administered the Grand Canyon in the years before it became a national monument and then park, and it welcomed the resources and political power of the Santa Fe Railway, whereas a little guy like Pete Berry served little use. Berry was unwilling to sell his land to the corporation that had ruined him. And who was the most outspoken enemy of railroad corporations that crushed the little guy? William Randolph Hearst. In the fall of 1913 Hearst traveled to the Grand Canyon to inspect the Grandview property and decided to buy it.

Hearst eventually owned about 200 acres there, in four sections. Today the best-known part of Hearst's land is Grandview Point, where he owned the 4.5 acres at its tip. He also owned the mining claims on Horseshoe Mesa below. To the southeast of Grandview Point, at the back of the drainage of Hance Creek, was the now-closed Grandview Hotel on five acres of land, and nearby was the 160-acre homestead of Pete Berry. Hearst bought the Berry homestead and the hotel site for $74,000. Years earlier Berry had sold Grandview Point and the Horseshoe Mesa mining claims to a mining company, and though the mine was not operating, its stocks were still active, and it would be 1927 before Hearst bought out those stocks and obtained Grandview Point and the Horseshoe Mesa claims. Hearst paid a total of $125,000 for all of this land.

Berry derived a spiteful glee in pitting Hearst against the Santa Fe Railway and the U.S. government. He wrote to Ralph Cameron that his persecutors had "been after me day and night. I then came to the conclusion that I was too hard a nut to crack. So I have sold out to William Randolph Hearst so as to give them something easy to but [*sic*] up against."[2]

The seeds of future conflict were sown by the fact that in places the Berry homestead didn't quite reach the canyon rim, leaving those portions government property. Hearst would go to great lengths to claim that thin strip of land.

When newspapers announced Hearst's purchase of Grandview, it set off extravagant rumors about his plans for the land. Residents of Flagstaff, which had lost out to Williams—the railroad junction—as the jumping off place for the Grand Canyon, were eager to believe that Hearst was going to restore Grandview to its prominence and boost Flagstaff's tourism economy. The *Coconino Sun* speculated that Hearst was going to build a railroad or highway from Flagstaff to Grandview, or an electric train run by power from the dam Hearst would build on the Colorado River:

> This purchase by the multi-millionaire…gives rise to many conjectures….
>
> This section of the Grand Canyon is undoubtedly the most wonderful of all…[which] naturally convince[s] the casual observer that the project is more than one of securing a home on the brink of the Canyon….
>
> Flagstaff and this practically unknown wonderland has needed someone with unlimited means to make it the most sought land in the whole west, and with William Randolph Hearst securing this special advantageous point…it would seem that a realization of pioneer hopes had come at last….
>
> Aside from the wonders of this country, which many a tourist has come all the way from Europe to see, there are possibilities of water power that would supply all of Arizona with power, as well as parts of Colorado and Utah.[3]

A month later, on January 23, 1914, a *Coconino Sun* headline announced that "Hearst Will Build a Palatial Residence to Entertain Friends Touring This Section of the Country."

Mr. Hearst will have built a lodge that will be in keeping with the natural wonderland of which it will form a part....

Here, also, in the midst of what is declared to be one of the most magnificent forests of pines in existence, will be erected a park with ...driveways throughout its extent of 160 acres....[At what] will be unlike any residential spot in existence, Mr. and Mrs. Hearst plan to entertain their many friends who journey from the Atlantic to California and from abroad to view the great natural wonder.

Soon the *New York Times*, no admirer of Hearst's endless scheming in city politics, found another motive:

PHOENIX, Ariz., Feb. 9—According to reports here, William Randolph Hearst aims to be the next United States Senator from Arizona. Mr. Hearst, it is said, will establish a residence in Arizona within the next few months, and in due time seek the Senatorial nomination to succeed Senator Mark Smith.

Real estate men say that Mr. Hearst has purchased a large tract of land on the Grand Canyon and is planning to erect a modern hotel that will be one of the most palatial and commodious in the entire West. Work on the structure, it is said, will be started soon....

Mr. Hearst could not be reached last night, but his secretary, Mr. O'Reilly, confirmed that part of the dispatch relating to the purchase of land.

"It is true that Mr. Hearst has bought some land in Arizona," said Mr. O'Reilly, "but the rest of the dispatch is merely presumption. Mr. Hearst does not intend to leave New York. He bought the site of an old hotel merely because its situation on the Grand Canyon appealed to him."[4]

A month later the editor of Hearst's Los Angeles newspaper passed through Flagstaff, after meeting with Hearst in New York, and provided more hope for Flagstaff:

Bostwick stated that the plans were being drawn for three distinct propositions, which included, first, a palatial residence for the owner, a resort hotel to accommodate a large number of tourists and the building of an electric railway from Flagstaff to the rim of the Grand Canyon with the terminus at Grandview....

As to when the railroad will begin building or from what source the power is to be drawn were facts not given publicity, but it is believed the immense undertaking will be practically initiated not later than June or July of the present year.

Speaking of reports in circulation and published throughout the country that Mr. Hearst was to make Arizona his home, to gain recognition as an aspirant for future senatorial honors from this state, Mr. Bostwick stated that such an impression was without any foundation whatever....

Mr. Hearst is to make New York City his base of operations, but will be a frequent visitor to Grand View, where he will maintain a home and entertain his friends without any other motive than that of a private citizen who has invested in the country, and who is appreciative of its marvelous scenic attractions.[5]

Hearst did enjoy making plans for Grandview. In 1914 he told his new architect, Julia Morgan, who later would design his San Simeon castle, to design a cottage for Grandview. Later Hearst had Morgan design for Grandview an elegant residence, a hotel, and a public museum for his substantial collection of Native American artifacts. He had bought many of these artifacts through Herman Schweizer, who managed Indian arts for the Fred Harvey Company, the Santa Fe Railway subsidiary that ran its tourist services, including at the Grand Canyon. In 1927 Schweizer informed Hearst that he had bought a large bell, weighing hundreds of pounds, and sent it to the Grand Canyon (he mentioned no plans for it), and Hearst was welcome to buy this bell for $1,500, which he did. But of Hearst's building plans for Grandview, nothing ever came of them—except myths.

A century after his purchase of Grandview set off a flurry of gossip and speculation, Hearst is still generating rumors. At least three books about Julia Morgan claim that her 1914 cottage was indeed built, and the publisher's blurb for one of these books claims that Hearst built a "famed lodge" at Grandview. This same book includes a photo of a cabin that is captioned as the Morgan/Hearst cottage, but it shows a wooden frame building, while Morgan's plans for this cottage show it as a southwestern-style adobe building.[6] These claims about the Morgan cottage are contradicted by NPS documents and by the statements of Hearst's attorney, Frank Lathrop, who handled much of his Grandview dispute. Lathrop often met with Frank Kittredge, the Park Service's western regional director based in San Francisco. (Kittredge's jurisdiction didn't actually include Grand Canyon National Park, but since he was in the same city as Hearst's lawyers, he would handle many interactions with Hearst.) After a 1938 meeting Kittredge wrote: "Mr. Lathrop emphasized that Mr. Hearst had always loved this property in Grand Canyon, and time and again had called in architects to discuss building but never had done so, perhaps because of his diversified and more pressing interests elsewhere."[7] A year later Kittredge wrote that Lathrop had said that Hearst had been "hoping to build on this property himself, but this being impossible...."[8] In preparing its condemnation of Hearst's land, the NPS made a thorough inventory of its contents, including 928 ponderosa pine trees and 7,123 feet of fences made of five-strand wire and steel posts. There was a highly detailed list of all the buildings, including Pete Berry's original cabin, now expanded to 750 square feet (at a cost of about $2,000) for use by Hearst's caretaker, Dick Gilliland; it was probably this cabin that was incorrectly identified as Morgan's cottage. The inventory makes no mention of any Julia Morgan cottage. Longtime Grand Canyon postmaster Art Metzger, who lived through the Hearst era, recalled for NPS interviewer Julie Russell that Hearst never built anything at Grandview, although Gilliland did fix up his cabin "pretty nice." Hearst documents indicate that he spent a total of $4,715 on improvements at Grandview, nearly half of which would have been for improving the cabin. In 1926 Grand Canyon National Park superintendent J. R. Eakin talked with Hearst at Hopi House and wrote to Stephen Mather: "He informed me that he had definitely decided to pull down the old buildings and build 'a little place.'"[9] In 1940 the park's acting superintendent, J. V. Lloyd, wrote: "At no time in the memory of old local residents has Mr. Hearst stayed on the ranch while at Grand Canyon, but during his rare visits he has always stopped at El Tovar Hotel. This probably is due to the fact that the existing buildings are old and unsuitable for this general use by Mr. Hearst."[10]

Yet at first Hearst seems to have made more use of Grandview. It's hard to track his visits to the canyon, as few sources mention them. One good source, however, is Harold G. Davidson's biography of Jimmy Swinnerton, a Hearst artist who played host at Grandview. Hearst was just starting out as a newspaperman in San Francisco when he hired Swinnerton in 1892, and he regarded him as his protégé. Swinnerton did illustrations, then cartoons, and then political cartoons. While still in his twenties Swinnerton contracted tuberculosis, atop his alcoholism, and his doctor predicted he would be dead in a month. Hearst sent him to the California desert to recuperate or die, and Swinnerton was amazed when he recovered. He credited the desert for saving his life and devoted himself to painting.

In 1914, six months after Hearst had bought Grandview, Swinnerton headed there to use it as a base for painting the Grand Canyon. Davidson's book includes one Swinnerton painting of the Grandview Hotel and one of its blacksmith shop, and two paintings of the view from Grandview. Hearst seems to have offered the Grandview Hotel as a vacation spot for his wide circle of friends, including famous artists and writers, and Swinnerton met them at the Flagstaff train station: "Jimmy was kept busy meeting and escorting such visitors as Zane Grey, William R. Leigh, and Mary Roberts Rinehart down the dusty road to Grandview."[11] Hearst came, too. "Jimmy waited at the depot on several occasions when the Hearst entourage came to town. Phoebe Hearst [Hearst's mother], "WR," and friends would often be unloaded from the Santa Fe cars and driven to Grandview."[12] When Swinnerton married in 1917, he took his new bride to Grandview. He stayed in Arizona several years, mainly in Flagstaff, and one outcome was the comic strip "Canyon Kiddies," which featured the adventures of Indian children set in southwestern scenes, including on the rim of the Grand Canyon. William Randolph Hearst was the pioneer of the Sunday comic strip, and "Canyon Kiddies" ran in his *Good Housekeeping* magazine for nearly twenty years.

One Hearst visit to the canyon is recorded in a Kolb brothers' photograph of Hearst, Will Rogers Jr., and others riding mules down the Bright Angel Trail on April 20, 1915. (Decades later, Will Rogers Jr.'s son would buy another private inholding on the canyon rim, a motel and bar at the Orphan mine site on the Hermit Road.) This photo was taken only five days after the premiere of the Kolbs' movie of their recent Colorado River boat trip, which

William Randolph Hearst (in rear) on Bright Angel Trail, April 20, 1915. Will Rogers Jr. is standing in the front. (*Grand Canyon National Park Study Collection*)

they would show in their South Rim studio for decades to come. Hearst was an avid photographer and had recently gotten into the newsreel and movie serial business (starting with *The Perils of Pauline*). He got to know the Kolbs and wanted them to take him on a Colorado River trip, but nothing ever came of it. Hearst later hired Ellsworth Kolb to photograph San Simeon; while working there, Ellsworth took a bad fall.

The Grandview Hotel was rustic to begin with, and by 1914 it was hurting from its nearly two decades of age and its years of being closed. It's not surprising that by 1926, when Hearst spoke with Superintendent Eakin, he had decided to tear it town. The hotel was removed a few years later, and its logs were donated to architect Mary Colter for use in her Desert View Watchtower, where they can be seen today in the ceiling of the round entrance room. The old trail from the rim to Horseshoe Mesa was also decaying, and in 1927 Hearst cabled his lawyer A. T. Sokolow about improving the trail, but it's not known if any work was done.

We have only one definite record of Hearst visiting the canyon in the 1920s, and that comes from Eakin's account. Hearst arrived one morning with a party of a dozen people, and they headed out to Grandview but were supposed to stay at El Tovar that night. When Eakin looked for Hearst at El Tovar, he found that Hearst had changed his mind and was leaving that evening, though he said "he was returning soon for a longer stay."[13] Eakin did speak with Hearst's attorney about Hearst's caretaker, Dick Gilliland, who showed "extreme antagonism toward the government."[14]

After the hotel was gone, Hearst had less incentive to visit or invite friends to Grandview. When the park engineer was making his 1939 inventory of Hearst's lands, he added: "It is reported that Mr. Hearst visited his holdings here twice in the past nine years, occupying quarters in the local El Tovar Hotel."[15]

Yet again, William Randolph Hearst spawned myths. Postmaster Art Metzger said that years later a star-struck writer for the Williams newspaper greatly exaggerated the celebrity life at Grandview. This may have been the version heard by Howard Stricklin, who was park superintendent in the 1960s and who, in an interview with park ranger Julie Russell in 1981, regarded Grandview as a love nest for Hearst's mistress Marion Davies: "And he bought the place for her. Then he'd come and visit her there."[16]

Hearst's neglect of Grandview was typical of him, for his acquisitive appetites far exceeded his time and budget for digestion. Hearst bought a castle in Wales and a ranch in Mexico, and he built a palatial "beach house" in Santa Monica, a Bavarian mansion called Wyntoon near Mount Shasta, and his Mediterranean-style castle at San Simeon, which began absorbing most of his attention and money a few years after he bought Grandview. Hearst spent an estimated $50 million on sculptures, paintings, furniture, and antiques, often through gallery catalogs, and much of it got shipped straight to his massive warehouses in three cities, where it sat—still crated and unseen—for decades. Hearst also hoarded real estate and newspapers, which he couldn't bear to sell even when they were losing serious money. Hearst was following the collecting passion of his mother, Phoebe, who had led the young William through Europe on her art-hunting trips. Hearst's aesthetic tastes did include a good view: he told Julia Morgan that the ocean view from his little mountain at San Simeon was its main asset, and that her buildings should be placed and designed to take full advantage of it. Grandview too offered a grand view.

Hearst, however, valued extravagant displays of wealth far more than he valued nature. At Harvard he had flunked natural history, and his idea of camping out was much like the scene in *Citizen Kane* where a "picnic" includes luxury tents and chefs. Hearst's newspapers showed little interest in conservation issues. In the years that President Teddy Roosevelt was trying to shape an American conservation ethic, the Hearst newspapers pummeled him with abuse. Hearst's *Los Angeles Examiner* campaigned incessantly to dam the Colorado River to provide water and power for California's growth. While John Muir was battling to save Hetch Hetchy from being turned into a reservoir, Hearst's only concern was whether it would be run as a private business or a public utility. Hearst believed in public ownership—but not for anything he owned.

In the same year—1914—that Hearst was making himself at home at Grandview, a mining executive named Stephen Mather wrote an indignant letter to the secretary of the interior complaining about how powerful private interests were threatening the national parks. The secretary wrote back that if Mather didn't like the way the parks were being run, he should come to Washington and run them himself, as the director of the new NPS. When Mather started, the NPS was a small agency with few resources and little political clout, and it was up against very powerful economic and political opposition. Mather devoted himself to establishing the authority of the new agency, to establishing new parks, and to fighting off numerous threats to the parks. One of his first goals was to get the Grand Canyon designated a national park. Even President Roosevelt hadn't been able to achieve that, for Arizona politicians were strongly opposed to the idea. For many westerners, the land was made for resource extraction—for mining, grazing, lumbering, and hunting; taking away the private lands of heroic pioneers was considered deeply un-American.

As Mather and his deputy, Horace Albright, campaigned to make the Grand Canyon a national park, they began encountering a mysterious and powerful opposition. They had calibrated the power of Arizona politicians, but this was something greater. Albright recalled the situation in a 1981 interview with park ranger Julie Russell:

> We found we were having an unknown enemy when the Park bill was going through, unknown enemy opposing it. I've forgotten how the opposition was being expressed—but anyhow it was effective. We found out one way or another…that William Randolph Hearst was back of it, backing the opposition. The reason was, he was afraid the National Park Service would take Grandview and that Berry property away from him. That's why he didn't want it made a park.[17]

Even if Hearst kept his land, he worried that the thin strip of land between his land and the canyon rim might fall into unfriendly hands. Mather and Albright reluctantly yielded to Hearst's power, agreeing to a provision in the bill creating Grand Canyon National Park that said:

> Where privately owned lands within the said park lie within three hundred feet of the rim of the Grand Canyon no building, tent, fence, or other structure shall be erected on the park lands lying between said privately owned lands and the rim.[18]

To the uninitiated this provision, which didn't mention Hearst by name, was quite mysterious. Why 300 feet? The private lodges and other businesses

"Hearst cabin" at Grandview. (*Grand Canyon National Park Study Collection*)

within the park were a lot closer to the rim than 300 feet. But 300 feet was the distance of the Berry-Hearst cabin from the canyon rim. "So when we got that arrangement made," said Albright, "why the opposition dropped and that ended our trouble." Ralph Cameron was still fighting the park bill, "but he didn't have the influence to stop the bill from going through."[19] The bill's sponsors, Arizona senator Ashurst and congressman Carl Hayden, also included a provision protecting the rights of other private landholders. But Mather and Albright never accepted this, and they were determined to root out private inholdings. It was especially galling that the NPS couldn't even build a fence on its own land because it might offend the almighty Hearst.

For years Mather sought to meet with Hearst to learn his intentions and persuade him to give his land to the park, but he had to communicate through intermediaries. In 1921 Ford Harvey, the head of the Fred Harvey Company, reported that he had run into Hearst's attorney in Chicago, who told him Hearst wanted to build "a fine residence" at Grandview, perhaps with one room devoted to a public museum for his Indian collection. Hearst was offended that the NPS owned the strip of land between his land and the rim, and he wanted it. Perhaps the NPS would give this strip to Hearst in exchange for an equal amount of his land. Ford Harvey, who understood

Mather's positions, thought Mather might agree to an exchange if it came with a promise that Hearst would refrain from any commercial development of his land and perhaps give the park an option to obtain it. Hearst's lawyer, A. T. Sokolow, told Harvey to forget about obtaining the land.

A few months later Sokolow held meetings with Albright and Mather and officially made Hearst's proposal. Soon Mather wrote directly to Hearst stating his position: the NPS wanted Hearst's land. One of Mather's top personal priorities, to which he had "given a considerable amount of money from my private funds, is the elimination of private holdings within the boundaries of national parks."[20] The NPS would agree to Hearst's land exchange only if he agreed to deed his entire holding to the NPS upon his death, or perhaps— Mather knew that Hearst was fifty-nine years old—his children's deaths. If Hearst refused this offer, he could obtain the land exchange only by agreeing to refrain from any commercial development of his land, and it would be best if he gave the national park five or six times the acreage it gave him and agreed to allow the public free access to the canyon rim along his lands. Two years later, Mather was still waiting to meet with Hearst to talk about a deal.

The next interaction between Hearst and Mather was initiated by George Parker, head of the Parker Pen Company. One of Parker's former employees, Arno Cammerer, was now one of Mather's top aides and sometimes served as acting director of the NPS. Parker was also well acquainted with Hearst's top executives. When Parker visited Grand Canyon National Park in June 1924, Superintendent Eakin drove him out to Hearst's land. Eakin wrote to Mather:

> I suggested to Mr. Parker that it would be a very gracious thing for Mr. Hearst to donate this property to the government; that we would preserve it in its original condition and establish a campground on this property. Furthermore…we would erect a suitable tablet stating that the property had been donated to the Government by Mr. Hearst and this tablet would be one of the very best means of perpetuating Mr. Hearst's name for all time.[21]

Parker passed this suggestion through to Hearst. Stephen Mather was not naïve enough to imagine that Hearst's lust for immortality would be satisfied by a plaque, but he wrote back to Eakin: "I hope something comes of it. It is always possible, of course. If it does go through I will feel more like erecting a tablet to Mr. Parker than perhaps to Mr. Hearst."[22]

In the midst of these communications, a map landed on the desks of both Hearst and the NPS. The NPS was planning to build a new road between Grand Canyon Village and Desert View, and the surveyors had selected a route that cut across one corner of Hearst's land. This route was shortest, required no grading, and offered a natural, solid road bed; it would save the park thousands of dollars. At last Hearst had something to bargain with. It took two years, but Hearst and Mather worked out a congressional bill exchanging the roadway land for the strip of rim land Hearst had wanted, with no further conditions attached. Mather did win the acreage contest, gaining 48.9 acres from Hearst while giving him 25.8 acres. More than half a year before the bill passed, Hearst gave permission to begin building the new road over what was still his land. But this land swap got Hearst into trouble with his wife, who was co-owner and reluctant to sign the transfer deed. Mrs. Hearst complained that William was signing away their children's inheritance. William huffed that this was "absurd" and finally got his wife to sign.

At some point—Albright's recollection has no date—Mather and Albright finally got to meet with Hearst. Albright recalled:

> I can remember how I was almost as thrilled and excited at seeing the great William Randolph Hearst as I was in seeing the Grand Canyon. I knew he was a very big man and reading his newspapers we regarded him as a ferocious character, a man of tremendous force and very difficult, and a man that a man would be afraid of. So when we finally had our appointment at the Palace Hotel in San Francisco, we were both shocked and surprised to find what a gentle fellow he was. He was just as gentle as a baby. Kindly eyes and friendly smile and charming and pleasant. We had one delightful visit with him. He said all he wanted Grandview for was to establish a museum for his silver collections, particularly his Indian collections he had. Mr. Mather said, "Would they be open to the public?" "Why, of course," he said, "it would be a museum for the public. I would like to have the pleasure of building that structure and putting my things in it." He collected all sorts

Horace Albright in ranger uniform. *(Grand Canyon National Park Study Collection)*

of things, you know, one of the world's greatest collectors. He said he wanted to be sure the stuff didn't get in the wrong hands.... Well, you couldn't argue with him about that. If he was going to develop it into a public museum and put all his collections in there, why it would have been a good thing for the Park. So we accepted his viewpoint and thanked him and after a very pleasant visit, we left him.[23]

By now Mather and Albright had fought many nasty battles with men and corporations that were determined to exploit and sabotage other national parks, so by contrast Hearst was a fairly benign problem, and the NPS left him alone for years.

Horace Albright had another reason to remain scared of William Randolph Hearst. At the start of 1929, soon after Albright had replaced Mather as director of the NPS, Albright was scared that Hearst was going to get him thrown out of his job. Herbert Hoover had just been inaugurated as president, and there was already uncertainty about Hoover retaining or replacing agency heads. "For about a month I sweated it out," Albright wrote in his memoir, *The Birth of the National Park Service*, "and I felt even more nervous when I heard a persistent rumor that was making the rounds. It seemed that George Hearst, one of the sons of the newspaper magnate, was being pushed by influential people for the job of Director of the National Park Service."[24]

George Hearst was grossly unqualified for the job. He was twenty-five years old, a serious alcoholic, a dropout after one year of college, and so incompetent working at one of his father's newspapers that his father had him fired. Even at Grandview, Dick Gilliland seemed aware of George's troubles: in June 1927 Gilliland wrote to a Hearst lawyer suggesting that George could buy some available land six miles from Grandview, just outside the park boundary, turn it into a great dude ranch, and become the ranch manager. Nothing came of this idea. It's surprising that his father would want to see George in a high-profile position like director of the NPS. But perhaps the "influential people" pushing for George Hearst was actually President Hoover. Hearst had endorsed someone else for the 1928 Republican nomination, and Hoover was anxious to win Hearst's support for his presidency. Then again, at this moment William Randolph Hearst was angry at Horace Albright, for he feared Albright was betraying his promise not to take his Grand Canyon land.

Hearst was angry over a proposal pending in Congress that would enable the NPS to acquire private lands inside national parks by either purchase or legal condemnation. This proposal was a response to an emergency at Yosemite National Park, where a timber company had the rights and the plans to cut thousands of acres of trees. But the congressional proposal was stated in general terms, and Hearst feared it could be applied to his Grand Canyon lands. A Hearst representative—and boyhood friend of Albright— called on Albright. On February 23, only a week before Hoover's inauguration, Albright wrote back that this proposal was not intended to apply to Hearst, who:

> ...has worked splendidly with the National Park Service in many matters.... I am perfectly willing to go on record, unofficially, not to proceed toward the acquisition of these properties, but to leave this to

future personal conferences with Mr. Hearst or his authorized representatives with the view of perhaps evolving something that would serve our purposes and at the same time entirely meet with Mr. Hearst's plans and ideas for their future.[25]

Albright kept his job, but he also kept the goal of obtaining Hearst's land eventually. Hearst attorney John Francis Neylan kept Albright's letter, for as Neylan wrote to Hearst: "If the Bill should pass, the enclosed letter, retained as a confidential document, will be very valuable in dealing with the matter in the future."[26] This letter would indeed reappear.

Hearst was correct to fear the NPS's new power of condemnation: ten years later the NPS used it to take Hearst's land. This outcome was set in motion just a few months after Albright pledged not to take such action against Hearst. In October 1929 the Wall Street crash triggered the Great Depression, which placed Hearst under tremendous financial pressure—and Franklin Roosevelt in the White House. Roosevelt loathed Hearst, a loathing he had inherited from his cousin Teddy. The Roosevelt family's hatred of Hearst went back more than three decades. Now it would be not just a small federal agency aimed against Hearst, but the full powers of the White House.

William Randolph Hearst and Teddy Roosevelt should have been political allies, for both were passionate progressives at home and chauvinists in foreign policy; Hearst had "provided the war" that made Teddy Roosevelt famous as a Rough Rider. But both men were politically ambitious, and with Hearst's move to New York City in 1895, both were living in the same city, and there wasn't enough space for both of them. In 1898 Teddy Roosevelt ran for governor of New York, and Hearst yearned to run against him. "That Theodore Roosevelt," wrote Hearst biographer David Nasaw, "who was less than five years older, was already so far ahead of him only whetted Hearst's ambitions. It is impossible to measure the depth of his loathing for Roosevelt...."[27] Hearst found it inopportune to run for governor in 1898 after living in the state so briefly, but in the pages of his *New York Journal* he launched against Roosevelt what Nasaw called "a brilliantly coordinated campaign of ridicule," complete with cartoons portraying Roosevelt as a brat, a humbug, and a cynical opportunist. Roosevelt won.

Two years later William McKinley chose Teddy Roosevelt as his running mate, and Hearst reprised his anti-Roosevelt campaign on a national level. Editorials and cartoons ridiculed everything about Roosevelt, including his love of the West. Roosevelt won. Once during the campaign, and once after McKinley won, the Hearst newspapers implied that McKinley deserved to be assassinated; before long, he was, making Teddy Roosevelt president. Hearst was widely and angrily blamed for the assassination.

Two years later, in 1902, Hearst finally got his own political career off the ground by getting elected to Congress. Soon he was seeking the 1904 Democratic nomination for president, to kick Teddy Roosevelt out of the White House. But Hearst was too controversial for most Democrats, and he lost the nomination three-to-one to the safer Alton Parker, who lost to Roosevelt in the greatest landslide in American history to that time.

Two years later Hearst announced he was running for governor of New York, and President Roosevelt saw his chance for revenge. "We must win," Roosevelt wrote to one congressman, "by a savage and aggressive fight against Hearstism and an exposure of its hypocrisy, its insincerity, its corruption, its demoguery, and in general its utter worthlessness and wickedness."[28] To an English friend Roosevelt wrote:

> It is a little difficult for me to give an exact historic judgment about a man whom I so thoroly dislike and despise as I do Hearst.... Hearst's private life has been disreputable. His wife was a chorus girl or something like that on the stage.... He preaches the gospel of envy, hatred and unrest.... he is entirely willing to sanction any mob violence if he thinks that for the moment votes are to be gained by doing so.... He cares nothing for the nation, nor for any citizen in it.... He is the most potent single influence for evil we have in our life.[29]

Roosevelt quietly planted reports and rumors about Hearst's personal immoralities. As Election Day approached and the race looked close, Roosevelt dispatched secretary of state Elihu Root to a public rally in New York to lead the attack on Hearst:

> I say to you, with the President's authority, that he regards Mr. Hearst to be wholly unfit to be Governor, as an insincere, self-seeking demagogue,

who is trying to deceive the workingmen of New York by false statements and false promises.... In President Roosevelt's first message to Congress, in speaking of the assassin of McKinley, he spoke of him as inflamed "by the reckless utterances of those who, on the stump and in the public press, appeal to the dark and evil spirits of malice and greed, envy and sullen hatred."...I say, by the President's authority, that in penning these words, with the horror of President McKinley's murder fresh before him, that he had Mr. Hearst specifically in mind. And I say, by the President's authority, that what he thought of Mr. Hearst then he thinks of Mr. Hearst now.[30]

The anti-Hearst newspapers repeated Root's message loudly. On Election Day 1.5 million New Yorkers cast their votes, and Hearst lost by 60,000 votes.

Observing all of this was young Franklin Roosevelt, who idolized and modeled himself on his cousin Teddy. In 1920 the Democrats nominated Franklin Roosevelt for vice president. Hearst, for the first time in his life, endorsed the Republican presidential candidate, Warren Harding.

Two years later Hearst once again set out to run for governor of New York, and Franklin Roosevelt worked to defeat him.

In 1932 Governor Franklin Roosevelt was the frontrunner for the Democratic nomination for president, and Hearst did his best to stop him, pushing the candidacy of an old friend, congressman John Nance Garner. Hearst organized Garner's campaign, which was mostly an anti-Roosevelt campaign. At the Democratic National Convention Roosevelt was about one hundred votes short of the two-thirds needed to win the nomination. Garner had about one hundred delegates. Roosevelt operatives pleaded with Hearst to throw Garner's votes to Roosevelt, since, after all, Hearst and Roosevelt shared basic progressive values. Hearst did like the idea of being a kingmaker, so he pushed Garner to support Roosevelt. When Garner was nominated for vice president, Hearst was sure it was his payoff. Hearst was expecting to play a major role in shaping Roosevelt's cabinet and policies, but Roosevelt was less responsive than Hearst felt he should be.

For awhile Roosevelt and Hearst tried to bury the hatchet, but as Roosevelt implemented his New Deal policies, Hearst found them intolerable. The New Deal imposed major restrictions on corporations and major taxes on the rich. Hearst's proletarian sympathies were now well buried beneath his self-interest as one of the richest businessmen in America. He was out-raged that the New Deal was pushing for fair wages and work conditions in the newspaper industry. Hearst declared that Roosevelt was violating the Bill of Rights and promised to fight his measures to the Supreme Court. He began calling Roosevelt a Communist and a dictator: "The people elected a Democratic Administration, not a socialist dictatorship. The people approved the well considered proposals of the Democratic platform, not the theories of Karl Marx and the policies of Stalin."[31] America, he said, was being ruled by "Stalin Delano Roosevelt." By the start of 1935, two years into the New Deal, Hearst launched all-out war against Roosevelt and became the national leader of the Roosevelt-haters. When Roosevelt ran for reelection in 1936, Hearst plucked Kansas governor Alf Landon out of obscurity and placed the full power of his media empire behind him and his running mate, Frank Knox, the editor of Hearst's Chicago newspaper.

Roosevelt, wary of Hearst's power, at first tried his famous charm on Hearst and tried to appeal to his old progressive values, but finally Roosevelt lost patience. "I sometimes think," said Roosevelt, "that Hearst has done more harm to the cause of Democracy and civilization in America than any three other contemporaries put together."[32] Roosevelt began counterattacking, sometimes openly, but more often indirectly, through secretary of the interior Harold Ickes.

In June 1935 Roosevelt announced a major tax increase on the wealthy, which Hearst branded as "essentially Communism." On the day the tax message was to be introduced in Congress, Roosevelt met with Harold Ickes and read it to him. Ickes wrote in his diary: "He told me that he thought it was the best thing he had done as president....At one place in the message he looked at me with a smile and said, 'That is for Hearst.'"[33]

Ickes, of course, was also in charge of the NPS, and he would be the one who would direct the seizure of Hearst's land at the Grand Canyon.

Franklin Roosevelt did not select Ickes as secretary of the interior because he had any background as a conservationist: Ickes had none at all. He wasn't even interested in the job. Instead he had wanted to be commissioner of the Bureau of Indian Affairs, where he could continue fighting for the under-dog. At the start of the twentieth century Ickes had been inspired by the progressive movement, by its outrage at the growing oligarchy and injustice in America. As a Chicago lawyer he had helped Jane Addams and her Hull House, took cases too radical for other lawyers, and served as president of the Chicago NAACP. Ickes became a major force in Chicago politics, a nasty world where his pugnacious personality fit right in. He idolized Teddy Roosevelt and remained a strong progressive even as America became much more conservative. When the 1920 Republican National Convention repudiated the Roosevelt tradition by nominating Warren Harding, and the usual motion was made to make the nomination unanimous, an outraged Ickes screamed "*NO!*" loudly enough to be heard all over the convention hall. In that fall's campaign Ickes worked for the Democratic candidates, James Cox and Franklin Roosevelt. Yet when Franklin Roosevelt was elected president a dozen years later, many old progressive leaders distrusted him, seeing a pragmatist with few convictions. Roosevelt wanted to reassure the progressives by appointing one of them to his cabinet.

Ickes saw conservation mainly as another form of progressive crusading against the rich and powerful. In the year after taking office, Ickes published a book, *The New Democracy,* to justify the agenda of the New Deal. He argued that the values of pioneer America, in which individual effort and an endless frontier promised both freedom and financial success, were no longer functional in an industrial, corporate world dominated by ruthless oligarchs. The Great Depression and environmental problems were both symptoms of the same disease: unregulated greed.

> Denuded forests, floods, droughts, a disappearing water table, erosion, a less stable and equable climate, a vanishing wild life—these are some of the notable results of unchecked and ruthless exploitation by men who euphemistically refer to themselves as "rugged individualists"...[34]
>
> Beautiful scenery that man with all his genius could never hope to duplicate has been destroyed or marred in order that some rugged individualist might be able to buy a Rolls-Royce for his feckless son or finance another fling with his favorite chorus girl....[35]
>
> National parks are a distinctly American institution. No other country has set aside in perpetuity such areas of great natural beauty.... In the middle ages the ruling classes appropriated to themselves great groves of trees and wide expanses of sylvan glade. One of the reasons

Harold Ickes laying the capstone on the new Interior Department building, with
President Franklin D. Roosevelt watching, April 6, 1936. *(Courtesy of the Franklin D.
Roosevelt Memorial Library)*

for the strong stand of the English barons when they forced King John
to sign Magna Charta was because the King had disregarded one of
their most cherished prerogatives—that of establishing great forests in
order to enjoy the pleasures of the chase. In the old times kings or
nobles or churchmen might set apart for their own enjoyment areas of
natural beauty. It was left to the United States to consecrate to the use
and enjoyment of the people thousands of acres of the most beautiful
and awe-inspiring scenery that...can be found anywhere in the world.[36]

These and other passages in Ickes's book read almost like a justification for
taking Hearst's land.

As secretary of the interior, Ickes often found ways to pursue his passion for
human rights issues. When Ickes built a large new headquarters for the Interior Department and an artist proposed a major mural on the theme of the
four elements—air, fire, water, and earth—Ickes preferred a mural depicting

the oppression of Native Americans and African Americans. It was Ickes who arranged for African-American singer Marian Anderson, when refused the Daughters of the American Revolution auditorium, to sing at the Lincoln Memorial. Since the Interior Department oversaw Native American policies, Ickes brought about major changes to make those policies more support- ive of tribal rights. Ickes also wanted geographical features in national parks to have Native American names, not Euro-American ones; he once fired off a memo complaining that places in Bryce Canyon had names like "Queens Garden."

Ickes took office less than a decade after the Teapot Dome scandal had badly marred the Interior Department's reputation, and he was determined to redeem and expand the agency. Ironically, he soon renewed the campaign of Albert Fall, the villain of Teapot Dome, to transfer the Forest Service from the Department of Agriculture to the Interior Department. Doubly ironically, Ickes's angry opponent was agriculture secretary Henry A. Wallace, the son of President Harding's secretary of agriculture, who had fought out this issue with Fall. Once again Gifford Pinchot weighed in against transferring the For- est Service, accusing Ickes of being driven by a lust for power.

Ickes's sympathies for the common man influenced his hopes and poli- cies for the national parks. Ickes denounced the practice of building luxury hotels in national parks—such as Grand Canyon's El Tovar—because they were playgrounds for the rich. In a speech to a 1934 gathering of national parks superintendents, Ickes declared:

> I think there was a wrong concept to begin with. I think accommoda-
> tions of that sort ought to be simple. The parks can perform a wonder-
> ful service in showing people that there is something more to life than
> jazz, and even radio.... The greatest service that we can do the people
> who come to our parks is to get them back to the simpler things of
> life.... That is what our parks are for. They are to be the great outdoor
> temple. And we ought not to desecrate them or permit them to be
> desecrated.[37]

Ickes considered it a desecration that greedy railroad corporations built and ran many of the tourist facilities in national parks: "I wish we had the statutory power and the money to take over all of those concessions and run them ourselves."[38] Ickes renounced the Mather-Albright emphasis on developing plenty of roads and facilities to draw tourists to the parks:

> I do not want any Coney Island. I want as much wilderness, as much nature preserved and maintained as possible.... I recognize that a great many people, an increasing number every year, take their nature from the automobile.... But I think the parks ought to be for people who love to camp and love to hike and who like to ride horseback and wander about and have...a renewed communion with Nature.... We lie awake at nights wondering whether we are giving the customers all of the entertainment and all of the modern improvements that they think they ought to have. But let's keep away from that, because if we once get started, there will be no end.[39]

Environmental historians credit Ickes with being the first secretary of the interior to declare that wilderness should be preserved for its own sake, not just for tourism or recreation. Ickes wanted to change the name of his department to the Department of Conservation. Perhaps it was the three summers the young Ickes had spent on a guest ranch in the Rockies that made such a deep impression on him. Or perhaps he was serving the vision of his first hero, Teddy Roosevelt. Ickes put a lot of effort into creating new national parks and monuments, including Olympic and Kings Canyon. He proposed three new national parks for New England and a 4.4-million-acre national monument for much of southern Utah, but local opposition blocked them. He also pushed for extensive national seashores: "When we look up and down the ocean fronts of America, we find that everywhere they are passing behind the fences of private ownership. The people can no longer get to the ocean...except by permission of those who monopolize the ocean front."[40]

Ickes was very aggressive in pursuing his goals, partly because that was his personality. He often irritated President Roosevelt and other cabinet members. Horace Albright said: "There is no denying he could be very hard to get along with. He could be impetuous and unreasonable. Also, he constantly kept his associates off-balance. None of us could ever be sure that we wouldn't walk in one day and get fired."[41] Some sources say that Ickes's bullying convinced Albright to retire six months after Ickes took office, and pushed Albright's successor, Arno Cammerer, into a heart attack. Ickes also fired a future director of the NPS, Conrad Wirth, only to soon apologize for his unfair wrath and rehire him. Yet President Roosevelt enjoyed aiming Ickes's combativeness against William Randolph Hearst.

Even as Hearst's attacks mounted and as the 1936 election neared, Roosevelt remained reluctant to fight back, but privately he was boiling. In his diary for November 15, 1935, Ickes wrote: "The President told me that...there was no man in the whole United States who was as vicious an influence as Hearst."[42] After Ickes delivered a speech blaming the rich for ruining American democracy, the Hearst newspapers ran a nationwide editorial "bitterly attacking me as a communist."[43] In January 1936 Ickes spoke with Roosevelt about "the question of William Randolph Hearst, who has been attacking the Administration viciously now for months. I think that there should be a counterattack....I believe that a real offensive ought to be opened up against Hearst with a determination to show him to the country for what he really is."[44] In February Ickes wrote in his diary: "It sounded today as if the President is about ready to turn someone loose on William Randolph Hearst. He has dug up a letter written by Theodore Roosevelt to Hearst in which he flays Hearst unmercifully, and he also has what Elihu Root said about Hearst when Root attacked him."[45] Franklin Roosevelt hadn't forgotten decades-old family grudges. When Hearst pushed the presidential candidacy of Alf Landon, Ickes urged Roosevelt to attack Landon by tying him to Hearst. On July 7, 1936, Ickes wrote:

> The President had apparently been thinking of it and discussing who might make such a speech with the greatest effect. He had me in mind but he doubted the propriety of a member of the Cabinet making an attack on Hearst. I reminded him that Theodore Roosevelt had delegated Elihu Root on one occasion to attack Hearst and that seemed to change his mind considerably. I told him that I was not anxious for the job because I realized that Hearst would smear anyone who went after him, but that the job ought to be done and that I was willing to do whatever he wanted me to do.[46]

Roosevelt decided that Ickes was the hatchet man for the job. Right before and right after the Republican National Convention, Ickes delivered nationwide radio speeches linking Landon with Hearst and lambasting Hearst. As Ickes's biographer T. H. Watkins described it, "He did it with savage delight."[47] Anti-Hearst newspapers gave Ickes's speech front-page, full-text coverage. As Ickes had predicted, Hearst counterattacked in a personal way: "Hearst opened up on me yesterday in a front-page story charging that my book, *Back to Work,* was written by members of the staff and, therefore, at the expense of the taxpayers. There was a long, detailed story full of moral indignation expressed against me."[48] Three weeks later Ickes made another radio speech against Hearst and Landon, and Ickes wrote, "Undoubtedly Hearst will keep up his attack on me now rather vigorously. As a matter of fact, there was an editorial in the *Washington Herald* this morning...an insinuation that I have been a dismal failure as the head of this Department and have done everything wrong."[49] Five days later: "That the Hearst press will overlook no opportunity to smear me from this time on there isn't any doubt."[50]

Ickes knew he was living dangerously, for Hearst possessed some damning personal information about him. Shortly after taking office Ickes had begun an affair with a much younger woman, which drove his wife to a suicide attempt. Someone began sending accusatory letters about the affair to newspapers, including Hearst's. To prove that these letters were being written by his lover's fiancé, Ickes had an Interior Department official gain entrance to the fiancé's apartment to find evidence. In March 1934 Ickes heard that Hearst's Chicago newspaper was going to print a story about the affair. Ickes called up Hearst himself in California and protested. Ickes lied and said the story wasn't true, and anyway, Hearst wasn't supposed to be in the business of publishing personal gossip. This was true: Hearst might be ruthless in his political attacks, but he had always refrained from exposés about love affairs and other personal dirt, if only because his own private life was so vulnerable. Hearst called up his Chicago editor, and the affair story was killed—but not forgotten.

A few weeks before the 1936 election Ickes wrote in his diary: "On Tuesday the President called me up on a departmental matter and I took occasion to tell him that, in my judgment, it was important for him to land with the full force of his right on Hearst's chin. I told him that no one else could do this for him.... The President said that perhaps he ought to 'take a shot at the old man.'"[51]

On October 1 "the old man" wrote in a front-page editorial: "Mr. Roosevelt declares that he is not a Communist, but the Communists say he is one. The Communists ought to know. Every cow knows its own calf."[52]

Roosevelt won in a landslide. After the next cabinet meeting, Ickes wrote: "The President made it clear that Hearst is *persona non grata* so far as the Administration is concerned. He said definitely that as to Hearst our attitude was to be thumbs down, and he made a physical demonstration of what he meant when he said 'thumbs down.'"[53]

Horace Albright had always remained "thumbs down" on Hearst's Grand Canyon lands. Before he retired in 1933, Albright made another attempt to talk Hearst into giving up his land and recalled Hearst's plans for a museum:

> Well, nothing happened. All those years went by and nothing happened.... But as Director I decided to tackle Mr. Hearst because I understood he was in financial difficulties. He had finished his castle and he was much older, of course. I thought quite possibly he might have changed his mind about the museum and better not take any chances on his selling Grandview. So I undertook to get a date with him through a lawyer.... Well, one of his lawyers got a date with him at the Ambassador Hotel. I had no reason to be afraid of him like I was before—I hadn't heard he'd changed temperamentally, anyway—only that he had had financial troubles.... I looked forward to possibly being successful in winning him to a point of view that he should give the land to the Park, even if we gave him a concession to build the museum, which we hoped he would. We had it all worked out as to how we'd handle it if he'd give us the land, or sell it to us for a reasonable sum if we could raise the money. I can remember going up to the hotel with a lawyer, but we couldn't get in because Miss Davies was with him and until that interview broke up, I couldn't see him. So I must have been there about an hour before the door opened and he and Miss Davies came out and he introduced me to Miss Davies.... The same thing happened, he was gentle and kind and friendly, but he still had his museum idea and he wanted to go ahead with it. He wasn't willing to turn over the property.

He complimented us on what we were doing on the administration of the park, said he had no apprehensions about anybody building up near him or anything. Being left as it was—that pleased him. He assured me that he was going to leave his property as it was; he wasn't going to do anything with it except build a museum sometime. He hoped to get it done and said, "I'm getting older all the time. I might not get it done." But he said, "I still have all my plans." So I couldn't do anything but thank him and go away.[54]

With Albright willing to leave the matter alone, no further action was taken for the next five years. Besides, with the Great Depression, the NPS had no money to spare. During these years the owner of the Rowe Well property, a private inholding just south of Grand Canyon Village, offered to sell his land. The NPS considered the Rowe Well property and the Hogan Orphan mine inholding on the rim to have a greater "nuisance value" than Hearst's land, for both places included bars at which locals often got drunk and got into fights. But the NPS had to forgo the Rowe Well purchase for lack of funds.

These were quiet years at Grandview. Dick Gilliland worked on improving his cabin, and the only trouble he reported was that "Last winter a horse broke through [the cistern cover] and it was just by chance that he did not go entirely down and it would have spoiled the water, beside drowning the horse."[55]

Hearst was indeed having financial troubles, and they got a lot worse over the next five years, until Hearst and his corporations were $30 million in debt. By 1933 the advertising revenue at Hearst's newspapers had dropped from $113 million to $40 million, and more than half his papers were losing money. Banks refused to loan him money, and he was forced to start selling off his art, his newspapers, and his real estate, even his castle in Wales, in which he'd invested millions of dollars for improvements. His Grandview property and plans were also affected.

Hearst may have been disingenuous when he told Albright that he only planned to build a museum at Grandview, for early on he had planned a residence, and not any cottage. When Hearst told Superintendent Eakin in 1926 that he was planning "a little place," this "little" was by San Simeon standards. By 1933 Hearst had had Julia Morgan draw up blueprints for his Grandview residence, and in 1936, even amid all his financial troubles, he was pressing ahead. Toward the end of June 1936 Hearst traveled to the Grand Canyon, and a few days later Julia Morgan flew to join him and look over the property. Two weeks later Hearst wrote to his construction superintendent, George Loorz: "The work at Grand Canyon must be done economically. I am not prepared to spend a lot of money there."[56] But by September Hearst was facing financial realities and cabled Morgan from Europe to "bring Wyntoon and San Simeon work to conclusion October first and hold up Arizona until my return which will be soon."[57] Six months later Hearst saw Morgan's construction plans for Grandview, but as Loorz told a contractor, "when Mr. Hearst heard they ran $180,000…he went up in the air. Much too much says he. Sorry, for if it had run a little over $100,000 I think we would have started there May first with a bang."[58] Soon Hearst was forced to shut down further work at his beloved San Simeon, so Grandview was out of the question.

Albright's feeling that a bankrupt Hearst didn't seem so fearsome was shared by the larger culture in which Hearst increasingly seemed a symbol of hubris—of American overreaching for success and power. In a March 1939 cover story, *Time* magazine ridiculed the fallen Hearst, concluding that "his appeal was not to men's minds but to those infantile emotions which he never conquered in himself: arrogance, hatred, frustration, fear."[59] Later that year Aldous Huxley, who had written for Hearst newspapers, published a satirical novel about Hearst, *After Many a Summer Dies the Swan*. Soon after, Orson Welles began work on *Citizen Kane*. And the Interior Department decided that it no longer needed to fear Hearst.

In August 1938 Hearst attorney Frank Lathrop went to NPS regional director Frank Kittredge and told him that Hearst needed to sell the properties that were least essential to him, and that this could include Grandview. Lathrop invited the NPS to make an offer. The NPS replied that it did not have any funds to buy Hearst's land. The only hope for such a purchase lay in a 1929 law—the law that had so worried Hearst—that authorized the secretary of the interior to pay half the value of private lands inside national parks if the other half could be obtained from private matching funds or as a donation from the landowner. Without this other half, the whole amount would need to be approved by Congress, which was very unlikely.

When Kittredge wrote to Grand Canyon superintendent Miner Tillotson about the proposal, word somehow leaked to Dick Gilliland, Hearst's caretaker. Gilliland wrote to Hearst complaining about this news, and Frank Lathrop stormed into Frank Kittredge's office and "raked me over the coals," as Kittredge described it to Tillotson. "Mr. Hearst went up in the air and said he would have nothing to do with the sale. This in spite of the fact that he had authorized his agent to go ahead with it, but he intended it to be kept entirely confidential.... the whole matter is supposed to be off...."[60] But Lathrop promised to raise the subject again with Hearst.

In the meantime, NPS managers started thinking about where they could get the other 50 percent of the funds needed to make such a purchase. Superintendent Tillotson talked with the Fred Harvey Company, and then he thought of approaching John D. Rockefeller Jr., who had been donating substantial lands for other national parks.

The Rockefeller idea came up through a chance inquiry. An agent for the Conoco Oil Company showed up at Tillotson's office and said his company wanted to open a gas station at the Grand Canyon. He was talking with Martin Buggeln, who owned a private inholding just east of Grandview, but Buggeln's land was a bit off the park road, so Conoco would need to build an access road on park land. Tillotson said the park would oppose that idea. The Conoco agent then asked if there were any other private inholdings where they could build a gas station. Tillotson kept his mouth shut, but this got him thinking that Standard Oil, owned by John D. Rockefeller Jr., might find Hearst's land a nice place for a gas station, if only they'd buy it from him. An added incentive would be that Standard Oil, which supplied the Fred Harvey gas stations at Desert View and Grand Canyon Village, would preempt competition from Conoco.

Frank Kittredge replied to Tillotson that after Hearst had left the land undisturbed for twenty-five years and offered to sell it to the park, it would look bad to build a gas station there. Kittredge doubted that Standard Oil would spend an extravagant amount of money for more than 200 acres of land for the sake of one gas station, and as for hoping for John D. Rockefeller Jr.'s personal help: "It is my understanding that the Rockefellers have been forced to give up some of their philanthropic activities."[61]

After Hearst's blowup over the confidentiality of his land sale proposal, Kittredge and Tillotson were taking pains to keep the whole subject secret, even from the NPS regional director, who had jurisdiction over Grand

Canyon National Park, which led to some bureaucratic ruffled feathers. But eventually secretary of the interior Harold Ickes heard about it.

Secretary Ickes was in the midst of another round of open combat with William Randolph Hearst. Three times in early 1939 he gave speeches denouncing the evil influences of Hearst and the rest of the monopolistic, conservative press. Later that year Ickes published a book, *America's House of Lords*, portraying the newspaper publishers as feudal barons who were oppressing the people. Ickes claimed that in 1910 Hearst had hired thugs who engaged in shoot-outs against other newspapers in the streets of Chicago, and that this was the beginning of the reign of gangsters in Chicago and across the nation. Hearst and other publishers struck back with what Ickes called "a violent storm of editorial abuse."[62] The editor who attacked Ickes most fiercely was Cissy Patterson at Hearst's *Washington Herald*. Patterson's spite had very personal motives, for she had once been in love with Ickes and had been jilted by him.

Ickes had met Cissy Patterson soon after FDR's inauguration. She came from a powerful and wealthy publishing family. Her grandfather was Joseph Medill, who had built the *Chicago Tribune* into a powerful newspaper, and her cousin still ran it. Her brother published the *New York Daily News*, and her daughter had married political columnist Drew Pearson. Patterson had wanted to be a publisher and offered to buy the *Washington Herald* from Hearst, but he declined and instead made her editor and gave her one-third of the newspaper's profits. After Ickes's wife died in a car accident in 1935, he and Patterson began dating seriously. Politically they were an odd couple, for Patterson was following Hearst into increasingly anti-Roosevelt stands. Then Ickes met a much younger woman, dumped Patterson, and married his new love. In her newspaper Patterson began attacking Ickes in such nasty, personal terms that he contemplated suing her for libel.

In 1939 Patterson finally purchased the *Washington Herald* from the financially ailing Hearst, and she made him a million dollar personal loan. She also wanted to buy his Grandview land. We don't know any details about this offer; we catch only a one-sentence glimpse of it in a letter Hearst wrote to one of his lawyers in 1941: "Mrs. Patterson tried to buy it from me for her private use."[63] In mid-1939, as Hearst was negotiating with the NPS about the Grandview land, he also began approaching wealthy people about buying it, and this was most likely when Patterson made her offer. One of Ickes's justifications for condemning Hearst's land was to prevent him from selling it to another private interest. If Patterson had bought Grandview, it would have turned the fight over Grandview into a romantic grudge match. Patterson would be attacking Ickes not just with editorials, but with a personal invasion of his bureaucratic turf.

Ickes was not above using his office in a personal grudge against a publisher. In 1935 the *Chicago Tribune* had launched a round of nasty attacks against Ickes, and he had started an investigation into whether the *Tribune* building in Chicago was complying with public water usage regulations and taxes.

For Ickes it may have been news that Hearst owned land at the Grand Canyon, but he quickly changed the nature of the game. In between his February and April speeches denouncing the newspaper barons, Ickes directed the director of the NPS to prepare a report on how Hearst had been using his Grand Canyon land, and he directed an Interior Department lawyer to examine the department's authority to condemn the land. Condemnation is the legal process by which a government agency takes over private lands for public use, against the will of the landowner, often for far less compensation than the landowner would demand. Ickes started the condemnation ball rolling even before there had been any formal negotiations between the NPS and Hearst; as of yet, no NPS documents had even mentioned a possible price for the land. Ickes wasn't interested in relying on the generosity of private donors like the Rockefellers. Ickes was also the director of the Public Works Administration, a jobs and construction program in which Ickes had dispatched huge sums of money. His solution would be to declare it a public works project to obtain the Grandview land and to obliterate every trace there of William Randolph Hearst.

The Interior Department lawyer soon reported a big problem with the condemnation option. The 1929 law that allowed for condemnation of private lands in national parks included an exemption for seven specific parks, including Grand Canyon, prohibiting condemnation against private lands that included a residence. This exemption had been written into the law by Montana senator Thomas Walsh, who owned some land in Glacier National Park. It was Walsh's dogged investigations that had blown open the Teapot Dome scandal and brought down Albert Fall, and no one had felt like punishing the hero of Teapot Dome by taking away his land. But now his exemption offered possible cover for Hearst. Hearst's lawyers knew of the exemption, and this was one reason Hearst had maintained a caretaker in residence at Grandview all these years. (Actually Hearst had two caretakers in residence, Dick Gilliland at the Berry homestead and a secondary caretaker at Grandview Point.) But the Interior Department lawyer believed that the department could evade this restriction on the grounds that Hearst himself did not use this land as a residence:

> It is my opinion that the restriction would not be applicable to this property. Even the assessed valuation of the improvements for tax purposes indicate that they are not such as to constitute a possible residence for Mr. Hearst. Certainly if the improvements are occupied in their entirety by the caretaker, I think the property cannot be said to be "occupied by the owner and used exclusively for residence" purposes.[64]

In response to Ickes's request for a report on Hearst's use of Grandview, A. E. Demaray, acting director of the NPS, indicated in a memo of April 28, 1939, that communications had been reopened between Hearst and the NPS and that Hearst was willing to sell his Grandview land for a tentative price of $150,000. A decade previously, in private communications regarding his land swap with the NPS, Hearst had repeatedly said that his Grandview land was worth less than $100,000. Demaray, who had once worked as a land surveyor in the Grand Canyon region and who now served as the number two man in the NPS and sometimes as acting director, found this $150,000 price "exorbitant." Demaray started a consistent NPS practice of low balling the value of Hearst's land. He cited the Coconino County tax assessment of the land's worth as $10,326—which counted only its 207.7 acres and its contents, such as barns and cows, not its extraordinary location or aesthetic value. Demaray admitted that a more realistic value was the $28,950 estimated by Superintendent Tillotson a few years previously. Demaray asked Ickes to authorize him to begin negotiations with Hearst, starting with an offer of $28,950.

Hearst tried to claim that the land's unique location and aesthetic value gave it huge financial value, but the Interior Department would refuse to concede this in their negotiations, even as they declared that the land's unique location and aesthetic value justified their condemning and obtaining the land for the park.

The NPS sought some independent assessments of the land's value, including from Jesse Kelly of the land acquisition department of the Standard Oil Company. The NPS was appalled when, on May 12, Kelly made a confidential report that the Hearst land was worth $168,170. Of course, Standard Oil was accustomed to assessing land as if it were going to be commercially developed. The NPS kept this report secret.

In June, Hearst lawyer Frank Lathrop came to NPS regional director Frank Kittredge and insisted that the land was worth $250,000, including the original $125,000 Hearst had paid for it plus all the related expenses and taxes and caretaker salaries and lawyers' fees for a quarter of a century. Hearst, however, was willing to sell his land for a bargain rate of only $200,000. Lathrop warned that an unnamed private interest—perhaps Cissy Patterson—had made a firm offer of $150,000 for the land, but Lathrop said that Hearst preferred to sell to the NPS. Indeed, Hearst would consider making the 50 percent private donation of the land (giving him a sizable tax break) if the NPS paid him the other half, $100,000, in cash. This was, in fact, the exact amount of money Secretary Ickes was in the process of obtaining from the Public Works Administration. But it seemed that only a portion of these funds could be used for land acquisition, with the rest earmarked for public works—such as tearing down Hearst's buildings.

Three weeks after this exchange, Harold C. Bryant, acting superintendent of Grand Canyon National Park (Tillotson had been promoted), reported that "wealthy men are being approached as possible buyers."[65] Lincoln Ellsworth, a famous polar explorer with considerable wealth, had called the park to inquire about Hearst's land, and soon after Bryant got a visit from the son of George Lorimer, publisher of the *Saturday Evening Post* and a long-time conservation ally of Stephen Mather. Lorimer's son had come to look over Hearst's land to consider buying it and building a memorial to his father, a conservation museum and library. Since George Lorimer had played a large role in promoting the establishment of Grand Canyon National Park, Bryant was torn between admiration for a worthy idea and dismay over the complication it could bring to acquiring Hearst's land. Bryant reported: "I carefully concealed any idea that immediate purchase was being considered."

Bryant's report crossed paths in the mail with a letter from Secretary Ickes announcing that he had obtained the $100,000, but "It is quite possible that condemnation proceedings eventually will be instituted for acquisition of this property."[66] This became more likely when, at the end of July, Hearst's attorney Frank Lathrop wrote to the NPS's Frank Kittredge: "...our separate ideas of value are so far apart that it would be fruitless to give further consideration to negotiations looking to putting these properties into public ownership."[67] Kittredge and others in the NPS weren't happy about the idea of condemnation. At least Hearst had honored park values, even leaving Grandview Point open for tourists. Kittredge wanted further negotiations with a higher offer. But Ickes pushed ahead, demanding an Order of Taking, which the Department of the Interior filed on September 16, 1939. Hearst would get $28,950, a sum soon deposited with the court. The justification was:

> The land is necessary for use in connection with a Public Works project which contemplates the conservation of natural resources, the prevention of soil erosion, forestation and reforestation, the preservation of scenic beauty, the building of foot trails, roadways, cabins, shelters and other structures and improvements necessary and appropriate to provide public facilities for picnicking, camping, and other recreational activities.[68]

The "forestation and reforestation" phrase was especially dubious, for Hearst was a fanatical tree lover. His lands at San Simeon and Wyntoon were heavily forested, and he refused to allow the cutting of a single tree. The logs for the large fireplaces at San Simeon were hauled in from mountains thirty miles away. One time when workmen noticed that one in a newly planted row of trees was dying, they painted its yellowing leaves green so that Hearst would not get angry and they could wait until he left to replace it. Another time movie mogul Samuel Goldwyn backed his car into a San Simeon tree, and Hearst spent $5,000 to move it to a safer location. At the Grand Canyon a timber company had built a railroad spur line just south of Hearst's land to conduct logging operations, and Hearst could have made some easy money off his trees, but he didn't. When park rangers were cutting down trees in the Grandview area to control a mistletoe infestation, they offered to cut infected trees on Hearst's land, but Hearst refused.

William Randolph Hearst did not like having his things taken away, either his trees or his land—especially by a communist. Hearst began pulling all his political strings.

Hearst flew to Seattle to talk with President Roosevelt's son-in-law, John Boettiger. When Hearst's presidential candidate Alf Landon had been clobbered in 1936, Hearst had been shocked and humbled, and as a peace offering, or influence offering, he had offered the editorship of his Seattle newspaper to the husband of FDR's daughter Anna, newspaperman John Boettiger, and given him more autonomy than any other Hearst editor. Now Hearst pressured Boettiger to help save his Grand Canyon land. On October 17, 1939, Harold Ickes wrote in his diary:

> John Boettiger called me up from Seattle. William Randolph Hearst had been up there to see him on Saturday to discuss with him our suit which I have authorized to condemn his holding on the rim of Grand Canyon. Hearst does not want to sell this holding, and I finally said to Boettiger that if Hearst were willing, we might be able to work out an arrangement by which we would take title at a fair, reasonable market price, subject to a life estate in Hearst and provided that Hearst did not make any improvements on the place or use it differently from how he has been using it in the past. John thought that this was fair enough.[69]

Ickes was repeating the till-death offer that Stephen Mather had made seventeen years before, but now it was seventeen years less generous: Hearst was seventy-six years old. Ickes did not repeat Mather's offer to let Hearst's children retain the land.

Hearst also contacted his friends in Congress. On November 19, 1939, Ickes wrote in his diary:

> Senator Hayden called on Monday about the Hearst property on the rim of Grand Canyon, which we are seeking to condemn. He said that when the bill went through creating the Grand Canyon National Park, he and Ashurst promised Hearst that no attempt would ever be made to bring in his property. He wished that he had been consulted. I told him that I had not known about any such agreement, since this park was brought in before my Administration. The NPS must have known of it but said nothing to me about it, although we have talked about this property for a long time. I told Hayden that we really ought to have this land which

Hearst has never used and that the thing for Hearst to do was to agree to a fair price at which he would sell to the Government, while reserving a life estate. According to Hayden, Hearst hates to give up any property that he owns but he has told people that he intended to leave this at his death to the Government. Of course, if this is what he wants to do, he could deed it outright with the reservation of a life estate.[70]

On November 30 NPS director A. E. Demaray sent a telegram to the superintendent at Grand Canyon, who had previously indicated he was ready to send in the Civilian Conservation Corps to demolish Hearst's buildings:

PENDING POSSIBLE SETTLEMENT FOR ACQUISITION HEARST PROPERTIES ON BASIS PERMITTING HEARST TO REMAIN THERE BALANCE HIS LIFE WHICH SECRETARY HAS INDICATED AGREEABLE TO HIM NO PLANS SHOULD BE MADE TO RAZE BUILDINGS UNTIL OPPORTUNITY TO ASCERTAIN FROM HEARST'S REPRESENTATIVES WHATEVER BUILDINGS DESIRED BY HEARST FOR SELF AND CUSTODIAN SHOULD BE ALLOWED TO REMAIN.[71]

Senator Hayden was not placated. He was angry at Ickes for turning him into a liar and a betrayer of a friend, a very powerful friend. On December 22 he wrote to Ickes:

When the bill to create that Park was first introduced, Mr. Hearst made inquiry as to whether the establishment of a National Park would in any way interfere with the use and enjoyment of his patented lands, and he was assured that all of his rights and interests would be fully protected. At a later date, when I introduced a bill to change the boundaries of the Grand Canyon National Park, an attorney representing Mr. Hearst stated that he would like to have the bill amended so as to specifically exempt the Hearst properties from acquisition by the Federal government. I assured him that such a legislative precaution was wholly unnecessary, and stated again that Mr. Hearst would not be disturbed.

Under these circumstances, I hope that the pending condemnation suit will be dismissed. As an additional reason for dismissal, I do not believe that in the present state of the Federal finances any money should be expended from the Treasury for the acquisition of property which is not absolutely essential to the proper administration of the National Park.[72]

Ickes responded:

> It has been the understanding for a number of years that, when Mr. Hearst found himself ready to give up his Grand Canyon holdings he would want the Federal Government to have them. Since representatives of his Estate initiated the negotiations which ultimately failed only because of an honest difference of opinion as to value, I do not see that we have violated any assurances given to Mr. Hearst in the past.[73]

Ickes also insisted he was trying to prevent "possible future alienation of the lands to some one else who might develop or use them adversely to the park welfare."[74] Months later Ickes was still trying to placate Hayden, writing a similar letter with many of the same lines.

Hearst also got California senator Hiram Johnson, a long-time progressive buddy of Harold Ickes and an ally in creating Kings Canyon National Park, to write a letter to the NPS. Hearst attorney John Francis Neylan told Senator Johnson:

> Of course, I think such use of the power of condemnation by the government is just as dishonest as were the antics of the railroads and others, in the old days when they overrode the rights of somebody whose property they desired.
>
> Coupling this use of the power of condemnation with these public works allotments, I think, is adding insult to injustice.
>
> I question seriously that there is any large amount of unemployment in the vicinity of the Grand Canyon, and to fake up another excuse for squandering some more money seems to me characteristic of the new public morality.[75]

When the condemnation suit was filed, Hearst angrily withdrew his offer of splitting a $200,000 price for the land. Hearst's lawyers now claimed that a fair price was $236,100 and that "they would fight the suit with all the force of the Hearst Estates in an endeavor to obtain what they consider a satisfactory price," as the NPS's Frank Kittredge noted after a meeting with Frank Lathrop and a Hearst executive. They protested that "they were singled out for condemnation when there are other tracts of privately owned land in Grand Canyon which are more troublesome, such as the Hogan property." Hearst's agents complained "that they had always cooperated with the National Park Service, had given access to the Grand View Point without charge to the public, and had complied with park regulations in all respects."[76] After all this, the NPS was trying to rob them. They soon produced Horace Albright's 1929 letter saying Hearst had cooperated "splendidly" with the NPS and promising not to proceed against Hearst's lands without his cooperation. Kittredge was sympathetic, and he wrote to NPS assistant director Demaray: "Mr. Hearst has been a good park-minded citizen in Grand Canyon, as far as anything I have ever known or heard. This is going to make the case a little more difficult, perhaps, if it goes to court." Kittredge also warned that Citizen Hearst's determination to fight the condemnation "to the limit" might apply not just in court, but in "the chain of newspapers which are under their control."[77]

Until the condemnation suit became official in the U.S. district court in Phoenix on November 21, 1939, the fight between Hearst and the NPS had remained behind the scenes, but now it hit the newspapers. Hearst didn't own a newspaper in Arizona, but he didn't need one to wage this campaign. Arizona was still a stronghold of Wild West values, in which the land was there for conquest and private wealth. Opposition from powerful Arizonans had prevented Grand Canyon from becoming a national park until nearly half a century after Yellowstone had become the first. And Hearst did have an effective agent for stirring up Arizona newspapers: his caretaker, Dick Gilliland, was no naive handyman. He had been a clerk at the Willard Hotel, the long-time hub of political life in Washington, D.C., where he had mingled with the politicians who lived there and witnessed the art of scheming. At the Willard, Gilliland had met Ralph Cameron, who brought him to the Grand Canyon to help manage his properties. Gilliland had absorbed Cameron's fierce hostility against the NPS, and as Hearst's man, Gilliland was a continuing source of hostility. Hearst paid Gilliland about $35,000 a year in today's dollars, plus generous expenses, so Gilliland had a lot to lose. Now he did his best to stir up public hostility against the condemnation suit. One of his tactics was to scare as many people as possible by claiming that the Hearst land seizure was part of a master plan to seize all other private property in the park, including that of the Santa Fe Railway, which was the largest taxpayer in Coconino County.

On January 26, 1940, the *Coconino Sun* headlined: "Department of Interior Scraps All Treaty Commitments Of Past to Grab Hearst Property: Ickes' Dictator Tactics of Confiscation." The article ridiculed Ickes's claim that $100,000 worth of public works funds should be spent on Hearst's 207 acres when the park contained over 1,000 square miles of equally worthy lands. It knocked Ickes for ignoring the pleas of Senator Hayden and for betraying a long history of commitments not to take Hearst's lands. It threatened that removal of Hearst's land from the tax rolls would force the county to raise taxes on everyone else (a laughable claim considering that in 1938 Hearst had paid only $248.30 in property taxes). It protested the NPS offering only $28,950 for land worth—Hearst's latest claim—$392,100.

Another long *Coconino Sun* article invoked the brave, noble, suffering pioneers who had sacrificed so much to conquer the West, a sacrifice the federal government was now betraying by seizing their hard-won lands. The noble pioneers they were referring to were Pete Berry and Ralph Cameron; the article quoted Cameron's pioneer diary at length and praised his "gallant battle" to retain control of the Bright Angel Trail.

A January 11, 1940, editorial in the *Williams News* was titled "Unprovoked Aggression," and portrayed Hearst as defender of democracy against tyranny:

> There is no positive stopping place for their aggression this side of undisputed authority, of absolute despotism…. Yet, in spite of federal encroachments, American democracy is still pretty free from shackles but year by year federal authority over the lives of Americans is being extended a little more and a little more. It behooves good democrats to oppose that extension wherever possible…. Thus the battle of the private interests to hang onto that which has been theirs within the boundaries of the Grand Canyon National Park, takes on more than

local interest. Each of these private holdings is an outpost needed to halt the aggression of federal bureaucracy. So long as these outposts can be held, democracy will be just that much safer.

In a March 1 article the *Coconino Sun* denounced "the imperialistic ambitions of the Department of Interior" and offered long quotes from a speech of Senator Henry Ashurst, accusing Harold Ickes of being drunk with "the heady wine of power."[78] Ashurst recalled how when he wrote the law creating Grand Canyon National Park, he had promised that private inholdings would be respected.

A February 9 *Coconino Sun* article quoted Dick Gilliland as saying he knew for a fact that after the NPS threw Hearst out, it was planning to seize the property of the Santa Fe Railway. The newspaper moaned: "Enormous property valuation would be lost to the county tax rolls if the railroad were taken over by the park. The ranchers, dependent on the Grand Canyon railroad, would also suffer." In its headline the article said that the new acting superintendent of Grand Canyon National Park, J. V. Lloyd, "Admits That Park Promises Are Scraps of Paper."[79] Worthless.

When this article came out, Gilliland headed for the telegraph office and sent a message to Ickes denouncing this "scraps of paper" outrage. Gilliland did get Ickes's attention. Ickes contacted NPS assistant director Demaray, who telegraphed J. V. Lloyd asking for an explanation. A nervous Lloyd wrote a long airmail denial: he never said this; the newspaper article never claimed he said this; the phrase was just a headline written by a hostile editor.

Reassured, Ickes sent a letter to Gilliland, misspelling his name in addressing him as "My dear Mr. Gilliand." Ickes said that "Owing to Mr. Lloyd's long service and acquaintance with the Department's policies, it is highly improbable that he would have made such a statement, which appears to be a newspaper canard."[80]

Gilliland sent a copy of Ickes's response to the *Coconino Sun*, which on March 8 commented: "Well, regardless whether the canard was committed by the newspaper or Lloyd (and we are betting in favor of the newspaper's report), we are surprised Park Service Lloyd would commit himself to any such personal opinion. Nevertheless, Gilliland writes us that he is preparing a magazine article and will call it 'THE STINK ON THE BRINK.'"[81]

Lloyd was annoyed and sent a letter to Demaray:

> This is another example of Mr. Gilliland's activities against the Service
> even though he is still being allowed the privilege of occupying land,
> the title to which now rests with the Government.... I wish to call your
> attention to the fact that the Coconino Sun...is quite evasive about
> such a statement. They offer to "bet" that such an assertion was made
> rather than back up their original statement, which was false. The gen-
> eral local reaction is that while Gilliland is an "old timer" he has gone
> too far with his vitriolic campaign against the Service.[82]

Various organizations also joined the attack. Ed Hamilton, a member of
the Coconino County Board of Supervisors, was especially alarmed by the
condemnation suit, for Hamilton owned the Rowe Well property, and he figured that if the NPS could get away with taking the land of the mighty William Randolph Hearst, he didn't stand a chance. Hamilton helped fan fears
about the government seizing everything in sight and ruining the tax base.
He got the board to pass a resolution condemning the condemnation.

The Arizona Hotel Association reprinted the county resolution in their
newsletter along with a cartoon picturing the Interior Department as a bear
chasing a cowboy labeled "private property of Arizona." The headline made
clear that this was a Russian bear and invoked the recent communist invasion
of Finland: "Will Arizona Become Another Finland? Or Have We Got Guts
Too?" The text warned that all of Arizona was being "Stalinized." "Whether
property belongs to a rich or poor man, don't let the government purloin it,
for such is un-American. In cold reality, it's Nazism and Russian tactics of the
lowest denominator."[83]

The Williams–Grand Canyon Chamber of Commerce passed a resolution
scoffing at the rationale for the condemnation, saying that Hearst could have
taken all those proposed conservation measures by himself. The government
power grab was "so far reaching" that "it is fraught with the possibilities of
vicious practice."[84] It was an attack on the U.S. Constitution.

NPS officials were appalled by these charges and launched a public relations campaign, writing letters and making public appearances and private meetings. Grand Canyon acting superintendent Bryant wrote to, "of all

groups," the Arizona Hotel Association, which depended on tourist dollars, and declared: "my reaction was most unpleasant." "What a glorious day it will be when time and trouble is taken to check and know both sides of a question.... [You] could have telephoned National Park Service representatives for the facts." The NPS version of events was that Hearst had approached the NPS wanting to sell his land; the NPS had engaged in long and honest negotiations but had been unable to agree on a fair price; now a jury of patriotic American citizens would assign a fair price; Hearst wasn't being dispossessed; and the NPS had no further plans or funds for acquiring any other private lands. Bryant signed off his letter "With deep regrets for the unfortunate imputations."[85]

Addressing the Williams–Grand Canyon Chamber of Commerce, Bryant said he was "astounded": "Looking at the name of the Chamber of Commerce it would appear to be voting against itself."[86]

Addressing the Coconino County Board of Supervisors, NPS director Arno Cammerer was also "astounded": "Grand Canyon National Park is a great asset to Coconino County.... Anything that improves the administration and usefulness of the Park makes more enthusiastic visitors and increases the travel, thus easily compensating for the loss of a few hundred dollars in assessable property within the Park."[87] In reply, the supervisors passed another resolution against the NPS. Even if Hearst wished to sell his land, they were opposed: "... when we think of the vast miles of rim line—the acres and acres in the Park available for recreation areas, we question the good faith of the Department of the Interior in its present action."[88]

The anti–NPS resolutions got sent to Arizona's senators and governor, and they complained to Secretary Ickes. Ickes answered Governor Jones: "The reason for this policy is that the exploitation of private lands in a national park may defeat the purposes for which the park is established."[89]

Among themselves NPS managers measured the progress and frustrations of what acting superintendent Bryant called their "good missionary work." To Assistant Director Demaray, Bryant wrote: "I spent January 3 at Flagstaff and Williams attempting to offset the activities of Mr. Gilliland.... Everywhere I went friends told me that his presentation of the situation was far different from the facts I presented.... I really feel that the Chamber of Commerce at Williams sincerely regrets having passed the hasty resolution urged by Mr. Gilliland."[90]

Yet a month later when J. V. Lloyd became acting superintendent and traveled to Flagstaff, he was a lot less positive: "I was greatly disappointed to find
such an unfriendly feeling existing toward the park, after years of patient
efforts to cultivate more cordial relations." Even with the local attorney for
the Santa Fe Railway and Fred Harvey Company, "I was amazed to find that
even he was rather pointed in his condemnation of the Service." At the Rotary
Club he "once again found the feeling against the Service to be quite bitter."
At a meeting of the Coconino County Board of Supervisors, he was "fully
conscious of the handicap of discussing any park problems or policies with
the Board of Supervisors or the average Flagstaff citizen at this time, when
they seem to be so disturbed."[91]

Four months later Demaray complained to Secretary Ickes that "Mr. Gilliland, has shown no appreciation of the Department's courtesy in allowing
him to remain on the property, but, on the contrary, has openly and vigorously assailed the action of the Department in acquiring it."[92]

The condemnation suit worked its way through the court very slowly. Gilliland testified after meeting with Hearst to plan strategy. In January 1940
Hearst's attorneys had filed their own countersuit, claiming that the land was
worth $392,100. Hearst's attorneys were doing their homework, studying what
other inholdings in national parks had been worth. In court, Hearst's attorneys
argued that the government was acting unconstitutionally. They were doing
their best to delay the proceedings, since the Public Works Administration
appropriation for the land needed to be spent on actual improvement work by
June 30, 1940, or the funds would expire. With this deadline approaching, NPS
managers got nervous and began discussing starting improvement work even
before they had won the suit. They had made lots of plans but frozen them
when Ickes renewed Mather's offer to give Hearst lifetime rights. It was already
too late to do genuine construction work, such as improving the road to Grandview Point or building picnic facilities, but it wouldn't take long to demolish
Hearst's buildings, which would qualify as an expenditure of the funds.

Regional Director Kittredge complained to Ickes that he had wanted to
continue negotiating over price, that the NPS should have offered as much
as $75,000. Ickes had weakened the NPS's bargaining power by diverting
$8,300 of the $100,000 appropriation to other projects, including the Statue
of Liberty. With two weeks to go before the June 30 deadline, Kittredge wrote
to Demaray: "It is my feeling that Mr. Hearst, as indicated in conversation

with the former Director [Albright], has been a very good park-minded citizen. With this in mind, it is hoped that every consideration may be given to Mr. Hearst's wish that the certain buildings requested may be allowed to remain."[93]

But with the deadline looming, the Interior Department prevailed upon the Justice Department to order Hearst to surrender his lands and remove Gilliland. Gilliland telegraphed Hearst to ask if he had to comply, and Hearst said yes. But this action wasn't final: the condemnation case was still going on in court.

On July 5 the *Coconino Sun* ran the headline: "Harold L. Ickes Outs Gilliland From Home." "Mr. Gilliland," it reported, "said that Hearst attorneys plan no compromise in their fight against the condemnation. Meanwhile, Mr. Gilliland, a pioneer resident at Grand Canyon, has been forced to leave his quarters on the Hearst property."

Weeks later the NPS was still trying to turn the bureaucratic gears to mobilize the WPA funds as quickly as possible. Acting Superintendent Lloyd now had a new justification for demolishing Hearst's buildings. The four-hundredth anniversary of the Coronado expedition, which brought the first Europeans to the Grand Canyon, was scheduled for that summer, and it included a history pageant on the canyon rim. Lloyd proposed that the pageant be relocated onto Hearst's lands, which would require the immediate razing of Hearst's buildings.

In August there was a new twist to the story. After having two acting superintendents, Bryant and Lloyd, Grand Canyon National Park finally got a new superintendent. It was Frank Kittredge, who had opposed Ickes's condemnation suit and who regarded Hearst as "a very good park-minded citizen."

Within days of taking office, Kittredge went out to Citizen Hearst's property to finally take a look at what he had been negotiating about. Accompanying Kittredge was long-time park naturalist-ranger Eddie McKee. Kittredge wrote a memo saying that McKee wanted a number of buildings preserved for their historic value or future park use. These included two log buildings Pete Berry had built for a blacksmith shop and an employees' bunkhouse; Emery Kolb had told McKee that these buildings had been there when he first arrived at the canyon in 1902. McKee also wanted a log corral saved, and the caretaker's cabin at Grandview Point "preserved and converted into a self-operating exhibit room." McKee also wanted Gilliland's cabin preserved:

"There is a possibility that there may be some park use for the structure and its presence will not interfere with any development." But Kittredge had his own motives for not wanting to tear down this building. This "so-called Hearst cabin was considered by the Hearst people as something of a symbol," and Kittredge didn't want it razed without his personal authorization.[94] Kittredge had started the whole process, only to have it ripped from his hands by the imperious Harold Ickes, but now Kittredge would finish it.

The condemnation suit dragged on for more than another year. On October 2, 1941, the court finally awarded the Hearst land to the NPS for the price of $85,000, plus 6 percent interest for its initial underpayment for the land.

When Hearst's attorneys asked the judge, David Ling, how he had arrived at this figure, he answered that there was no realistic way to determine what such a unique property was worth, but he had decided that the Hearst claim was too high and the NPS claim was too low. Hearst's attorneys supposed that Judge Ling had simply split the difference, leaving a figure that was three times the NPS claim and one-third the Hearst claim. But Judge Ling's $85,000 figure was extremely convenient for the government. Secretary Ickes had diverted $8,300 of the original $100,000, and the nearly two years of 6 percent interest owed by the NPS came to $6,264, leaving only $85,436. If Judge Ling had declared that the land was worth $86,000, the whole deal could have been wrecked.

Hearst's attorneys had no doubt that Ickes had malicious motives, but in court they had been unable to offer such a case. Attorney Henry MacKay Jr. explained to Hearst:

> The right of the Government to condemn for the purpose of a National Park is unquestioned and could not be successfully attacked. Our only point was the right of Secretary Ickes to condemn these lands for National Park purposes under the guise of a PWA project, and thus seek and use PWA funds to accomplish his purpose. However, the Declaration of Taking and the Declaration of Necessity are regular on their face. The trial court would not permit us to go behind the face of these documents to impeach these official statements by taking the testimony of Secretary Ickes and his subordinates, and it is extremely doubtful that the Circuit Court would do so either. In other words, the determination

of necessity is also a question of fact delegated to the Secretary of the Interior, which the Courts will not question in the absence of fraud.[95]

Hearst was incensed, and he wanted to appeal the decision. His attorneys talked him out of it. A majority of the judges on the appeals court were New Deal appointments, and they would not be friendly to Hearst. A new decision might award Hearst even less money. Hearst couldn't demand the price he had paid in 1914, for the courts determined only the current value of a property, and in the Depression property values everywhere had declined. The Grandview property was indeed, as Judge Ling said, so unique that it was impossible to assess its market value. The government, too, was unhappy with the decision, and if Hearst provoked them further, they might file their own appeal. Further proceedings could take years and lots of money. This case had already cost Hearst $16,745 in legal fees, and many thought he should settle for what he'd gotten. There was some solace in having "nicked" Ickes for three times what he had offered.

Attorney Henry MacKay advised Hearst that at least he could get an income tax break from the court decision if he declared and could prove that the Grandview property was not for personal use but had been an investment property, on which he'd lost money. This was contrary to what Hearst had always told the NPS about his land, but he now dutifully wrote a letter to one of his lawyers declaring that Grandview had always been an investment property. Hearst also vented his anger:

> I am terribly distressed and disappointed at the values fixed by the court upon the Grand Canyon property. They are greatly below its worth.
>
> There is very little privately owned Grand Canyon property.
>
> I bought mine knowing that its rarity and its unique location would make it an extremely profitable investment.
>
> I did not make any mistake in my estimates as far as private bidders were concerned.
>
> I could have sold it at a handsome profit for commercial purposes, and Mrs. Patterson tried to buy it from me for her private use.
>
> I held out for twice what I paid for the property and I know I would have secured it except for the fact that the government insisted on

ridiculously low values and the courts were apparently afraid to render a fair verdict.

I think we should appeal the case.

There is no reason why the government should plunder me of this beautiful property for half of what I paid for it.

I should get a reasonable profit or at least what I paid for it.

The testimony of the vast majority of experts proves largely increased value.[96]

Since the NPS had almost nothing left of its $100,000, there was now no money to do actual work on the land. Besides, very soon World War II would break out. A decade later, most of the buildings were still there, still decaying.

There is no word about Franklin Roosevelt's reaction. We don't know exactly what role he played in Secretary Ickes's actions. But the president had always supported Ickes's open combat against Hearst and the rest of the conservative press. Roosevelt was surely aware that Ickes was moving to take Hearst's land. Roosevelt must have taken some sweet, mischievous pleasure in this triumph over Hearst.

At the end of 1948, NPS officials were still trying to figure out if they had the legal right to tear down the Hearst buildings. Since the land had been taken on the premise of being a public works project, but no public works had been performed, was the whole deal solid? Assistant Director Demaray pointed out that, in fact, very quietly, while the court case was still proceeding, $3,000 had been authorized and spent on the land, including razing some buildings. This satisfied the NPS's claim to the land. There is no word as to how the NPS replaced that $3,000, which it needed to purchase the land.

Two years later the rest of Hearst's buildings were demolished.

Today some remnants of the buildings are still there, but often they are not even noticed by people walking right past them on their way to Hearst Tanks, two small ponds developed as a water supply, now a good bird-watching spot. Few visitors to Hearst Tanks realize how that name originated.

BRIGHTY OF THE GRAND CANYON

History Becomes Fiction, and Fiction Makes History

When Marguerite Henry's novel *Brighty of the Grand Canyon* was published in 1953, rangers at Grand Canyon National Park began receiving questions and letters about Brighty. Was there really a Brighty? How much of the novel was true? What happened to Brighty after the novel ends?

There was indeed a real Brighty. He was more real than much of the novel and the movie made from it. Brighty fully deserved to be turned into an enduring symbol of the wild grandeur of the canyon. His real story also contained many of the elements of a Wild West novel, especially his death, a story Henry didn't dare tell. For many years the park gave its letters about Brighty to longtime park librarian Louise Hinchliffe for her to answer, and she didn't have the heart to tell children the full truth either, so she said, "during one of the cold North Rim winters, when he was captured by horse thieves, he froze to death."[1]

Here's the real story of Brighty's life and death, and the stories of how Brighty got turned into a novel, a movie, and a controversial statue.

Most of what we know about Brighty comes from the writings of Thomas McKee, who with his wife, Elizabeth, managed the first tourist facility on the North Rim, starting in 1917. Elizabeth Wylie McKee's father, William Wylie, had opened one of the first tourist camps in Yellowstone National Park in

1893. When the Union Pacific Railroad reached southern Utah and wanted to set up tourist facilities at Zion and the North Rim of the Grand Canyon, it turned to William Wylie. Wylie's camps consisted of tent cabins with wooden floors and roofs but canvas walls. A former teacher and director of public schools in Montana, Wylie also offered campfire entertainment and interpretative programs, which may have influenced the National Park Service's tradition of ranger programs. Wylie himself ran the camp at Zion, and he sent Elizabeth and her husband to the North Rim. Elizabeth had studied astronomy at Wellesley College, and upon graduation she applied for a job at California's Lick Observatory, the leading observatory of the time. Lick's director admitted that Elizabeth was just as qualified as the male applicants, but he turned her down because she was a woman. Elizabeth and Thomas remained on the North Rim for a decade, until the Union Pacific, by then convinced of the value of building an expensive lodge there, sent them packing.

In the wintertime the McKees lived in southern California, and Thomas, who had worked as an editor before his tourism career, wrote magazine articles and radio programs. He wrote an article about Brighty that was published in *Sunset* magazine in August 1922. Thirty years later Marguerite Henry discovered this article, and it inspired her to write her novel.

When the McKees arrived at the canyon, Brighty had been living there for almost three decades, as nearly as Thomas McKee could figure out from the very few people who had encountered Brighty. Thomas heard a story suggesting that Brighty was first seen in the canyon in 1890. The previous year, on the first attempted Colorado River expedition since John Wesley Powell's expeditions, Frank Brown, a railroad company president from Denver, had drowned only a dozen miles into the Grand Canyon. Brown's wife refused to give up hope that he might still be alive at the bottom of the canyon. She sent a plea to John Fuller, a herdsman who lived at the top of Bright Angel Canyon on the North Rim, asking him to search for Frank. John Fuller knew the Colorado River and the canyon well enough to realize that Mrs. Brown's plea was a foolish fantasy. It was extremely unlikely that Fuller would even find Brown's body, which could have washed up anywhere—or nowhere—in the seventy-five miles between where he disappeared and where Fuller could reach the river at the mouth of Bright Angel Creek. Still, unlikely things did happen in the canyon, and Fuller hated to refuse a desperate widow's plea. With his friend Harry MacDonald, Fuller headed into the canyon.

At that time the route from the North Rim was a rough deer trail. Fuller and MacDonald couldn't get their pack horses down the trail and had to proceed on foot. When they got to the junction of Bright Angel and Phantom Creeks, about a mile from the Colorado River, they were amazed to find a little tent there, with a grey burro standing beside it. There was no one else around. Fuller and MacDonald spent four days searching the river shore for as far as they could hike or see with binoculars. Giving up and heading back up the trail, they stopped again at the tent, and still no one was there but the burro.

This time Fuller and MacDonald gave the camp a closer inspection. They found two cots inside, two nearly new Winchester rifles, and an Elgin gold watch that had run down from not being wound. A campfire and Dutch oven, with food still inside, looked like they hadn't been used in about a week. Fuller and MacDonald, experienced trackers, followed the tracks of two men and two horses to the river, where the tracks disappeared. Fuller and MacDonald decided that the men had come down from the South Rim and were trying to go back up for supplies, but they had misjudged the river's current and been swept to their deaths. In their tent was a written receipt for supplies from Babbitt's store in Flagstaff, and a letter from the fiancée of one of the men warning him against his often reckless behavior. Later, Fuller heard about two men with a burro who, soon before Fuller's trip into the canyon, had passed through Flagstaff and into the canyon. No one knew who they were, and no one ever heard from them again.[2]

The burro finally gave up waiting for the two men to return and began roaming Bright Angel Creek and Canyon, for which he would be named. Brighty figured out that he could escape the summer heat by heading up to the North Rim, where lush meadows offered much better food. When snow started falling on the rim, he headed back into the canyon. He repeated this cycle for over thirty years.

On the North Rim Brighty liked to hang out near the cabin of "Uncle" Jim Owens, the Forest Service game warden, famous for killing hundreds of North Rim mountain lions.[3] In his diary, McKee notes that Owens first met Brighty at a surveyor's camp, though he gives no details. Brighty enjoyed humans for their company—and their pancakes. Occasionally hunters showed up and tried to capture Brighty for use as a pack animal, but he usually got away. When the McKees and the tourists showed up, Brighty usually hung out with them. Uncle Jim and the McKees honored Brighty's free spirit

Brighty the burro with the McKee family and camp staff on the North Rim. *(Grand Canyon National Park Study Collection)*

by letting him come and go as he wished, never trying to tie him up. Marguerite Henry captured the spirit of their friendship when she portrayed Uncle Jim and Brighty together: "There was no visible tie rope between the man and the burro, but it was there all the same—a tie rope of such stuff as could never thin out and break apart."[4]

Brighty also enjoyed a friendship with the McKees' son Bob, who was seven years old when the family first arrived at the canyon. Brighty helped Bob haul water for the camp from its only source, a spring about two hundred steep feet below the rim, about half a mile away. In the morning Bob went to the kitchen door and yelled, "Pancakes, Brighty!" and Brighty, who usually bedded down nearby, almost always showed up. Bob led Brighty up and down the path to the spring several times a day, and at the end of each trip Brighty got pancakes left over from breakfast. He wore a packsaddle that held two ten-gallon metal cans made for Model T Ford gas tanks; when full, the tanks weighted close to two hundred pounds. Decades later, Bob recalled:

Brighty took his own sweet time, and would stop when he was winded. Since Brighty was well along in years, we understood, and never pushed him. When he had rested, he would start up the trail on his own. Many times, I went on ahead, knowing that the burro would come right up to the unloading point by himself as soon as he was ready."[5]

In a 1954 letter to Marguerite Henry, Thomas McKee recalled:

The mischievous girls, waitresses and maids, put up on this tree a sign: "Wylie Water Works. Power Plant, Brighty; General Manager, Bob." A girl one day asked: "Bob, which is the boss of this shebang, you or Brighty?" Reply: "Neither. We are pardners." They used to tease Bob in fashion like this: One to another in Bob's hearing: "I do believe that Bob and Brighty are together so much that they are beginning to look alike." Retort: "I'll lend him to you for a while if you think it will improve your looks." O, we used to laugh a lot in those dear dead days![6]

Brighty also enjoyed giving rides to the smaller children in the camp. "But when the larger boys mount him and demand too much either in speed or endurance he will promptly kick up his heels and pitch them off. He can be coaxed but not driven, and the limits of the service he renders are set by himself."[7]

In the winter of 1920–21, when Brighty was at the canyon bottom, a construction crew arrived and built the first footbridge across the Colorado River. Brighty took a keen interest in their activities:

He fraternized with the men of the crew and at times lent his back to aid in the enterprise. When the structure was completed the question arose as to who should be permitted to make the first official crossing. By acclamation and by the consent of the authorities the honor was bestowed upon Brighty as the oldest and most distinguished inhabitant of the place.[8]

But the bridge opened up Brighty's winter refuge to trouble. The next winter a man came down from the South Rim, crossed the bridge, and captured

Brighty. He was running from the law after stealing $6,000 in Liberty Bonds from the home of an elderly man in southern Arizona. No one had noticed the theft right away, so the thief got a good head start. He led Brighty up the trail to the North Rim, though it was now winter, and the snow was deep.

It seems that the thief had already planned his escape route out of Arizona. The previous July he had arrived at the canyon from the north and gone down the trail and crossed the new footbridge. On his way to the canyon he had stopped at the log cabin headquarters of the Bar Z Ranch, located at today's Kaibab Lodge. He had eaten dinner with the cowboys and stayed the night, and he asked a lot of questions about the cabin. Did anyone live there in the winter? No. Was any food left there over the winter? Some. Later on, the cowboys recalled that the man had given the cabin a close inspection before he left in the morning.

From the cabin the man walked seventeen miles to the rim, and there he encountered another camp of cowboys eating lunch. The man stopped and talked with them, and by chance Brighty walked up for a snack. The man asked about Brighty and was told that he always spent the winters along Bright Angel Creek, and that he was so friendly, anyone could walk right up to him.

That December the thief showed up at the South Rim carrying a heavy pack. "By mere chance," wrote Thomas McKee in an unpublished article about Brighty's death, from which this account is taken, "a ranger saw him going down into the Canyon by way of an old, abandoned trail far to the westward from all habitations. The ranger at a distance inspected the fellow through field-glasses and...supposed him to be one of those inveterate prospectors who haunt the warm Canyon in winter."[9] The thief was trying to avoid the busier trails; when he got to the Tonto Plateau he headed east along it until he reached the Bright Angel Trail and descended it to the footbridge. Across the river, he found Brighty. A pack animal and trail breaker might come in handy. The thief was planning to spend the winter in the Bar Z cabin. He may not have realized that the cabin was at about 9,000 feet, and winters there were very hard.

The winter of 1921–22 was unusually hard, with constant snowstorms. The trail out of the canyon was treacherous, and the seventeen miles from the rim to the Bar Z cabin took two days. In the snow and fog the thief couldn't be sure of the direction to the cabin. Thinking he must be near, and thinking he would lighten his load, he hung his pack, with his food and gun and wool blankets on a tree limb, planning to return for it soon. When he found the cabin, it was near nightfall, too late to return for his pack. In the morning he found that the snow had erased his footprints, and he could not find his pack. He had been counting on his gun to supply him with meat, if only squirrels. In the weeks to come he continued searching for his pack, but never found it. In the cabin the thief found that the only food was about ten pounds each of beans and flour. There were no blankets.

By an unlikely chance, another desperate man was about to arrive at the Bar Z cabin. He was a former U.S. Marine who had fought in the battle of the Marne and thought of himself as a tough guy. He was heading from Salt Lake City to southern Arizona, where he had been offered a mining job. He had hitched rides to the Utah-Arizona border and had decided that the shortest route was to go straight across the Grand Canyon on its trail and the new footbridge he'd read about. The man found his way to Jim Owens's winter quarters, a ranch twenty-four miles northwest of the Bar Z cabin, at a much lower and warmer elevation. When the ex-marine told Owens his plan, Owens warned him against it. The snows were already deep; a blizzard was visible on the plateau above; and the head of the trail into the canyon was tucked away in a nook that was hard to find even in summer. The ex-marine answered that he had grown up in Michigan winters and was a hardy woods-man. Owens reluctantly gave him directions and drew him a map of the trail-head, and told him to spend his first night at the Bar Z cabin.

The man made poor progress up the plateau and failed to reach the cabin that night. The next day he saw the cabin but didn't make the detour to it and kept going. After another hard day he reached the canyon rim, but in the snow and fog he could not find the trailhead. He camped on the rim that night and spent the next day searching for the trail. He camped for a third night in the blizzard, now without food, and without a fire because his matches were soaked. He knew that his feet were dangerously cold, going numb. He started a life-or-death retreat to the Bar Z cabin. He pushed on with frozen feet, through the night, until at dawn he found the cabin—and saw smoke rising from its chimney.

The thief saw the ex-marine coming and stepped onto the porch, raised an axe, and ordered him to go away. The ex-marine was shocked. He pleaded his desperation. The thief lunged at him with the axe, and the ex-marine, who had once dodged German bayonets, dodged the axe, knocked it away, overpowered the thief, and pulled a knife. The thief now shared his own desperation, stuck in a snowbound cabin with too little food for two. The ex-marine was too exhausted, his feet too incapacitated, to fight further. The two settled into a tense truce.

The ex-marine inspected his feet and found them severely frozen. He would have to stay there awhile, and he would need the thief's help to get to Owens's place. The thief hadn't known about Owens's place and didn't know the way to it, so he would need the ex-marine's help to find it.

When the two men assessed their food situation, they decided there was only one thing to do. As Thomas McKee put it, "the two desperate men went into Brighty's room, hit him with the axe and killed him. That night and for many a night after there were burro steaks for supper."[10]

The two men remained in the cabin for about three months. The snow continued piling up until it was up to the roof. To fend off the cold, they kept the fire burning constantly, obtaining wood by disassembling a log shed. They slept side by side for warmth, but never stopped fearing each other. At night they placed their axe and knife in the other room and barred the door. They quarreled constantly.

The ex-marine's legs were terribly painful. On one foot the ends of three toes were gone, and on the other foot large strands of flesh were rotting and sloughing off. He coated the wound with fat from Brighty's body. He made crutches and hobbled about. He also made two pairs of skis, with rawhide bindings made from Brighty's skin.

They watched Brighty's meat diminish. They set aside just enough to get them to Jim Owens's ranch. When their main food supply was gone, they cracked Brighty's bones and boiled them for soup, with alfalfa.

At last they were forced to head for the Owens ranch. The ex-marine wrapped his arm over the thief's shoulder, and they struggled through the snow. It took all day to get ten miles. That evening they built a platform out of logs, lit a fire, and roasted some of their meat. They next day the ex-marine was weaker, and they made only eight miles. The next day, heading down the edge of the Kaibab Plateau, they could see the Owens place six miles away.

The thief offered to go ahead to the ranch and bring back help, but the ex-marine feared he would be abandoned and insisted they continue together. The thief slugged him, knocking him into the snow, and took off.

When the thief reached the ranch, Owens was amazed by his gaunt condition and by his story that he had recently come across the Grand Canyon. The thief fell into bed and a deep sleep. Hours later, when Owens went out to feed his horses, his hunter's keen eyes spotted a speck about three miles away, a speck that seemed to move. Owens rode out to it and discovered it was the ex-marine he had advised months before. Owens took the man to his cabin, and when the ex-marine saw the sleeping thief, he drew his knife and would have killed him but was restrained. Owens was appalled by the man's frostbitten feet, now rotted to naked bone. Owens and his employees nursed the man for two days, and then two employees took him to Kanab for medical care. Both feet were amputated.

After the ex-marine left, the thief became eager to leave himself. He told Owens he wanted to get to Utah but didn't want to pass through the Arizona town of Fredonia along the way. He decided to head for Hurricane, Utah, though it was seventy roadless, uninhabited miles away. Owens reluctantly gave him some supplies and watched him trek off into a looming blizzard. The thief was never seen again.

When the Bar Z cowboys returned to their cabin in the spring, they found Brighty's skinned hide. They buried it with ceremony and sorrow for an old friend.

The story of Brighty became a legend that Thomas McKee told around his campfires. In his diary for September 7, 1923, McKee noted: "MATHER (Head of Nat. Park Svc) and 6 G arrived. Told Brighty story @ campfire."[11]

Memories of Brighty could have faded away, as have so many stories from the canyon's pioneer years. But McKee had written that *Sunset* article, and the public library in Elgin, Illinois, had saved its issues of *Sunset*. Thirty years later a lady walked into the library to do some research about burros for a book she was writing on horses and their relatives. She had never even seen a real burro. When the librarian found the *Sunset* article, the researcher was delighted. *This* was a great story.

The researcher was Marguerite Henry, America's favorite writer of horse stories, including *Misty of Chincoteague*. The daughter of a Milwaukee book publisher, Henry grew up surrounded by books, but also by a large city. For her the countryside was an exotic and romantic realm of green pastures and elegant horses. As a teenager she discovered the novels of Zane Grey and the idea of a West of open spaces, beautiful landscapes, freedom, horses, and adventure. At age seven Henry decided to be a writer, but she was nearly forty when she published her first book for children, in 1940. A few years later Henry wrote her first horse novel, *Justin Morgan Had a Horse*, based on a true Vermont story, though she invented a boy named Joel who rescues a mistreated horse. After the success of this novel, Henry traveled to the Virginia coast to check out another true horse story. Long ago a Spanish galleon had shipwrecked off Assateague Island, and the horses on board had swum to the island. Eventually the settlers from nearby Chincoteague Island began making an annual trek to Assateague Island to round up wild ponies and swim them to Chincoteague, where they were auctioned off. Henry not only fell in love with this story, she fell in love with one of the ponies, whom she named Misty and brought home to her backyard stable and corral.

Henry studied Misty's behavior carefully as she wrote a novel about her. She was better than most authors of animal stories in trying to portray animal behavior realistically, though she couldn't resist a certain amount of cuteness. Her illustrator, Wesley Dennis, with whom she collaborated on seventeen books, also took pains to make his drawings realistic. *Misty of Chincoteague* was a huge success, and so was her next horse book, *King of the Wind*, which won the Newbery Award.

When Henry discovered the story of the tough, free-spirited Grand Canyon burro, she knew it was her kind of story. She tried to get in touch with Thomas McKee, but her letters to him at various Grand Canyon addresses were all returned as "Addressee Unknown." Curiously, in his *Sunset* article McKee had never identified himself as the owner of the North Rim tourist camp. Henry traveled to the Grand Canyon and talked with rangers, wranglers, and lodge managers, but she couldn't find anyone who even knew who Thomas McKee was. She did, however, find lots of stories about Brighty, about his free spirit, his friendliness, and his adventures.

Marguerite and her husband, Sid, who was terrified of heights, rode mules from the North Rim to Phantom Ranch, and she took lots of notes about the scenes, plants, and wildlife Brighty would have known. She did her best to see the canyon through Brighty's eyes, drinking from Bright Angel Creek because "I wanted to know just how cold and delicious it was. And I sampled the burro browse that grew in sprigs up through rock crevices; I had to know how it would taste. And I hiked part of the way, making believe I *was* Brighty."[12]

On the rim Henry sought out a large overhang on the Cliff Springs Trail where Teddy Roosevelt and Jim Owens had spent a night during their mountain lion hunt in 1913. Henry believed that Brighty was along on this trip. Park rangers warned her that she might be visited by a mountain lion coming for a drink, and indeed in the middle of the night she woke up to a whimpering cry and the sound of cat feet landing nearby: "Terrified, I dived deep into my sleeping bag, like a headless turtle. I had come especially to see a mountain lion, but I was too much a coward to look! Next morning I took pictures of the paw prints in the wet sand around the pool within the cave. They were— lion tracks!... It was easy to write that scary mountain lion chapter the next morning!"[13]

Henry wanted to take home a Grand Canyon burro, just as she had taken Misty home. It would help her write more realistically. She tried to persuade park superintendent Harold Bryant to catch a wild burro for her, but he declined. Bryant tried to sound like he was doing her a favor: "Already you have created in your mind a warm image of him. If you were to own one of these wild critters, he might be an ornery fellow and ruin that image."[14]

When Henry got home, she found a burro in her own neighborhood. His name was Jiggs, but she renamed him Brighty and moved him in with Misty. She studied Brighty's behavior and his interactions with a neighbor boy named Tex, who often rode and played with the burro. Tex would become the model for the boy in the novel, Homer Hobbs.

Henry created *Brighty of the Grand Canyon* from three main sources: McKee's *Sunset* article, the stories and experiences she got at the canyon, and her own literary imagination. It seems that some of the stories she heard at the canyon were already pretty imaginative, making the novel a mixture of reality and fiction.

McKee's *Sunset* article emphasized Brighty's free spirit, starting with its title: "Brighty, Free Citizen: How the Sagacious Hermit Donkey of the Grand Canyon Maintained His Liberty for Thirty Years." (The word *burro* is the Spanish word for donkey.) It was this free spirit that had inspired Henry's interest, and she emphasized it in the novel. She avoids saying that Brighty was brought to the canyon by humans and says only that a prospector named Old

Timer found Brighty "running wild" in the canyon. She begins the novel with Brighty asleep amid the canyon's wildness: "he seemed part of the dust and the ageless limestone that rose in great towering battlements behind him."[15] Several chapters later, beneath a Wesley Dennis drawing of Brighty in the nighttime canyon, Henry muses: "Daytimes the canyon was all he wanted— winds rumpling his mane, birds whistling at him, and Bright Angel Creek talking and laughing. But sometimes at night a loneliness crept in and he would bray to the winking stars as if asking them to come down and play with him."[16]

Brighty does like people. He is happy to see Old Timer, who has found a promising vein of copper. But a bad guy, Jake Irons, shows up and murders Old Timer for his ore and takes his gold watch. When Uncle Jim and the sheriff come along, Irons flees. When the sheriff tries to turn Brighty into a pack animal, Brighty flees. Brighty spends a night under the overhang at Cliff Springs, and a mountain lion attacks him, but Brighty fights it off. Uncle Jim finds the wounded Brighty and leads him up to his North Rim cabin, where he nurses Brighty back to health. President Teddy Roosevelt shows up for a mountain lion hunt, and Uncle Jim takes Brighty along, but when the dogs tree a mountain lion, it jumps onto Brighty. Someone, maybe President Roosevelt himself, shoots the mountain lion right off Brighty's back. Roosevelt admires Brighty's bravery. Uncle Jim ties the dead mountain lion onto Brighty's back. That night they camp under the Cliff Springs overhang.

Just as in McKee's article, Brighty spends the summer hanging out with the people at the Wylie camp. McKee's article never said anything about how his son employed Brighty to haul water from a spring, but Henry may have heard this story, for she invents a camp owner's son, Homer Hobbs, who does just that. Where McKee mentioned that Brighty would give rides to small children but not larger children, Henry adjusts this to say that Brighty gives rides to kids but "turned demon" if an adult tried to ride him.

When the novel's Brighty returns to the inner canyon for winter, he is caught by Jake Irons, who tries to haul him across the river on a cable car, but Brighty breaks out, falls into the river, and swims for his freedom. Another summer, Brighty watches the construction of the footbridge across the canyon, and for the dedication ceremony President Roosevelt shows up. Roosevelt is supposed to be the first to cross the bridge, but he defers to Brighty.

Another winter, Brighty is again captured by Jake Irons, who is trying to escape the law by heading to Utah. Irons and Brighty trudge through a North Rim blizzard and take shelter in a deserted cabin. There's a knock on the door, and it's Homer Hobbs, who has ignored the warnings of Uncle Jim and is trying to hike to the canyon and across the bridge to get to Flagstaff and a job as a lumberjack.

Clearly, Henry had heard the story of Brighty's demise. One of her sources was an account by A. E. Demaray, who worked as a surveyor in the Grand Canyon region before becoming assistant director of the National Park Service. Demaray's article was published in *Outing* magazine in February 1923. In Henry's novel, as Jake Irons grows hungry, his "eyes studied the burro as if he had never seen him before, weighing the ounces of meat on the ribs, counting the mouthfuls.... He brought the gun to his shoulder and pointed at the wide space between Brighty's eyes."[17] Just then Uncle Jim arrives and captures Irons. But one night when Homer is supposed to be guarding Irons, he falls asleep, and Irons grabs the rifle. He tries to shoot Uncle Jim, but Brighty jumps in-between and takes the shot in his shoulder. A rescue party arrives and hauls Brighty on a sled to safety.

The novel ends with the suggestion that Brighty's spirit lives on today: "Especially on moonlit nights a shaggy little form can be seen flirting along the ledges, a thin swirl of dust rising behind him. Some say it is nothing but moonbeams caught up in a cloud. But the older guides swear it is trail dust out of the past, kicked up by Brighty himself, the roving spirit of the Grand Canyon—forever wild, forever free."[18]

Marguerite Henry did turn Brighty into an enduring symbol of the Grand Canyon, but occasionally she got carried away, especially in her suggestion that it was Brighty, in migrating in and out of the canyon, who had created the trail from the North Rim to the river.

Another dubious claim involves the mountain lion hunt of Teddy Roosevelt and Jim Owens. This hunt really did happen, in 1913, after Roosevelt had left the White House, but it is questionable whether Brighty was along. Neither Thomas nor Bob McKee ever mentioned that Brighty was on the hunt or had even met Teddy Roosevelt—but then, the McKees didn't arrive at the canyon until four years after Roosevelt's visit. Roosevelt wrote an account of the hunt and even named two of the three burros on it, but he didn't mention

Brighty: "When we started on our cougar hunt there were seven of us, with six pack-animals. The latter included one mule, three donkeys—two of them, Ted and Possum, very wise donkeys—and two horses."[19]

Both Thomas and Bob McKee gave good reasons why Jim Owens would not have trusted Brighty as a pack animal, especially on a trip with a former president. According to Bob, "Uncle Jim had been dubious about Brighty as a regular pack animal, since the burro had not done any work for years."[20] Brighty was probably about twenty-five years old at the time of the hunt, and it was only five years later that, as Bob described, Brighty was moving very slowly when hauling water for the camp. Thomas McKee spent half of his *Sunset* article detailing Brighty's dislike of serving as a pack animal and his strategies for escaping it. He repeated some of this in a 1954 letter to Marguerite Henry: "Brighty could divest himself of a pack load.... He was known as a free agent and sometimes was forcibly seized and made to pack hunter's loads. Uncle Jim used to smile when he saw such. He knew what would happen before long.... Brighty's technique was to sneak away from his kidnappers; then rub the pack against trees until the lashings loosened and the load fell off."[21]

The archives at Grand Canyon National Park include a photograph of Roosevelt, Owens, and three burros ready for their hunting trip, but no identification of the burros. I took this photo, plus a photo of Brighty with the McKees, to the Grand Canyon mule barn and showed it to the wranglers, who have plenty of experience at telling apart burro-like creatures, and they said that the hunting trip burros didn't look like Brighty. Since Henry went to the trouble of camping under the Cliff Springs overhang where Roosevelt's party had stayed, taking her chances of meeting a mountain lion, she probably sincerely believed that Brighty had been there. Perhaps she had picked up a canyon legend that Brighty was on the hunt. Or perhaps, since Henry was a big admirer of Teddy Roosevelt, she couldn't resist the idea of putting them together. She concludes the hunt chapter with a scene of Roosevelt writing lines of poetic praise for the Grand Canyon, lines that are nearly a quote from his true account of the hunt.

A few months after *Brighty of the Grand Canyon* was published, Elizabeth McKee went into a bookstore shopping for a gift for her granddaughter—Bob's daughter—and she discovered the novel. Thomas McKee wrote to introduce himself to Henry: "We have read it, and it makes us homesick because we are the people who managed the summer camp on the North Rim, and Brighty was a resident of our camp for several years."[22] McKee sent her a photo of Bob sitting on Brighty's back on the canyon edge: "As my wife and I read your book, we knew in a twinkling that our son was the Homer Hobbs of your story!" Henry was delighted to learn that her character was real. She and McKee enjoyed a long correspondence, and he shared more memories and photos of Brighty. McKee said he wasn't surprised that Henry hadn't found anyone at the canyon who had known him, since around 1920 the North Rim was very isolated, and the people on the South Rim, with its fancy El Tovar Hotel, always looked down on the crude camp on the opposite side.

Brighty's story got turned into a movie in the same serendipitous way it was turned into a novel.

In 1963 a young mother named Betty Booth walked into a suburban Detroit bookstore looking for books that would keep her three young sons entertained on a long road vacation. The clerk suggested *Brighty of the Grand Canyon*. As Betty read it to her family, her husband, Steve, also found the story captivating. Steve was a thirty-nine-year-old newspaperman and television producer who had done some corporate films. It seems that Steve wanted to do something more ambitious, and he decided that Brighty's story would make a wonderful film, especially for kids. Five months later he acquired the film rights to the novel, but when he tried to find a Hollywood studio to fund and make the film, he ran into great skepticism. Animal movies for kids were almost a Walt Disney monopoly, and it would be hard for other studios to compete with Disney at their own game. And it sounded like filming a movie inside the Grand Canyon would be especially challenging and expensive. Booth was forced to raise money from private investors, which proved difficult, and the project nearly foundered, but then Booth found a director who gave the project high credibility.

Norman Foster started his Hollywood career as an actor in the 1930s; he was the husband of Claudette Colbert. Foster later became a director, mainly of formula movies like the Charlie Chan pictures. In 1942 he won more respectability by finishing a movie started by Orson Welles, *Journey into Fear*. In the 1950s Foster started working for Walt Disney, and he cowrote and directed the phenomenal hit *Davy Crockett: King of the Wild Frontier* and its sequel, *Davy Crockett and the River Pirates*. Now that Foster was an expert on rivers, Walt Disney sent him into the Grand Canyon to scout locations and potential problems for filming the Disney movie about John Wesley Powell, *Ten Who Dared*. Foster didn't direct that movie, but now he knew the Grand Canyon, and he also knew burros from having worked with them in several westerns.

Foster brought with him an actor who gave the Brighty movie even more credibility. Back in 1942 Foster had worked with the star and cowriter of *Journey into Fear*, Joseph Cotten, a close associate of Orson Welles. Cotten's first Hollywood movie was *Citizen Kane*, in which he played a close associate of Orson Welles's character, Charles Foster Kane. Next Cotten starred in Welles's *The Magnificent Ambersons*, and soon *Gaslight*. Cotten's screen persona was a smart, sophisticated, soft-spoken gentleman. In *Brighty* he played the rugged Jim Owens. If it was true that Cotten's career was going downhill, he gave a large boost to the image of Jim Owens.

To play Homer Hobbs, Foster came up with an Arizona boy, Richard "Dandy" Curran, who had already appeared in one Hollywood movie thanks to his mother having been Miss America of 1949.

But who would play Brighty? Foster "auditioned" many burros but couldn't find the right star. During a frustrated phone conversation with Marguerite Henry, Henry said that she had the star right there: her own Brighty. Skeptical, Foster traveled to Illinois to meet him, and he won the part. Brighty too was skeptical about being a movie star, about leaving the familiar flat prairie and riding in a van to Arizona and hiking into the weird Grand Canyon and being coaxed to behave in lots of strange ways. To keep Brighty calm and willing, he was placed under the care of Henry's neighbor Tex, who had ridden and taken care of Brighty since both were kids. In a newsletter she wrote to her fans, Henry said that she was waking up in the middle of the night and worrying about the dangers facing Brighty in the canyon.

The filming took three and a half months in the spring and summer of 1965. Only about a month of that was at the canyon. For most of the North Rim scenes, Foster substituted the high country of Dixie National Forest in southern Utah, where his crew rebuilt a house used in the 1943 movie *My Friend Flicka*. They also built a replica of Jim Owens's cabin based on old photos. Booth and Foster were proud of not using any sound stages for *Brighty*.

They did film a few scenes on the real North Rim, including one of Teddy Roosevelt giving some lines from his famous "leave it as it is" speech.

To film inside the Grand Canyon, Booth rented a helicopter, which made about 1,200 flights to haul film equipment, props, and people in and out.[23] Booth also used a thirty-five-mule pack train. A trailer near Bright Angel Lodge served as headquarters, with radio communications to the bottom. The actors stayed at Phantom Ranch and at the rim lodges. All these expenses raised the cost of making the movie to half a million dollars, which might have been cheap by Disney standards, but was a lot for a small, independent company like Booth's.

By the time canyon filming was wrapping up at the start of June, it was 112 degrees at the bottom. The actors didn't need to act at being hot and tired.

Inside the canyon the film crew had to be careful not to catch glimpses of 1965, such as a footbridge across the river or a backpacker on a well-groomed trail. The biggest problem was that the transcanyon water pipeline was being built, and the construction company had its own helicopters flying overhead frequently. Park superintendent Howard Stricklin told Booth that his film crew would need to stay out of the way of the construction crew, which was camped four miles north of Phantom Ranch. But Foster broke the rules to film a scene of Brighty at Ribbon Falls, nearly six miles north of Phantom Ranch. On June 15 the National Park Service filed a complaint against Booth in U.S. district court, saying that he "did drive livestock over trails closed to public use due to hazardous and dangerous conditions...." Foster had ignored a "plainly marked sign as follows: 'Trail closed to livestock travel—hikers may be delayed.' Said sign on trail north of Phantom Ranch. Above named defendants driving up trail from Phantom Ranch one mule and three burros causing damage to construction work."[24] At least Brighty didn't get arrested. The novel, which includes a drawing of Brighty at Ribbon Falls, said that "Brighty could never resist the pretty beckoning finger of Ribbon Falls."[25]

Booth probably got off to a bad start with the National Park Service when he asked them to supply him with a cage full of Kaibab squirrels for extras; the superintendent told Booth to go find his own squirrels in the wild. Booth did bring along his own mountain lion for one scene. The lion was actually tame, as well as defanged and declawed, and the trainer had to prod it with a stick to get it to snarl. It took the trainer four days to get Brighty to make a half-hearted kick at the lion, but then Brighty and the lion got into the spirit of the thing. The scenes showing the Roosevelt lion hunt used another, wild lion that had been captured for the movie. The scene in which Brighty breaks out of the cable car and jumps into the river was carefully staged to avoid any real danger, and it used Brighty's stunt-double. Marguerite Henry was relieved that Brighty came home from the canyon in great shape.

The story in the movie follows the novel fairly closely, with a few Hollywood indulgences. It gives Brighty credit for discovering Old Timer's mine; it changes the mine from a copper mine into a gold mine; and it adds a literal cliffhanger ending with Jake Irons dangling from the edge of the canyon. It skipped a few scenes, such as the bridge dedication, which would have been impractical to film. The movie ends with a summary of Marguerite Henry's closing lines about Brighty's spirit living forever.

The movie had its world premiere in November 1966 in the Detroit suburb where Steve Booth lived. It was a long way from Hollywood. The movie didn't do very well at the box office; Booth didn't have the clout or resources to get major national distribution.

Bob McKee had mixed feelings about the movie: "The burro was well cast—a ringer for the original. Uncle Jim Owen was much more of a frontiersman than the one depicted—rough beard and a slouch hat." Bob was a bit miffed that Homer Hobbs, who might be mistaken for himself, had messed up: "the boy is quite unnecessary as part of the story. About the only important thing he does is to go to sleep when he had the duty of guarding the prisoner."[26]

Having become very fond of Brighty, Steve Booth commissioned sculptor Peter Jepsen to make a life-sized, bronze statue of him that cost $15,000, along with dozens of smaller, ten-pound copies that Booth gave to people involved with the movie. He donated one to Grand Canyon National Park in March 1966, and it was placed in the South Rim visitor center with an exhibit on early canyon tourism. In December 1967, after the original statue had served its publicity duties, Booth donated it to the park as a "Christmas gift." The park planned a dedication ceremony, with Booth, Jepsen, and Henry present, but a winter storm cancelled those plans. The statue first went into the visitor center but later was moved to the outdoor patio. Some park rangers felt that the statue belonged on the North Rim, Brighty's true home. In late 1968

Brighty statue in the South Rim Visitor Center, 1967, with sculptor Peter Jepsen.
(*Grand Canyon National Park Study Collection*)

the park's chief naturalist, Merrill D. Beal, wrote to Marguerite Henry reassuring her about the proposed move, which was rumored to be a demotion, and Henry wrote back: "Of course you are right!... His real place, as you say, is there... [and] with the new Visitor Center Brighty will again be the center of loving hands. Our own real-life Brighty is very doleful unless he is surrounded by admiring children."[27] Yet it would take fifteen years, and a major controversy, before Brighty arrived on the North Rim.

Park rangers may have had another motive for wanting to move Brighty to the North Rim, where he would be admired by only 10 percent of the tourists seeing him on the South Rim. For many years the park had been worried by the problem of feral burros. Brighty wasn't the only one that prospectors had left behind. Over the decades the canyon's burro population had grown into the thousands. Burros were natives of Africa, introduced to America by the Spanish, and their behavior patterns were a bad fit for the American desert. The cute-looking burros are actually more aggressive and territorial than the native desert bighorn sheep, and phalanxes of burros were preventing bighorns from using springs. Burros were also much more destructive of vegetation. By the 1960s visitors at South Rim overlooks looked down on a Tonto Plateau that was a maze of burro trails. The bighorn population had been dwindling, and even hikers seldom saw any, but they did encounter burros that blocked trails or camping spots. The park had been dealing with the burro problem, quietly and sporadically, by shooting them, but these efforts had little lasting effect.

As the idea of ecosystems became the foundation of wildlife management policies, the National Park Service began more actively protecting native species and opposing invasive species. In the early 1970s the park planned to send military helicopters into the canyon with rangers armed with rifles to shoot burros, but this became a very public and heated controversy. The ecosystem concept may have won public respect, but it didn't carry nearly the appeal of cute burros. For most people, a news report about Grand Canyon burros invoked an image of Brighty. How could park rangers *murder* Brighty? Twelve thousand outraged letters flooded in.

As they read angry letters and editorials about the proposed burro hunt, park managers could look out their windows to the patio where the Brighty statue still remained, with families happily admiring him. Realizing that the National Park Service had helped create its own public relations problem, in April 1978 superintendent Merle Stitt decided to remove the statue and place it in storage.

Now the furor around the burro removal plan turned into furor over removal of the Brighty statue. The Wild Burro Protection Association, based in Tucson, Arizona, issued a press release calling for Stitt's resignation:

> Superintendent Stitt's illegal and unethical actions to remove wild burros from the Grand Canyon, and his capricious and paranoid removal of the life sized statue of the famous wild burro "Brighty of the Grand Canyon" indicate a loss of touch with reality....
>
> In 1967 the National Park Service recognized the burro's contribution to the historical and cultural dimensions of the Canyon by sanctioning the erection of a 600 pound, life-sized bronze statue of Brighty....
>
> Brighty... is part of the folklore of the Southwest....
>
> In place of the Brighty statue, the Park Service has mounted an exhibit explaining the alleged problems caused by wild burros....
>
> If necessary we will go to court to have Brighty returned. [28]

The press release announced the launch of a national "Bring Back Brighty" campaign, which included petition and letter-writing drives. The petition read: "We demand that immediate steps be taken to return the statue of Brighty to its rightful place."[29]

Another organization, the Southwestern Donkey and Mule Society, protested in a letter:

> Do you really think that the removal of this statue will make us forget the burros? All you are doing is rubbing salt in a very sensitive wound.
>
> How many appeals have you received in behalf of the Big Horn Sheep you so ardently protect? How can a few men decide which of God's creatures is deserving of this protection? It appears that the Big Horn Sheep have done nothing for mankind to deserve the "award" they are receiving....
>
> Perhaps you might consider thinning out the herd of Big Horn Sheep if you must do some thinning, and leave more "flora" for the burros.[30]

In an attempt at damage control, park managers drafted a form letter that was a bit more diplomatic than the internal memo from which it started. The memo offered all the reasons why the Brighty statue was inappropriate. Park museums were supposed to present facts, and the Brighty novel "is fiction and not based on either historic or biological fact." The novel represented a pre-ecological worldview in which "Burro life is an enchanting, make-believe world within the park in harmony with all other 'good' animals." The novel endorsed the anti-ecological view that predators are evil, and it glamorized the practices of Jim Owens. The memo claimed that the Brighty statue was just a promotional gimmick for a private film company. Mainly, the novel and statue gave a friendly face to burros: "Many people do not disassociate make-believe from fact about feral burros in the park. This is evidenced by the thousands of letters the park has received.... Ironically, many persons base their comments on this serious environmental problem solely on the story of 'Brighty' or the existence of the 'Brighty' statue."[31] The park's form letter also emphasized that it was the duty of the National Park Service to protect the natural environment, and that scientific studies now made it clear that the burros were causing serious damage.

Marguerite Henry didn't see the ecological light. When the Brighty statue was removed, the head of the Wild Burro Protection Association called her up, and Henry began adding a postscript to all her correspondence with children:

> P.S. I've just learned, to my sorrow, that the wonderful life-size bronze sculpture of Brighty has been removed from its place in the Visitors Bureau at the Grand Canyon. The people who put it in storage claim that all the burros in the Canyon should be destroyed before they cause a shortage of food for the bighorn sheep.
>
> In reality, the possibility of such a shortage is remote because the burros graze on the Tonto Plateau within the lower canyon, while the bighorn sheep graze in the highest mountain tops. As to the number of burros in the Canyon, the figure is exaggerated beyond belief by the enemies of all the little "Brightys" in the world.
>
> If you want to have the statue of Brighty put back where it belongs and—even more important—if you want to save the real burros, it would help to write a letter stating your feelings to....[32]

If only Superintendent Bryant, a quarter of a century before, had given Henry an ornery wild burro that ruined her "warm image" of Brighty. All those children writing outraged letters about the murder of Brighty were a public relations disaster for the National Park Service, which finally gave up its plans for mass executions of burros. Instead it began, with the help of private organizations, to round up the burros and remove them from the canyon, even using helicopters to airlift them out, at a huge expense.

The statue of Brighty remained hidden away until after the wild burros were safely out of the canyon and the uproar about them had died down. By 1983, if not earlier, Brighty had been released from captivity and placed in the lobby of Grand Canyon Lodge on the North Rim, in his old neighborhood. The park was still shy about publicity for the statue. When Steve Booth heard about its new location, he wrote to the park superintendent and proposed a long-delayed dedication ceremony. The superintendent wrote back apologizing for not having informed Booth about the Brighty statue's having been moved, but he declined the idea of any dedication ceremony.

The Brighty statue is still on the North Rim today, with a very shiny nose from tens of thousands of children—and adults, and even park superintendents—rubbing his nose for good luck and friendliness and a connection with the history of the Grand Canyon.

KING OF THE ROAD

Roger Miller's Big Adventure

It was the height of the British Invasion. If Roger Miller was playing his radio as he drove into Grand Canyon National Park, chances are he was hearing the Beatles or another British band. It seemed that rock and roll was taking over the musical world, sweeping aside folk, jazz, country, Broadway, and crooners—even Sinatra was worried. But not Roger.

He drove past the old Motor Lodge and its campground, where he had lived one summer a dozen years before. He had worked "two hours pushin' broom" to live in a "trailer for rent," about "eight by twelve." The trailer had "no phone, no pool, no pets." He had been "a man of means, by no means." But he was seventeen years old, seeing the country for the first time, having a great adventure. The trailer was tiny and run-down, but it was on the rim of the Grand Canyon.

The trailer was next to the railroad tracks, right where the trains slowed down and turned around. Even in 1953, well after the high tide of Great Depression homeless men riding the rails, a hobo would occasionally ride a freight car into Grand Canyon Village (most food and supplies still came by train) and hop out of the "third boxcar." It's not likely that any of these hobos would hop onto the "third boxcar; midnight train; destination Bangor, Maine," but hey, what are you going to rhyme with "train"? "Williams" just doesn't cut it.

Roger may have had a chance to meet some of the hobos and hear about their life on the road. If the hobos tried to bum cigarettes off him, he may have told them, "I ain't got no cigarettes." But in his job he did spend a lot of time cleaning cigarettes and cigars off the ground. Since he worked next to the parking lot of El Tovar, the Grand Canyon's luxury hotel, he had plenty of chances to "smoke old stogies I have found, short but not too big around." At least he didn't have to "pay no union dues."

Roger also had a chance to "know every engineer on every train, all of their children and all of their names." Just like today, when passenger trains parked at the canyon station, their crews would wander up the hill to get coffee at El Tovar or a candy bar at the shops.

Driving past the Motor Lodge (which later would be replaced by Maswik Lodge), Roger didn't see his old "trailer for rent."

He drove up the hill to Verkamp's store. He walked inside and asked if his old boss, Jack Verkamp, was still there. Verkamp came out, pretty surprised that Roger Miller would visit him now that he was a huge star. Especially since Verkamp had fired him and kicked him out of his "trailer for rent." But at least Roger always had a good sense of humor about things.

Miller's sense of humor had helped make him a star. The songs he wrote were popping with clever, humorous wordplay. His success also came from his ability to blend musical styles. In the early 1960s, when country music seldom branched out from its roots, it was rare for country music stars to have hits on the pop music charts. Twenty years later, in 1985, Miller would win a Tony Award for writing *Big River*, a hit Broadway musical about Huckleberry Finn. Roger was the only country music star ever to win a Tony Award. The producer of *Big River* drafted Miller to write its music, convinced that he was the only person who could combine the folksiness of Mark Twain's voice and Huck Finn's life with a musical style that would satisfy sophisticated Broadway audiences. This blending of folksy material and beyond-country musical style produced Miller's biggest hits, allowing him to compete with the Beatles. Between 1964 and 1965 Miller won eleven Grammy Awards, more than the Beatles at the peak of Beatlemania, a two-year record that would stand for two decades.

Roger's biggest hit was "King of the Road," which won the 1965 Grammy for best song in both the country and rock-and-roll categories, beating out the

Beatles' "Yesterday." It even hit number 1 on the pop charts in Britain. "King of the Road" resonated with Americans' love of the open road, a theme that ran from Daniel Boone through Whitman and Steinbeck and that in the 1960s was practically the only theme that appealed equally to hippies and rednecks. The song's imagery of a down-and-out hobo roaming the country was right out of the folk tradition of Miller's fellow Oklahoman Woody Guthrie. But the words were set to music that was much more upbeat, its syncopation more like jazz than country. The song's mood, too, was upbeat. Though the hobo's clothes are threadbare and he is picking up "old stogies" off the ground, he knows his way around, he has friends along the way and he's having an adventure. He is king of the road. This mood was an expression of Miller's upbeat personality, and it also fit the times—the swinging sixties— better than Woody Guthrie's despairing victims. Miller had taken an old folk image, kept the poignancy, yet given his hobo an optimism that ran deep in the American spirit.

If Jack Verkamp was surprised to see Roger Miller walk through his door a dozen years after he'd fired him, it was partly because Verkamp hadn't realized what the job had meant to Roger. Born in 1936, in the depths of the Great Depression, Roger had grown up in Oklahoma on Route 66—the mother road, the queen of the roads—and he had watched real Joads living the *Grapes of Wrath*, overloading their old trucks and heading west for a better life in California. Later on, in better times, Roger saw tourists heading into the mythic West, the land of cowboys and Indians and the Grand Canyon. Roger had loved playing cowboy. And now here he was, in the real West, looking out over the Grand Canyon every day, living in a place those tourists were merely visiting. He was living out an American myth; he was the king of the road.

Now Miller had even more reason to appreciate his time at the Grand Canyon. He had just achieved a huge hit with "King of the Road."

"He ended up at the railroad depot," Jack Verkamp explained, recalling how Roger Miller came to work for him in 1953. Verkamp and his wife, Betty, were interviewed in 1995 by Grand Canyon National Park archivists Carolyn Richard and Mike Quinn. "Sam Turner was the agent at that time. He went in there and hit him up for a job. Sam didn't have anything for him but he did call me. I said, 'Well, I might be able to put him on as a clerk.'

So he came up and we happened to have a little old trailer over in the old Auto Camp."[1]

Betty added, "Just big enough for one person."

"Kind of a travel trailer," continued Jack. "So I put him over there. He worked out pretty good until this big influx of Boy Scouts came in." Verkamp was referring to a 1953 invasion of the South Rim by trains carrying 20,000 Boy Scouts to a national Boy Scout Jamboree. When the Boy Scouts swarmed the store like locusts,

> I saw him leaning on the counter top talking to a couple of the young girls we had working there, and these guys, they were just all over the place, so I got him out of that deal. Then after lunch, same thing happened. I said, "Roger, you're fired." These old gals were just working their butts off and he was [Verkamp makes a jabbering sound] with these young girls. So I just fired him right on the spot. He used to come back and see us. First time he came back he says "I got something to thank you for. I wrote that 'King of the Road' when I was in that little trailer. I want to thank you for getting me started on my road."

Roger's "road" forced him to finally get serious about his musical career. He soon headed for Nashville. At least, that's what Miller told Verkamp about the origins of "King of the Road." I would discover that Miller told quite a few stories about it.

To learn more about Miller's time at Verkamp's, I spoke with the children of Jack and Betty Verkamp: Susie, Steve, and Mike. They grew up in the house above the store and were six to eleven years old when Miller worked there. Steve remembered Miller as "a character," a skinny kid who would bring his guitar into the store and play it, mostly strumming chords, when he was supposed to be working. Miller was already a good musician. Steve said that his father repeatedly had to tell Roger to stop playing his guitar and get back to work. Susie remembered Roger playing the "drums": "He drove my father nuts beating out rhythms on the glass display cases."[2] Miller's job included quite a bit of "pushin' broom," certainly the two hours of it mentioned in the song. Miller was almost the only male in the store, and pushin' broom was a man's job, and a constant job, since the store was only sixty feet from the rim, and updrafts blew dust out of the canyon and into the store all the time. Steve Verkamp said that his father was "a fanatic" about keeping the store clean.

Miller also had to clean the front porch, where tourists often sat and smoked, and the grounds around the store, including the space between the store and the rim, though this was National Park Service property. Miller was actually getting paid to pick up the "old stogies I have found" in the song. Steve Verkamp said that the trailer where Miller lived was "really shabby, about twelve feet long," exactly the length in the song. Mike Verkamp recalled Miller as "a very attractive and social guy with probably more charisma than ten regular blokes." Miller didn't have any trouble getting dates for the dances at Bright Angel Lodge. In one incident Miller seems to have been practicing for a future incident in which he fell asleep right in the middle of a meeting with top record company executives, which convinced them that Miller was a hopeless slacker: one day Jack Verkamp carried some new merchandise into the store's basement, only to find Roger sleeping on a box of merchandise. Both Mike and Steve Verkamp remembered Miller returning to the store after he was a star and talking with their dad. Miller had come back to say thanks. The Verkamps still had a receipt for one of Roger's paychecks; he was paid seventy-five cents per hour.

To me, Roger Miller's happy-go-lucky attitude while working at Verkamp's seemed a lot like that of the hobo in "King of the Road." But there was one line in the song that didn't make sense for a hobo. Hobos tried to stay invisible from train crews, and they rode lots of different trains, so they would not "know every engineer on every train, all of their children and all of their names." But at Verkamp's, just up the hill from the train depot, Miller would have had a good chance to "know every engineer on every train."

Would Miller have also met hobos at the canyon? I asked Grand Canyon railroad historian Al Richmond about whether there were hobos at the South Rim, and he said, "Although I have never heard any stories of them I am sure some must have made their way to the canyon on the occasional freights. The passenger trains would have been almost impossible to hop a ride without detection."[3] Grand Canyon historian Mike Anderson added, "I don't know of any specific mention of people riding the rails to the canyon, but I wouldn't doubt it." Anderson said that during the Great Depression many dust bowl refugees heading for California came up to the South

Verkamp's store in 1951, two years before Roger Miller was "pushin' broom" there. (*Grand Canyon National Park Study Collection*)

Rim, camped in the forest, and often found work inside the park. "NPS documentation," said Anderson, "indicates there may have been as many as 500 of them there during the 1933-35 period."[4] Twenty years later there weren't so many hobos, but freight cars were still free, and even hobos can be curious to see the Grand Canyon.

One October I followed Roger Miller's road back to his hometown of Erick, Oklahoma.

Erick sits nearly on the Texas border, and on the Hundredth Meridian. Its town history museum is called the Hundredth Meridian Museum. Erick was a proof of John Wesley Powell's thesis that beyond the 100th Meridian the settlement patterns that had worked in the East could no longer succeed. There wasn't enough rainfall or good topsoil for the traditional 160-acre American family farm to support a family. Like most of the high plains, Erick had been losing farms and ranches and population for a century. The dust bowl years had hit western Oklahoma especially hard. In 1975 the new interstate bypassed Erick's Route 66 main street, and many of its old businesses were wiped out. Today most of its downtown consists of empty and

Roger Miller (left) play-
ing guitar at Bright Angel
Lodge, 1953. (*Courtesy of the
Roger Miller Museum*)

decaying buildings. Roger Miller had grown up in this discouraging, decaying world, and this may have left its imprint in "King of the Road," in which
a hobo is riding the rails, searching for something better, and somehow keeping up his spirits.

A few years ago Erick tried to lift its spirits by turning an abandoned but
nice old bank building into the Roger Miller Museum. I visited on the day
of their annual Roger Miller Festival. The museum held lots of memorabilia
from Miller's life, including his guitars, albums, awards, and photographs.

One photo showed five guys in cowboy hats playing music on a small
wooden stage, with a background wall of half-cut logs. The caption read:
"Grand Canyon, Az. (circa 1953) Roger Miller (left)." This was the year Roger
Miller worked at Verkamp's. Roger looked pretty young. Along with his
white cowboy hat he wore a bandana, cowboy boots, and blue jeans, and he
was playing a guitar.

Three other names were listed on the photo: Ray Mansel, Robert Salmon,
and Cotton Holley. When I checked into these names, I found that only Ray
Mansel had enjoyed a musical career that had left much of a trace. In 1955
"Ray Mansel and his Hillbilly Boys" had released a single from a Houston,
Texas, record label, which seems to have led to better things. On March 3,
1956, *Billboard* magazine reported that Ray and his boys were appearing twice
weekly in a fifteen-minute show on an Amarillo, Texas, TV station and daily
on an Amarillo radio station. Later *Billboard* articles announced the release
of (unpromising) Mansel records but didn't mention the names of Mansel's

band members. Was this Bright Angel photo showing Mansel's band, perhaps on a tour down Route 66?

After this photograph was published in the *Ol' Pioneer*, the magazine of the Grand Canyon Historical Society, two canyon ol' timers contacted me and said they recognized the fifth, unidentified man in the photo, the fiddle player. It was Tram Bowman, the long-time fiddle player of the cowboy band that had played at Bright Angel Lodge for many years. This photo was undoubtedly the local cowboy band.

I got in touch with Tram Bowman's wife and son-in-law. They told me that Tram had worked at the canyon for twenty-seven years, mainly in stores, including the newsstand and curio shop in Bright Angel Lodge. The cowboy band provided the only regular musical entertainment in the park and was greatly appreciated by park employees. At that time the park's live music venue was in what later became the History Room in Bright Angel Lodge. The Saturday night dances were so popular that they overflowed onto the covered patio outside. Folding chairs were set up to accommodate everyone. The walls were decorated with cowboy hats. Over the years the band grew and shrank, sometimes including drums and a saxophone. Tram was always the fiddle player. Mrs. Bowman didn't recognize the other names listed on the 1953 photo.

Mrs. Bowman hadn't been married to Tram in 1953, but she did recall him talking about how Roger Miller had wanted to write songs and perform them with the band. But Tram wasn't so sure about letting a kid play his own songs. Mrs. Bowman didn't know how Roger had come to be at the canyon, but she told me that Tram came to the canyon from the town of Cheyenne, Oklahoma—which is only twenty-five miles from Miller's hometown of Erick.

Had Miller known Bowman back in Oklahoma? Was Bowman's band the reason Roger had come to the canyon? Mrs. Bowman told me that she didn't think Roger and Tram had known each other in Oklahoma. Tram Bowman's son-in-law told me the same thing.

But the walls of the Roger Miller Museum held another photograph. This photo showed an even younger Roger playing in Cheyenne, Oklahoma, circa 1950. He was with three other musicians, in a band called The Lonesome Valley Boys. There wasn't any geographical Lonesome Valley in this part of Oklahoma, so this must have been one of those Lonesome Valleys you find in the lonely state of Country Music.

I contacted the historical society in Cheyenne, and they put me in touch with a local historian, Arthur Trammell, who had known Tram Bowman after he moved back to Cheyenne for awhile. Arthur told me that Tram would tell him stories about his musical adventures.

Tram Bowman was fifteen years older than Roger Miller, and as far as Arthur knew, the two hadn't known one another in Oklahoma. But Roger knew *about* Tram, and Tram was why Roger headed for the Grand Canyon. Cheyenne and Erick were part of the same small musical world, where, in the Great Depression years, people had to rely on their own talents for entertainment, often holding dances in people's homes. Tram Bowman organized a few musicians into a band, and they wanted to have a better chance at making some money, so they headed west. When they got to the Grand Canyon, they found that it had no regular band, and they talked some lodge manager into letting them perform steadily. But there was no pay or housing for musicians, so they had to find regular day jobs. This wasn't the best deal for musicians, so band members came and went.

Roger Miller probably heard about Tram Bowman in Cheyenne, where he would go to take music lessons. The wife of a Cheyenne banker was a renowned music teacher, and Roger began studying with her, but she declared that he had no talent and would never make it as a singer. At some point Roger heard about a man from Erick—Arthur couldn't remember his name— who was planning to go to the Grand Canyon to join Tram Bowman's band. Tram had arranged for a job and housing for this man. Roger decided to go along. When Roger showed up at the canyon and asked to join Tram's band, it put Tram in a bind, since he didn't have a job or housing for him.

Tram Bowman did appreciate Roger's talent. Roger was already writing his own songs, and Tram let him perform them when the band was taking breaks. But Tram didn't approve of Roger's sense of cowboy style. His band members were supposed to tuck the bottom of their jeans inside their cowboy boots, but Roger kept coming on stage with his jeans outside his boots, and Tram would have to nag him about it.

Arthur said that Roger Miller always remembered Tram Bowman fondly. After he became a big success, he tried to direct his agent to take some interest in Tram, but nothing came of it. In the 1990s Roger invited Tram to visit his home in New Mexico.

When I first saw the photo of Roger Miller at the Grand Canyon, I assumed it was taken in today's live music venue, the lounge in Bright Angel Lodge. Later I learned that today's lounge hadn't been constructed until 1958, five years after this photo was taken. Steve Verkamp confirmed that in 1953 the entertainment venue had been down the hall, in what was now the History Room. Steve said he attended many musical events there, including the local cowboy band on Saturday nights. But he couldn't recall seeing Roger Miller playing with them. On Sunday mornings this room was converted into a church for the local community, which sometimes got some odd stares from tourists who had seen the lively cowboy band there the night before.

I took a copy of the 1953 photo into the History Room and tried to match it with the walls there, but I couldn't find a match. I showed the photo to the History Room's long-time host, Lowell Fay. He agreed that the photo's rough-cut logs, some vertical and some horizontal, had the correct Bright Angel look. Lowell pointed out the remnant of a stage-like area behind the history exhibits, but the background wall didn't match the photo. Lowell told me that Bright Angel Lodge had been remodeled extensively several times over the decades, so lots of old arrangements had disappeared. I searched several archives for photographs of the Bright Angel interior in the 1950s, but I couldn't find photos of any stage.

At the Roger Miller Festival I attended a talk by Don Cusic, who teaches music history at Belmont College in Nashville and has written biographies of several major country music stars. Cusic was starting research for a biography of Roger Miller, which, surprisingly, would be the first full-scale one written on him. The only previous book about Miller was *Ain't Got No Cigarettes*, a collection of interviews with Miller's friends and musical colleagues conducted by Lyle Style.

In response to an e-mail query, Style told me he'd never heard about Roger Miller working at the Grand Canyon. In his interviews Style had asked a number of people about the origins of "King of the Road," but no one had mentioned the Grand Canyon. Style told me that over the years there had arisen quite a few stories about the origins of "King of the Road," some of them encouraged by Roger Miller. During one of his interviews Style interrupted the speaker and said, "A lot of people have mentioned that song and how it came to be written, and every story has been different!"[5] Style told me, "There could be a documentary done on that song and what the real story is."[6]

I next talked to Don Cusic, and he too said that it was news to him that Roger Miller had worked at the Grand Canyon. Cusic said that the summer Miller worked at the canyon was right after he'd been kicked out of two high schools in and near Erick, so he might have quit town and headed west. I explained Miller's circumstances at the canyon, and how they were a good fit for the lyrics of "King of the Road." Cusic said that he didn't know of any other time when Roger had lived in a trailer and earned it by pushing a broom and picking up old stogies. Then again, every week Cusic ate breakfast with Jerry Kennedy, Roger's record producer, who had recorded "King of the Road," and Kennedy had never mentioned any Grand Canyon connection.

Cusic took me back into the museum and introduced me to Mary Miller, Roger's wife. Cusic asked Mary about Roger working at the Grand Canyon, and she beamed, saying she knew all about it. One time in the 1980s they'd been driving across Arizona and Roger took her on a detour to the South Rim. They walked into Verkamp's, and Roger introduced her to Jack Verkamp, his boss from thirty years before. Clearly, Roger was still fond of his time working there. Mary said she recalled seeing the housing area for Verkamp's employees, but she didn't recall Roger ever mentioning living in a trailer, or mentioning any connection between the Grand Canyon and "King of the Road." Roger did like to tell a joke about looking into the Grand Canyon and saying, "Just think what God could do if he had money."

Cusic told me he wasn't surprised I was having trouble pinning down the origins of the song. He had heard lots of stories about it, some of them encouraged by Roger. Roger was always telling stories, sometimes tall tales. But despite his outgoing persona, he was actually a very private person who seldom talked about his own life or work. This hadn't made things easy for a biographer.

The Roger Miller Museum had two artifacts that were related to the origins of "King of the Road." One was a carved, wooden folk art hobo standing on a pedestal that said "King of the Road." Cusic said that in 1964 Roger was driving to Chicago when he saw a sign that said, "Trailer for sale or rent," and this struck him as a great start for a song. A few weeks later Miller was in

Boise, Idaho, and the song began coming together. He wrote the first verse in a hotel room, but he couldn't finish the song. Cusic told me that this was normal for Roger, who had a short attention span. But Roger kept at it. He saw this hobo statue in an airport gift shop, and it helped him to finish the song. In his public performances Roger sometimes credited Boise for the song.

The other artifact, framed on the museum wall, was a credit card application for Western Airlines on which Roger had written the initial lyrics to "King of the Road," lyrics slightly different from the words he later recorded.

Thus, we concluded, it wasn't possible that Roger had written the song when he had worked at Verkamp's in 1953, as he had indicated to Jack Verkamp. It was unimaginable that a struggling young songwriter like Roger would sit on such a great song for a decade. Roger's claim to Jack Verkamp was one more tale he'd spun about the song.

Nevertheless, after Cusic listened to my list of all the lines from the song that fit Roger Miller's circumstances at the Grand Canyon, he said he found it quite plausible that Roger had drawn upon those experiences in writing the song. When Roger saw that sign that said "trailer for sale or rent," it could have brought back his memories of when he had rented a little rundown trailer beside some railroad tracks and paid for it by pushin' a broom and picking up old stogies.

Cusic mentioned that somewhere along the way Miller had developed a fondness for the Southwest. He had settled in Santa Fe and kept an Indian pot beside his bed. A pot, I thought, a lot like the ones sold at Verkamp's.

In a way it was appropriate that "King of the Road" had gathered some folklore around it. The song already embodied a lot of American folklore, which had helped to make it an American classic. As I told various people about Roger Miller's time at the Grand Canyon, I was amazed at how many people, old and young, could not only recognize lines from the song but recite them, half a century after it had been a hit. Roger Miller had lived and given words to a core part of the American story. When he was young and free, he had heard the beckoning call of a western song and hit the open road and gone searching for something. He had heard train whistles constantly playing the song of the open road. He had followed the Mother Road. He had discovered himself to be the King of the Road.

THE HOTEL ON THE EDGE OF FOREVER

Early Tourists React to the Grand Canyon

For the first tourists who stepped off the Santa Fe Railway at the South Rim in 1901, the Grand Canyon was a startling new experience. It had not yet become a ubiquitous image in calendars, postcards, and advertising. While a handful of cultural pioneers such as painter Thomas Moran and writer Clarence Dutton had offered important interpretations of the canyon by the 1880s, in 1901 there were still very few writers who had seen the canyon and offered the public clues about how they might experience it. Even these writers were often puzzled by the canyon. The expectations of the average tourist may have been formed only by a few black-and-white photographs and by Santa Fe Railway advertising brochures. There was plenty of room for surprise—for tourists to figure out the canyon for themselves.

Someone at El Tovar, the South Rim's luxury hotel, seems to have recognized the value of recording tourists' reactions to the canyon. For a decade after it opened in 1905, El Tovar offered guests a book in which to share their thoughts and feelings about the canyon. At the top of each page was printed: "IMPRESSIONS OF THE GRAND CANYON. Guests are respectfully invited to record their impressions of the Grand Canyon of Arizona, signing name, also giving home address and date."[1] These *Impressions* books offer a rich record of Americans trying to grasp the canyon's meaning. Their comments reflect the broader historical and cultural currents of the time, a time of expansive national pride, a time when the modern conservation ethic was taking shape, and a time when science and religion were contending to be the highest authority for explaining the world. One of the strongest themes running through the *Impressions* books is whether the Grand Canyon should be attributed to God or to Nature, and sometimes this theme breaks out into open debate, with guests writing critical comments about one another's impressions.

The *Impressions* books were probably inspired by a guest log kept by John Hance at his tourist camp near Grandview, the first tourist facility at the canyon. In 1899 G. K. Woods, the manager of the Grand Canyon Stage Coach line, which ran from Flagstaff to Grandview, compiled eight years of comments from Hance's log books, starting in 1891, into a book titled *Personal Impressions of the Grand Cañon of the Colorado River, Near Flagstaff, Arizona, as Seen Through Nearly Two Thousand Eyes, and Written in the Private Visitors' Book of the World-Famous Guide Capt. John Hance, Guide, Story-Teller, and Path-Finder.* Woods may have intended this book to publicize his stagecoach line, but it has served as a valuable source for historians. It gave us a few often-repeated comments about the canyon, such as Buckey O'Neill's, "God made the canyon, John Hance the trails. Without the other, neither would be complete." The El Tovar *Impressions* books offer an even richer source of reactions to the canyon.

We can begin with some basic sociology about who was visiting the Grand Canyon between 1906 and 1915. It seems that some of the *Impressions* books have been lost, as there are several gaps in the record. The surviving *Impressions* logs include 1,718 entries, of which nearly 1,500 include an address. Only 6 percent of visitors—or at least log entries—came from outside the United States, two-thirds of these from Europe. Germany, England, and France appeared in about a dozen entries each. Visitors from Canada made a dozen entries, and Latin Americans eight. Asians made only six, Australians and New Zealanders four, and South Africans four.

The 1,379 entries that give American addresses reveal the economic divisions of American society in the first years of the twentieth century. Two-thirds of American visitors, or 895, came from northern states (the Northeast, Great Lakes, and Midwest states), while only 146 entries were made by southern visitors, nearly half of these (70) from Texas. Ohio visitors alone made more entries, 78, than eleven southern states combined, not including Texas. El Tovar opened only forty years after the Civil War, and the South was still impoverished, while the North was now the world's industrial power-house. Visitors from New York State made 157 entries, Pennsylvania 87, and Massachusetts 57. By contrast, visitors from Georgia made 11 entries, Virginia 7, and Louisiana 3. It's likely that El Tovar patronage exaggerated national economic disparities, as the less affluent were staying at the Bright Angel Hotel.

If the *Impressions* book was kept in the El Tovar lobby, other canyon visitors would have had access to it since plenty of tourists wandered into El Tovar. Yet we don't know exactly where the book was kept. The limited numbers of photographs showing the El Tovar lobby from that period don't show the *Impressions* book. If the book was kept on the registration counter or in one of the activity rooms, then it was less likely to have been used by non-guests.

Another demographic void is from the Mountain West. With the exception of Colorado, whose residents made 48 entries, very few visitors came from other mountain states: only 2 from Montana, 3 from Utah, and none from Nevada. It's likely that people from these states, thinly populated to begin with, were visiting their own nearby wonders, such as Yellowstone and Zion. Arizonans, who made 64 entries, took advantage of their proximity to the canyon.

Being on the route of the Santa Fe Railway also boosted totals. Missouri residents made 86 entries, but the farther north people lived, the more they were in the realm of the Northern Pacific Railway, which was promoting Yellowstone and its own newly opened Old Faithful Inn; thus Iowans made just 28 entries, and Minnesotans, at the head of the Northern Pacific line, made only 19. Kansans—on the Santa Fe line—made 33 entries, while Nebraskans made 14, and visitors from South Dakota and North Dakota combined made only 5. Visitors from the states at either end of the Santa Fe line made two of the three highest totals: Illinois with 142, and California with 187—the highest total. California's top rank makes a curious contrast with Arizona's eastern neighbor, New Mexico, which was also on the Santa Fe line, but whose residents made only 7 entries. This contrast may again point to the importance of affluence in Grand Canyon tourism, especially in El Tovar patronage. In 1910 California still had a smaller population than Wisconsin or Georgia, so its top rank wasn't guaranteed by mere numbers. But the specific addresses recorded by

John Hance (standing) with former President Teddy Roosevelt (on mule) in front of the El Tovar Hotel. (*Grand Canyon National Park Study Collection*)

Californians tend to represent more affluent cities, such as Pasadena and San Francisco. New Mexico was a poorer state. Since affluence tends to correlate with educational levels, the affluence of El Tovar log writers probably accounts for comments rich in intellectual and literary content. A roughly equal number of men and women wrote entries in the *Impressions* books.

While the Grand Canyon may seem timeless, the *Impressions* entries did reflect a particular time in history. It was, above all, the time of Teddy Roosevelt. Even after Roosevelt left the White House in 1909, he remained a dominant figure in American life, and not just as a politician; he exemplified the American spirit at a turning point in the country's history. The United States had become one of the world's leading economic powers and was eager to be respected for it. With the Spanish-American War and the Philippines conquest, America had ventured into competition with European empires. With the Panama Canal, America had crowned an age of heroic technology. Teddy

Roosevelt expressed an exuberant pride in America, a pride that included America's natural wonders. Several *Impressions* entries simply used Roosevelt's favorite exclamation to describe the canyon: "Bully!" Roosevelt had made it okay for even macho hunters to gush purple about natural wonders. The *Impressions* books contain plenty of purple gushing and national pride, and just enough mentions of Roosevelt—usually just "Teddy"—to see his presence in people's minds. A man from Houghton, Michigan, called the Grand Canyon "The greatest freak of nature except Teddy." Several people paraphrased Teddy's now-famous speech about leaving the canyon for your children and your children's children. Someone called the canyon "A bigger bluff than T. Roosevelt," a line that another person crossed out. A man from New Jersey said, "It's a bigger ditch than Panama, and must make Teddy jealous."

At the same time, Roosevelt himself was worrying about the loss of the frontier and advocating a new ethic of protecting America's natural wonders. The *Impressions* logs show the stirrings of new attitudes about conservation and economic development, as we'll see below. Roosevelt was also worried that the transformation of America from a frontier and rural society into an urban one would zap the American character, and he was urging Americans to pursue a life of vigorous outdoor adventure, for which the Grand Canyon was one of his favorite stages.

The most fascinating thing about the *Impressions* logs is how people were attempting to come to terms with what they were seeing. Early Grand Canyon visitors showed a genuine and deep astonishment that seems much less common today. Visitors conscientiously tried to figure out what the canyon meant. Some visitors compared it to other natural wonders. Many tried to figure out how it fit into their theology or philosophy. Others tried to come up with images that did justice to it.

Nearly a hundred people compared the Grand Canyon to other famous places, mainly a few of the world's iconic natural wonders: Niagara, Yosemite, Yellowstone, the Alps, or Vesuvius. A few people compared it to famous man-made landmarks. Most such comparisons were favorable to the canyon.

In an entry titled "Mt. Vesuvius Vs. Grand Canyon," Reverend S. M. Bernard of San Dimas, California, wrestled with his impressions, describing his climb up and into Vesuvius: "It was grander to me than Grand Canyon but not so beautiful. The view of Grand Canyon from the open space just below the half-way house is the most picturesque natural scenery I have ever observed, and I have traveled in 13 foreign lands." Another visitor, who signed himself simply "One Who Sees," added a note alongside Reverend Bernard's entry: "I also have seen Vesuvius, which is positively devoid of color. There is no comparison." Jules Hexter of Victoria, Texas, wrote, "I thought Yellowstone, the so-called home of the devil, was beautiful, but the Grand Canyon beats it to smithers, for this is the ideal place for the angel's dwelling." Julia Randall tried to share the glory: "The Yosemite is the palace of the gods, Yellowstone park their play ground, and the Grand Canyon their tomb." But A. E. Ballard held that "Grand Canyon is all right but the Grand Canyon of Yellowstone can go it one better." A man who signed himself only as "a guide at Yellowstone park" admitted only "She sure is some hole." J. W. Flood of Louisville, Kentucky, compared the canyon to another hole: "Who would have thought that Mammoth Cave can be seen out here with the 'lid off.'" A New Yorker compared the canyon to the skyscraper canyons of New York City. No one compared the canyon to an iceberg until after the sinking of *Titanic* in 1912, and then Mr. and Mrs. R. Samuel of New York City found it "awe-inspiring as a mammoth iceberg." An Englishman compared it to "the deep and wonderful subterranean passages of the ancient temples of Thebes and Karnak of the upper Egypt region."

Reflecting a time when many Americans felt that touring Europe was obligatory to being sophisticated, M. J. McLean of the U.S. Forest Service in Washington, D.C., complained, "Many Americans who visit and revisit the toy scenery of Europe have never seen the Grand Canyon." Agreeing with him was Robert Miller of Lancaster, Pennsylvania: "After seeing the natural wonders and man-made wonders of Europe, Asia, and Africa, I feel that it is but a fitting climax to my travels to view the greatest wonder of God's handiwork— The Grand Canyon of Arizona." A bit more provincial was Charles Peacock of Randolph Street, Chicago, Illinois: "As compared with Randolph Street, Chicago—well—forget Randolph Street." Twelve-year-old Thomas Moronly reached deep into his experience of grandeur and exclaimed: "I loves you Coney Island, but oh! you Grand Canyon."

Such comparisons were often contaminated by a national inferiority complex and by sectional pride. More than thirty Americans made comparisons with Europe, including Celeste Nellis-Ryns of Los Angeles, California: "There is nothing in all Europe to compare with this 'Titan of Chasms.' I am proud it is in America." HRL of St. Paul, Minnesota, was ready to die for the canyon: "When there is war, be patriotic and remember that the Grand Canyon is only one of the many things that we should fight for." Sometimes sectional pride was debatable, as when Alexander Warner of San Francisco said, "After seeing the Grand Canyon, see Yosemite. Grand Canyon is the tail to the kite. Yosemite beats it out of sight for sure." But another San Franciscan answered, "I am a loyal Californian, but I must in all justice, place Yosemite second to Grand Canyon." Sometimes sectional pride was silly boosterism about Indiana corn, New York products, or Texas size, but Fairfax Lee Carter of Virginia set off a nasty exchange when he declared, "The Grand Canyon is a keen disappointment. It does not compare with some of the sublime scenery of the Grand Old Blue Ridge. After all Virginia is the finest state in the union and produces the best ham." To which someone answered, "He is one of those damned old 'You Alls.'" To which "a little rebel from Georgia" answered, "The above lines were written by a negro loving blue bellied Yank." To which there were three more retorts. An Englishman got tired of American bombast and complained, "If the absolute silence so noticeable in the Grand Canyon had been preserved as regards the majority of these 'advertising personal impressions,' the book would be worth reading and the grandeur of the canyon not have been vulgarized."

Many people offered mainly adjectives, especially "Sublime," "Beautiful," and "Wonderful." Two people just made a line of exclamation marks. Dr. Boning of the University of Pennsylvania made a line of question marks. Several people imitated the fancies of Romantic poetry, seeing the canyon as the work of giants, elves, and fairies. Al Vaughn of Peoria, Illinois, saw: "A wonderful old fortress city, captured, and then deserted, ages and ages ago." W. H. P. MacDonald of San Francisco marveled at "What pranks the elfs have played among these dismal chasms. The awful silence makes the beating of the heart sound like the thumpings of a tortured monster, and ones breathing like the groans of the restless sea."

Dozens of people came up with original images and comments. Frederick Gunster of Birmingham, Alabama, saw "The setting of an opera, the music of which will never be written." Dr. Harry Watson of New York City preferred silence: "It is more expressive than words and more silent than the Sphinx."

Several people found themselves in dreamland, such as Helen Lincoln of Santa Barbara, California: "I feel like a child, who has had a wonderful dream and on awakening, found it true." A school teacher from Commerce, Texas, became a student: "I feel like a child grappling mentally with an arithmetic problem that is beyond him. It's too big for me—I can't grasp it in its entirety, but get only occasional glimpses of light." Charles May from Peoria, Illinois, claimed he had conducted a test of the canyon's size: "Yesterday...I accidentally dropped a new hat over the edge. I watched it fall for a few minutes, then went in and ate dinner, borrowed a telescope and went back and watched it fall all afternoon." Someone from Livingston, Montana, may have been waiting for dinner when he wrote: "The world's greatest commissary of food for the human mind." George Fredric Wheeler of "Everywhere" wrote, "My first impression was that all the vari-colored tents of the Arabs had been pitched here and the gray dust of ages had settled over all." A politically incorrect lady from Kansas City, Missouri, said, "It looks like Sambo had been here making funny noises with a pick and shovel." Otie Doak said, "It looks like the hole feels after your tooth has been pulled." Arthur Fisk of San Francisco said, "Looks almost as big to me as my first week's salary did." Several people from Missouri, the "Show-Me State," said that the canyon had "shown them." A man from Los Angeles admitted that the canyon was better than a movie theater. Florence Richardson of Brookline, Massachusetts, may have been admiring El Tovar's arts-and-crafts style when she wrote: "To my mind the Grand Canyon is an exhibition of the arts and crafts of Nature." The male guests often found more manly comparisons. H. M. Johnson of Boston saw "A royal flush, can't be beat." Two men projected a "sporty" golf course onto the canyon. A man from Paris imagined it filled with champagne; a man from near New Orleans imagined it as a container for a "New Orleans gin fizz"; and a man from Wisconsin said, "The Grand Canyon looks greater to me than 1,000 barrels of Munich beer in the middle of the Sahara Desert." But for Ben Benson of Kalamazoo, Michigan, the canyon was sobering: "After once the canyon's walls you see/ you will surely decide not to go on a spree." J. W. Brook preferred another poison: "I always thought Star Tobacco was the finest thing on earth, but this comes up to it." B. M. Terry of Coffeyville, Kansas, noted the canyon was "Some irrigation ditch." At least Paul Smith Livermore of Ithaca, New York, felt a twinge of poetry: "If the baby did not need shoes, and the Ithaca Gun Company my valuable presence, I would spend the rest of my days gazing at the most wonderful sight on Earth—the Grand Canyon." But for some, like Florence Tyler of Chicago, one visit was satisfying enough: "A wish of my life has been granted, to visit the Grand Canyon."

Nearly ten people wished that some famous artist, writer, or musician had seen the canyon. W. Miller said, "A great pity Dante did not see the Grand Canyon from the rim, or go down the trail to the Colorado River before having written the Inferno." Henry Doggett of Evanston, Indiana, said, "If Doré had visited this place before he painted his pictures of Dante's Inferno, he would have obtained many more impressions of sublimity than he did out of his own brain." Others who visitors thought should have seen the canyon included Jules Verne, Dickens, Poe, Coleridge, Schiller, Beethoven, and Raphael.

In the absence of Dante, over seventy-five people tried writing their own poems about the canyon. They range from sunset-purple prose to silly doggerel to the genuinely imaginative. H. P. tried his own Dante in "The Canyon So Grand":

> When Lucifer, god of the morning, fell
> From Heaven in fiery flame,
> Condemned forever to Hell,
> To hide forever his shame,
> Then interposed Mother Earth,
> Her broad loving bosom to save;
> She clasped him, not heeding the breath
> That seared, burning deep, till a grave
> Was made for the god on her breast;
> And where once was smiling green land,
> He laid himself down and found rest,
> Where now lies the Canyon so Grand.

With a bit less polish, M & J too saw the devil's mark:

> The canyon is a fearsome place, Is't not?
> Damned spot
> Devil's grot

Rimmed rock
Imps lot
And yet the fool contends the devils not.
What! No Devil? When the wind blows weird?
Nay but I saw him grin
When I looked in.

More people saw God in the canyon, including Leigh Hodges:

I stood upon the outer rim and said,
There are no words this majesty to laud,
And then some spirit brushed my soul, and led
My faltering tongue to lisp—"A Living God."

Also, E. R. Hyatt from Brooklyn, New York:

We did not need this lesson, Lord, to make us bend the knee,
For everything that moves and breathes proclaims thy majesty;
But here where in the ages past the Red Man owned thy sway,
We thank thee God! Our eyes have seen thy wondrous works this day.

But another Brooklyn poet wasn't so serious:

The Canyon simply baffles all description.
It's like a nightmare, which some old Egyptian
Of high degree, commanding countless folk
Compiled in this abyss, just for a joke.

Then there was:

There was a young lady named Hasdum
Went to view the big chasm,
She looked long at it,
Then fell in a fit,
And had spasm, pon' spasm, pon' spasm.

One person played it safe and simply quoted Shakespeare, and a man from Scotland quoted Homer—in Greek. But far more people gave up trying to describe the canyon. The largest single response in the *Impressions* logs, written by about 220 people, was to declare the canyon to be indescribable. Several people broke off in midsentence and made declarations like: "—oh hell, what's the use." Many people said, "You have to see it to believe it." Yet people did try to describe why the canyon was indescribable.

Samuel Steiner of Newark, New Jersey, said: "There is only one word which gives a description of the canyon and that word is 'indescribable.'" Gary Sparkes of Prescott, Arizona, said, "You never realize how incomplete Webster is until you visit the Grand Canyon." Several people proposed inventing new words to do justice to the canyon. Mrs. Henry Lustig of Kansas City, Missouri, proposed, "There should be more than one Grand in the name of the canyon." Alfred Bernheimer of New York City said, "The following lines by my pen describe the unrivaled grandeur of the canyon as adequately as any which I have read: [he leaves the line blank]." No sucker said, "No one but a Barnum's circus press agent would dare to try to describe the Canyon." After Dr. Gillard of Port Clinton, Ohio, wrote, "No words can describe the grandeur of the canyon, particularly when mounted on a donkey," M. W. Stanton of San Francisco critiqued his sentence structure: "Atlas carried the World on his shoulders, but behold! Ohio's poet mounts the Grand Canyon on a donkey." After D. J. K. McDonald of Prescott, Arizona, wrote, "The Grand Canyon, like the women and the soul of man, defy the brush and pen," a wag added, "Why, wouldn't she receive your letters?" Helen Lowenthall of New York City said: "It is an eternal model for the 'impressionist,' an everlasting despair for the 'expressionist.'" But J. A. Laird of New York City wasn't impressed: "There have been 57 varieties of language used to describe the Grand Canyon, but after all *it's* only a big hole."

The question of whether the Grand Canyon was just a big hole or a work of God engaged about 1 out of 6 writers, and 217 of them, or 78 percent, attributed the canyon to God, while 62 others attributed it to nature, although often a capitalized Nature, which in the Romantic mind could be a mask of God.

Many believers simply quoted Bible verses, such as "In the beginning God created…" or "Behold what God hath wrought." Others worked harder at canyon theology. C. W. Leffingwill of Knoxville, Illinois, said, "Looking into the

Grand Canyon is like facing eternity—and conversing with the infinite, 'Put off thy shoes from thy feet, for this is holy ground.'" H. G. James of Independence, Kansas, said, "When God looked out upon the earth and pronounced it good, methinks He stood in the Garden of Eden on the brim of the Grand Canyon, looking down into its marvelous depths and beauty." On the other hand, Joseph Rout of Kansas City, Missouri, wrote, "The Grand Canyon was once the city of Sodom; the Lord left it beautiful." Homer Humphrey of Boston preferred the Book of Revelation: "A fitting scene for a Last Judgment." LeRoy Anderson of Prescott, Arizona, was typical of many in saying, "This is the one thing in nature that *compels* man to know that there is a God." William Hall Moreland of Sacramento, California, said, "The Grand Canyon ranks next to the Incarnation itself as a revelation of God. It is a sacrament of the Divine wisdom and glory." For Sophia Wolf, "The Grand Canyon is God's seal of approval on a beautiful world." R. C. Graves of Oklahoma City saw it as "God's autograph on nature's page." For Elizabeth Moore of Topeka, Kansas, it was "God's own cathedral." Another person from Topeka declared, "If heaven is like the Grand Canyon, I want to go there." Ed Robinson of Mansfield, Ohio, wrote, "To the omnipotent mind—of which the universe is but a thought—All Hail!" A few people tried to draw moral lessons, including George Robertson from California: "Here we learn God was never in a hurry." And H. C. Bradley of Waterbury, Connecticut, advised, "Yield not to temptation—a man can sink to greater depths in the Grand Canyon than any other place I know of."

There were some friendly doubters, such as E. Weber from California: "It seems to impress the majority as resembling either heaven or—the other place. Seems to me it's a bit desolate for the first, and as for the second—I've never heard that it snowed in Hades." And leave it to children to question the emperor's new theology. Dorothy Wilson, age five, asked, "What did God dig such a big hole for?" And Emerson Miller, age four, from Needles, California, asked, "Why did the dear lord make it so big?"

A child from New York City offered the simplest statement of the alternative to canyon theology: "It certainly is a swell bunch of rocks." More sophisticated attributions to nature include one from J. M. Jamison of Phoenix, Arizona: "The monument to the remains of the greatest of titanic struggles between nature's forces." Carl Bruce of Chicago saw "A large impression in this earth of indefinable forces of centuries ago." A New Yorker saw the canyon as "Nature's greatest battlefield!" W. S. Lowell of Honolulu, perhaps considering Hawaiian volcanoes to be greater battlefields, said, "Tis but a wrinkle on the cheek of our aged Mother Earth." But a Californian saw "A bleeding wound on the bosom of Mother Nature." Many people saw natural forces as titanic and violent; fewer offered pretty images, such as that of Robert Burns of Cambridge, Massachusetts: "Nature, all dressed up in her Sunday gown." Mrs. Bessie Knox of Clinton, Iowa, saw nature violated: "Some titanic surgeon of prehistoric times cut deep into the bowels of old mother earth (looking for her appendix?). Frightened at the bleeding wound he left his work incomplete. The blood still flows (in the Colorado River) and that is the reason why the wound never healed."

Clearly, people were struggling with the mismatch between the Grand Canyon and their expectations about natural beauty, expectations defined by a century of Romanticism. For the European romantics natural beauty was often pastoral, a rolling green countryside with blue streams and lakes, Edenic flowers and trees, grazing sheep, and perhaps a few broken Greek columns. At the extreme, natural beauty was the Sublime, an alpine chasm so huge and inhuman it would force humans to feel their smallness before nature. Yet even the Sublime usually held water, trees, familiar rocks with familiar colors, and perhaps familiar—if pagan—gods. Now visitors were discovering that the Grand Canyon was more extreme than the Sublime. It was a wasteland of dryness and decay, full of rocks with weird shapes and weird colors, hostile plants and poisonous reptiles, and tribes with weird religions. Even the painter Thomas Moran had felt obligated to fake his Grand Canyon scenes to make them conform to public expectations about natural beauty.

Some visitors seemed most bothered by the absence of life inside the canyon. Marguerite Baumann of New Jersey declared, "A vulgar display of rock!" And EWF of Rockford, Illinois, wrote: "Lifeless, supporting no life in its terrifying depths, the Grand Canyon repels me beyond expression. I can see nothing but its desolation and waste." Hildah Devlin found it "The most terrible thing nature ever did. It hurts one to look." George Baird of Chicago couldn't quite decide: "A monstrous freak of Nature. Awful! Stupendous! Grand! Indescribable!" C. Schoen of Milwaukee, Wisconsin, found that the canyon explained "why the Indians formed such a weird and superstitious religion." Sherwood Chapman struggled to find the Christian God in the wasteland:

> The Grand Canyon seems to represent God's own monument to the battles and conflicts through which this world has gone—a region magnificent in its dignity; certainly not to be gushed over or called beautiful! It has all left too great an impression of majesty and awesomeness upon me for me to view it in any spirit of "scenery." It is dead—nothing could be more lifeless—and being so completely estranged from the living world, makes one think—and try to discern a hidden Voice.

The distance between the Grand Canyon and the Garden of Eden encouraged freethinkers to dismiss the many testimonials to God, as did Carla: "This natural phenomenon is certainly far greater than our wildest imaginings regarding the works of any divinity." And E. H. de Smet, Veteran of the 9th Minnesota Volunteer Infantry: "We do not think a god had anything to do with it." After Pat Marion McCarthy of Boston wrote, "A Masterpiece by the Great Architect of the Universe," the next entry—on the same date—was from Louis McCarthy of Boston: "A Grand, Awful, and Peculiar Masterpiece of Nature's two most powerful elements, Fire and Water." Someone who signed as "Non-Sentimental" wrote, "Truly wonderful, but only a ditch on a large scale. Water, earth, rock and time are the forces at work, and that have always worked. It is foolish to talk as if it is a work of God, Infinite, etc." Several people wrote retorts to this, one calling the author an "idiot."After Benjamin Franklin Marx of New York City exclaimed, "Throne of the Infinite!" someone retorted, "Would you put Him in a hole?" Someone who signed as "Scientific" wrote, "It is foolish for as wonderful things as man finding God in a big ditch. Let him consider himself. Don't be superstitious." After Mr. and Mrs. W. W. Wescott wrote, "A greater sermon than was ever preached by man," someone scribbled, "Oh, bunk!" Some Christian testimonials included arguments like that of C. J. Jones: "Some say the canyon was made entirely by erosion. Nonsense. It is the moulds in which God made the mountains." Yet Thomas Hogan of Boston found God in erosion: "Carved from the most stubborn substances by the most yielding and facile of elements, it is God's greatest lesson teaching us the potentiality of existence." Someone who signed as

"Aint it the Truth" said, "The lad who was talking the most about this 'wonderful work of the Almighty' on the way down the trail was swearing the loudest at the mule on the way up."

One thing that Christians and atheists agreed upon was that the canyon inspired humility. Nearly forty people offered expressions of humility. K. P. Hooper said, "I have been in many places but until *ascending* Bright Angel's trail I have never before fully realized the infinitude of nature and the helplessness of man." E. Mayer wrote, "Here one feels as if a voice had said 'Stand back, you are nothing.'" Ed Wolff of San Antonio, Texas, described the canyon as "the muffler of infinity on the vocal exhaust of human presumption." To which someone added: "Toot! Toot!" For Ida Smutter of Buffalo, New York, "This is the veil through which I cannot see. There is much of the Grand Canyon and little of me."

Humility was not always so obvious when it came to American attitudes about land use. It was still the age of Manifest Destiny, the tail end of the Gilded Age. One person scoffed, "Why all this bosh about the canyon. It is crude, massive, and unnecessary. A drainer of the life giving waters for all vegetation and an impediment to travel. The present age would appreciate something one quarter as large." Several people reacted against this, one of them saying, "I'll bet this sucker loves money." A man from Greeley, Colorado, loved how canyon acreage "could be watered by the Colorado River and made good irrigated potatoland. At $50 per acre this would be $80,000,000 per year from potatoes—not to say what sugar beets would do. El Tovar may have 50 guests paying per day at $3 each—profit of $150 per day—$4,000 per month—$50,000 per year—Just compare with the potato crop!" Mr. Old from Galway, Ireland, said, "The canyon would be a good place to dig for building material." Leon Jewett from Los Angeles saw "A splendid place for a bill board." W. C. Harrison from Painesville, Ohio, said, "Uncle Sam owes to its citizens a railroad on the edge of its rim," but someone answered, "*NEVER.*" The visionary J. R. Haskin of Los Angeles knew that the future lay not in railroads but in flight: "Come back in 1920…and you will go down in an air ship." For Anna Kaufmann of San Antonio, Texas, the canyon proved "the power of man. Man has conquered this Grand Canyon, by scaling its walls and exploring its bottom." Herman Gillette of Dighton, Kansas, was already counting the profits: "We need something like the Grand Canyon to draw people to Kansas."

But others were worried about Americans' fondness for money. F. W. from Los Angeles said, "The Grand Canyon is all right but don't let the Los Angeles boomers know it, or you will lose it." J. D. Eastin of Emporia, Kansas, said, "The wonder is that some man from Los Angeles don't buy it and subdivide it." They weren't entirely joking about Los Angeles attitudes; one man from Los Angeles wrote, "Grand Canyon does not express it. Wonderful. Glorious. But why in this far away country—it should have been near Los Angeles." A. W. Daniels from Boston said, "Perfectly wonderful! Hope nobody removes it before I can come again." This was, after all, the age of the Panama Canal, of moving mountains for human progress and national glory. Jerome Twitchell of Kansas City, Missouri, said, "Should have moved this down to Panama." Yet for more people, like F. Graham of Philadelphia, the Panama Canal was a lesson in humility: "The Grand Canyon makes the Panama Canal, the greatest work man ever accomplished, seem like a child's plaything." M. D. Austin of Chicago said, "No *graft* in the digging of a bigger ditch than Panama." Nature was also superior in the arts, according to W. E. Cleary of Brooklyn, New York: "The Grand Canyon is a great illustration of the superiority of natural grandeur and beauty over the artificial. Majestic nature disappearing into insignificance the noblest artistic artificial productions of man." Yet, surprisingly, not one person ever mentioned the need to protect the Grand Canyon as a national park or monument. Perhaps the *Impressions* book for 1908 included some discussion of Teddy Roosevelt making the canyon a national monument that year, but that volume has been lost. At the least, a number of people advocated that the canyon should be considered one of the Seven Wonders of the World.

There was also a discussion about El Tovar and the Fred Harvey Company that ran it, with most people pleased with them. But Mrs. G. R. Brubaker of Los Angeles complained:

> *The El Tovar may be a "holdup"*
> *The "Hopi House" a bluff,*
> *But of this grand old canyon,*
> *I can never get enough.*

Another lively topic of discussion was the adventures and misadventures people had on the Bright Angel Trail. B. E. Dutton said, "The trip down to the river is best of all and after seeing the Corkscrew one might imagine that they had seen the Bottle too." Harry Zellinger of Philadelphia said, "The modern 'Cliff Dweller' who spends his days in a tall office building and his nights in an equally tall apartment house will find the journey down the trail to the pre-historic dwellings of his ancestors a stimulant to his jaded imagination and a constant succession of emotions and thrills." As ever, three guys bragged about their fast time hiking to the bottom and back up. But S. J. Carter of Houston, Texas, admitted, "I came, I saw, I was conquered and fatigued by the trail to the Colorado River." J. K. Turner of Cleveland, Ohio, moaned, "The first hour I was afraid the mule would slip & fall down the precipice—the last hour I wished he would." J. Weaver of Milwaukee, Wisconsin, offered, "Advice: Get a short mule. Every turn & Molly turned either her head or tail hanging over. Not for the faint hearted." A Texas family ran into a landslide and proclaimed, "It was the devil's trail instead." Maurice Caton of Chicago said, "Not for a $1,000 would I miss 'Bright Angel' to the river and not for another $1,000 would I repeat it."

As the years went by, people mentioned that they were making their second or third visit. This included Andrew Carnegie, who said, "Farewell, there is no farewell to scenes like these." A few other famous names appear in the logs. John Jacob Astor wrote, "It's a cute little ditch." At least, someone wrote this—a few months after Astor drowned on the *Titanic*. Also of dubious authenticity, but summing up both the Grand Canyon experience and the humor of El Tovar guests, was a comment from Helen Keller: "It's the best place I've ever seen."

"THESE INFINITIES OF BEAUTY AND TERROR"

Poets and Writers Discover the Grand Canyon

Even today, every person who comes to the Grand Canyon discovers it anew. Every visitor sees the canyon with their own personalities, perceptions, and beliefs. Many visitors come thinking they already know the canyon, having seen it in a lifetime of photographs, only to be shocked by its real scale and shapes and colors.

For the visitors who stepped off the first Atchison, Topeka, and Santa Fe Railway trains at the Grand Canyon in 1901, there was much more room for surprise. Photography had not yet become a ubiquitous part of the media; books, magazines, newspapers, and advertising posters still relied on illustrators. The canyon photographs that tourists had seen were black-and-white and of limited quality. The Santa Fe Railway placed its promotional trust in artists, especially Thomas Moran, but Moran's romanticized depictions of the canyon were misleading, leaving out its true colors and geological strata. The El Tovar Hotel guest logs show average visitors struggling conscientiously to recognize the canyon, compare it with their expectations about natural beauty, and grasp its meanings. For intellectuals visiting the canyon, this struggle was often quite a bit more serious, and it gave rise to much more elaborate writings.

Among the early visitors to the Grand Canyon were some of America's leading poets, novelists, and nature writers. They too were surprised by the canyon, often quite emotionally. They saw it with naked minds, without the templates provided by previous authors. They had to figure out the canyon for themselves. Coming from different backgrounds as people and as authors, they saw the canyon in different ways, yet most of them saw it as a realm of ultimates, of the deepest workings of nature or of God. They felt that the Grand Canyon was challenging them to rise above the usual concerns of personal life or American history. It was asking them canyon-deep questions and offering them deep meanings for human life. Not all of their musings were brilliant or artistically successful, but the canyon did succeed at stirring some serious men and women into serious thought and telling imagery.

While this chapter is about the career poets and writers who explored the Grand Canyon in the first quarter of the twentieth century, any discussion of Grand Canyon poetry should acknowledge John Wesley Powell and Clarence Dutton. Powell was the canyon's first river explorer, in 1869, and Dutton was the first geologist to extensively study the Grand Canyon region, in the 1870s. Powell and Dutton were the canyon's first explorers not just physically but poetically, helping to define how we should see this strange new landscape. Powell and Dutton had absorbed much of nineteenth-century literary culture, and they did quite well at employing the best of its poetic traditions in their books. Because both men saw the land with geological eyes, and because their encounters with that land had included life-and-death hardships, they did not take seriously the worst of Romanticism's poetic traditions, which saw landscapes as nothing but imaginary realms such as fairy gardens and giants' castles.

Dutton shared his perceptions not just in eloquent books but in evocative place-names. As the American people settled a vast continent, they needed to come up with many thousands of names for landscape features and towns. In contrast with Native Americans, whose landscape names held deep familiarity and spiritual meanings, American names were often superficial, honoring the first pioneer to get there or to die there, or a politician or railroad president who'd never get there. Powell's landscape names came mainly from this pioneer tradition, honoring his crewmates, his wife, his political patrons, and expedition mishaps, with other names being more descriptive, such as Vermilion Cliffs. Dutton, however, felt that the Grand Canyon held such deep grandeur that only religious names could do it justice, and he started the tradition of naming canyon features for religious shrines, such as Brahma Temple. Dutton was influenced by the long Romantic tradition of seeing in nature spiritual purposes, mythological images, and architectural shapes.

Three types of writers came to the Grand Canyon: poets, nature writers, and novelists, and each group had a distinct experience of the canyon.

The first well-known writer to visit the Grand Canyon was novelist Charles Dudley Warner in 1891. Yet novelists, who deal in human dramas rather than in landscapes, were the writers least drawn to the canyon, and those who did come had the least to say about it.

The poets who encountered the Grand Canyon—including three Pulitzer Prize winners—were by far the most philosophically ambitious about it. They saw the canyon as a great puzzle about the ultimate nature of reality, demanding an answer. They often saw the canyon as a symbol of the whole cosmos. But was the cosmos a place of order or chaos? Was the canyon evidence for God or for ancient and massive natural forces? Did the canyon point toward immortality or decay? If nature was the power behind the canyon, what was the reality of nature? Was it generous or malevolent? For many Grand Canyon poets, these questions weren't abstractions, but powerful personal questions that drove their lives and poetic work. These questions were especially alive in the early years of the twentieth century, when science was dramatically changing the universe and challenging familiar religious frameworks. In 1901 one future Grand Canyon poet, Edgar Lee Masters, was the law partner of Clarence Darrow, who in the Scopes trial would plead the case of evolution. But for human society, hopes for evolution led not to progress or utopia but to the mad, mechanized slaughter of World War I, a deep shock to the basic optimism of Western culture.

The nature writers—John Muir, John Burroughs, John C. Van Dyke, and Mary Austin—had much more confidence in nature as an ultimate and benevolent reality. They were willing to see spiritual realities behind nature, but they didn't worry about it nearly as much as the poets did. They were mainly interested in figuring out how the Grand Canyon fit into nature's order; how time, geological forces, and erosion worked and looked; how a desert landscape could still be beautiful; and how the canyon compared with other natural wonders, like Yosemite.

As different as these writers were, they shared some common reactions to the canyon, especially a strong sense of surprise and puzzlement. For one writer the surprise and puzzlement might be metaphysical; for another, geological; for another, aesthetic. Some writers reveled in the shock of something very new to them and to human culture.

But many writers felt frightened by the canyon. They shrank back as if it were going to swallow them, or as if they feared they might throw themselves into it. John C. Van Dyke devoted much of the first chapter of his book *The Grand Canyon of the Colorado* to this suicidal impulse:

> ...the rock platforms down below seem to heave, the buttes sway; even the opposite Rim of the Canyon undulates slightly. The depth yawns to engulf you. Instinctively you shrink back. If it were not for the presence of companions you might cry out.
>
> Ah! the terror of it!
>
> And, worse than that, the mad attraction of it, the dread temptation that lies within it! The chasm repels and yet draws. What does it mean? Why before this most prodigious beauty of the world does one feel tempted to leap over the edge?[1]

Van Dyke claimed that "almost everyone at the Canyon for the first time knows this impulse."[2] This might be an exaggeration, but Van Dyke had a personal interest in this impulse: a dozen years previously, his cousin, Henry Van Dyke, a popular and confidently Christian poet, had published the book *The Grand Canyon and Other Poems,* in which he confessed that the canyon had brought on a sudden existential vertigo. John C. Van Dyke suggested that such a fear was actually a fear of our own darkest impulses. Probably, it also came from tiny human identities suddenly being invaded or overwhelmed by a vast, inhuman, lifeless, mysterious reality. This reaction is much less common in writers today, and would probably be dismissed as personal pathology. But the frequency of this reaction a century ago suggests it was a cultural phenomenon, or rather a lack of cultural preparation for meeting and perceiving a new, strange, powerful reality. Today's visitors have been trained to expect something beautiful, and nature writers have been trained to see nature not as any threat to human identity but as an innocent victim of human threats.

Almost no writer expressed conservationist concerns for the canyon. John Muir admitted that he'd had misgivings about the railroad reaching the rim, but when he finally rode the train there, he declared, "In the presence of such stupendous scenery they are nothing. The locomotives and trains are mere beetles and caterpillars, and the noise they make is as little disturbance as the hooting of an owl in the lonely woods."[3]

In the years the Grand Canyon was being discovered, Romanticism was still a dominant cultural force, and most writers saw the canyon through its eyes. Romanticism placed a strong emphasis on nature and saw it as a realm more perfect than the human realm, and often as a spiritual realm. On its more serious side, Romanticism saw nature as a gospel written in stone and forests, or as embodied spirit. On an aesthetic level, Romanticism saw nature as the source of ultimate beauty, maybe metaphysical beauty. On its more superficial level, Romanticism saw nature as the enchanted playground of non-Christian spirits, of giants, elves, fairies, and Greek gods; mountains were their castles, forests their gardens. Such enchantments had become such a strong literary convention that few Grand Canyon authors avoided it. Some noted that they had read Clarence Dutton, so perhaps they were following Dutton's lead in mixing architectural and mythological images in the canyon. Or perhaps the Romantic temptation to see castles was a function of the human brain trying to find familiar patterns in a new and confusing environment.

There were two writers who objected to filling the Grand Canyon with Romantic castles, and they were the two writers who best knew southwestern landscapes. After years of living and traveling in the Mojave Desert, John C. Van Dyke published *The Desert* in 1901, and Mary Austin published *The Land of Little Rain* in 1903. Both authors challenged Americans to see and appreciate the desert on its own terms; to stop seeing it through the eyes of the English Romantics; to stop seeing it and calling it ugly for what it lacked; to start seeing that naked rock had its own identity and beauty. Twenty years later Van Dyke and Austin wrote about the Grand Canyon. Austin complained about some of the fanciful names and warned visitors to "be careful whom you ask to point the place out to you, lest you be answered by one of the silly names cut out of a mythological dictionary and shaken in a hat before they were applied to the Grand Cañon for the benefit of that amazing number of Americans who can never see anything unless it is supposed to look like something else."[4] Van Dyke felt that the Grand Canyon had been insulted: "...the parlor-car poet was abroad in the land and in consequence the mock-heroic and the absurd have been put upon the map. A series of numbers would have been less agonizing and quite as poetic."[5] Austin and Van Dyke agreed that Native American names would have been more appropriate.

Yet even as many poets saw castles in the canyon, most of them were struggling, sometimes painfully, with the transition between Romanticism and modernism, not just in literary style, but philosophically. The powerful cultural tradition that saw nature as a realm of perfection, beauty, and spirit was being challenged by the hard-to-evade power of science, which saw a universe of vast spaces and strange forces, with large roles for chance and chaos.

Novelist Charles Dudley Warner is best remembered today as the coauthor, with Mark Twain, of *The Gilded Age,* Twain's first novel, which gave the name to the post–Civil War era of expansion, opulence, greed, and corruption. Americans still had no doubt that the frontier was endless, that they would conquer it, and that it would make them rich. A typical episode in the novel involves a company formed to straighten and dredge a river and build a canal, but the company pays out so many bribes to congressmen that it goes broke. When Warner saw the Grand Canyon, he found a realm beyond river-straightening conquest, and far beyond the New England scenery where he lived. If Mark Twain, who was one of a small group of Americans who had roamed the desert Southwest, had told Warner how different it was from normal ideas of beauty, Warner was still shocked by the canyon. His surprise and puzzlement were typical of many early canyon visitors:

> Our party were straggling up the hill: two or three had reached the edge. I looked up. The duchess threw up her arms and screamed. We were not fifteen paces behind, but we saw nothing. We took the few steps, and the whole magnificence broke upon us. No one could be prepared for it. The scene is one to strike dumb with awe, or to unstring the nerves; one might stand in silent astonishment, another would burst into tears.
>
> There are some experiences that cannot be repeated—one's first view of Rome, one's first view of Jerusalem. But these emotions are produced by association, by the sudden standing face to face with the scenes most

wrought into our whole life and education by tradition and religion. This was without association, as it was without parallel. It was a shock so novel that the mind, dazed, quite failed to comprehend it....

Wandering a little away from the group and out of sight, and turning suddenly to the scene from another point of view, I experienced for a moment an indescribable terror of nature, a confusion of mind, a fear to be alone in such a presence. With all this grotesqueness and majesty of form and radiance of color, creation seemed in a whirl. With our education in scenery of a totally different kind, I suppose it would need long acquaintance with this to familiarize one with it to the extent of perfect mental comprehension.[6]

Warner was familiar with the writings of Clarence Dutton, who "tried by the use of Oriental nomenclature to bring it within our comprehension." Warner, too, tried to tame the canyon by finding human architectural shapes in it, seeing temples, castles, pagodas, and train wrecks: "There is no end to such devices." But the canyon "was a city of no man's creation nor of any man's conception." In the end he conceded that the canyon was the realm of inhuman geological forces, of "immense antiquity, hardly anywhere else on earth so overwhelming as here. It has been here in all its lonely grandeur and transcendent beauty, exactly as it is, for what to us is an eternity, unknown, unseen by human eye."[7]

In 1902 Hamlin Garland, who had become famous for the prairie stories of *Main Traveled Roads,* traveled to the bottom of the Grand Canyon and witnessed a sunset and moonrise there. He was a friend of John Wesley Powell and had written a poem, "The Stricken Pioneer," inspired by Powell and the American pioneer experience. Yet as a writer, Garland was out of his depths at the Grand Canyon, lacking Powell's honest rapport with the landscape. He described the sound of the nighttime Colorado River as "like some imperious nocturnal animal—a dragon with a lion's throat." As the moon rose, Garland turned it into a fake melodrama: "For an instant my blood thickened with fear. Was it some ghost of the river's dark caverns?"[8]

Willa Cather was another writer who knew the Southwest well, featured it in several novels, and gave good descriptions of Mesa Verde and Walnut Canyon. Yet when it came to the Grand Canyon, she seemed to admit defeat.

In *The Song of the Lark,* published in 1915, Cather described the notebook of someone who had attempted to describe the Grand Canyon: "The pages of that book were like a battlefield; the laboring author had fallen back from metaphor to metaphor, abandoning position after position. He would have admitted that the art of forging metals was nothing to this treacherous business of recording impressions, in which the material you were so full of vanished mysteriously under your striving hand."[9]

Zane Grey and Owen Wister, who created the genre of the western novel in the same years that tourists were first seeing the Grand Canyon, gave Americans a strong reinforcement of their tendency to see western landscapes as a mere theater of the national story, of the heroic conquest of wilderness and Indians, and the discovery of gold and other sources of wealth. Still, both writers occasionally saw that western landscapes might offer something more. In Wister's introduction to Ellsworth Kolb's 1914 book about he and his brother's Colorado River trip, Wister concluded: "This canyon seems like an avenue conducting to the secret of the universe and the presence of the gods."[10] Then again, the fact that the Kolbs were more interested in adventure and film-making than in finding "the gods" may point out the dangers of Romantic rhetoric.

The first important poet to see the Grand Canyon was Harriet Monroe in 1899. Actually, Monroe was less important for her own poetry, which was rather conventional, than for founding *Poetry* magazine in Chicago in 1912. Through *Poetry*, she became the midwife of modern poetry, the mentor of Yeats, Eliot, Pound, Stevens, and many others who transformed the genre. Monroe and *Poetry* broke the long dominance of Victorian poetry, which consisted of well-ordered rhymes, logical arguments, moral instruction, charming images, and noble but exaggerated sentimentality. Today literary historians regard the decades between the publication of Whitman's *Leaves of Grass* (1855) and 1912 as a stagnant era in American poetry, leaving little of lasting value. American poets were writing as if Whitman had never lived; they venerated New England aristocrats like Longfellow, who sought their inspirations in Europe, not in American nature. *Poetry* magazine opened a flood of new styles, free verse, serious subject matters, and a poetry not of didacticism but of images and symbols. Monroe's circle of poets knew that she loved the Grand Canyon, and this encouraged several of them to send her poems about it, poems that bore all the marks of modernist experiments in style.

Harriet Monroe. *(Special Collections Research Center, University of Chicago Library)*

It was only by accident that Monroe discovered the Grand Canyon. She was raised in a prominent family in Chicago and was taught all the conventions of European culture. She won local fame for writing the official ode for Chicago's 1893 world's fair, the Columbian Exposition. In the custom of the time for affluent young Americans, she spent a year and a half on a grand tour of Europe. On returning home, she came down with severe pneumonia, which refused to fade in a Chicago winter, so her parents sent her off to Phoenix, Arizona. She recalled, "[My] illness gave me the West—a gift of incalculable value."[11]

From her convalescent chair Monroe spent hours every day watching the desert mountains changing colors. As she recovered, she started going on long horseback rides into the desert. Like Mary Austin and John C. Van Dyke, Monroe adjusted her definitions of natural beauty:

> The desert, lying silver in the sunlight, had a weird and hoary beauty of its own, very unlike the beauty of green fields and thick forests but quite as potent. It seemed the most ancient thing on earth. It suggested

immensities of time. One measured it not by years but by geological ages.... At first [the saguaro cacti] seemed monstrous, foolish...as if a tombstone should flower. But gradually I felt convinced of entering another world, accepting unfamiliar laws. Here were not companionable trees and shrubs, but the afterglow of an ancient earth.... Humanity had no rights in this enormous desolation; I intruded upon its profound mysterious beauty.[12]

Monroe now looked back on European culture, where she'd seen scholars "devoting their lives to the analysis of Giorgione's color and Donatello's silver line," as terribly superficial compared with the colors and lines of the Arizona desert, where "Nature is not conciliatory and charming: she is terrible and magnificent...upon whose fundamental immensity and antiquity our boasted civilization blooms like the flower of a day."[13] It was this sense of trespassing upon a vast, ancient, inhuman nature that defined Monroe's experience of the Grand Canyon.

Monroe nearly left Arizona without seeing the canyon, but at the last minute she received a $30 check from a publisher, and this afforded her a stagecoach trip to Grandview. She wrote three descriptions of her Grand Canyon experience, the first published in the *Atlantic Monthly* in 1899 and the second two in her autobiography four decades later. The contrast between the 1899 account and those in her autobiography reflects the changes of literary style that Monroe helped instigate in the world of poetry. The 1899 account is full of Romantic rhetoric and imagery, and spiritual messages:

Prophets and poets had wandered here before they were born to tell their mighty tales—Isaiah and Aeschylus and Dante, the giants who dared the utmost. Here at last the souls of great architects must find their dreams fulfilled; must recognize the primal inspiration which, after long ages, had achieved Assyrian palaces, the temples and pyramids of Egypt, the fortresses and towered cathedrals of mediaeval Europe. For the inscrutable Prince of builders had reared these imperishable monuments....[14]

In Monroe's autobiography, such Romantic habits have largely disappeared. But she insists that the main experience she described in 1899 wasn't rhetorical but powerfully real and life-changing. With her new but still unsteady desert-trained eyes, Monroe was deeply shocked by the Grand Canyon's vast inhuman spaces: "I leaped to an emotion too big for me, a blinding flash of beauty and terror, a lift to the sublime."[15] She felt like an intruder in a realm where human life wasn't even allowed. In her 1899 article she wrote:

> Everywhere the proof of my unfitness abased and dazed my will.... The strain of existence became too tense against these infinities of beauty and terror. My narrow ledge of rock was a prison. I fought against the desperate temptation to fling myself down into that soft abyss, and thus redeem the affront which the eager beating of my heart offered to its inviolable solitude. Death itself would not be too rash an apology for my invasion—death in those happy spaces, pillowed on purple immensities of air. So keen was this impulse, so slight at that moment became the fleshy tie, that I might almost have yielded but for a sudden word in my ear—the trill of an oriole from the pine close above me. The brave little song was a message personal and intimate, a miracle of sympathy or prophecy. And I cast myself on that tiny speck of life as on the heart of a friend—a friend who would save me from intolerable loneliness, from utter extinction and despair. He seemed to welcome me to the infinite.... I made him the confidant of my unworthiness; asked him for the secret, since, being winged, he was at home even here. He gave me healing and solace; restored me to the gentle amenities of our little world; enabled me to retreat through the woods, as I had come, instead of taking the swift road to liberty.[16]

In spite of this moment of existential dread, or perhaps because of it, Monroe became devoted to the Grand Canyon. In her autobiography she wrote:

> From that first look to the latest of many visits the Canyon has been my house of dreams. I have lived there for weeks at a time, quietly and intimately, with episodes of more adventurous exploration. I have camped on the mesa halfway down and waked to a mountain lion's roar.... Above all, one of my visits was during a rare season of heavy rains; and I stood, by good luck, at one of the great viewpoints while a thunderstorm trailed its grey robes up and down the vast abyss.... For two hours

I watched the great drama—the most sublime spectacle I ever expect to see.[17]

This sublimity didn't require any Greek gods or alpine castles, only the reality of nature. Monroe wrote two poems about the Grand Canyon, but neither is nearly as interesting as her personal accounts.

In her praise of the Grand Canyon, Monroe was comparing it with the greatest landscapes of the American West, for she traveled, hiked, and camped widely. Her experience of hiking the Hetch Hetchy Valley with the Sierra Club led John Muir to recruit her to testify before Congress on behalf of saving it from being turned into a reservoir (an effort that failed).

Monroe's journeys to the West and the Grand Canyon were made easier by the Chicago-based Santa Fe Railway, which built the tourist facilities on the South Rim and often gave Monroe free railway passes. The Santa Fe Railway also became a financial patron of *Poetry* magazine, and it included Monroe's 1899 article in its 1902 book *Grand Canyon of Arizona*. The railway didn't seem worried by Monroe's suggestion that the canyon could prompt suicidal impulses.

Illinois was also the home base of John Wesley Powell, whom Monroe acknowledged in her 1899 article. Two of Monroe's star poets, Carl Sandburg and Edgar Lee Masters, were Illinois boys with a keen interest in American history. Both of them wrote Grand Canyon poems, and Sandburg acknowledged the Illinois connection: "then came Powell, Hance, the Santa Fe, the boys shooting the rapids, and Fred Harvey with El Tovar."[18]

In preparing to launch *Poetry* magazine, Monroe spent months reading the works of contemporary American and British poets, and she made a list of modernist-inclined poets she would invite to submit work to *Poetry*. One of those on her list was George Sterling, who was among the best-known American poets of the time. Sterling probably knew of Monroe's enthusiasm for the Grand Canyon, for one of the poems he submitted was "At the Grand Canyon," which was published in the third issue of *Poetry*.

Sterling was both a forerunner and a victim of the modernist revolution in poetry. When in 1903 he published his first book, *The Testimony of the Suns*, he was hailed as an avant-garde poet who was shedding Victorian sentimentality for realism; he was a bohemian rebelling against conventionality; he was exploring the new realities revealed by science. Yet in style, his poetry remained stuck in the nineteenth century. Only three years after publishing his Grand Canyon poem, Harriet Monroe wrote a review of Sterling's body of work, dismissing him as an anachronism, full of "shameless rhetoric," "the worst excesses of the Tennysonian tradition," and "the frippery of a bygone fashion."[19] Sterling knew he was being left behind. After his Grand Canyon poem and two others were printed beside the cutting-edge poems in *Poetry*, Sterling wrote to Monroe: "When I saw them next to Yeats I regretted more than ever that they were not my best work...."[20]

Sterling was the founder and hub of the Carmel, California, arts colony. He moved there in 1905, seeing it as his own Walden Pond, a place for simple living and natural beauty. When the earthquake of 1906 rendered most of San Francisco's bohemian community homeless, many writers and artists headed for Carmel. Sterling became close friends with Ambrose Bierce and Jack London, who shared his naturalistic and often dark world view, and London turned Sterling into a character in his novel *Martin Eden*—prophetically, one who commits suicide. Sterling was obsessed with the idea of suicide, and in 1926 he finally killed himself with cyanide.

His friend Upton Sinclair declared that Sterling had been killed by "the nebular hypothesis," which referred to the landscape of Sterling's *The Testimony of the Suns*. As astronomers in the 1880s and 1890s revealed an ever larger, older, and stranger universe, Sterling was both enthralled and appalled. The universe was full of stars that had their own lifecycle, far beyond the scale of human lives. Stars were born out of nebulae, lived many millions of years, and then collapsed or blew up and unraveled back into nebulae. Sterling pictured the universe as a "war" of stars, stars colliding in a Darwinian jungle of stars. Amid such massive destruction, human hopes for a universe of love and immortality were pathetic vanities. And yet, out of dead-star nebulae new suns and new planets and new life would arise.

When George Sterling looked into the Grand Canyon, he saw it with the same eyes with which he saw the testimony of the suns. He saw massive, ancient, violent forces, amid which human lives were negligible. Sterling's poem "At the Grand Canyon" contains the traditional Romantic fancy of seeing a landscape as the home of gods, but for Sterling these gods were not noble Greeks or charming giants or fairies, but warring gods, geo-Darwinian gods. In his astronomical poetry Sterling often offered a bleak, nihilistic vision, only to end on a softer, more upbeat note. Perhaps he was trying to placate readers who weren't ready to follow him into despair. In his Grand Canyon poem, too, Sterling ends by turning a bleak universe into a good excuse for human pleasures:

> It seems as though a deep-hued sunset falls
> Forever on these Cyclopean walls,
> These battlements where Titan hosts have warred,
> And hewn the world with devastating sword,
> And shook with trumpets the eternal halls
> Where Seraphim lay hid by bloody palls
> And only Hell and Silence were adored.
> Lo! the abyss wherein the wings of Death
> Might beat unchallenged, and his fatal breath
> Fume up in pestilence. Beneath the sky
> Is no such testimony unto grief.
> Here Terror walks with Beauty ere she die.
> Oh! hasten to me, Love, for life is brief![21]

The same issue of *Poetry* that included Sterling's Grand Canyon poem also introduced a twenty-seven-year-old poet, John Gould Fletcher, who would win the Pulitzer Prize for poetry a quarter of a century later. Fletcher's first inspiration as a poet came from the landscapes of the Southwest. While a literature student at Harvard, he took a train trip from his home in Arkansas to southern California, and he was enthralled by the desert. He wrote in his journal, "A huge splintered mass of rocks stands on an endless plain...some vast nightmare of a castle (a good idea for a poem.)"[22] Two years later, hoping to reconnect with his southwestern muse, he joined a Harvard archaeological expedition to Colorado, where he saw how "Once the great ocean rolled over/ these mesas."[23]

Fletcher moved to Europe, thinking it was the only place for a serious poet to be, and his first collection of poems, *The Book of Nature*, was a standard Romantic tour of Europe's castle-like landscapes. Yet Fletcher was also stirred by the modernist revolution in the arts—he was in the audience for the legendary premiere of Stravinsky's *The Rite of Spring*—and he began to change his style.

The outbreak of World War I forced Fletcher to return to America. He went through Chicago and introduced himself to Harriet Monroe, and then he headed for the Southwest, including the Grand Canyon. He wrote a series he called the "Arizona Poems," and when he went back through Chicago, he handed them to Monroe. Fletcher was broke, so she put him up for a few days. The next year, 1916, Monroe published the "Arizona Poems" and awarded Fletcher *Poetry's* annual Guarantor's Prize, worth $100. Twenty years later Fletcher found it easy to talk Monroe into devoting a whole issue of *Poetry* to southwestern authors.

Fletcher's poem "The Grand Canyon of the Colorado" begins—much like Monroe's *Atlantic Monthly* article of sixteen years before—with the experience of emerging from a pine forest and beholding an unreal canyon landscape. Twice Fletcher says that the canyon is "not of this earth." This seems a failure of geological imagination, for of course nowhere else is the earth revealed more completely. Fletcher sees the canyon as a realm of stability: the cliffs are "strong-built," "durable," "forever completed," "unscarred, unaltered/ the work stands finished," "molded and fashioned forever in durable ageless stone"—and "It is finished." Again, this is a curious thing to say about the world's greatest display of erosion-in-action. Perhaps Fletcher's desire to find stability in the canyon arose from the chronic instability of his own life. Emotionally volatile, he suffered from depression, failed relationships, and suicidal impulses. At the time he wrote his Grand Canyon poem, Fletcher was broke, homeless, and horrified by the ongoing slaughter in European trenches.

The Grand Canyon's seeming eternity was so appealing to Fletcher that he imagined it as his final resting place:

> One single thing I would ask for,
> Burn my body here.
> Kindle the pyre
> Upon this jutting point;
> Dry aromatic juniper,
> Lean flame, blue smoke,

Ashes and dust.
The winds would drift the ash
Outwards across the canyon,
To the rose-purple rim of the desert
Beyond the red-barred towers.[24]

It was not to be. In 1950, at age sixty-four, Fletcher finally gave in to the urges for self-annihilation expressed in his poetry: he walked into an Arkansas lake and drowned himself. He wasn't cremated, but buried in a Little Rock cemetery near his parents.

A few months after launching *Poetry* magazine, Harriet Monroe met the young Sara Teasdale and invited her to visit Chicago. Five years later Teasdale won the first Pulitzer Prize awarded for poetry. She had discovered the Southwest in 1908 when a female philosophy professor at the University of Arizona, who admired Teasdale's first book, hosted her for over two months. She would write about "those vehement stars" of Tucson, and she had strong interests in astronomy and botany, but Teasdale seldom wrote about nature for its own sake; more often she used it as a backdrop for her emotional life. Teasdale didn't see the canyon until 1920. According to her biographer, William Drake, "She stopped for a day at the Grand Canyon, where she had to rest for an afternoon because the spectacle overwhelmed her."[25] To Monroe, Teasdale wrote, "It makes me feel that immortality must Be, after all, since the ages have worked for such harmonious splendor there."[26] She found a similar reassurance in the night sky, more there than in the Bible. Like John Gould Fletcher and many other poets, the disaster of World War I left Teasdale shaken and yearning for greater stability. Although she didn't write a poem about the Grand Canyon, she did use the stars as symbols of the grand if mysterious design of the cosmos: "If ever I started a religion," she wrote Monroe in 1926, "it would be star-worship."[27] But neither the canyon nor the stars brought stability to Sara Teasdale: she too ended her life.

Harriet Monroe discovered several young poets who went on to major careers, the foremost of whom was Carl Sandburg, twice the winner of the Pulitzer Prize for poetry. A year after Sandburg's death in 1967, his North Carolina home was designated a national historic site, the first time an American writer was so honored. When the National Park Service inventoried

Carl Sandburg playing cowboy. *(Courtesy of the Carl Sandburg Home National Historic Site)*

Sandburg's possessions, it counted five copies of Ferde Grofé's *Grand Canyon Suite* and seven pages of yellowed, unused stationery from El Tovar Hotel. Sandburg wrote two long Grand Canyon poems, each the final poem of the books they were published in.

Sandburg modeled himself after Walt Whitman in his free-verse style, his folk voice, and focus on the lives of "the People." When Monroe published her first Sandburg poem, with its opening line about Chicago being the "Hog butcher of the world," it was considered a shocking, crude violation of poetic prettiness. As Sandburg celebrated the American people through the national ordeals of the Great Depression and World War II, he became such an appreciated voice that President Franklin Roosevelt urged him to run for Congress.

In the 1920s Sandburg earned his living as the movie critic for a Chicago newspaper; he was the Siskel and Ebert of his day. Movies were a new art form, and Sandburg recognized their artistic possibilities, but he also appreciated them for showing the pulse of the people. He loved westerns, partly just for their scenery; Sandburg was a nature lover and wrote about it often in his poetry. Of one Zane Grey movie Sandburg wrote that the scenery "out does every human action in the picture": "Here the deserts and mountains fight. Here the Indian gods had a terrific wrestle one time when the world was congealing out of the mists and putties of chaos. Jagged remnants gesture upward and the deserts pull and wear at them, torture them, century in, century out, to drag the rocks down to dust."[28] Sandburg finally got to see the real West, including the Grand Canyon, on a 1921 train trip to Hollywood, where he interviewed stars like Charlie Chaplin and Will Rogers Jr.

Sandburg begins his Grand Canyon poem "Slabs of the Sunburnt West" with the image of a train winding its way through southwestern landscapes: "Stand up, sandstone slabs of red/ Tell the overland passengers who burnt you." The landscape is full of the ghosts of prairie schooners and forty-niners. It's typical of Sandburg to approach the Grand Canyon in the context of American history and human activities, so when he describes a donkey rider arriving at the canyon rim, readers might assume this is a cowboy or tourist. But soon there are signs that this is some Christ-like figure arriving in a Jerusalem of ultimate realities. The canyon makes the rider's sense of reality waver, and he begins what Harriet Monroe called his "interview with God." The rider recalls his boyhood image of God as a man "with long whiskers in the sky," but "they lied." The canyon implies that God must be much larger than this—if God can be found at all:

> How can I taste with my tongue a tongueless God?
> How can I touch with my fingers a fingerless God?
> How can I hear with my ears an earless God?
> Or smell of a God gone noseless long ago?
> Or look on a God who never needs eyes for looking?[29]

The rider does feel:

> The power and lift of the sea
> and the flame of the old earth fires under,
> I sift their meanings of sand in my fingers.
> I send out five sleepwalkers to find out who I am,
> my name and number, where I came from,
> and where I am going.[30]

But the sleepwalkers offer no answer. The rider is left puzzling on the canyon rim:

> *I walk the high lash of the frozen storm line;*
> *I sit down with my feet in a ten-mile gravel pit.*
> *Here I ask why I am a bag of sea-water fastened*
> *to a frame of bones put walking on land....*[31]

When Sandburg describes the canyon's shapes, he sees modern, proletarian images: "trucks hauling caverns of granite," "somersaults of telescoped railroad train wrecks," "memories of work gangs and wrecking crews," "tumbled skyscrapers and wrecked battleships."

As Sandburg broods about ultimate meanings, he occasionally interrupts the poem and repeats three simple lines that imply that other forms of life skip philosophy and simply go on living:

> *A bluejay blue*
> *and a gray mouse gray*
> *ran up the canyon walls.*

Sandburg can't arrive at any conclusion, and he ends the poem with these ambiguous images:

> *The worn tired stars say*
> *you shall die early and die dirty.*
> *The clean cold stars say*
> *you shall die late and die clean.*
>
> *The runaway stars say*
> *you shall never die at all,*
> *never at all.*[32]

A few years later Sandburg tried again to wrestle the Grand Canyon for its meanings. H. L. Mencken heard that Sandburg was writing a "high-toned" Grand Canyon prose poem and demanded it for his *American Mercury* magazine. In "Many Hats" Sandburg once again uses the canyon to calibrate the location of God:

> *The Grand Canyon of Arizona, said one, this is it, hacked out by the*
> *broadax of a big left-handed God and left forgotten, fixed over and embellished*
> *by a remembering right-handed God who always comes back.* [33]

Sandburg has various "hombres" approach the canyon and see different things. One sees Time, another sees Law and Order. One sees the Garden of Eden, with:

> *Adam and Eve satisfied and sitting pretty till the day of the Snake Dance*
> *and the First Sin; and God was disgusted and wrecked the works; he ordered*
> *club-foot angels with broken wings to shoot the job; now look at it.*
> *Comes another hombre all wised up, This was the Devil's Brickyard; here*
> *were the kilns to make the Kitchens of Hell; after bricks enough were*
> *made to last Hell a million years, the Devil said, "shut /'er down"; they*
> *had a big payday night and left it busted from hell to breakfast; the Hopis*
> *looked it over and decided to live eighty miles away where there was water....* [34]

This time Sandburg doesn't really expect to find any answer; he is fascinated by the questioning itself. Near the beginning of "Many Hats" he asks, perhaps thinking of Harriet Monroe:

> *Why did one woman cry, The silence is*
> *terrible? Why did another smile, There is sweet gravity here? Why do*
> *they come and go here and look as in a looking glass?* [35]

Near the end of the poem two men speak:

> *...one man says, There goes God with an army*
> *Of banners, and another man, Who is God and why? Who am I and why?* [36]

In the same way that in "Slabs of the Sunburnt West" Sandburg had interrupted his broodings with an image of contented animals, Sandburg frames

"Many Hats" by beginning and ending with the same graceful image of the eternal sunrise:

> *The drums of the sun never*
> *get tired, and first off*
> *every morning, the drums of*
> *the sun perform an intro-*
> *duction of the dawn here.*[37]

Edgar Lee Masters wrote one of the most popular poetry books of the twentieth century, *Spoon River Anthology*, a national bestseller in 1915. In it are the stories of two hundred dead people, speaking from a small-town ceme-tery about their deepest secrets, regrets, longings, and reflections on life. The anthology explored universal human themes, yet it was also an insider's attack on America's nostalgia for the idyllic life of small towns. Masters grew up in two Illinois towns, one near the Spoon River, the other on the Sangamon River—about which he would one day write a book in the "Rivers of Amer-ica" series. Masters took an early interest in nature and wrote some of his first poems about it. After reading the works of atheist Robert Ingersoll, he decided he couldn't believe in a traditional Christian god, and nature became more important to him as a substitute. His nature was a mixture of Emerson's transcendental nature, Shelley's mystical nature, and especially Spinoza's pan-theistic nature, in which the cosmos is really just a thought in God's mind. Masters's longing for a better world also led him to become a Progressive era political activist and a lawyer defending underdogs and agitators. In 1904 he and his law partner Clarence Darrow argued a case before the U.S. Supreme Court, but the court dismissed their client as "an anarchist."

The success of *Spoon River Anthology* allowed Masters to write full-time, mainly about American history, but his literary reputation shrank steadily, and his finances and personal life were chaotic. His constant philandering ruined two marriages and many friendships. Masters intellectualized his phi-landering by saying he was searching for the perfect poetic soul, but he also seemed to concede the Christian case against atheism, saying: "No one knows what nature intends; so we are warranted in following our desires and our reasons, conveniences, tastes, since nature gives us no basis for morality."[38]

In the 1930s Masters was living in New York City's Chelsea Hotel—poor, lonely, embittered, and despairing. Yet he was spending summers in the mountains and river valleys of upstate New York, and this rekindled his youthful love of nature and inspired him to write a book of nature poems, *Invisible Landscapes.* The title referred to the mystical depths of nature seen by Shelley and Spinoza, which offered a greater pattern and purpose and peace to human life. In his autobiography Masters said, "in this year of *Invisible Landscapes,* my brother, the god, has returned to me after a long absence.... The country is the haunt of something universal and deathless and infinite which broods upon the earth and reflects itself in it. In communion with nature we can wrest from the gods images identifying life with eternity...."[39]

One of the poems in *Invisible Landscapes* was "The Grand Canyon." Masters had visited the canyon in 1925, and he must have been intrigued by the Southwest, for the next year he traveled to New Mexico to see the Pueblo people and their villages. Like much of *Invisible Landscapes,* whose metaphysical abstractions limited its sales to only nine hundred copies, "The Grand Canyon" is opaque reading. But it does seem to triangulate Masters's whole life. In his youth he was inspired by the Romantic vision of a spiritual nature. As a writer, especially with *Spoon River Anthology,* he became a leader of naturalism, which looked at the world without sentiment, including without religious sentiment, seeing it as a difficult, Darwinian struggle. As an old man Masters was looking back on the wreckage of his life and seeking some kind of redemption. He stares into the canyon with a "searching heart" and asks if the universe is nothing but matter in chaos, but then he suggests that the canyon is the emblem of something greater, a great thought with a great order, a Spinozan God who resides in all matter and all flesh:

> *If this gorge came from that which is not Love,*
> *Nor Will, nor Vision gazing many-eyed,*
> *A force alone which pours out fair, venene*
> *Life as a blind and heedless tide;*
> *And we thrown here are of*
> *Its unconcern, nor planned for, nor foreseen—*
> *Yet that which awakens thought is it but thought,*
> *Seeing it taxes man beyond his power?*

That which stirs love is it risen and wrought
Of flame no brighter than man's passionate hour?
That which creates, if without love and blind,
If without thought and without mind,
Is yet a forehead brooding like the dawn,
Instinct with genius, inevitable and swift.
And as the wandering dove, or songless swan,
Or the bee on summer winds adrift
Find home again, so That from which you came,
Great Canyon, by its own subconscious gift
Shaped what it dreamed: rocks, flesh, a soul, a flame.[40]

But in the poem's conclusion Masters retreats from any conclusion:

Though whence we came and what we are,
Souls, or but sparkles on the foam
Of waves whose rolling on is accident,
Is by this canyon shown not, but concealed;—
Though on the heart long made to roam
This beauty, evil or beneficent,
Makes deeper wounds than those it healed,
The hurt, somehow, finds wings whose flight is meant
To point the long way home.[41]

Another man on Harriet Monroe's list of worthy poets was Alfred Noyes, who appeared in *Poetry* in its first year. Noyes was a popular British poet, and during the years Monroe was launching her magazine, he was teaching at American universities. While Noyes was at Cal Tech, one of his students was Frank Capra, who was aiming for a career in engineering. Noyes inspired Capra with the power of language and storytelling, and Capra switched to a career as a filmmaker, today most identified with *It's a Wonderful Life*. Capra sometimes sneaked lines from Noyes's poetry into his films, including what became Capra's personal credo, "There are times in every man's life when he glimpses the eternal," which Capra used in both *Lost Horizon* and *State of the Union*.

Noyes was present when in 1917 astronomer George Hale opened his new hundred-inch telescope at Mount Wilson Observatory, high above the Cal Tech campus. This was the telescope Edwin Hubble would use to prove that the universe is expanding. Noyes became inspired by the mystery of the universe and by the human quest to understand it, and he began working on a three-book, eight-hundred-page epic poem about the progress of science, *The Torch-Bearers*. The first book, *Watchers of the Sky*, begins at Mount Wilson Observatory and traces the history of astronomy. The second, *The Book of Earth*, published in 1925, begins and ends at the Grand Canyon and explores the ideas of geology and biology.

Of all the works in which the Grand Canyon plays a role, *The Book of Earth* is the most ambitious, both artistically and intellectually. Noyes spends the first twenty-seven pages of the book introducing the Grand Canyon. He stares:

> *Into the dreadful heart of the old earth dreaming*
> *Like a slaked furnace of her far beginnings,*
> *The inhuman ages, alien as the moon,*
> *Aeons unborn, and the unimagined end.*[42]

Noyes spends the day riding along the rim and spends the night in a cabin "upon the monstrous brink." In a section called "Night and the Abyss," Noyes announces his purposes for this book. The abyss is both the Grand Canyon and the spiritual abyss into which many modern people are thrown by the visions of science. Noyes intends to find the true meaning of geological time and forces. But from the start, he makes it clear that in the end he expects to find God:

> *Below me, only guessed by the slow sound*
> *Of forests, through unfathomable gulfs*
> *Of midnight, vaster, more mysterious now,*
> *Breathed that invisible Presence of deep awe.*
> *Through the wide open window, once, a moth*
> *Beat its dark wings, and flew—out—over that,*
> *Brave little fluttering atheist, unaware*
> *Of aught beyond the reach of his antennae,*
> *Thinking his light quick thoughts; while, under him,*
> *God opened His immeasurable Abyss.*[43]

After three hundred pages in which he gropes for meaning and explores the worlds of Pythagoras, Aristotle, Leonardo, Linnaeus, Lamarck, Goethe, and Darwin, Noyes concludes that geology is really God's scripture written in stone. At the Grand Canyon, by morning, he ends the poem:

> *Far away*
> *Along the unfathomable abyss it flowed,*
> *A harmony so consummate that it shared*
> *The silence of the sky; a song so deep*
> *That only the still soul could hear it now:*
> *New every morning the creative Word*
> *Moves upon chaos. Yea, our God grows young.*
> *Here, now, the eternal miracle is renewed*
> *Now, and for ever, God makes heaven and earth.*[44]

When Harriet Monroe was preparing to launch *Poetry* magazine, she received lots of advice from Ezra Pound about which poets to include. When Pound needed an example of poets who were too traditional and trite, he said, "You don't want the Henry Van Dyke kind."[45]

He was referring to the cousin of John C. Van Dyke, the author of *The Desert* and *The Grand Canyon of the Colorado*. Henry was a Presbyterian clergyman and a Princeton English professor whose often-religious poetry was widely popular. In the 1890s he wrote two Christmas stories, *The First Christmas Tree* and *The Other Wise Man*, which are still shared today. In 1906 he chaired the committee that wrote the first Presbyterian liturgy, *The Book of Common Worship*, and in 1914 he published *The Grand Canyon and Other Poems*. The title poem, six pages long, begins with a sunrise over the canyon and then offers a standard Romantic image of the canyon as the realm of Titans. But suddenly Van Dyke feels himself to be a tiny human body threatened by vast inhuman dimensions:

> *How still it is! Dear God, I hardly dare*
> *To breathe, for fear the fathomless abyss*
> *Will draw me down into eternal sleep.*[46]

As Van Dyke broods over the meaning of the canyon, he considers the possibility that the blind artistry of the Colorado River symbolizes an entire universe ruled not by God, but only by force. His existential doubt is just as vivid as that of George Sterling or Edgar Lee Masters. Addressing the river, he says:

> *At sight of thee, thou sullen laboring slave*
> *Of gravitation,—yellow torrent poured*
> *From distant mountains by no will of thine,*
> *Through thrice a hundred centuries of slow*
> *Fallings and liftings of the crust of Earth,—*
> *At sight of thee my spirit sinks and fails.*
> *Art thou alone the Maker? Is the blind*
> *And thoughtless power that drew thee dumbly down*
> *To cut this gash across the layered globe,*
> *The sole creative cause of all I see?*
> *Are force and matter all? The rest a dream?*
>
> *Then is thy gorge a canyon of despair,*
> *A prison for the soul of man, a grave*
> *Of all his dearest daring hopes! The world*
> *Wherein we live and move is meaningless,*
> *No spirit here to answer to our own!*
> *The stars without a guide! The chance-born Earth*
> *Adrift in space, no Captain on the ship!...*
> *And man, the latest accident of Time....*
> *Man is living a lie,—a bitter jest*
> *Upon himself,—a conscious grain of sand*
> *Lost in a desert of unconsciousness,*
> *Thirsting for God and mocked by his own thirst.*[47]

It's possible Van Dyke's expression of despair was not sincere but merely an acknowledgment of the intellectual currents of the time. A moment later, he appeals to the canyon in a different way:

> *Speak to my heart again and set me free*
> *From all these doubts that darken earth and heaven!*

Who sent thee forth into the wilderness
To bless and comfort all who see thy face?
Who clad thee in this more than royal robe
Of rainbows? Who designed these jeweled thrones
For thee, and wrought these glittering palaces?
Who gave thee power upon the soul of man
To lift him up through wonder into joy?
God! let the radiant cliffs bear witness! God,
Let all the shining pillars signal—God!
He only, on the mystic loom of light,
Hath woven webs of loveliness to clothe
His most majestic works....
Now, far beyond all language and all art
In thy wild splendor, Canyon Marvelous,
The secret of thy stillness lies unveiled
In wordless worship! This is holy ground,—
Thou art no grave, no prison, but a shrine,
Garden of Temples filled with Silent Praise,
If God were blind thy Beauty could not be![48]

For all their creativity and soul searching, the poets had a relatively small audience and little influence on public perceptions of the Grand Canyon. A far larger influence was had by the nature writers, especially John Burroughs and John Muir, who were already well-known and whose Grand Canyon essays were published in one of the leading magazines of the time, *Century Illustrated Monthly Magazine*. Burroughs and Muir helped set the tone that was adopted by journalists and travel writers, who had the largest audience of all. Burroughs, Muir, and Mary Austin seemed fairly immune to existential doubt, and they and John C. Van Dyke helped create the Grand Canyon that today's visitors expect to find: a scene of deep beauty and peace.

John Muir first visited the Grand Canyon in 1896, and on his return in 1902 he wrote his *Century Illustrated* account of it. Muir and Burroughs came to the canyon together in 1909, and Burroughs wrote his account then. By 1909 Burroughs had been America's leading nature writer for forty years; John Muir had emerged relatively recently with the 1894 publication of *Mountains of California*.

John Muir (top) and John Burroughs (third down) on Bright Angel Trail, 1909. *(Grand Canyon National Park Study Collection)*

Muir and Burroughs had trained their perceptions and their pens in landscapes that were quite different from the desert Southwest: Burroughs in New York's Catskill Mountains; Muir in the Sierra Nevada, with its mighty trees and lush meadows. Both men were nearly the same age, sixty-five in 1902, an age when it isn't easy to adjust one's perceptions. Muir felt out of his element at the Grand Canyon, telling his editor at *Century Illustrated* that writing his canyon article was "the toughest job I ever tackled."[49] He puzzled over the desert vegetation, finding the cacti "strange, leafless, old-fashioned plants...making the strangest forests ever seen or dreamed of."[50] Yet at least Muir was accustomed to the raw grandeur of western landscapes. A typical John Burroughs essay would find him amid pleasant pastoral scenery, perhaps bird watching on a farm. When Muir and Burroughs had traveled to Alaska together a decade before their Grand Canyon trip, Muir was openly scornful of Burroughs's inability to get enthralled by rugged landscapes. At the same time that Muir was struggling to write about the Grand Canyon in 1902, thirty-four-year-old Mary Austin was living in the Mojave Desert just east of the Sierra and writing *Land of Little Rain*, and forty-six-year-old John C. Van Dyke had finished writing *The Desert* only seven months before. Both Muir and Burroughs resorted to the kind of Romantic "frippery" that would have made Austin and Van Dyke gag. Yet because the canyon was such a contrast with the nature familiar to Muir and Burroughs, both men worked conscientiously to come to terms with it, and they brought to this task a greater depth of knowledge about nature than did Austin or Van Dyke.

Both Muir and Burroughs begin their accounts with how the canyon surprises people seeing it for the first time, how it defies their past experience or their ability to grasp it. Burroughs relates stories of people overwhelmed by the canyon, including the experiences of Harriet Monroe and Charles Dudley Warner. Burroughs then relates his own vicarious fright: "One's sense of the depths of the cañon is so great that it almost makes one dizzy to see the little birds fly over it, or plunge down into it. One seemed to fear that they, too, would get dizzy and fall to the bottom."[51] Both men confess their inability to describe the canyon. Muir wrote, "It is a hard job to sketch it even in scrawniest outline.... I cannot tell the hundredth part of the wonders of its features." And for Burroughs, "Of the many descriptions of it, none seems adequate. To rave over it, or to pour into it a torrent of superlatives, is of little avail." But then, of course, both men set out to describe it.

Both men try to give a sense of the scale of the Grand Canyon by comparing it with other famous wonders. "Niagara," wrote Burroughs," would be only as a picture upon your walls…the pyramids, seen from the rim, would appear only like large tents." Yet Muir was annoyed by comparisons made by other authors, starting with Charles Dudley Warner's claim that Yosemite would disappear in the Grand Canyon, and Muir spent about three hundred words defending Yosemite's honor: "None of the sandstone or limestone precipices of the cañon…approaches in smooth, flawless strength and grandeur the granite of El Capitan." But Muir is ready to dismiss other wonders, like Yellowstone, in favor of the canyon.

Both Muir and Burroughs indulge in the Romantic frippery of seeing mythological and architectural shapes in the canyon, "which must play," says Burroughs, "a prominent part in all faithful attempts to describe it." Burroughs saw in the canyon "truncated towers," "balustrades on the summit of a noble façade," "immense halls," "three enormous chairs," "temples and tombs, pagodas and pyramids, on a scale that no work of human hands can rival." Muir sees "a huge castle with arched gateway, turrets, watch-towers, ramparts, etc., and to right and left palaces, obelisks, and pyramids fairly fill the gulf, all colossal and all lavishly painted and carved…the prevailing style is ornate Gothic, with many hints of Egyptian and Indian." Muir goes on and on describing "nature's own capital city," with its "fairy embroidery."

John Muir's account offers a broad survey of canyon phenomena, including geology, wildlife, botany, weather, the river, the trails, the mule rides, the rim roads, Native American ruins, and the canyon's changing appearances through sunrise, sunset, and rain storms. John Burroughs, however, is mainly interested in the canyon's geology, and, surprisingly, he gives a better feel for geological time and forces than does Muir. Burroughs turns his eastern eyes into an advantage by contrasting East and West: "Erosion, erosion—one sees in the West as never before that the world is shaped by erosion.… In the East the earth's wounds are virtually all healed, but in the West they are yet raw and gaping, if not bleeding." Burroughs found it reassuring that the canyon "was not born of the throes and convulsions of nature—of earthquake shock or volcanic explosion. It does not suggest the crush of matter and the wreck of worlds. Clearly it is the work of the more gentle and beneficent forces. This probably accounts for the friendly look." A gentle, friendly man, Burroughs usually found nature to be friendly as well.

Both Muir and Burroughs had been raised to fear a severe, vengeful God, and both rebelled and found a grander and friendlier god in nature. Earth wasn't a fallen world but the incarnation of divinity. Yet Burroughs was uncomfortable with the outright piety in much of Muir's writings. He ends his Grand Canyon article with a simple statement: "The remainder of our lives will be the richer for having seen the Grand Cañon." Muir was a more lyrical, rhapsodical writer, which is one reason his writings continue to have wide readership. Of the Grand Canyon, Muir glowed:

> It seems a gigantic statement for even nature to make, all in one mighty stone word, apprehended at once like a burst of light, celestial color its natural vesture, coming in glory to mind and heart as to a home prepared for it from the very beginning. Wildness so godful, cosmic, primeval, bestows a new sense of earth's beauty and size. Not even from high mountains does the world seem so wide, so like a star in glory of light on its way through the heavens.

Muir ended by comparing the Grand Canyon to "a grand geological library":

> And with what wonderful scriptures are their pages filled—myriad forms of successive floras and faunas, lavishly illustrated with colored drawings, carrying us back into the midst of the life of a past infinitely remote. And as we go on and on, studying this old, old life in the light of the life beating warmly about us, we enrich and lengthen our own.

When you crossbreed Muir's romanticism with the desert realism of John C. Van Dyke and Mary Austin, and later Joseph Wood Krutch and Edward Abbey, you come out with today's perceptions of the Grand Canyon.

Like Harriet Monroe, John C. Van Dyke never had any intention of setting foot in the Southwest until illness forced him to. Van Dyke was a professor of art history at Rutgers and a popular author of books on art, including the Dutch masters. The Dutch, of whom John C. Van Dyke was one, were supposed to be the best at seeing light in all its subtleties. Then in 1897 Van Dyke developed severe asthma, and his doctor exiled him to the desert to recover. Van Dyke was shocked by the desert's light, colors, and landforms, which

violated every theory of art he'd ever known. He became obsessed with seeing the desert, taking long, solitary trips into it, getting lost and running out
of water, risking his health and his life for the sake of beauty.

Van Dyke's background in art history was both his strength and his weakness as a writer. More than anyone else who wrote about the Grand Canyon, he was focused on aesthetics, the definitions of natural beauty. Van Dyke
wrote long passages describing all the subtleties of scenes and lighting, as in
his detailed description of the Supai Formation's varying tones of red: "In the
early morning when in shadows it is beef-blood red; at noon it is a dark terracotta; at sunset almost a fire red."[52] He also carefully compares the look of one
butte with others, as he compared the canyon's Shiva Temple with Europe's
Mont Blanc. More important, Van Dyke tells us why we should accept desert
colors and forms as beautiful. Yet Van Dyke's aesthetic vision also often limited him to seeing landscapes as if they were nothing but paintings, nothing
but appearances. The subtitle of his Grand Canyon book is "Recurrent Studies in Impressions and Appearances."

Van Dyke offers quite a bit of geology in his canyon book, but sometimes
with the apologetic air of a professor teaching a compulsory class. He presents geological facts, observations, and theories, but he mainly seems interested in geology as the painter of his favorite visual effects. Only occasionally
does he join Muir and Burroughs in seeing landscapes as but the momentary, ever-changing face of powerful, ancient, ever-flowing geological forces.

There was one thing about the Grand Canyon that inspired Van Dyke into
Muir-like poetry. For Van Dyke the desert is most powerful as a symbol of creation, of eternity and ultimate mystery, against which all of human history is
but a tiny thing. This was the source of his annoyance at humans seeing in
the canyon landscapes only their own architectural glories. In his Grand Canyon book Van Dyke is trying to describe the "temples" when he once again
flies into exasperation:

> There never was a temple of Shiva or Brahma that lifted five hundred
> feet or could hold five thousand people, but here we have the carved
> forms of Nature that reach up nearly seven thousand feet, and, if hol
> low, might hold a million souls! In all their many centuries of existence
> they have never heard the footfall or the voice of priest or worshiper,

or had any association with humanity. How easily, securely, undeviatingly from the perpendicular they have stood through the ages, while the Indian temples have been falling away stone by stone, crumbling under their own weight, flattening into their own dust!

The pyramid of Cheops at Gizeh was the labor of thousands of slaves over many years. When the capstone was put on the top, the height reached was four hundred and eighty-two feet. But here at the Canyon the so-called Cheops Pyramid was the labor of Nature over thousands of centuries, and today, after ages of erosion, it still lifts skyward over five thousand feet. Perhaps the first marauder who broke into the tomb in the heart of the Gizeh Pyramid was brought to a standstill by seeing in the dust of the floor a naked footprint—the footprint of the last attendant who had gone out and sealed the door behind him five thousand years before; but here in the under-strata of the Canyon Pyramid are the sand-ripples left by the waves of a primal sea perhaps five million years ago. You can almost see to a nicety just where the last wave broke. These are the footprints of Creation, beside which those of the human seem so small and so inconsequential.[53]

Throughout his book Van Dyke takes jabs at the Romantic fancies other writers were inflicting on the canyon, such as portraying the river by moonlight as "an angel's pathway." Even after decades of familiarity with the Southwest, Van Dyke is spooked by his journeys to the canyon bottom: "One cannot imagine anything more uncanny than these inner Canyon walls"; "they are almost too creepy for enjoyment. They are grim and unearthly"; "Wind and storm and lightning are an old story, but the mad plunge of a canyoned river is something unique."[54]

While Van Dyke saw landscapes mainly in aesthetic terms, Mary Austin saw landscapes through their human stories, through the eyes and history of the people who lived there and knew it best: the local sheepherders and Native Americans. Yet soon after writing *The Land of Little Rain*, Austin followed George Sterling to Carmel and became one of the leaders of the Carmel arts colony. This increasingly led her away from nature and into social issues and cultural trends, then to New York and Europe. After a dozen years of living in New York City, Austin felt lost and sought to reconnect with her literary and spiritual roots. She explored Arizona and New Mexico, including the Grand Canyon in 1923, wrote *The Land of Journeys' Ending* about them, and settled in Santa Fe for the rest of her life. She immersed herself in Native American culture and religion, eventually compiling a collection of southwestern tribal songs published by Harriet Monroe.

Austin described the Grand Canyon more accurately than most writers, yet she also came up with some vivid poetic images: "The dawn came up, as it does in the Navajo country, a turquoise horse, neighing joyously."[55] In her poem "The Grand Cañon," Austin imagined that all the world's beautiful sky colors ended up in geologized form in the canyon:

> Now I know what becomes
> Of the many-colored days,
> Rose red evenings,
> Red mornings…
> They are on their way to the Grand Cañon.
> There they lie, overlapping
> In motionless unreality.[56]

Austin wasn't being fanciful, but stating her personal spirituality, when in *The Land of Journeys' Ending* she describes seeing Native American spirits in Grand Canyon clouds: "I am not sure that the other tourists saw anything but the changing configuration of the cliff through the cloud-drift, but that was their misfortune. It is only as they please that Those Above show themselves in the rainbow…or the moonbow…."[57] Austin was ahead of other Grand Canyon authors in being a serious student of Native American tribes, whose connections with the land have become another strong element in today's perceptions of the Grand Canyon and the Southwest.

The last word in this chapter goes to John C. Van Dyke, but only because he realized there would be no last word about the Grand Canyon. At the end of his book he passed judgment on all canyon writings:

> Many a poet has come away from the Canyon with a fine frenzy in his eye and a thick feeling in his throat, but by the time he has his emotion down on paper it has proved merely a disjointed rhapsody. You cannot

absorb the Canyon mentally and body it forth in verse as you do the New England mill-pond or the poppies in Flanders fields. The mass of form and color, the bewildering display of light, are baffling. For all the verseful eulogies and rhythmic odes, the beauty of the depth remains unrevealed, its splendor not half told. The Canyon still lacks a poet.[58]

Sorry, cousin Henry Van Dyke, this includes you. It also, John C. Van Dyke confessed, included himself.

Writers have continued coming to the Grand Canyon for over a century, and each one has seen the canyon differently. The canyon has been like a Rorschach ink blot onto which people have projected their own personalities, needs, philosophies, and literary styles. As Carl Sandburg put it in "Many Hats":

> *For each man see him-*
> *self in the Grand Canyon—*
> *each one makes his own Canyon*
> *before he comes, each one brings*
> *and carries away his own Canyon....* [59]

Poets have come and gone, generations have come and gone, trendy styles and philosophical urgencies have come and gone. The Grand Canyon never noticed. The canyon endures.

HAUNTED BY TIME

British Writers Discover the Grand Canyon

When the Grand Canyon was opened to mass tourism in 1901, Americans did their best to turn it into a national icon. But the canyon itself was oblivious to patriotic pride, and it offered itself to anyone who was ready to find beauty and meaning in it. It soon became world famous and began drawing international visitors. Many of them were British, including some of Britain's leading writers, such as poet Alfred Noyes, considered in the previous chapter. These writers proved Carl Sandburg's claim that each person sees him- or herself in the Grand Canyon, for the writers' reactions to it were quite personal and varied. But writers were often seeking in the canyon something universal—an ultimate revelation of nature, a source of meaning for human lives.

At the start of the twentieth century most American writers still considered British literature more sophisticated than American literature, but this was probably not true when it came to perceptions of the Grand Canyon. For three centuries Americans' encounters with wilderness had been one of the central elements of the national experience. While many American novelists tried to imitate British novels of high-society manners, it was often the novels that encountered the forces of nature—*Huckleberry Finn, Moby Dick*— that endured. It was Thoreau's personal encounters with living nature that eclipsed Emerson's sermons on abstract "Nature." Britain had long ago been tamed and urbanized; British novelists were preoccupied with British society; and an elite British education placed a fog of abstract ideas and cultural self-references between a writer and nature. But British culture did include the rich traditions of Romanticism, with its reverence for nature, and much of this tradition had been created by British writers and artists. With this mixture of intellectual tradition and a lack of personal experience with a powerful wilderness, British writers sometimes struggled to figure out the Grand Canyon. They saw it as a source of order, beauty, peace, and perhaps divinity.

For three British writers, John Galsworthy, J. B. Priestley, and Vita Sackville-West, the Grand Canyon was especially meaningful.

John Galsworthy won the Nobel Prize for literature in 1932, only the third British author to do so. He won mainly on the strength of his series of novels called *The Forsyte Saga*, which began with *The Man of Property* in 1906. The series portrayed the sordid realities behind the public face of a proper, upper-class British family. While many British novels dealt with class issues, they were usually written by authors, like Dickens, who were on the outside and looking in. John Galsworthy was an upper-class insider who pulled back the curtain on his own world for all to see in rich, scandalous detail. In 1967 the BBC turned *The Forsyte Saga* into a twenty-six-part television series, and the audience response was so positive that the BBC created the still popular series *Masterpiece Theater* to continue this idea of TV literature.

John Galsworthy wrote *The Forsyte Saga* not out of sociological sympathies for the poor, but from strong personal anger at the rich. As a young, single man he fell in love with Ada Cooper, who would become the center of his life. But Ada was already married to John's cousin. It was an empty marriage to a nasty man, but she was trapped by British propriety. John was tortured to see Ada abused and humiliated by her husband, who wore a public mask of upper-class respectability and righteousness. As John and Ada conducted a years-long, semisecret relationship, John too was subjected to the hypocrisies and meanness of upper-class society.

Galsworthy was pursuing a career as a novelist, against his father's wishes that he go into a respectable business or legal career. His father sent him on an around-the-world sea voyage, hoping to encourage John to take an interest in maritime law, but by chance John met a young Polish seaman and aspiring novelist named Korzeniowski, soon to be world famous as Joseph Conrad, and the two encouraged each other and became lifelong friends. Ada, too, encouraged John's writing, another source of his loyalty to her. His first novels were flat, full of unreal characters and stereotyped plots, but when Galsworthy began writing the story of Ada and her husband and himself, as well as their social world, the writing was full of passion and strong characters and events. Eventually Ada got a divorce, and she and John married. By 1912, the year they visited the Grand Canyon, Ada had been the center of Galsworthy's world for nearly two decades. But now their marriage was threatening to fall apart; its fate would be decided at the Grand Canyon.

The Man of Property made John Galsworthy famous—and made him interesting to other women. At forty-four, a typical age for a midlife crisis, John fell for a beautiful, nineteen-year-old actress and dancer, Margaret Morris, and she fell for him. Morris, who studied dance with the brother of the iconic dancer Isadora Duncan, would go on to a major career as a dancer and dance teacher. She had a vitality that Ada Galsworthy had never had. The attraction between John and Margaret remained chaste, but intense enough that he was almost ready to abandon his wife. Ada was very hurt, and her already frail health imploded. Galsworthy was very conflicted. All he was able to do was decide, quite abruptly, to take Ada abroad and place some distance between himself and Morris. From France he wrote to her that seeing Ada tortured was torture to him, and that they must give each other up. But he was still in love with her, and still conflicted, and his frequent letters to Morris left her hoping. Then he booked passage to New York City, where one of his plays was being produced, and from there he and Ada took a train to the West and the Grand Canyon. The desert might be good for Ada's health.

At the canyon Galsworthy wrote in his diary: "Morning and afternoon, walking and gazing at that marvelous, mysterious, beautiful, rhythmic piece of shifting form and colour." And the next day: "Rode with A. down into the Canyon on mules. Seven hours' steep riding. Interesting, but better to stay on the top. Sublimity is lost as you go down."[1] Sublimity could also be lost as you go down from looks into a love affair.

In a letter from El Tovar Hotel, Galsworthy wrote to Morris:

> This Grand Canyon of Arizona is the greatest sight in the world. It is one of those few wonders of Nature that are real masterpieces of art—as

if every line, hollow, dome, shadow, and hue had been designed in subordination to a tremendous theme. It has the emotionalizing rhythm of great art.... The first effect is almost crushing so that you feel your life—man's life—of no importance whatever. The second feeling, and that which stays with you, is that of exaltation, for you perceive that this stupendous thing before you is the result of the same forces at work in yourself and cause you to live your life and do your work in the way you must and do do it. In other words that you are a midget representation of this inspiring marvel before you and you get a sense of cosmic rhythm and Deity which one is always looking for and so seldom catches.

I've seen a few other sights in my time that give me something of the same sense of Unity.... But none of them can touch this for sheer grandeur of form and colour. I will give the rest of America for this sight.[2]

In comparing himself with the canyon and looking for a greater power there, Galsworthy seemed to be seeking an ideal, a moral compass, something larger and truer than his own limitations and desires. It was then, he later told his nephew Rudolf Sauter, that he made up his mind about Ada and Margaret. Galsworthy's biographer Catherine Dupré interpreted the psychology of this decision:

It was also here, according to Rudolf Sauter, as he stood at the edge of the Grand Canyon, that John finally resolved to be faithful to Ada. Until this moment the issue was, in his own mind at least, not quite decided; to have Margaret as well as Ada was now obviously impossible; to take Margaret with all her youth and vitality for his own—could he inflict this final devastating wound on Ada? For his happiness, even for his fulfillment as a writer, it was perhaps the obvious course; Margaret could give him the freedom he needed to develop his talent and explore the depths within himself. To live with Ada must be to accept the essential superficiality and limitations of her character.... Now, as he viewed the marvelous landscape of the Grand Canyon...he was struck perhaps by his own insignificance, by the comparative unimportance of his own suffering; one is "a midget representation of this inspiring marvel before you and you get a sense of cosmic rhythm and Deity which one is always looking for and so seldom catches."[3]

Galsworthy cut off his relationship with Morris, who would never stop loving him, and remained with Ada, though they would never again be as close.

If Galsworthy needed any further symbolism of the smallness of human lives against nature's power, he soon heard about the sinking of the *Titanic*. He and Ada had been booked to return to England on its second voyage.

Later that year Galsworthy wrote an essay, "Meditation on Finality," that was framed by his Grand Canyon visit. On the surface it's a rather abstract musing on art and literature, but when we know of Galsworthy's personal turmoil at the canyon, his discussion of the human dislike of uncertainty suggests more personal meanings:

> In the Grand Canyon of Arizona...Nature has so focused her efforts, that the result is a framed and final work of Art.... Having seen this culmination, I realize why many people either recoil before it, and take the first train home, or speak of it as a "remarkable formation." For, though mankind at large craves finality, it does not crave the sort that bends the knee to Mystery. In Nature, in Religion, in Art, in Life, the common cry is: "Tell me precisely where I am, what doing, and where going! Let me be free of this fearful untidiness of not knowing all about it!"[4]

Later in the essay Galsworthy describes a scene of romantic tie and trial:

> Traveling away, I remember, from that Grand Canyon of Arizona were a young man and a young woman, evidently in love. He was sitting very close to her, and reading aloud for pleasure, from a paper-covered novel, heroically oblivious of us all: "'Sir Robert,' she murmured, lifting her beauteous eyes, 'I may not tempt you, for you are too dear to me!' Sir Robert held her lovely face between his two strong hands. 'Farewell!' he said, and went out into the night. But something told them both that, when he had fulfilled his duty, Sir Robert would return...." He had not returned before we reached the Junction, but there was finality about that baronet, and we well knew that he ultimately would.[5]

Ada's health did benefit from the desert climate, and she and Galsworthy returned for several more winters, staying at guest ranches in Arizona or California. In 1926 he and Ada were touring America with his nephew Rudolf Sauter and his wife, Violet. Sauter recalled:

> ...in later life, my uncle became more and more allergic to sight-seeing, avoiding all but the most cursory visits to the subjects that appear in travel-brochures. But there was one place which he and Ada had visited before and which they said must on no account be missed; this was the Grand Canyon of Arizona.[6]

Sauter, an artist, was thrilled by the canyon, and the two couples stayed at El Tovar for three weeks so that he could paint the canyon. During their stay Galsworthy and Violet arranged to go horseback riding on the rim. Sauter recalled:

> "Out-West," all English folk had a reputation for being superb horsemen.... So, when word got about that John Galsworthy himself was visiting the Canyon, stables prepared in advance their best animal, feeding him oats for a week, to ensure that the V.I.P. should have a first-class ride. It was known, too, that he preferred an English saddle and one was specially furbished up.
>
> When the horses were brought round for him and Vi, she naturally climbed into the Western saddle to which she had become accustomed...by some mischance the saddles had been switched.
>
> Off they went together without any feeling of unease. But it was not long before Vi's horse, delighted (as it would seem) to be relieved of my uncle's prospective weight, proceeded to run away with her along the rim of the canyon, weaving in and out among the trees at full gallop, with a drop of several thousand feet below—a very white-faced but helpless uncle following as hard as he could on what was so evidently the staider animal. Much to his relief, the rarefied air at 6,000 feet eventually brought the horses to rest before disaster occurred; and they were able to make their way back in more sober fashion—to the hotel, already in an uproar of anxiety (for the mistake had become known).

Vi's "stock" as a horsewoman soared sky-high, so that in future she was always given their trick mule for rides down canyon trails....[7]

Sauter also recalled:

The awe with which my uncle regarded the canyon was never too great to prevent him from looking at it with an air of detached speculation. I can see him now, sitting on the terrace drinking coffee after lunch, in front of what is one of the world's most amazing phenomena, and proceeding to calculate how long it would take a golfer, teeing up on the terrace and driving out over space, to fill the canyon with golf balls— somehow managing to invest the absurd problem with a kind of cosmic significance.[8]

After Galsworthy and Ada had benefited from their winters in Arizona, he recommended Arizona to his friend J. B. Priestley. In the 1930s Priestley was becoming one of Britain's leading novelists and playwrights, but his wife, Jane, was not thriving in London's cold, damp winters, and her doctor told her to find a warmer and drier refuge. Priestley's first wife had died of cancer when he was twenty-nine years old, leaving him with two children, so he was ready to go the distance for the sake of his second wife's health. The Priestleys spent the winters of 1934–35 and 1935–36 in Wickenburg, Arizona, famous for its rustic guest ranches. The next year they tried Egypt, but Priestley discovered that he cared about nature more than human artifacts: "No strange emotions, no magical memories of other existences, disturbed my mind as I stared at the Pyramids or the Sphinx.... Nothing really happened inside my mind; there was no genuine *click*. I felt more in one minute when I first looked into the Grand Canyon than I felt during all those weeks in Egypt."[9]

The next winter they returned to Arizona. Priestley had become fond of the Wickenburg guest ranch, whose owners had built a hut beside the Hassayampa River just for him to use as a writing studio. But mostly he loved the desert, and the Grand Canyon. Priestley had imagined that Wickenburg would be a good base from which to travel to Hollywood to do some film writing, but he found Hollywood even less genuine and magical than Egypt, and Hollywood made him appreciate the desert even more. Priestly wrote a memoir about his second Arizona stay, *Midnight on the Desert*, and its concluding section on the Grand Canyon has become a favorite source of quotes for Grand Canyon books, calendars, and ranger-led park programs.

In the first two pages of *Midnight on the Desert*, Priestley explains why he is there:

> The New World! It seemed to me the oldest country I had ever seen, the real antique land, first cousin to the moon. Brown, bony, sapless, like an old man's hand. We called it new because it was not thick with history.... Man had been here such a little time that his arrival had not yet been acknowledged. He was still some season's trifling accident, like a sudden abundance of coyotes or cottontails. The giant saguaro cactus, standing like a sentinel on every knoll, was not on the lookout for us, had not heard of us yet, still waited for trampling dinosaurs.... The country is geology by day and astronomy by night. It offers a broad view of what is happening generally in the solar system, with no particular reference to Man.[10]

This image of timelessness was a powerful image for Priestley, a man haunted by time and tempted by the possibility of timelessness. His most famous plays and novels dealt with time-haunted people, the nature of time, and the possibility that the past was redeemable—or not really gone. Priestley's longing for timelessness was at the core of his fascination with the Grand Canyon.

Perhaps Priestley's obsession with time and timelessness began with personal losses: the loss of his mother soon after his birth, reemphasized by the loss of his first wife. But it was World War I that left him with a powerful sense of shattered time and lost futures. Priestley was twenty years old in 1914, the age when most young men feel themselves to be striding into a glorious future. Britain, too, was confident of its future, and the whole human race seemed confident of "Progress" of one sort or another. But 1914 brought the Great War, and after his years in the trenches, being wounded and seeing his friends killed, Priestley returned to a Britain where the bright future had vanished. He was too realistic to indulge in false nostalgia for some idyllic past— and with his working-class background and socialist sympathies he wasn't longing for the lost glories of the British Empire—but like much of his generation he felt a powerful sense of being robbed of time and possibilities and hope. In his 1946 autobiographical novel *Bright Day* Priestley looks back to 1914: "When all allowance has been made for my youth and innocence, I am certain these people lived in a world, in an atmosphere, that I have never discovered again since 1914, when the guns began to roar and the corpses piled up."[11] He generalized this sense of loss and blamed "Time" itself: "I hate that beastly clock in the corner.... I feel it's just ticking us away." Priestley used similar lines about life-robbing clocks in his plays and in *Midnight on the Desert* when he discussed the Grand Canyon. At Phantom Ranch, Priestley went for a walk along Bright Angel Creek, and he puzzled over why this was the most powerful memory of his Phantom Ranch stay:

> All this and more came back to me now, yet the little walk I had up the creek that first evening remained the dominant memory and I found myself constantly returning to it. I remembered very little of what I must have seen.... No, all that remained was the quality of that hour, the deep satisfaction, the peace. My memory clung to it as if every step I had taken along that path had been set to exquisite music. The time value was queer, perhaps significant. It lasted hardly any ordinary time at all, at most an hour, yet...it seems to have had more real time in it than some whole years of hurrying and scurrying I have had. Or you can say, with equal truth, that it had a timeless quality; there were no ticking clocks gnawing it away.[12]

Priestley's longing for timelessness attached itself to two metaphysical theories about time. In 1927 he discovered the book *An Experiment with Time* by British aeronautical inventor J. W. Dunne, who argued that time was not one-directional, but that the past and future existed simultaneously and eternally. In dreams humans could occasionally break through the illusion of linear time and glimpse the future or past; immortality consisted of permanently merging with endless time. During his *Midnight on the Desert* winter in Arizona, Priestley discovered *A New Model of the Universe* by the Russian mystic P. D. Ouspensky, who agreed that linear time is an illusion and offered his own theory that time is an eternal, six-dimensional spiral, on which humans can

J. B. Priestley (in front of door), family members, and mule wranglers at Phantom Ranch, mid-1930s. *(PRI21_5_8, Special Collections, J. B. Priestley Library, University of Bradford, used with permission)*

transcend their flaws and become perfect and eternal. Priestley was enthralled with these ideas, and they inspired several plays. Sailing from Los Angeles to Britain after his Arizona stay, he plunged into writing the play *I Have Been Here Before*, and right after that, *Time and the Conways*. As with his later and most popular play, *An Inspector Calls*, these dramas combined family stories or love stories, twilight-zone moments of strange time, and longings and recognitions of lost or future time.

Priestley's enthrallment with these metaphysical ideas about time soon entangled itself with the Grand Canyon. In his 1964 book *Man and Time*, which explored how human cultures have related to time, Priestley said that his first visit to the Grand Canyon, during his 1934–35 stay, offered proof of the reality of precognitive dreams:

The...dream belongs to the middle 1920s. I found myself sitting in the front row of a balcony or gallery in some colossal vague theater that I never took in properly. On what I assumed to be the stage, equally vast and without any definite proscenium arch, was a brilliantly colored and fantastic spectacle, quite motionless, quite unlike anything I had ever seen before. It was an unusually impressive dream, which haunted me for weeks afterward.

Then in the earlier 1930s I paid my first visit to the Grand Canyon, arriving in the early morning when there was a thick mist and nothing to be seen. I sat for some time close to the railing on the South Rim, in front of the hotel there, waiting for the mist to thin out and lift. Suddenly it did, and then I saw, as if I were sitting in the front row of a balcony, that brilliantly colored and fantastic spectacle, quite motionless, that I had seen in my dream theater. My recognition of it was immediate and complete. My dream of years before had shown me a preview of my first sight of the Grand Canyon.[13]

Priestley was being too generous to his memory of this event, for in *Midnight on the Desert* he had described the same event much more tentatively:

After I had spent several hours, staring at it from various viewpoints, I had a growing feeling that I had seen it before…it was only after I had spent some time looking at it that I began to ask myself why I should feel that somehow once before I had stared at this scene and more or less as I was doing it now, across and down from some high place. Then at last I remembered. Some years before I had had a dream.…[14]

Yet for Priestley the Grand Canyon meant far more than just evidence for his metaphysical ideas about time. He was also ready to see geological time there, and he saw it more vividly than most writers:

This incredible pageantry of sunlight and chasm, I thought, is our nearest approach to fourth-dimensional scenery. The three dimensions are on such a scale that some of the fourth has been added. You do not see, hung before you, the seven million years that went to the making of these walls and their twisted strata, but you feel that some elements of Time have been conjured into these immensities of Space. Perhaps it is not size nor the huge witchery of changing shapes and shades that fill us with awe, but the obscure feeling that here we have an instantaneous vision of innumerable eons.[15]

Priestley even saw a connection between the canyon's deep time and its silence:

> There must be the profoundest of silences there because all the noises made throughout these years have no existence in this instantaneous vision of the ages, in which the longest time that any individual sound could take would be represented by the tiniest fraction of an inch on these mile-high walls.[16]

Priestley begins the Grand Canyon chapter of *Midnight on the Desert* with the same scene that frames much of the book, one of him burning unsatisfactory novel manuscripts and Hollywood scripts he'd worked on that winter. He had devoted most of the winter to a novel set in London, *They Walk in the City*, in which the Grand Canyon makes a brief appearance when a small-town person tries to describe London: "It's a wilderness. It's the Amazonian jungle. It's another Grand Canyon. Whole tribes live there, buried away; no one knows much about 'em."[17] Priestley's burning of manuscripts suggests the futility of human efforts, and in the book, talking to himself, he admits to ennui: "You are still, my dimension-juggler, feeling a little lost, a little bewildered, vaguely unhappy." Then he recalls how happy he was during his Grand Canyon visit, with his vision that humans belong to a larger scheme of things.

Priestley recalls how his first, mist-curtained visit to the canyon had begun with ennui. He had arrived on the train at night, sleepless. By then he had seen enough cheesy American tourist attractions that he was expecting the worst from the Grand Canyon:

> The little station looked dreary. The young man waiting with the hotel bus...looked all wrong, for he wore a ten-gallon hat and an embroidered cowboy coat with English riding-breeches and long boots, like a cowboy in a musical comedy. The bus turned two corners and landed

J. B. Priestley on the canyon rim with El Tovar Hotel in the background. *(PRI21_5_13, Special Collections, J. B. Priestley Library, University of Bradford, used with permission)*

us at the front door of an hotel that was so tremendously Western that it might have been created by a German scene-designer who had never been farther west than Hamburg. I felt grumpy about all this. A lot of nonsense. The interior of the hotel took my breath away, not because it was very beautiful, but because it was overheated and seven thousand feet above sea-level. I continued to disapprove of everything....[18]

But that changed when Priestley walked the rim and the mist cleared:

...a miracle had happened. At last, in all my travels, I had arrived and there had been no anticlimax, and my imagination, after weeks or months of expectant dreaming, had not cried, "Is that all?" Reality, stung by my many jeers at its poverty, had gone to work to show me a thing or two....

I have heard rumors of visitors who were disappointed. The same people will be disappointed at the Day of Judgment. In fact, the Grand Canyon is a sort of landscape Day of Judgment. It is not a show place, a beauty spot, but a revelation....The Colorado River made it, but you feel when you are there that God gave the Colorado River its instructions. It is all Beethoven's nine symphonies in stone and magic light.[19]

In speaking of visitors who were unimpressed by the canyon, Priestley was probably thinking of George Bernard Shaw, Britain's most famous playwright, whom he happened to meet on the rim during his second visit to the canyon in 1936. In *Midnight on the Desert* Priestley comments only on the implausibility of their meeting: "To meet the Grand Canyon and Bernard Shaw on the same morning—what an adventure!" But twenty-five years later in his memoir *Margin Released,* Priestley complained about Shaw's always mocking attitude: "He was peevish. He refused to wonder and exclaim at the Grand Canyon, muttering something about Cheddar Gorge. The truth was, I am afraid, that he was determinedly resisting the spell of this marvel…the most ego-shrinking of all earth's spectacles."[20] In his 1957 essay "Shaw," Priestley suggested that Shaw couldn't face having his ego shrunk. Shaw was "a very vain old super V.I.P. I remember once coming across him at the Grand Canyon, and found him peevish, refusing to admire it, or even look at it properly. He was jealous of it."[21]

Or perhaps Shaw was reluctant to admit there might be something admirable about the United States. He had always disliked it and refused to visit. Most of his images of America were from skeptical authors like Mark Twain and from movies. Shaw regarded Americans as shallow people, obsessed with money and social climbing. In a 1920 newspaper article called "Why I Won't Go to America," he explained:

It takes a foreigner to understand your institutions, simply because he has a perspective on them which you have not. Why, then, go to America and lose the perspective? To see skyscrapers? If I saw them tomorrow they'd hold no surprise for me…. The beauties of nature? I've seen Niagara Falls, Yellowstone Park, the Grand Canyon, Yosemite, and what not at the cinema.[22]

Shaw finally visited the United States in 1933, at age seventy-seven, and three years later he returned and took an overnight train from California just to see the Grand Canyon. He spent twelve hours there and returned to California. A brief account of his visit appeared in the *New York Times* and gives Shaw more credit than Priestley did. Shaw even seems to have noticed that many canyon overlooks were named for Native American tribes:

A strangely solemn George Bernard Shaw saw the Grand Canyon today and said "It reminds me of religion."

"Science changes every twenty years, and we must change our views on many things," he said, "but the canyon and the truths of religion are always the same."

Attracted by the many beautiful birds, Mr. Shaw expressed regret that "the extent of my knowledge is to distinguish a parrot from a canary."

"If we decide to name one of the scenic points in the canyon formations for you, what name would you suggest," a park official asked.

"Shawnee," he replied.[23]

Priestley had another unlikely literary encounter at the El Tovar newsstand: it was selling Franz Kafka's novel *The Castle*. Priestley took a copy down to Phantom Ranch, where the novel's surrealism seemed the perfect match for the canyon's otherworldly landscapes. His ride into the canyon on a white mule named Marble brought out Priestley's sense of humor; watching Marble stopping to eat anything he could grab, Priestley decided "it was Marble who had eaten out most of the Grand Canyon."[24] The ride also enthralled him with the canyon's changing shapes and colors. When he arrived at the ranch, Priestley took the solitary walk up Bright Angel Creek that he found so joyful and became his most lasting memory of that trip.

At Phantom Ranch, where Priestley and his family spent two nights, he observed the camp of the Civilian Conservation Corps:

> They had some decent work to do for the good of their own community, and they were being reasonably well sheltered and fed and paid in one of the most enchanting places on earth. And when I remembered that these brown, husky lads who waved at us were the new American equivalent of the unemployed English youths who stand outside our labor exchanges and at slushy street corners, just miserably kept alive by the dole, I could not see that we could teach the Americans much about social services.[25]

Priestley was often critical of American society for the same reasons Shaw was, but he also loved America's democratic spirit, including how the

Wickenburg cowboys made no class distinctions and treated everyone the same: "To return to England, after a few months of this, is like dropping back into the feudal system."[26] Priestley hoped American society could live up to the greatness of its land, its Grand Canyon:

> Even to remember that it is still there lifts up the heart. If I were an American, I should make my remembrance of it the final test of men, art, and policies. I should ask myself: Is this good enough to exist in the same country as the Canyon? How would I feel about this man, this kind of art, these political measures, if I were near that Rim? Every member or officer of the Federal Government ought to remind himself, with triumphant pride, that he is on the staff of the Grand Canyon.[27]

When Bruce Babbitt was inaugurated as secretary of the interior in 1993, he quoted those lines.

In the spirit of this Priestly quote, Vita Sackville-West wrote her novel *Grand Canyon* to challenge Americans to rise to their political destiny. When she got the idea of writing such a novel in 1933, she was one of Britain's leading literary celebrities. Two years previously she had published *All Passion Spent*, her most enduring novel. Sackville-West was the model for the hardly disguised central character in Virginia Woolf's 1928 novel, *Orlando*, which has been called a long love letter from Woolf to Sackville-West. The two were lovers, even while both were married to prominent men. Woolf and Sackville-West were part of the Bloomsbury circle of artists, writers, and intellectuals who were encouraging new ideas in the arts, politics, psychology, spirituality, and human relationships. The two women became leading feminist voices, depicting the burdens of traditional female roles and restrictions. In literature it was a time of bold experiments, some of which, like Woolf's novels, have become cultural landmarks. Sackville-West's novel *Grand Canyon* was this kind of experiment, but it was not so successful. For two decades her novels had been published by Hogarth Press, run by Woolf and her husband, Leonard Woolf, but *Grand Canyon* was rejected.

In 1933 Sackville-West went on her only trip to America, with her devoted husband, Harold Nicolson, a diplomat, biographer, and member of the House of Commons. She made the rounds of American cities and colleges, where her lectures drew enthusiastic audiences. Vita and Harold disliked America's commercial values. To Virginia, she wrote, "Los Angeles is hell.... The Americans have an unequalled genius for making everything hideous."[28] But she loved nature, a central element of her novels and poetry, and she found much of it to love in America. In *Orlando* Woolf depicts the Sackville-West character as a nature lover who endlessly devotes herself to her epic poem "The Oak Tree." The real Sackville-West first sought out Niagara Falls, with which she was thrilled. After Los Angeles, she and her husband retreated to a cottage at a California desert guest ranch, as Galsworthy and Priestley had done. "Magnificent stars overhead," she wrote to Woolf, "and mountains all around. The desert itself is carpeted with rosy verbena.... We are as happy as larks."[29] It was at this ranch that Sackville-West conceived of her Grand Canyon novel, which like *All Passion Spent* would be about personal transformation and renewal. Her husband wrote in his diary:

> It is about a middle-aged woman who has had some deep sorrow in her life and becomes benevolent and neutral. It is divided into two halves. One half is in life and the other half in death. The life part is to take the form of the Grand Canyon.... The death part is to take the shape of a wind-jammer from which, at stated intervals, people tumble overboard.... It is the sort of thing which only she could carry off....[30]

Sackville-West conceived this idea before she had actually seen the Grand Canyon, but on April 1, she and her husband arrived and checked in at El Tovar Hotel. During their visit they went for rim walks, watched the Hopis dance, shopped for Indian jewelry, and traveled to the Desert View Watchtower, from which they admired the Painted Desert in the distance. To Nicolson the canyon was like "twenty Matterhorns blazing with alpine glow and situated many thousands of feet below one."[31] He was disappointed by the Hopi dances though; having just come from Hollywood and a meeting with Gary Cooper, he was probably expecting Hollywood Indians. But Sackville-West was very interested in Native American spirituality, and she would begin her novel *Grand Canyon* by relating the Hopi belief that the spirits of their dead enter the canyon to reach the underworld. Nicolson reported: "Vita is very impressed by the Grand Canyon. So am I."[32] At sunset they walked from El Tovar to Powell Memorial. Nicolson wrote:

> It is approaching sunset and we get the best view of the Canyon we have seen. The shadows are slate-blue and the rocks a dominant sang-de-boeuf trailing off to pink in places and in places to orange. We walk back thinking out comparisons. I say it is like a wood-fire—looking into the glow of the logs. Viti says it is like nothing on earth. She adds that she feels "increased." I say that I do too. We dine hungrily, look out again by moonlight—but there is only half a moon and the Canyon opens a dim cold greenness....[33]

From South Carolina, near the end of her American trip, Vita got out a piece of El Tovar stationery and wrote to Virginia:

> Oh, the things we've seen and the people we've met! I don't think I wrote to you from the Grand Canyon which is the most astonishing thing in the world. We're going to come back to America in order to motor all through Texas, Arizona, California, and Mexico, taking tents with us in order to camp in the desert. You can't imagine, Virginia, what the Painted Desert is like. It is every color of the rainbow, broken by great pink cliffs.... And the sun blazes every day.... Why don't you and Leonard come with us? January, February, and March would be the time to go, and the first bit of April. Nor can you imagine the desert flowers.... Doesn't it appeal to you?[34]

This trip never happened, and Virginia Woolf never saw America. But she was responsible for Sackville-West writing *Grand Canyon*. It appears that Virginia had suggested to Vita that her American trip might supply her with the raw materials for a novel. Upon returning to England, she made a brief attempt at a start, but, as she wrote to Virginia: "Didn't start it, so much as returned to a bit of vomit I spewed in America—the novel you said I was to write—all about deserts and hurricanes. I don't know if I can make anything of it."[35] She set the idea aside for seven years, returning to it only because of

Virginia's encouragement. In 1940 Vita dug out another piece of El Tovar stationery, with its image of the Grand Canyon, and wrote to Virginia:

> Thank you for letting me come to stay with you and for being so per-
> manently loving towards me—
>   Your friendship means so much to me. In fact it is one of the major
> things in my life—...
>   Isn't this a nice piece of writing-paper I have found for you?
>   I am so grateful to you: you sent me home feeling that I really ought
> to go on with my novel—Before I came to you, I was in the dumps
> about it.
>   Then I told you something about it, which I would never have said
> to anybody else, and you said just the right thing.
>   So instead of despairing about it, I fished it out again this evening
> instead of trying to avoid it....
>   *Your Orlando.*[36]

Vita would retain her idea about a story with a life half and a death half,
but she would abandon the death half's ocean setting and place it in the
Grand Canyon also. A larger change occurred because World War II was now
raging, and she turned the novel into a political allegory. Combining her
original personal/metaphysical story with a political story resulted in a novel
that Sackville-West scholar Michael Stevens called a "failure" and referred to
as "this strange book."[37]

With the outbreak of World War II Harold Nicolson became a war min-
ister in Churchill's cabinet, and one of his duties was writing a book, *Why
Britain Is at War,* to rally the world's sympathy, especially in neutral America.
Nicolson was well-positioned to observe America's ambivalence about the
war. He had written a biography of American diplomat Dwight Morrow, and
in 1933 he and his wife had visited him and gotten to know his daughter Ann
and Ann's husband, Charles Lindbergh, who soon would become the most
influential voice against America aiding Britain. Sackville-West also had some
expertise on American-British relations. Her grandfather had been Britain's
ambassador to the United States in the 1880s, and her mother had become a
star in Washington social circles. According to family legend, the widower

President Chester Arthur became smitten with her mother and proposed marriage, but she turned him down.

Sackville-West had considered herself a pacifist, but now she encouraged her two sons to be proud soldiers. In the darkest days of the war, when German planes filled the skies and an invasion seemed imminent, Vita and Harold were so horrified at the possibility of defeat that they both carried a vial of poison. With Americans still resisting the war, before Pearl Harbor, Sackville-West began writing *Grand Canyon* to arouse Americans about the German threat. She labored on the "bloody book" through many midnights, since it was "The only form of happiness I can find."[38]

In 1942 she sent the completed manuscript to Leonard Woolf at Hogarth Press; Virginia was no longer there, for she had committed suicide the year before. Hogarth Press had already given Vita a contract for the novel and advertised it as a forthcoming book, so she was shocked when Woolf rejected the manuscript.

He explained that the novel's portrayal of British defeat and German world conquest was just too bleak and demoralizing. "This is," he wrote to her, "one of the most unpleasant letters I have ever had to write, primarily because as an author you have always treated us so extraordinarily well that it seems almost unthinkable that the Hogarth Press should reject a book of yours."[39] He was referring to the fact that Sackville-West had stayed with Hogarth Press even when the success of her novels meant she could have jumped to a larger and more lucrative publisher. Privately, to his business partner John Lehmann, Woolf expressed his doubts about the novel's literary merits: "It is not a good book, I'm afraid, and I doubt whether, were it not by Vita, one would consider it."[40] It was, he said, "in many ways absurd."[41] Sackville-West sent the manuscript to another major publisher, who also turned it down. After some revisions, a third publisher took it. Hogarth Press had published fourteen of Sackville-West's books, but she would never return to them. On the basis of her reputation the novel drew eight thousand prepublication orders, but then it drew what the author called "some bloody reviews."[42] At least her American publisher, Doubleday, stuck by her, but on their jacket blurb they promised readers a happy ending and made no mention of the novel's metaphysical elements or its depiction of the United States being conquered by the Germans.

The first half of *Grand Canyon* is titled "The Hotel" and is set at El Tovar.

The novel begins as a typical British novel of manners, observing the little society in the hotel. The main character, the British Helen Temple, is basically Sackville-West herself and voices many of her opinions. Observing a couple with children, Helen says, "They are decent people—so decent that one wonders how they ever brought themselves to commit the grotesque act necessary to begat children."[43] Helen meets a British man, Lester Dale, a perpetual wanderer who comes to the Grand Canyon every year: "Like the Indians, he could believe that the canyon held the secrets of life and death."[44] Helen and Lester observe the doings of the Americans. Unlike J. B. Priestley, with his proletarian sympathies, Sackville-West was an aristocrat and indulged in the long British habit of snobbery toward lesser peoples: "Americans never grow up at all—they remain permanently adolescent; that's their charm if they only knew it, though they don't like being told so."[45] At dinner time, "The dining room filled up with people and chatter as the hour for feeding approached. The animals must be fed, be fed. The animals in the Grand Canyon Zoo couldn't be allowed to go hungry."[46] Of the Indian dancers: "What's the good of having a canyon if you don't exploit it? The management exploited it for all it was worth."[47]

Only well into the novel is there any mention that this is a time of war. The Nazis have conquered Britain and much of the world. The Americans are too innocent to grasp the reality and strength of "Evil" and to prepare to fight it. The Grand Canyon is the hub of huge American military maneuvers, and the hotel is full of servicemen. We discover that the manager of the hotel is a Nazi secret agent, with the mission of setting the hotel afire at night to guide German bombers to a surprise attack on the American forces. When the bombers appear and an alarm sounds, Helen opens her jewelry case to get her vial of poison, and then she and many other guests flee toward the Bright Angel Trail. "The burning hotel was dramatic enough in its own way, but the magnificence of the canyon cheapened it into a mere little bonfire. The quick disaster of man showed up cheaply against the slow carving of Nature."[48] The bombs fall, and there's a "big crash." Only later do we discover that this blast has killed everyone.

In the second part, "The Canyon," Helen and Lester and the others descend the Bright Angel Trail to Phantom Ranch, where they catch radio reports of the massive German attack against the United States. In New York, the Statue of Liberty is destroyed. But the author hints that something remarkable has happened to her characters: a blind man can now see, a deaf man can now hear, a tubercular Harvey Girl waitress is now well, and no one is bothered by the heat or hunger.

The characters then proceed to carry on implausible and didactic conversations that allow Sackville-West to voice her own opinions. Human psychology may leave humans separated "as wide and deep as the Grand Canyon," but they can build "a broad and substantial bridge connecting even the most completely incommensurable of psychological universes."[49]

At last we learn that the characters are actually spirits, but "They... felt so remarkably alive, more alive than they had ever felt in their ordinary lives before.... There was indeed a great deal to be said for being dead...if being dead meant that one gained this new angle of proportion on life.... So Mrs. Temple and Mr. Dale wandered among the immensities of the canyon...."[50] The canyon was now "*their* territory, *their* domain, in its inexhaustible beauty and surprise.... It was necessary to spend...seasons, years, for its magnitude and beauty fully to enlarge and enrich the soul. This opportunity was theirs now."[51]

In an implausibility that tops all the others in the novel, the German bombing of New York City triggers a fault line to rupture, toppling skyscrapers and leaving—right down Fifth Avenue—a canyon that "reminded him of a section of the Grand Canyon of the Colorado. He said that he seemed to look as deep into the earth and that the tumbled masonry of the buildings suggested the natural rock formations of that region."[52] Nature or God had endorsed the self-destruction of humanity.

Humans may be hopelessly mad, but Helen and Lester are content in nature's embrace: "We know that other mountains and other hills shall in time be washed into the sea, and coral reefs and shales and bones and disintegrated mountains shall be made into beds of rock, for a new land where new rivers shall flow. But in the meantime let us enjoy the strip of beauty that has been granted to us."[53]

The idea of finding peace in nature had always been important to Sackville-West, and now, as German bombers thundered over her home, she was probably wishing she had a Grand Canyon in which to hide. She had to settle for her garden, for which she became famous.

With its hybrid origin, its implausibility, its didactic rhetoric, and its passing moment of history, *Grand Canyon* wouldn't satisfy many readers or endure. Yet Sackville-West does deserve credit for at least attempting to make the canyon the setting for a meaningful, literary story. Almost all Grand Canyon fiction has used the canyon as a stage for melodrama, whether it be the Wild West variety, romantic melodrama, or river running adventures. While poets readily saw the Grand Canyon as a realm of ultimate questions, and nature writers saw it as one of nature's ultimate expressions, few serious novelists have seen much use for it. Novelists deal in human stories, and the Grand Canyon seems an inhuman realm, as inaccessible by a novelist's pen as it is by boot or boat. At least Vita Sackville-West tried to use it as a philosophical landscape.

There were two other British novelists who should have written about the Grand Canyon.

D. H. Lawrence spent nearly two years in New Mexico in the 1920s trying to reinvent paganism for the modern world out of a mixture of nature romanticism, tribal spirituality, and sex. When he first traveled from San Francisco to New Mexico, he had a vague plan to visit Yosemite and the Grand Canyon, but he was feeling poorly, and he said, in the words of biographer David Ellis, "he would drop dead if any more stupendousness assailed him."[54] In 1924 Lawrence journeyed to Arizona to see the Hopi Snake Dance, but this was as close as he got to the Grand Canyon.

The outbreak of World War II stranded Aldous Huxley in America for six years. He lived in southern California, an easy train ride from the Grand Canyon, which held a Huxley Terrace, a butte named for Aldous's grandfather, Thomas Huxley, the public champion of Charles Darwin. Yet Aldous didn't seem to feel much rapport with the canyon. He had visited on his first American visit, in 1926, spending a day there and taking the bus tour of the South Rim. Having just come from Hollywood and a visit with Charlie Chaplin, Huxley wrote to a friend that he had now seen America's "two most remarkable natural phenomena—the Grand Canyon and Charlie Chaplin. Both were splendid."[55] But Huxley seemed more interested in Chaplin. To another friend Huxley wrote:

> The Grand Canyon was quite up to specifications and only man was vile. (But then, poor devil, he can hardly fail to be when he is as closely

concentrated as he necessarily must be round the point where the railway touches the canyon.) One trundles in motor buses along the brink of the chasm. Of if one has more time or, being a woman, likes the shape of one's haunches in breeches, one mounts a mule and goes off with a movie cowboy down into the gulf. The breeches, I must say, added something to the charms of the scene.[56]

The canyon's main literary influence on Huxley was that it introduced him to Native American culture in the form of the dancers at Hopi House. Five years later in *Brave New World* Huxley explored Puebloan life and ceremonies; he has two characters visit a New Mexico "Savage Reservation," where the Indians are imprisoned by an electric fence that gets its "current from the Grand Canyon hydroelectric station."[57] In contrast with Lawrence's "Noble Savages," Huxley's Indians are far from utopian. Like Lawrence and Priestley, Huxley was frustrated with science and searching for more spiritual realities, but he couldn't believe in Lawrence's prescription for a more primitive life and preferred a purer form of mysticism. Aldous Huxley might have found more inspiration in Buddha Temple than in Huxley Terrace.

Huxley, Lawrence, and Shaw agreed with Galsworthy, Priestley, and Sackville-West in disliking American pomposity and social values, but when the three latter writers gave the Grand Canyon a chance, it quickly broke through the sociological veil and spoke to them on its own greater terms. They found in the canyon a realm of ultimate beauty and order and peace, a peace that could reach through the turmoils of love and war and doubt, and grant its timelessness to troubled human hearts.

TROPIC OF CANYON

Henry Miller's Moment of Truth

Grand Canyon river guides often witness the canyon's power to change lives. When people are cut off from their usual social realities and immersed in nature's power, they sometimes perceive themselves in new ways and decide that they cannot return to their old lives. Such moments of truth also happen on Grand Canyon hikes and even on visits to the rim, but these experiences tend to be more private, less likely to be witnessed and remembered by others. One such transformative experience happened to a prominent American writer, Henry Miller.

For several generations of American writers and artists, leaving America for Europe became an essential rite of passage. Yet leaving America was a different experience for writers than it was for artists. For artists it was a practical career necessity. The best artists and art schools and the latest trends were in Europe. But for writers it was a deeply problematic act. Being an American writer was supposed to mean that you wrote about the American experience. By going to Europe, writers cut themselves off from both their personal and national experience. If American writers imagined that they could write about Europe, they quickly realized that they lacked the authenticity to do so. At best, they might write about being an American in Paris. For artists, painting a face, a flower, or a mountain in Europe was not fundamentally different from painting the same subjects in America. But for writers there usually came a moment of truth at which they realized that to be writers at all, they needed to go home and write about the American experience. This was a difficult realization, since most of them had gone to Europe as an act of rejecting American society. America was a land of philistines who didn't value literature, while Europe was the land of intellectual sophistication. In New York City cafes, businessmen talked about the stock market and advertising gimmicks, while in Paris cafes bohemians talked about the latest ideas, books, and art movements.

The magnetism of Paris cafes was especially powerful in the 1920s. In America the Progressive movement had fizzled out and given way to an era of conservative politics and stock market mania; American moral values remained Victorian; and with the Scopes trial, it had become a criminal act to talk about ideas. Most annoying of all, America's triumph in the Great War had left it with a smug sense of superiority. Disgusted, many young Americans fled to Europe, becoming the Lost Generation. When they realized that to find their voices, they needed to go home, they faced many dilemmas, and they came up with different solutions. Ernest Hemingway, like Gershwin in music, wrote about being an American in Paris. William Faulkner, like Thomas Hart Benton in art, returned to the place of his birth and found a regional expression of universal human longings. Many writers, like Sinclair Lewis, decided that it was their mission to be adversaries of American society.

For Henry Miller, returning to and reconnecting with America was especially problematic. His novel *Tropic of Cancer*, published in Paris in 1934, had been banned in the United States. Miller had taken this as the banning of himself; he had no intention of returning to America. Still, his feelings about America continued gnawing at him. There were some things about it that he missed powerfully: not his family, with whom he had fallen out long ago, but the land itself, especially the landscapes of the American West.

At age twenty-one, in 1913, Henry Miller had taken a trip across the Southwest, and he'd been enthralled. The more time he spent in Paris—with its narrow lanes, crowds, noise, and artificial fashions in clothing and food—the more he remembered the open horizons of the American West. He remembered its people, the Indians who lived with a simplicity and authenticity that was so different from Parisian life. It was ironic that Parisians frequently asked him about the American West: Did you ever meet any Indians? Are desert sunsets beautiful? Have you been to the Grand Canyon? To the latter question he was chagrined to have to answer, "No." He had been through Arizona, but he hadn't been to the canyon. And now he had left this land behind, only to discover that the sophisticated Parisians found it all quite fascinating.

In his imagination Miller started planning a journey across America. This was strictly a fantasy trip, since Miller was a starving artist. In his journal he occasionally wrote down places to explore. "I remember distinctly," he wrote later, "the thrill I had when putting down such words as Mobile, Suwanee River, Navajos, Painted Desert...."[1]

In 1940, after a decade as an expatriate, Miller finally returned to America, but in his mind he was not returning, he was coming to settle accounts and to say good-bye for good. "I felt the need to effect a reconciliation with my native land," he said introducing the book he wrote about his journey.

> It was an urgent need because, unlike most prodigal sons, I was returning not with the intention of remaining in the bosom of the family but of wandering forth again, perhaps never to return. I wanted to have a last look at my country and leave it with a good taste in my mouth. I didn't want to run away from it, as I had originally. I wanted to embrace it, to feel that the old wounds were really healed, and set out for the unknown with a blessing on my lips.[2]

Miller would end up staying in America, living and writing in a rustic house perched atop a wilderness cliff, an entirely different universe from Paris. One thing that helped change his mind was the Grand Canyon: "For over thirty years I had been aching to see this huge hole in the earth."[3]

Miller's fame as a novelist came from his sensuality. He did get some respect for his stylistic innovations, especially for picking up elements of surrealism and Dadaism and working them into fiction. But it was the candid sexuality of his characters that made him unique—and notorious. Miller became the focus of the most famous censorship battle in American history, which ended in 1964 when the U.S. Supreme Court ruled that the thirty-year ban on his books was even naughtier than the four-letter words in them. By then Miller had become a cause célèbre among American writers, artists, civil

libertarians, and everyone who had ever been frustrated by American phi-
listinism. Famous writers, including Norman Mailer, rallied to his defense
and wrote elaborate justifications as to why his books weren't smut but art,
even the greatest art. Miller, they proclaimed, was the American James Joyce,
using stream-of-consciousness to tell the deepest secrets of human life; Miller
was the American Proust; he was the greatest literary innovator since Shakespeare; and all that sex was actually spiritual, the Dionysian force in all nature,
a celebration of life. But after the Supreme Court ruling, literary folks wondered if they might have gotten a bit carried away. It might be nice if Miller's
novels had a bit more structure, even a plot. He did seem to ramble. Perhaps
narcissistic self-indulgence was not the same as exploring "the Self." Miller's
preoccupation with sex did seem pretty adolescent at times. When feminist
literary criticism got going—and got going on Miller specifically—it turned
out that he was a male chauvinist pig and a dirty old man after all.

Yet Miller did have a Dionysian inclination, a philosophy that nature was a
powerful transcendent spirit that manifested itself through humans. He was
born in Manhattan at the moment Walt Whitman was dying there, and it was
Whitman who most inspired Miller's philosophy, free-flowing literary style,
exuberance, and embrace of sensuality. In his youth Miller read the American Transcendentalists—Emerson and Thoreau—and adopted their vision of
nature as divinity. Surrounded by the squalor of Gilded Age New York City,
Miller decided that the American Indians, surrounded by nature, lived a far
purer life than white Americans. In Europe Miller was fascinated by thinkers
like Nietzsche, Freud, and Henri Bergson, who portrayed humans as puppets
on the hand of a powerful and creative nature.

At age twenty-one Miller made a run for it, leaving New York for the
American West. This turned out to be a traumatic experience, for in his fer-
tile imagination he had turned the West into a transcendentalist symbol that
the real West could never live up to. Miller's trip was also inspired—he later
told a French biographer—by growing up during the presidency of Teddy
Roosevelt, who had celebrated the West as a realm of adventure and vigor, an
image irresistible to any American teenage boy. Miller envisioned becoming
not just a cowboy hero, but a spiritual cowboy. Instead, he ended up working
in very mundane jobs on a California ranch and in a lemon grove, "working
like a slave...wretched, forlorn, miserable...."[4]

The discrepancy between the real West and the West of his longings first hit him when he stepped off the train in Arizona. Miller recalled this shock in the autobiographical *Tropic of Capricorn*, the companion to *Tropic of Cancer*. It is worth quoting this experience at length, since the conflict between reality and imagination would be the key to Miller's experience of the Grand Canyon three decades later:

> I remember now that it was already night when I first set foot on Arizona soil. Just light enough to catch the last glimpse of a fading mesa. I am walking through the main street of a little town whose name is lost. What am I doing here on this street, in this town? Why, I am in love with Arizona, an Arizona of the mind which I search for in vain with my two good eyes. In the train there was still with me an Arizona which I had brought from New York—even after we had crossed the state line. Was there not a bridge over a canyon which had startled me out of my reverie? A bridge such as I had never seen before, a natural bridge created by a cataclysmic eruption thousands of years ago? And over this bridge I had seen a man crossing, a man who looked like an Indian, and he was riding a horse and there was a long saddlebag hanging beside the stirrup. A natural millenary bridge which in the dying sun with air so clear looked like the youngest, newest bridge imaginable. And over that bridge so strong, so durable, there passed, praise be to God, just a man and a horse, nothing more. This then was Arizona, and Arizona was *not* a figment of the imagination but the imagination itself dressed as a horse and rider. And this was even more than the imagination itself because there was no aura of ambiguity but only sharp and dead isolate the thing itself which was the dream and the dreamer himself seated on horseback. And as the train stops I put my foot down and my foot has put a deep hole in the dream: I am in the Arizona town which is listed in the timetable and it is only the geographical Arizona which anybody can visit who has the money. I am walking along the main street with a valise and I see hamburger sandwiches and real estate offices. I feel so terribly deceived that I begin to weep. It is dark now and I stand at the end of a street, where the desert begins, and I weep like a fool.[5]

Three decades later when Miller planned his real trip across America, he seemed eager to give the Southwest another, more mature test. "I want desperately to get to Arizona," he wrote to his Paris publisher.[6] This time he would see the Grand Canyon: he already had a title for a chapter about the Grand Canyon, "The Grand Canyon and the Culebra Cut." Miller's exact intentions for this chapter aren't clear, but they're not hard to guess. The Culebra Cut was the man-made canyon cut for the Panama Canal. Originally a French project, it was crippled by disease, bankruptcy, and a serious underestimation of the difficulty of carving canyons. When the Americans took over, the Culebra Cut so plagued them with landslides that some experts predicted that the canal was hopeless. When the Cut was completed, it was hailed as the greatest engineering triumph in human history. Given Miller's skepticism about technological progress, we can guess that he was planning to use the Grand Canyon to ridicule the pride of humans in their puny little canal. But the Culebra Cut wouldn't show up in Miller's writing about the Grand Canyon; it seems that his real experience there swept aside his polemical scheme.

When Miller got to New York City he talked a publisher into grubstaking his trip in exchange for a book about America, though the publisher imposed one rule: no sex. Miller bought a car and set forth to explore America by road, which in 1940 was still considered a daring idea. Route 66 was barely a decade old, and most roads, especially out west, were still dirt. There were relatively few highway services such as motels and gas stations. Kerouac's *On the Road* and Steinbeck's *Travels with Charley* were two decades in the future; indeed, Miller's road trip helped to create them and many other literary adventures. Miller's plan was even more adventuresome because, as he freely admitted, "I had never owned a car, didn't know how to drive one even."[7] He took a few driving lessons from poet Kenneth Patchen and hit the road.

Miller envisioned his trip as a Whitmanesque adventure. For a notebook he had obtained from a publisher the unbound proof pages of *Leaves of Grass* and wrote on the backsides. He must have realized before he started, however, that he could not emulate Whitman's celebration of America. Miller had already decided that his book's title would be *The Air-Conditioned Nightmare*, implying that America's technological comforts only housed a poverty of values and human spirit. Right from the start he began attacking America. Sometimes these complaints were perceptive: "Topographically the country is magnificent—and terrifying. Why terrifying? Because nowhere else in the world is the divorce between man and nature so complete."[8] Yet his scathing attacks were often embarrassingly overwrought, even by the standards of 1930s left-wing literary culture. Considering that he was writing as Hitler was conquering Europe, which prompted even the devoted pacifist Albert Einstein to urge others to join the army and inspired the communist Woody Guthrie to write patriotic ballads, Miller's alienation from America seems even more obsessive. Indeed, by the time he finished his manuscript, after Pearl Harbor, his publisher backed out, for no one was in the mood for virulent America bashing. The book wouldn't be published until after the war.

In *The Air-Conditioned Nightmare* it soon becomes clear that Miller's 1940–41 journey is guided by the same Romantic philosophy and longing as his 1913 journey. Between Pittsburgh and Youngstown,

> an Inferno which exceeds anything that Dante imagined, the idea suddenly came to me that I ought to have an American Indian by my side, that he ought to share this voyage with me, communicate to me silently or otherwise his emotions and reflections.... Imagine the two of us standing in contemplation before the hideous grandeur of one of those steel mills.... I can almost hear him thinking—"So it was for this that you deprived us of our birthright...burned our homes, massacred our women and children, poisoned our souls, broke every treaty which you made with us and left us to die."[9]

After a scorched-earth campaign in which Miller criticizes everything about America except for a few obscure artists and religious eccentrics, he arrives in the Southwest, and here his mood changes:

> Somehow, ever since I hit Tucumcari I have become completely disoriented. On the license plates in New Mexico it reads: "The Land of Enchantment." And that it is, by God! There's a huge rectangle which embraces parts of four states—Utah, Colorado, New Mexico, and Arizona—and which is nothing but enchantment, sorcery, illusionismus, phantasmagoria. Perhaps the secret of the American continent is contained in this wild, forbidding and partially unexplored territory. It is the land of the Indian par excellence. Everything is hypnagogic, chthonian

and super-celestial. Here nature has gone gaga and dada. Man is just an irruption, like a wart or a pimple. Man is not wanted here. Red men, yes, but then they are so far removed from what we think of as man that they seem like another species. Embedded in the rocks are their glyphs and hieroglyphs. Not to speak of the footprints of dinosaurs and other lumbering antediluvian beasts. When you come to the Grand Canyon it's as though Nature were breaking out into supplication.[10]

Driving toward the town of Cameron and the canyon, Miller had an experience similar to his 1913 train-window vision of the dreamlike Indian horseman:

For about forty miles I don't think I passed a human habitation.... Three cars passed me and then there was a stretch of silence and emptiness, a steady, sinister ebbing of all human life, of plant and vegetable life, of light itself. Suddenly, out of nowhere, it seemed, three horsemen...just materialized, as it were...then spurred their horses on into the phantasmal emptiness of dusk, disappearing in the space of a few seconds. What was amazing to me was that they seemed to have a sense of direction; they galloped off as if they were going somewhere when obviously there was nowhere to go to.[11]

The similarity of this experience with his *Tropic of Capricorn* experience might make us wonder if Miller was plagiarizing himself or posing for literary effect, but in fact his Grand Canyon visit is also recorded in his letters to his French lady friend Anaïs Nin, and in these letters his experiences, including the surrealistic horsemen, are often described even more vividly and emotionally than in *The Air-Conditioned Nightmare*. This similarity between Miller's 1913 and 1941 experiences should have made him nervous, for his youthful journey had ended in tearful disillusionment. If he now feared putting his foot through his romantic dream again, he was about to face the ultimate test, the ultimate southwestern landscape. The Grand Canyon had been hyped by everyone from artists to travel writers to the Atchison, Topeka, and Santa Fe Railway. Could the reality possibly match the dream? From Cameron, where Miller camped in the back seat of his car, he wrote to Nin: "Tomorrow the grandiose will reach its apotheosis at Grand Canyon. The river gorge here is about 300 ft. deep and looks impressive in its moonlike desolation. But at Grand Canyon it is *one mile* deep!!"[12] Miller was also seeking spiritual depths at the Grand Canyon. From Albuquerque he had written to Nin that he was now heading for "the Canyon, which I love—next to Tibet the greatest spot on earth."[13]

Miller's first experience of the Grand Canyon was intense, including intense relief, for the canyon did indeed live up to his dream. On May 1, 1941, he wrote to Nin from Bright Angel Lodge: "First glimpses of canyon suburb—no deception, no letdown. In fact I *trembled* looking into it and got to laughing. I took a room for a week."[14]

In *The Air-Conditioned Nightmare* Miller not only trembles but weeps with joy, tears that finally wipe away and cancel out the tears of disillusionment he shed as a young man. The Lost Generation had been disillusioned so many times that finally they refused to believe in anything; they had made a god out of disillusionment. But now, after all the phoniness Miller had found in his trip across America, here was something real, overwhelmingly real—actually so surreal that it surpassed all the surrealistic art and writing he had admired:

> It's mad, completely mad, and at the same time so grandiose, so sublime, so illusory, that when you come upon it for the first time you break down and weep with joy. I did, at least. For over thirty years I had been aching to see this huge hole in the earth. Like Phaestos, Mycenae, Epidauros, it is one of the few spots on earth which not only come up to all expectation but surpass it. My friend Bushman, who had been a guide here for a number of years, had told me some fantastic stories about the Grand Canyon. I can believe anything that any one might tell me about it, whether it has to do with geological eras and formations, freaks of nature in animal or plant life, or Indian legends. If some one were to tell me that the peaks and mesas and amphitheatres which are so fittingly called Tower of Set, Cheop's Pyramid, Shiva Temple, Osiris Temple, Isis Temple, etc. were the creation of fugitive Egyptians, Chinese or Tibetans, I would lend a credulous ear. The Grand Canyon is an enigma and no matter how much we learn we shall never know the ultimate truth about it....[15]

Two days after his arrival at the canyon Miller wrote to Nin:

> Well, it's one of the places on earth I dearly wanted to see. It's no let-
> down. The rocks are cut as to resemble the facades of Hindu or Siamese
> temples. Some of the rocks which jut up alone and isolate are named
> after ancient temples. It is a tremendous drama of geology. I'll send you
> a little book on it soon—it's fascinating. Now it's pouring (we've had
> unusual weather in this country where it's so dry) and the canyon is
> steaming—like a huge cauldron. At night, when you can see nothing, it
> is awesome. You *feel* this big hole—a mile deep. I haven't been down it
> yet—afraid to walk it because I might not get up—it's like climbing up
> five Empire State Buildings.... I'd like to live down at the bottom for a
> week or so. Only Indians could live in such a place.[16]

Miller stretched his stay at the canyon to ten days. On day seven he
reported to Nin: "I didn't get down *in* the Canyon—just walked and drove
around the rim, viewing it from all angles in all sorts of atmospheric conditions. It changes perpetually, like a chameleon."[17] Miller also reported that "I
gave up *all* medicines about 3 days ago—and, oddly enuf, I feel better.... Must
be psychological too...." He closed with:

> The sky now is perfect here—especially toward sunset. That electric
> blue I first noticed in Greece. And the stars at night like pinpricks on
> a cloth of unseizable velvet. The canyon itself is covered with green, a
> faded Byzantine green, of suede. Striking. I don't go into it in a letter
> because I want to write about it at length. I'm grateful to have seen it.
> One of the wonders of the universe.[18]

In *The Air-Conditioned Nightmare* Miller dwelled on several canyon experiences. The sight of a discarded newspaper served as a symbol of the smallness
of human lives compared with geological time:

> ...as I was taking my customary promenade along the rim of the Can-
> yon, the sight of a funny sheet (Prince Valiant was what caught my eye)
> lying on the edge of the abyss awakened curious reflections. What can

possibly appear more futile, sterile and insignificant in the presence of such a vast and mysterious spectacle as the Grand Canyon than the Sunday comic sheet? There it lay, carelessly tossed aside by an indifferent reader, the least wind ready to lift it aloft and blow it to extinction. Behind this gaudy-colored sheet, requiring for its creation the energies of countless men, the varied resources of Nature, the feeble desires of over-fed children, lay the whole story of the culmination of our Western civilization.[19]

As Miller walked among the tourists, he "caught the weirdest fragments of conversation, startling because so unrelated to the nature of the place."[20] Miller couldn't resist making fun of tourists who were more interested in their western-style fashions, their ice cream, or their social pretensions than in the canyon.

In front of Verkamp's store Miller ran into young Jack Verkamp polishing the rim telescope. When Jack mentioned that his dad's store sold film, Miller was almost triggered into another tirade against American commercial values. But he seems to have recognized the absurdity of venting in front of a young boy who lived on the edge of the canyon and obviously loved it, so for once in the book Miller lightened up and wrote a double-edged tirade that was also a parody of his own self-righteousness:

But to him everything was phenomenal and interesting, including the hotel on the opposite side of the canyon—because you could see it clearly through the telescope. "Have you seen the large painting of the Canyon in my father's shop?" he asked, as I was about to leave him. "It's a phenomenal piece of work." I told him bluntly I had no intention of looking at it.... He looked aggrieved, wounded, utterly amazed that I should not care to see one of the greatest reproductions of Nature by the hand of man. "When you get a little more sense," I said, "maybe it won't seem so wonderful to you...." I was fuming to think that a young boy should have nothing better to do than try to waylay tourists for his father at that hour of the morning. Pretending to be fixing the telescope, polishing it, and so on, and then pulling off that nonsense about "man imitating God's handiwork"—on a piece of canvas, no less, when there before one's eyes was God himself in all his glory, manifesting his grandeur without the aid or intervention of man. All to sell you a fossil or a string of beads or some photographic film. Reminded me of the bazaars of Lourdes.[21]

Miller devoted one chapter to "The Desert Rat," a dusty old prospector with whom he'd talked for hours over lunch at Bright Angel Lodge. "He went on about the virtue of living alone in the desert, of living with the stars and rocks, studying the earth, listening to one's own voice, wondering about Creation."[22] The hermit talked about how the land spoke to him more profoundly than any book could; about the wisdom of the earth and of the Indians; about the craziness of cities and civilization. Writing to Nin, Miller called it "The best talk I've had with anyone since leaving New York. All I told you of my intuitions about the Indians…he confirmed. He knows them—lived with them. Is a solitary prospector in the desert near Barstow, Cal. And a mystic and philosopher…. And at the end he apologized for 'not being educated.' I learned more from him than from all the professors."[23]

There was a reason why Miller became so absorbed in a conversation about nature versus cities, earth versus books, simple restaurants versus stylish cafes. This was the very argument that Miller was waging within himself as he tried to figure out where to go and what to do with the rest of his life. This internal conflict surfaced in the second letter he wrote to Nin from the Grand Canyon as he coaxed himself toward a different life than the one he had lived in Paris: "Of course I realize the change that is coming. I ask nothing better than to sit down and live simply…. I know how to go without and not feel disoriented. I don't even miss the movies."[24]

Only nine days after Miller left the Grand Canyon, even as he was settling into Hollywood, it seems he was feeling a new direction, at least subconsciously. He wrote to Nin about his plans: "Guess it will be San Francisco next, though I'm not sure. May stop off in between at Big Sur about which Robinson Jeffers wrote—the wildest part of the Pacific Coast."[25] Miller found Big Sur as captivating as Jeffers had, and he would spend sixteen years there in a cabin with no electricity perched atop cliffs above the ocean—cliffs a bit like those of the Grand Canyon. He would live a life closer to that of the Mojave Desert prospector than to that of Paris intellectuals in their cafes, theaters, and art galleries. On his way up the Pacific coast Miller had checked out Carmel, but he told Nin, "Didn't like the looks of the place—so arty."[26] In Paris Miller had reveled in such places, but now he was turning his back on art in favor of nature—an extension of the pride he took in refusing to step into Verkamp's store and see art of the Grand Canyon when he could embrace the real thing.

In her diary Anaïs Nin recorded Miller's struggle for direction. In December 1940 he had returned from the American South to New York City, where Nin was living. She wrote, "Henry returns from his wanderings. He tells me about America.... He has been looking for something to love. Nature, yes, that was extraordinary. He tells me about a stalactite cave, the wonder of it.... Henry is not impressed with size, power. He looks for a deeper America."[27] He would soon set out for the West.

In the end, it's not possible to prove how much influence the Grand Canyon had upon Miller's change of direction. He never stated this in print. Miller's biographers and scholars often skim over the whole *Nightmare* road trip around America and barely mention the Grand Canyon; they are interested mainly in Miller's novels, and most of them come from an academic perspective where the only reality is human culture and it can be hard to imagine nature having anything important to say to anyone. But all the indications are that Miller's encounter with the Grand Canyon fit powerfully into his midlife crisis and helped to resolve it. In his youth he had felt a powerful pull to the American Southwest, but then he had lost faith in his own impulses, and then in America entirely. Miller's homecoming road trip may have done little to heal his alienation from a phony society, but he did discover that, in nature, America holds something powerfully real, powerfully surreal, something besides which human society didn't really matter, something that allowed him to return home and begin a new life atop a remote cliff.

Miller did give us one strong hint about the influence the Grand Canyon had on him. After settling in Big Sur, he sought out and became close friends with two people who were closely associated with the Grand Canyon and the Southwest, Lawrence Clark Powell and Edwin Corle. Powell was a southwestern historian and the librarian at UCLA. Back in 1932 Powell and Miller had taught English at the same boy's school in Dijon, France. Now both found a spiritual home in the American West. In 1960 Powell wrote, "If an astrologer had told Henry Miller thirty years ago in Paris that the crowning years of his life would be spent on an isolated stretch of the Central California coast, he would have changed astrologers."[28] Powell became Miller's lifeline to the literary world, sending him a constant stream of books from the UCLA library. His other close friend, Edwin Corle, was a novelist, and he would later write the introduction to one of Miller's novels. He also wrote the midcentury's most popular book about the Grand Canyon, *Listen, Bright Angel*. This title should have caught the imagination of a man who had spent ten days at Bright Angel Lodge trying to listen to his own heart, and who had sat for hours in the hotel's restaurant listening to a desert hermit talk about listening to nature.

In 1975 a *Rolling Stone* reporter went to interview Miller. "On one wall is a hand-inscribed poster listing the names of scores of places Miller has visited around the world—with marginal comments." It included: "Grand Canyon (still the best)."[29]

13

TALL CLIFFS AND TALL TALES

The Origins of John Hance

As Americans pioneered a vast and powerful continent, they developed a style of storytelling that did justice to their experience. From Europe many emigrants had brought with them a tradition of tall tales, but the American experience tended to make those tales quite a bit taller. America's mountains and trees were taller, its rivers and prairies were bigger, and its weather and wildlife were wilder. And its canyons were deeper. The men and women who were measuring themselves against the American wilderness felt challenged to be taller and braver and more ingenious. They needed heroes to inspire them. They felt they were characters in a national epic. They spun stories about adventures and misadventures that were as big and wild as the land. Some of their stories involved fictional characters like Paul Bunyan, while others involved real people like Davy Crockett.

When American pioneers finally arrived at the Grand Canyon, they faced a landscape and a challenge that was gigantic even by the standards of the American experience. Some of the prospectors who came to the canyon rim took one look and considered the effort it would take to explore the canyon, build a trail into it, and haul ore out of it, and they turned around and left for easier landscapes. It would take a larger-than-life man to inhabit this place. That man was John Hance, the first white settler on the canyon rim, and the first prospector to build a trail into the canyon. Hance came from a region where the art of the tall tale was especially well developed, but he recognized that the Grand Canyon required some very tall tales to do it justice. Hance was equal to that challenge too. For a lover of tall tales, the canyon provided a mother lode of material.

Hance especially liked to tell one tale about snowshoeing across the canyon on top of the fog. On evenings when there was mist shrouding the canyon, Hance would walk up to guests sitting on the El Tovar Hotel porch, snow-shoes slung over his shoulder, and announce that the fog was looking thick enough for him to walk on it across the canyon. He would walk up to the rim, stick a foot out to test the fog, and then announce that he'd go along the rim to Yaki Point to make the crossing. He'd tell guests to watch for his campfire on the North Rim that night. When Hance saw those guests the next day, he'd ask if they'd seen his campfire, and if they said no, he'd say that, of course, the fog was too thick to see through it. Hance told how one time the fog thinned out before he'd made it across, and he was lucky to reach Zoroaster Temple, atop which he was stranded for days without a thing to eat. The fog refused to thicken, but after days of losing weight, Hance was thin enough to walk atop the thinner fog.

For over thirty years John Hance told tall tales to Grand Canyon visitors, and his tales made Hance himself a tourist attraction. At first there were only a few who would find their way to Hance's cabin near the rim in the Grandview area. Hance had found a rich asbestos lode near the bottom of the canyon and built a trail to it. When that trail washed out, he built another. Tourists would ask him to take them down the trail, and they offered him money for food and shelter. Hance soon realized he could make easier money from tourists than from mining, and he became the canyon's first tourist host and guide. He became such a legend that when the Santa Fe Railway arrived, it hired him just to guide and entertain tourists. Hance hung out at the Bright Angel Hotel and lived in a cabin nearby. Visitors who wrote about their canyon experiences often mentioned their encounter with John Hance. Novelist Hamlin Garland called him "a powerful and astonishing fictionist. Consciously he is a teller of whopping lies.

Unconsciously he is one of the most dramatic and picturesque natural raconteurs I have ever met."[1]

Hance's tall tales included some foggy tales about his own life, which has left some of the basic facts obscure or distorted. In the case of his Civil War record, he had a good motive for lying, but he played games even with his date of birth.

Hance apparently told one guest at his cabin that he was born in 1850, for on Sept. 7, 1898, this guest recorded in Hance's guest book that it was Hance's forty-eighth birthday. On a voting record in 1906, however, Hance claimed he was sixty-four, meaning he was born in 1842. But two years later, on another voting record, Hance said he was sixty, giving him a birthdate of 1848. In a legal affidavit from 1902, testifying about the work Ralph Cameron had done on the Bright Angel Trail, Hance stated he was fifty-one, meaning a birthdate of 1851. In the 1870 U.S. census Hance listed himself as twenty-nine, implying a birthdate of 1841. In the 1880 census Hance was thirty-seven years old, meaning a birthdate of 1843. In the 1900 census Hance said he was forty-nine, and he claimed a birthdate of 1850. In the 1910 census Hance was sixty-four, meaning a birthdate of 1846. In 1917 Hance published a newspaper article declaring that it was his eightieth birthday, meaning a birthdate of 1837. He told his brother George that he was born in 1838, and George repeated this for John's obituary in the *Coconino Sun* on January 17, 1919, but George, who was many years younger, seemed cautious about this, saying "I have only his statement as to his age." George also said that John was born on September 11. A week previously, the newspaper had listed Hance as "about 88 years old," for a birthdate of 1831. But Hance's obituary in the *Arizona Republic* listed him as eighty-four years old, for a birthdate of 1835. The truth about John Hance is more interesting than his tall tales. When we see where he came from, not just geographically but culturally, then his life as a Grand Canyon prospector and storyteller seems more likely as an outcome.

We can take a fairly good aim at where Hance was born. He told someone he was born at Cowan's Ferry, Tennessee, but there never was a town with that name. There was, however, a ferry by that name that crossed the French Broad River a few miles east of Dandridge, in Jefferson County. This was Appalachian Mountain country: Cowan's Ferry was about twenty-five miles north of today's Great Smoky Mountain National Park. The French Broad River is one of the major tributaries of the Tennessee River, and the ferry had been established by a prominent local family that had pioneered Jefferson County in the 1700s and farmed seven hundred acres along the river. The ferry was located at the junction of the French Broad River and Indian Creek, and was approached from the east by Cowan's Ferry Road. In 1837, according to the Jefferson County deed book, fifty acres at the junction of Indian Creek and the French Broad River were sold by Martin Bunch to Green Hance, short for Greenberry, John's father. Martin Bunch was Green's brother-in-law, having married his sister Elizabeth. John was probably named for his grandfather John Hance, who had moved his family from South Carolina in 1811, judging from the census note that his first seven children were born in South Carolina and the next six, born after 1812, were born in Tennessee. It appears that in the 1830s Hance's grandfather moved from elsewhere in Tennessee to Jefferson County and settled in the Muddy Creek area a few miles west of Indian Creek.

The 1840 census found Hance's grandfather and four of his sons, including Green, living in Jefferson County, and Green and his wife, Elizabeth, now had two sons. Unfortunately the 1840 census did not list the names or ages of children, merely their gender and age range. Green's two male children were listed only as "Under Five." One of these sons should be our John Hance, who was Green's second son. The 1850 census said that John Hance was then ten years old, implying a birthdate of 1840. It's possible that the 1870 census was correct in listing Hance as twenty-nine years old; if his birthday was in September and the census was taken slightly after his birthday, the 1870 census would have recorded him as being twenty-nine.

Why was Hance later so mischievous about his age? He remained a bachelor, so perhaps a lingering hope of romance prompted him to consistently understate his age. Then again, his public persona as a wise old frontiersman would seem to call for him to exaggerate his age. All we can say for sure is that Hance grew up in a place where telling mischievous tales was a way of life.

Hance was the child of a strong river, rugged mountains, and forests still full of bears. He was the child of a land that was not wanted by most people. The first English settlers had claimed the rich farmlands along the east coast of America, and by the time Hance was born, their grandchildren were bypassing the Appalachian Mountains to settle in the Ohio River valley. The mountains offered only dense forests, steep slopes, rocky soil, poor farming, no room for plantations, and bears in the backyard. They were left for Scotsmen, who were accustomed to poor, rocky lands, and Irishmen, who were accustomed to poverty and would be satisfied to own any land at all. As the American frontier moved steadily westward, the Appalachians were left as an enclave of frontier culture, where log cabins were the norm and survival might depend on hunting and fishing. In remote hollows, entertainment depended on fiddles and moonshine and storytelling. Storytelling was a long Celtic tradition, but tales of the American frontier were even more greatly exaggerated, full of heroic but stoic frontiersmen taking on the land, the elements, the beasts, and the Indians.

As Hance was growing up in Jefferson County, he would have heard tall tales about a man who'd grown up there forty years previously and was now America's Superman of tall tales: Davy Crockett. The Crockett family moved to Jefferson County around 1795, then to the next county over, where Davy's father ran a tavern. Crockett was good at telling his own tall tales, and his real frontier exploits soon made him a magnet for anyone who needed to attach a tall tale to someone larger than life. Crockett's Alamo death in 1836 only further inflated the stories about him.

The Appalachian talent for tall tales is still alive today. America's world series of storytelling, the National Storytelling Festival, is held in Jonesborough, Tennessee, about fifty miles north of where Hance was born. Longtime Grand Canyon interpretive ranger Stew Fritts, who has been known to tell a tale or two in his evening programs, is a devotee of the Jonesborough festival, which includes many days and many large tents full of stories. Fritts agrees that Hance's brand of tall tales has an Appalachian accent; even in the 1940s radio stations didn't penetrate the mountains, so people had to do their own storytelling.

Hance had another story he liked to tell tourists who wanted to hike down his trail. If someone asked nervously if there were any snakes in the canyon, Hance would tell them how one time he'd seen four hundred snakes at once, but they were moving in a big circle, one snake eating another, until finally there was only one left, and then it grabbed its own tail and ate itself, and ever since, there have been no snakes in the canyon.

Yet even the best stories couldn't substitute for poor lands. In the 1850s Tennessee led the nation in the percentage of population that was leaving the state. By far the largest destination for Tennesseans was Missouri. In the 1840s most of the Hances left for Pulaski County, Missouri, the portion of it that in 1857 would be split off to create Phelps County, its county seat the town of Rolla. Pulaski/Phelps County was on the northern edge of the Ozark Mountains.

The 1850 census found Green Hance and at least six of his siblings living in Pulaski County. He now had a second wife, Rebecca, and five children, the youngest of whom, George Washington Hance, had been born in Tennessee in 1848, indicating that the family had arrived in Missouri after then. Green's brothers were having children at a steady pace, and the dividing line between births in Tennessee and births in Missouri allows us to plot the dates at which the Hance brothers were following one another to Missouri. The children of Andrew Jackson Hance and Samuel Hance were born in Missouri in 1844; Jonathan Hance's daughter was born in Missouri in 1845; and Croseph (or Crow) Hance's first Missouri-born child came in 1850. The Hance brothers had moved their parents to Missouri, and their father John died there in 1846. The 1850 census shows their mother, Rachel, living with the family of Jesse Rhea, the next-door neighbor of Green Hance. Only one of the brothers, John Jr., remained in Tennessee. Hance apparently told someone that his parents had moved to Missouri in 1852, but this was probably the honest mistake of a boy who was less than ten years old at the time.

Several Hance brothers settled in a valley called Kaintuck Hollow (translation: Kentucky), a dozen miles southwest of Rolla. Green Hance settled halfway between his brothers and Rolla, in township 37N, range 8W, section 19. I once sought out this location and found a hollow between ridges about a hundred feet high, with a creek flowing through it and a flat bottom full of lush green grass and happy cows. Since the road ended at a private gate, I was unable to investigate if there was any trace of the 1850s Hance homestead.

The Hances' migration to the Ozarks was part of a much larger migration of Appalachian people to the region. This migration partook of Manifest Destiny, of the dream of a better life in the West, but it was also a fatalistic migration, for the Ozarks held many of the same disadvantages of the Appalachians: steep, rocky hills covered with forests, demanding hard labor for poor

John Hance on the porch of his cabin. (*Grand Canyon National Park Study Collection*)

farmland. At least the Ozarks offered hunting and fishing far better than on the plains. Once again, Appalachian people took land no one else wanted. In the Ozarks, Appalachian people continued their culture of log cabins, hunting, storytelling, home remedies, moonshine, and old-timey music. It would be this culture that gave Americans their main images of hillbilly life, partly because the 1960s TV show *The Beverly Hillbillies* featured a family from the Ozarks. These images also came from Branson, which by the 1990s had become America's top musical destination, drawing more tourists than the shows of Broadway, Nashville, or Las Vegas. Branson started out as just a few hillbilly music shows in a small vacation town known for good fishing, and it still revels in its hillbilly identity. The fishing and hunting lifestyle of the Ozarks gave birth to the massive Bass Pro Shop, now a national chain, and to some of the leading manufacturers of fishing boats, such as Tracker. And it's possible there was a touch of Ozarks storytelling style in the voice of Mark Twain, a contemporary of Hance's who grew up about 120 miles north of where Hance did.

The Ozarks also offered good geological preparation for John Hance's Grand Canyon career. His family settled in an area of limestone cliffs as high as four hundred feet—which is tall by midwestern standards—with lots of mining.

In Phelps County the Ozarks Plateau drops off toward the drainage of the Missouri River to the north, and the Gasconade River cuts through, creating a further complexity of topography—of cliffs and ridges, valleys and hollows. These cliffs have entrenched the Gasconade River in the way that southwestern rivers become entrenched in canyons. The river winds 300 miles to complete 120 crow-flight miles, and in one section near Phelps County, a boat has to travel 15 miles to complete 2 crow miles. Such a trip wouldn't have taken long in the flood of 1879, when the Gasconade River reached 120,000 cubic feet per second. John Hance's father drowned in another flood in 1888, but there are no details about this accident other than that his body was never recovered. Hance's asbestos mine was on the north side of the Colorado River, but his trail came down from the south side, requiring him to cross the river in a small wooden boat. That section of the river has a swift current and strong eddy lines, so Hance would have been often reminded of the dangers of rivers and his father's fate.

The drop of the Ozarks Plateau toward the Missouri River brings underground water to the surface, creating lots of springs, sinkholes, and caves. Missouri has more caves than any other state, and of Missouri counties, Phelps has the second highest number of caves. The long string of caves along the northern flank of the Ozarks includes some famous tourist caves, including Meramec Caverns. Today one Pulaski County cave near the Gasconade River holds a restaurant.

These caves have inspired some Ozarks-style tall tales, such as the Lost Fiddler. Having heard about the wonderful acoustics and echoes inside a cave, a fiddler goes to try it out. A few friends go with him, but remain outside to listen to the echoes. Then the fiddling stops. When the fiddler fails to emerge from the cave, his friends fear he has taken a wrong turn and go searching for him. The fiddler, who is indeed lost, tries using his fiddle to summon help, but with all the chambers and passageways and echoes, his friends get confused and never find him. The fiddler was lost forever.

Another one of Hance's favorite stories recounted how he tried to jump across the Grand Canyon on his horse Old Darby. But Darby didn't get enough of a running leap and started to fall into the canyon. Fortunately Hance had

trained Darby well, so a few feet before Darby and Hance hit bottom, Hance
yelled out, "Whoa!" and Darby stopped. Hance stepped off Darby onto solid
ground. In another version, Darby doesn't quite make it across the canyon
and Hance lands in a cave below the rim, impossible to climb out of, with
nothing to eat. When tourists would ask Hance what happened next, he told
them that he'd starved to death.

The many caves in the Hances' backyard was also due to the type of rock
there, dolomite limestone, which erodes into a topography called karst, a
Swiss cheese of underground streams, sinkholes, and caves. These dolomites
were deposited in the Cambrian period, at the same time the Muav Limestone was being deposited in the future Grand Canyon region.

In the 1820s a group of Native Americans traveling from Missouri to Washington, D.C., to meet the Great White Father stopped for the night at an Ohio
farm. The farmer, Thomas James, noticed the hematite (iron) of their face
paint and asked where it had come from. The Indians described a vast deposit
of it next to a large spring. Intrigued, James traveled to Missouri and found
this deposit, a mother lode, in the future Phelps County. In 1826 he opened
the Meramec Iron Works, which over the next fifty years produced 300,000
tons of iron. Phelps County iron became the cutting edge of Manifest Destiny, used as plows, guns, kettles, rails, steamboat shafts, and wheels for covered wagons. The only drawback was the mine's location, which required
hauling the iron by wagon to the Gasconade River. The solution was a railroad, which arrived in 1860. Given the centrality of mining to the county
economy, locals organized the Missouri School of Mines and Metallurgy in
Rolla in 1870, one of the few American colleges devoted primarily to geology
and mining. This college still exists as the science and engineering branch of
the University of Missouri, and it still has a strong emphasis on geology and
mining. The campus symbol is a half-scale replica of Stonehenge, made of
granite that was cut by students in their high-tech mining lab.

The activity and wealth generated by the Meramec Iron Works inspired
a lot of local youths to take an avid interest in mining. About twenty-five
miles down the Meramec River from the iron works lived a boy named
George Hearst who loved working in his father's small lead mine, loved
hanging out with the miners, loved reading geology books. When the 1849

Gold Rush began, Hearst lit out for California. When he came back to Missouri ten years later to take care of his dying mother, he was rich, co-owner of the Comstock lode and on his way to a mining empire that would include the Homestake and Anaconda mines. While in Missouri, George married a teacher at the Meramec Iron Works schoolhouse, Phoebe Apperson. The couple soon returned to San Francisco and had a son, William Randolph Hearst. William became more interested in newspapers and politics than in mining, but in 1938 he did buy John Hance's old asbestos mine inside the canyon. This was a separate purchase from the Grandview and Horseshoe Mesa properties that Hearst had bought earlier from Pete Berry. Park officials could never figure out why Hearst bought the Hance mine, since unlike Grandview it was inaccessible and held little real-estate value. At the least, there was some symbolism in this acquisition. The careers of John Hance and George Hearst had started from the same place and inspiration, the Ozarks iron country. It's quite possible that Hearst encountered John Hance at one of the South Rim hotels, and William Randolph Hearst himself was definitely a skilled practitioner of tall tales.

The Hance brothers were "quite interested in mining," according to Ruth Hance Thayer, granddaughter of George Hance, John's brother and a long-time judge in Camp Verde, Arizona. "The story is told that George ... had an old black copy of Dana's *Mineralogy* on which he swore all of his witnesses instead of the Bible—holding the two books of equal importance. John's early trips into and around the Grand Canyon were on mine hunts."[2] George Hance's great-grandson Mike Mauer thinks this story about George swearing in people on Dana's *Mineralogy* is just another Hance tall tale, but in any case, John Hance had caught mining fever early on; according to the obituary George wrote for him, John Hance had joined the Pike's Peak gold rush in 1859. In Arizona he would try many other pursuits, but the Arizona mining boom of the 1870s and '80s probably rekindled his interest. The Hances probably never forgot the model of Thomas James, who had followed a hunch into a wilderness and ended up living in a mansion there, and the Hances probably knew that George Hearst had started from where they had. Few prospectors were willing to take on a landscape like the Grand Canyon, but John Hance's boyhood in a land of big cliffs, big rivers, big mines, and big dares was a better preparation for the canyon than most prospectors ever got.

When the Hances moved to Missouri, they joined an equation of conflict that would soon lead to the Civil War. More than most places, in Missouri the Civil War really did pit brother against brother, and it would divide the Hance family.

Missouri was originally settled by southerners, who filled up the rich farmlands along the Mississippi and Missouri Rivers, bringing slaves and setting up plantations. They were followed by German and Irish immigrants who had fled European feudalism only to find that a similar system, with lords and manor houses and pomposity and cruelty, still reigned in Missouri. The state's southerners did their best to take Missouri into the Confederacy, but the Germans and Irish resisted, with the result that neighbors were ambushing one another and burning one another's barns. For Appalachian migrants to Missouri, the equation was even more complicated. Appalachia was the one part of the South that was unsympathetic to slavery. This wasn't out of regard for the slaves so much as resentment of plantation society. Appalachian farmers, who did their own work, were at a big disadvantage in markets dominated by slave labor, and they felt politically powerless in states dominated by a few dozen wealthy plantation families. These resentments led West Virginia to secede from Virginia and remain in the Union, and they left mountain Tennessee alienated from the Confederacy.

Missouri's Pulaski and Phelps Counties were dominated by southerners, but only some of them were Appalachians. The name "Rolla" was a southern-accented phonetic spelling of "Raleigh," the capital of North Carolina. In the Civil War, Pulaski County provided only fifty-nine soldiers to the Union army, but about four hundred to the Confederate army. Phelps County had more Union supporters, partly because of the influx of Irish workers to build the railroad and work the mines. When the war broke out, Rolla's southerners forced the local, pro-Union newspaper to close, raised a Confederate flag, and formed a militia to patrol town. When a Union regiment arrived from St.Louis to secure the railhead, Confederates scattered into the countryside and formed guerilla groups to bushwhack Union sympathizers and supply wagons. Since Rolla held the closest railhead to the Ozarks, it became a major staging area for Union operations in southern Missouri and northern Arkansas. Huge amounts of supplies moved through town, and in the winter of 1861–62 about twelve thousand Union soldiers camped there. They made life very uncomfortable for local Confederates.

The most common story about John Hance's role in the Civil War is that he first joined the Confederate army, was taken prisoner, and then joined the Union army; however, in 1948 Hance's niece Francis Hance Rose (George's daughter), wrote a letter to Lon Garrison, assistant superintendent of Grand Canyon National Park, who was writing an *Arizona Highways* article about Hance, and she insisted that her uncle couldn't have been in the Confederate army. Rose said that her father, George, was an ardent abolitionist, and she would have heard if there had been any Confederates in the family.

It seems that George Hance was good at keeping secrets: John Hance's military record shows that he enlisted in the Confederate army on August 1, 1862, in Oregon County, Missouri, which was on the Arkansas border, a safer location than Rolla at which to organize Confederate troops. He joined Company D of the Tenth Regiment of the Missouri Infantry, which was a reorganization of several other regiments.

A few days after John Hance enlisted, his seventeen-year-old brother, Andrew Jackson Hance, enlisted in the Confederate 8th Infantry, also mustering in Oregon County. Andrew's military activities are mentioned several times in the diary of his commanding officer, Eathan Allen Pinnell.[3] Andrew campaigned in Arkansas, got sick a couple of times, was assigned to a pontoon bridge crew in Little Rock and then to a steamboat on the Red River in Louisiana, where he surrendered in May 1865.

Two of John Hance's uncles, Jonathan and Johnson, who were twins and seemed to think alike, also joined the Confederate army. Johnson was a Kaintuck Hollow neighbor of his brothers Samuel and Crow Hance, but both of them sent sons into the Union army: Samuel's son, Joseph, and Crow's son, Harrison. Also joining the Union army was a Green Hance, who presumably was another of Samuel Hance's sons, not John's father Greenberry. (Because the Hance brothers began naming their sons for one another, the same names proliferated, leaving things confusing even for Hance family genealogists. Even today there's a Greenberry Hance in the Rolla area.)

George Hance (John's brother) served the Union cause in the Quartermaster Corps, hauling supplies by wagon. This was a logical career for someone from Rolla, with its huge amounts of supplies going from the railroad onto wagons and then hundreds of miles to the front. It was this job that, after the war, would take George and John Hance to Arizona. This job was also the beginning of George Hance's long friendship with Lorenzo Hickok (brother of Wild Bill), who served as a Union wagon master based out of Rolla. When the war ended and shipping dried up, Lorenzo tried to open a saloon in Rolla, but this didn't last long, and soon he was commanding army wagons in Kansas alongside George and John Hance.

John Hance's Tenth Regiment was organized by W. O. Coleman, a Rolla merchant who earlier that year had been leading guerilla attacks against Union wagon trains. This raises the possibility that John might have attacked wagon trains driven by his brother George, but there is no indication that this happened. There is nothing to support the suggestion of Lon Garrison in his June 1949 *Arizona Highways* article that John Hance was associated with William Quantrill, the bloodiest of Missouri Confederate guerillas.

We do know that Hance fought in the battle of Helena, Arkansas, a disaster for the Confederates and especially for the Tenth Regiment, which entered the battle with 525 men and emerged with 236. Most of those losses were men who were captured, including John Hance.

Helena was an important port town, and an important link in the Union army's plan to take control of the Mississippi River and split the Confederacy. In February 1863 Union general Benjamin Prentiss took command of Helena and began fortifying it with heavy artillery. Prentiss was the hero of the battle of Shiloh, where in the Hornet's Nest, with the help of an artillery commander named John Wesley Powell, he had held off the Confederates long enough to bring a Union victory. Now Prentiss had 4,129 soldiers to hold off a Fourth of July attack by 7,645 Confederates who sought to retake Helena and break Union pressure on Vicksburg downriver. But the Confederate attack was poorly planned and poorly coordinated. Hance's regiment, along with seven others, was under the command of General Sterling Price, who failed to start his attack from the planned location or time. Nevertheless, Price's men managed to seize their target, Union Battery C on Graveyard Hill, through a brave charge against heavy artillery and rifle fire. Even the Union officers were impressed, one of them calling the charge "a splendid spectacle," and General Prentiss credited "a courage and desperation rarely equaled." Yet Price's thinned ranks then foolishly tried to charge the neighboring Union battery, and they were quickly beaten back. A Union counterattack soon recaptured Graveyard Hill and captured about 350 Confederates there, a majority of them from the Tenth Regiment of the Missouri Infantry, presumably including John Hance.

Hance spent the rest of the war in prison. He was sent up the Mississippi River to Alton, Illinois, where an abandoned state prison had been reopened as an army prison. Built in 1833, it had been abandoned after being deemed unfit for human habitation. In 1846 reformer Dorothea Dix had visited the Alton prison and denounced it as filthy, with its mere five hospital beds located in a basement that flooded during rains. The prison had only 236 cells, but the Union army now stuffed them with up to 5,000 prisoners. Sanitation and ventilation were terrible; there were no bathing facilities; and smallpox swept through, killing over a thousand prisoners. For two weeks in December 1863, and for a week in January 1864, John Hance was listed as being in the prison hospital, with no reason given.

On February 29, 1864, he was transferred to Fort Delaware, a moated stone fortress on a seventy-five-acre island in the Delaware River. The Fort Delaware prison began as a temporary holding station for prisoners who were soon exchanged for Union prisoners, but this changed with the arrival of about 10,000 Confederate soldiers captured at the battle of Gettysburg. For the next two years Fort Delaware's prisoner population would range between 5,000 and 10,000, and by one estimate it peaked at 16,000, making it the largest city in Delaware. Severe overcrowding, collapsing barracks, poor sanitation, foul air, insufficient food, disease, and a harried guard force of only 300 men, made Fort Delaware a notorious hellhole dreaded by Confederates and branded by some historians as "the Andersonville of the North." Andersonville was the Georgia prison where 13,000 Union soldiers died from its harsh conditions. At Fort Delaware, three prisoners died every day on average, for a total of 2,460 deaths.

By the time John Hance arrived at Fort Delaware, the prisoner exchange system had broken down, so he was there for the remainder of the war, over a year. We catch a glimpse of his arrival in the diary of a Yankee guard, A. J. Hamilton, who noted for March 4, 1864: "We have been receiving a new installment of Rebels and today receive the last of 1,700."[4] For November 22 Hamilton reported, "The weather is very cold, everything frozen up tight as a brick, we nearly freeze when in quarters."[5] November 22 was also the day that Hance was admitted to the prison hospital, and he was not discharged until February 23, three months later, but there is no record of his illness. Waves of smallpox, malaria, scurvy, intestinal disorders, and other illnesses meant that most prisoners who entered that hospital died there.

Hamilton's diary also reveals his impatience with the Confederates. On July 10, 1863, looking at newly arrived Gettysburg prisoners, he wrote, "Many of them admit they are sick of war and wish peace was restored on any terms. Others are determined to fight it out to the bitter end and apparently have no doubt of their success. Poor, deluded wretches. Lousy, filthy, exhausted and almost naked. What can you gain?"[6] One thing Confederates could gain was their freedom, by taking an oath of loyalty to the Union, but few did. John Hance did not.

The miserable conditions and high frustration inside Fort Delaware led to fights, escape attempts, and guard cruelty. In spite of these challenges, it appears that John Hance's mischievous sense of humor was alive and well. The only glimpse we get of Hance in prison is the periodic Roll of Prisoners, which normally is impersonal, but with each roll call he varied his name: he is John Hantz, or Hans, or Hands, or Hants, or Hance. While these could have been clerical errors, these variations sound so much like Hance's later games with his birthdate that it's plausible he was having some fun with his captors.

On April 22, 1865, with the war essentially over, Hance was part of a prisoner exchange. He was shipped to New Orleans, and then, on May 2, sent up the Mississippi to the mouth of the Red River, where his military record ends. He ended the war as he began it: as a private. His later use of the name "Captain" was apparently just a nickname, an honorary term often used by mountain men, especially those who had served as guides for army units or exploratory expeditions. Even Native American chiefs sometimes adopted the title "Captain" for themselves.

And what of the claim of Hance's niece, Frances Hance Rose, that John couldn't possibly have been a Confederate? In researching this chapter I communicated with her grandson, Mike Mauer, who assumes that Frances, along with the rest of the family, was merely engaging in wishful thinking: they simply didn't want the most famous Hance to be a Johnny Reb. But George had plainly spelled out John's true military record in his 1919 obituary in the *Coconino Sun*. Mauer said that John Hance never talked about his Civil War experiences, and he believes that he simply wanted to bury his horrible memories. Another possible reason for Hance's reticence about the war was that in a family whose youngsters, like Frances, were eager to admire their Hance war heroes, there would be little welcome for a traitor who had fought against Frances's father. Also, when Hance went to work driving wagons for the army after the war, he was surrounded by Union veterans. In the early years of Grand Canyon tourism most tourists came from northern states, and some were Union army veterans, so Hance's popularity depended on his carefully cultivated persona as an American frontier hero, not a rebel.

Nearly twenty years passed between the end of the Civil War and John Hance's arrival at the Grand Canyon, which is usually dated at 1883, although there is some uncertainty about this too. The one date we can pin down is June 15, 1884, which is when Hance filed a claim for land on the canyon rim, according to a legal notice published in the Flagstaff newspaper, the *Arizona Champion*, on January 22, 1887.

Hance's life in the years between the war and the canyon is sketchy. But the key to it was George's job as an army wagon master. At the end of the war George had been transferred to Fort Leavenworth, Kansas. He doesn't mention it in his autobiographical notes, but this transfer may have been owed to his friendship with Lorenzo Hickok. In her letter to Lon Garrison, Frances Hance Rose said that George and John started working for Lorenzo Hickok out of Fort Leavenworth. Certainly George and Lorenzo had become good friends. By one account, it was George who connected the name "Wild Bill" to Lorenzo's brother. In *Wild Bill Hickok: The Man and His Myth*, Joseph G. Rosa says, "According to legend, James Butler Hickok won the name Wild Bill in 1862, when he stopped the lynching of a bartender at Independence, Missouri. The source of this story is George W. Hance, a fellow wagon master and family friend. He served during the Civil War in this capacity, sometimes with Lorenzo Hickok, and first met both brothers at Rolla, Missouri. Tradition asserts that a woman in the crowd yelled 'My God, ain't he wild!' and Wild Bill was born."[7] However, in an article George wrote about Wild Bill Hickok for the Topeka *Mail and Breeze* on December 20, 1901, he made no mention of any role in the naming of Wild Bill, and his great-grandson Mike Mauer had never heard this story. Mauer does recall a nicknaming that worked in the other direction. Around 1900 Lorenzo was visiting George at his home in Camp Verde, Arizona. Upon seeing George's daughter Frances, he commented that she was "as pretty as a posie," and afterwards the Hances called Frances "Posie."

In September 1865 George Hance, and probably John, joined an expedition of 186 mule teams heading from Fort Leavenworth to establish and provision army forts across Kansas, as far as Hays. After this, George became a dispatch rider based at Camp Riley, carrying messages to General George A. Custer, who was in charge of suppressing Indian troubles in western Kansas. In 1867 George was appointed assistant wagon master on an expedition to Fort Union in New Mexico. By June 1868 George and John were at Fort Sumner, New Mexico, where they helped transport the Navajos back home after their disastrous Long Walk exile. Most of the Navajos had to walk home, in a line that stretched ten miles, but the army provided fifty-six wagons to carry the aged and infirm, as well as supplies. As soon as he was done with this job and had returned to Fort Union, George resigned from the army and headed back to Arizona, along with John, their younger brother Jim, and over a dozen others. They arrived in Prescott at the start of December 1868. But George soon reconnected with the army. He moved along with John and Jim to Camp Verde, where he went to work at the army sutler's store, and with their bull team they began taking contracts to haul wood and hay to the fort. John Hance supervised Mexican workers at cutting hay. The Hances also helped build roads and ditches. When the army decided to remove the Apaches from the Verde Valley to the San Carlos Reservation, the Hances were hired to help transport the aged and infirm. In John's obituary in the *Coconino Sun* on January 17, 1919, George Hance said, "He was here in early Indian times and was slightly wounded skin deep on one side in the center of ribs under one arm, on the other about same depth of wound on opposite arm and may have been in other fights in other parts of Arizona or New Mexico, as he was on the go or run-about in early days." John Hance would add "Apache fighter" to his public persona, but this could have been simply a brawl during the Apaches' eviction.

John Hance seems to have caught the bug for Wild West adventure, but George settled down and became a leading citizen of the Camp Verde area. In 1877 George went into the tourist business. He had bought a ranch on the south rim of the Verde Valley, and since it was on the busy road between Camp Verde and Prescott, he began offering lodging and meals. Arizona state historian Sharlot Hall paid tribute to George's hospitality in her obituary of George in the Prescott newspaper *The Courier* on August 2, 1932: "For many years he owned the beautiful Cienega Ranch between Camp Verde and Prescott and not only farmed and ran cattle but operated a road station popular with all travelers on that route. It was not an unusual sight to see half a dozen old time freight outfits, Army ambulances, and the mail and passenger buckboard all camped under the trees of the Cienega Ranch waiting for one of the fine dinners served by Mrs. Hance and her helpers." We don't know if John ever worked in George's tourist operation, but he surely was aware of how popular it was, and it probably prepared him to set up a similar operation on the South Rim of the Grand Canyon.

Little is known about Jim Hance except that he settled in Flagstaff for many years but then moved back to Missouri. Family members recall that both George and Jim possessed a sense of humor similar to John's. One story about Jim has survived, and it seems pure Hance. While living in Flagstaff Jim bought a cow, only to discover that it refused to be milked by a man, cooperating only with a woman. But Jim found he could fool the cow by dressing in women's clothing. One time for a Flagstaff parade Jim paraded in a dress and won the award for best costume.

John Hance continued to pursue various activities. In the 1870s he was running his own bull team. George's granddaughter Ruth Hance Thayer said that John also tried mining: "In the sutler's Ledger Book at Fort Verde on November 10, 1876, John Hance derived the handsome sum of two hundred thirty dollars ($230.00) for two mares and a colt. No doubt this entire sum was applied to his account, for at that time he and John Ricketts were in some sort of venture together and had purchased many supplies."[8] The Yavapai County deed book for 1877 shows John Hance buying 160 acres, but borrowing a thousand dollars from George to do so.

This period of Hance's life inspired a tall tale almost a century later. The January 1967 issue of *True West* magazine carried a story claiming that in 1881 John Hance was driving a Wells Fargo stagecoach near Flagstaff when he was held up for $125,000 in gold coins; the robbers hid the treasure and then were killed by a posse. According to northern Arizona historian Richard Mangum, this *True West* tale was bogus, written by a novelist who often mixed fiction into his history articles. Perhaps the spirit of John Hance encouraged taking such liberties. This article kept Flagstaff residents searching for the lost treasure for years.

It was buried treasure of a different sort that lured John Hance to the Grand Canyon to go prospecting. He did find a rich asbestos lode, but clearly he also fell under the canyon's romantic spell.

Long after Hance died, his asbestos mine was involved in a near-repetition of the epic struggle between the National Park Service and William Randolph Hearst. By 1930 the abandoned mine owed $1,742.62 in back taxes. In 1938 Hearst bought the mine and 325 acres that went with it for $2,500, including the back taxes. When the Interior Department filed its condemnation suit to claim Hearst's Grand Canyon lands, the old Hance claims were not included. Hearst continued owning it, and his heirs inherited it. In 1960 the heirs approached park officials about trading this land for property in California's Shasta National Forest, but neither the National Park Service nor U.S. Forest Service had the authority to trade lands between themselves. The park superintendent tried to raise money from private sources to buy the Grand Canyon parcel, and tried to talk the Hearsts into donating it. The Hearsts wanted $150,000 and threatened to develop the land for tourism—such as a helicopter pad—if the National Park Service refused. After the National Park Service claimed that the land was worth only $35,000, the Hearsts offered to sell it for $40,000 on the condition that they receive lots of favorable publicity. The National Park Service then made an offer, which the Hearsts accepted— but they then withdrew their acceptance with no reasons given. In 1967 the Hearsts again requested a land exchange, and negotiations went on for over ten years. The National Park Service threatened to condemn the land but never did. As of 2012, a century after Hearst bought the Grandview land, his heirs still owned John Hance's old asbestos mine, the only remaining private inholding inside the original boundaries of Grand Canyon National Park.

Nearly a century after his death John Hance is still a Grand Canyon legend, with a trail, a creek, and one of the Colorado River's most infamous rapids named for him. For years interpretative ranger Ron Brown has performed a living history program dressed as Hance and telling his tales. History buffs seek out Hance's grave. Thus it is surprising that the Hances back in Missouri have completely forgotten him.

In researching this story I contacted the thirty Hance families in the Rolla area phone book, and they placed me in touch with more far-flung Hances, some of whom had done family genealogy research. But I couldn't find a single one who had ever heard of John Hance. The family holds an annual reunion in the area, and I found a Hance to act as my scout at the event, but she could find no memory at all of John Hance. Of course, these were Hances I was dealing with, so it was possible they were all lying.

But it seems that the Arizona Hances simply lost touch with the Missouri Hances. On January 19, 1906, the Saint James, Missouri, *Journal* mentioned, "James Hance, formerly a resident of this locality, returned to his home in Arizona Tuesday. This is Mr. Hance's first visit here in twenty-five years." Though James (Jim) Hance later moved back to Missouri, he seems to have settled near St. Louis, not among the old Hance families, and he never had any children. George Hance visited Missouri in 1912, the first time in nearly fifty years. As far as we know, John Hance never returned home. But the Missouri Hances were delighted to learn from me that, somehow, their family history and places and spirit had spawned a man who was the right match for the spirit of the Grand Canyon.

John Hance is still playing games with us, for his tombstone says he was eighty years old, meaning a birthdate of 1838, a date probably derived from George's obituary.

I never did discover how John Hance had lost the tip of his index finger, so perhaps it was also true that he "plum wore it off, pointing out the scenery to visitors."

14

THE YELLOW BRICK ROAD

A Personal Reflection on History

At the long-abandoned homestead of John Hance, the first white settler on the rim of the Grand Canyon, I reached down and turned over a broken yellow brick.

It could have been years since anyone had touched it. The homestead was seldom visited. Only a few Grand Canyon history buffs even tried to find it, and sometimes they couldn't. There wasn't much to see there: a foundation outline, with bricks and stones scattered around it; a stone well that now offered water to no one; some rusty old hardware and tin cans. No, there wasn't much to see, except for the ghost road of American history, the road that within twenty years had turned John Hance from a hermit into the public persona of one of America's most celebrated landscapes.

Imprinted into one side of the yellow brick were four letters: "ON MO." I immediately surmised where this brick had come from: the town of Fulton, Missouri, which was only twenty miles from where I'd grown up. I'd seen Fulton's abandoned brick factory quite a few times. My hometown and many small towns in Missouri still had plenty of old brick streets, sidewalks, buildings, and walls whose bricks were imprinted with the name of the town or factory where they were made, including the Fulton imprint. But I was surprised to find a Fulton brick way out here, more than a thousand miles away.

There must have been many perfectly good brick factories that were closer, some of them much closer. By what logic or chance of history had a Fulton brick found its way here? There was a story here, a mystery, and perhaps it was the story of John Hance himself, of America itself—the story of a road, a westward tide, that had carried not just bricks and men but a whole nation to its western destiny.

Fulton bricks were loaded with history, though very few people knew it. One of the few who did was the man who was president of the United States on the day I found the Fulton brick at Hance's old place. A pile of Fulton bricks had collapsed on him, pushing him onto a railroad track, into the path of an oncoming train. The train ran him over, severing his legs. But it turned out that the train didn't really run over his legs: his legs were amputated by a sadistic doctor who wanted to make sure that his daughter didn't marry a man who was beneath her.

If you're having trouble remembering which recent American president had his legs amputated by a sadistic doctor, it's not because you are a poor student of American history—only movie history. I first visited the Hance homestead in 1988, when Ronald Reagan was president. If Reagan had been able to land more roles like that of Drake McHugh in *Kings Row*, he probably would have remained a Hollywood actor and never switched to politics. Film critics agree that *Kings Row* was Reagan's best movie. Reagan thought so too. It was based on a 1940 bestselling novel by Henry Bellamann, a native of Fulton, Missouri. The fictional town of Kings Row wasn't nearly fictional enough for Fulton's residents, who were appalled at seeing themselves depicted as sadists, murderers, swindlers, mental cases, snobs, and pompous hypocrites. To this day some Fulton residents resent *Kings Row*.

Reagan's character in the movie, Drake McHugh, works in the local train yard after being robbed of his savings by a runaway banker. One winter night he is waving a signal lantern beside a moving train when the stack of bricks behind him falls. In the novel, the bricks are on a wooden wagon that is sitting atop an earthen bank that collapses due to a recent thaw. In the movie the bricks are sitting on the train platform and collapse for no obvious reason; in fact, the engineer yells out a warning a split second before the bricks begin to fall. We see Reagan disappear beneath the bricks, and then we see his tin coffee pot being crushed by the train wheels. When he wakes up in bed, he looks beneath the blanket and cries out in horror, "Where's the rest of me?" With the help of his steadfast girlfriend, played by Ann Sheridan, Drake McHugh recovers his self-confidence and goes into business building a sub-division for the workers of the clay pits and brick factory.

In the novel and movie the brick accident is set in 1900, when John Hance was still living at his original homestead. Later he would move to a cabin near the Bright Angel Hotel, where he would entertain tourists with his tall tales. If Hance was writing this chapter, then the very bricks that knocked down Drake McHugh/Ronald Reagan would be gathered up and put onboard a train heading west. The bricks would pass cowboys and Indians and aging Wild West towns like Dodge City and head into the mountains and find their way to John Hance's homestead. Anyway, the bricks here had taken part in the unlikely adventure of migrating to the Grand Canyon and sheltering a character like John Hance.

I wandered around the Hance homestead and found an unbroken brick inscribed with "FULTON MO," but most bore no name. The majority were light yellow, meaning they were firebricks, manufactured to withstand greater heat than the red bricks used for most construction purposes. Perhaps these firebricks had formed Hance's fireplace or chimney. Or perhaps when tourists began staying here, Hance had built an outdoor grill to cook for them. Or perhaps Hance was so far from the nearest hardware store that he had to take whatever bricks he could get.

I found only one other brick that was inscribed with the name of a town: "COFFEYVILLE," a town in Kansas. Coffeyville too was baked with history, with Wild West lore. In the late 1800s it was a cow town where cowboys brought cattle to the railroad and then lived it up and shot it out. Although never as famous as Dodge City, Coffeyville won its spurs one day in 1892 when the Dalton gang rode into town to rob two banks and got into a gun-fight with citizens who killed most of them. If Hance was telling this story, he would no doubt point to a knick on his Coffeyville brick and swear it was from a bullet that had struck a pile of bricks on the platform at the Cof-feyville train station, bricks waiting to be loaded onto a train to Arizona. Hance might also claim that his brick was manufactured by the same hands that had wielded a gun and shot at the Dalton gang.

I decided that sometime when I went through Fulton, Missouri, I'd try to learn more about its brick history. Both the novel and movie of *Kings Row* begin with an image of bricks, of "the public-school building—Kings Row's special pride.... It was a red brick building, luxuriantly gothic—a bewildering arrangement of gables, battlements, and towers."[1] On the same page we see "the old brick sidewalks, uneven after many years."[2] After learning that both the richest man in town and the poor European immigrants live in brick houses, we visit the town cemetery: "Absently, he noted the brickwork supporting the moss-covered slab.... He thought the brickwork was a good job— 'A damn good job,' he said aloud."[3]

A century after this scene, I walked into a downtown still full of brick buildings, sidewalks, and streets. There are lots of Missouri towns made mostly of brick because there is lots of clay there—high-quality clay for making high-quality bricks, especially firebricks. There is lots of clay because during the Pennsylvanian period, about 300 million years ago, when the Appalachian Mountains were at their peak, far larger than the Rockies today, rivers full of sediment were draining off to the west and forming thick deposits. Twenty miles north of Fulton these deposits would give rise to a firebrick factory, in a town called Mexico, that would supply the bricks to build many major steel mills and later the launch pad that absorbed the fire of Apollo moon rockets. Mexico still calls itself "the firebrick capital of the world."

This was one good reason why Fulton bricks might end up at the Grand Canyon: they were good bricks. But not, apparently, good enough for Fulton. I walked up Main Street to where half a block of the street had been excavated to repair underground pipes. Workmen were laying the old bricks back atop the filed-in dirt, carefully arranging them like jigsaw pieces. They were laying the bricks with their inscribed side facing down, but from a stack of bricks I could see the inscription "MOBERLY MO." Moberly was forty miles away. I asked the workmen why Fulton, with its huge brick factory only a mile from here, didn't have Fulton bricks on its own Main Street. They only laughed. Soon afterward I visited Hannibal, Missouri, and I noticed that the old brick street in front of Mark Twain's boyhood house also consisted of Moberly bricks. So why wasn't it Moberly bricks or Mexico bricks at John Hance's homestead?

I walked back down Main Street, looking at all the brick buildings, some of them made entirely of yellow firebrick. The woodwork on the buildings was nicely maintained and painted. Like thousands of American towns, Fulton had by the 1950s decided that nineteenth-century brick and wood were old-fashioned and began covering them with steel sheeting and tile. But in the 1980s Fulton decided that maybe brick wasn't really so ugly.

I went into the county history museum. They had one exhibit about Fulton bricks, including photos and several sample bricks. The first firebrick factory in Fulton opened soon after the Civil War, but it was a modest operation, using shovels to fill a barrel with clay and using "a gentle mule," harnessed to a wooden shaft, to walk around the barrel and stir it up. In 1885—soon after John Hance settled on the South Rim—an ambitious brick operation began, intending to market bricks outside of town, though sometimes the factory sat idle due to lack of orders. Gradually business improved, and the factory expanded, employing 130 men by 1930. A major breakthrough occurred when railroad companies began buying Fulton firebricks to line the fireboxes of their steam locomotives, appropriate for a town named for Robert Fulton, inventor of the steam engine. Perhaps John Hance's bricks smoked their way west in a Santa Fe Railway locomotive and then got replaced and discarded. Or did the Santa Fe Railway bring a supply of Fulton firebricks to the South Rim when it arrived in 1901? But here the timing is wrong. The railways didn't adopt Fulton bricks in a big way until 1909, and by then Hance had abandoned his homestead and no one was visiting.

Someone did haul some Fulton bricks to Anita, the copper mines about fifteen miles south of the South Rim. The Anita mines were opened by Buckey O'Neill in 1897. Over a century later archaeologists examining an Anita mine shaft recorded that it held Fulton bricks. If the Anita mines had a pile of extra bricks, Hance could have obtained his from there.

I drove out to the abandoned Fulton brick factory. Along the way I came to a railroad crossing with a stop sign, the spur to the factory. It had been abandoned years ago, and the tracks removed and paved over, but the old stop sign was still there, requiring everyone to stop for ghost trains, for the roar of the past. This was the sort of town Fulton was, a town still enthralled by the glories of the past, especially the Confederacy. In 1861 Fulton was so enthralled by the Confederacy that it seceded from the United States even when the rest of slave-owning Missouri didn't. In the county history museum I'd overheard two local ladies looking through old photographs and saying how glorious it would be to find a photo of their ancestor wearing his Confederate uniform. It was such pomposities that had given Henry Bellamann rich raw material for his novel, and that made many locals regard Bellamann as a traitor even today.

Along the way to the factory I paused at the original brickworks, which had been abandoned in 1948. Today it was the city maintenance department yard, yet it still held one kiln and one smokestack. It was this brickworks that Harvey Butchart saw in operation when he moved to Fulton in 1939 to teach college. Butchart would become the most legendary of all Grand Canyon hikers, a character in the same larger-than-life class as John Hance.

For three years Butchart smelled the smoke of the factory that made the bricks that somehow found their way to the rim of the Grand Canyon. He was only a few years away from finding his own way to that rim, and to John Hance's trail into the canyon, and to decades of obsession with hiking the canyon. Did Butchart ever wander over to Hance's homestead, turn over a brick, and smell that old Fulton smoke again?

The original brickworks was right next to William Woods College, where Butchart taught math. William Woods was a women's college in the southern style, where Scarlett O'Haras came to become proper southern ladies, learning the essential skills of horseback riding, music, and fashionable dress—but not math. To this day the campus is dominated by huge horse stables and arenas, and many students walk around campus in breeches and boots. Butchart was teaching in Fulton when *Kings Row* was published and came out as a movie, and he undoubtedly knew how outraged the locals were about it. After three years he left for a more prestigious college, Grinnell, in "Yankee" Iowa.

I found my way to the much larger brick factory that had opened in Fulton in 1948. Its huge metal building and water tower were rusting; its old clay quarries were full of weeds. In 1962 this factory had produced 100,000 bricks every day, but the age of American steel mills, steam locomotives, and basement furnaces had ended.

On my way out of town I stopped at the other college in Fulton, Westminster. It was the college's venerable British name, plus its location in President Harry Truman's home state, that prompted Truman to invite Winston Churchill to Westminster's yellow-brick gymnasium to deliver his "Iron Curtain" speech in 1946. Today the campus commemorates the speech with a chapel designed by famed architect Christopher Wren, bombed out in World War II and later shipped to Fulton and rebuilt. The basement holds a Winston

Churchill museum. One exhibit is a chaotic pile of broken bricks, portraying a bombed London house. I tried to pick up a brick to see if it was actually a Fulton brick, but it was glued down. I thought of how the asbestos that John Hance mined from the Grand Canyon was reportedly shipped to London for use as fireproofing; perhaps it helped to save buildings in the war.

A display on Churchill's personal life included three bricks and a trowel. Two photos showed him enjoying his hobby of bricklaying at his estate: "Churchill constructed several new buildings with his own hands.... Proud of his skill as a bricklayer, he took out an apprentice card in the Amalgamated Union of Building Trade Workers."

As Churchill entered the yellow-brick college gymnasium, did he glance up to inspect its workmanship? If history had twisted differently, the bricks that ended up on the rim of the Grand Canyon, shielding John Hance's labors to obtain the asbestos that aided Winston Churchill's labors to save London from fire, could have ended up being admired by Churchill's glance. Or Churchill could have failed to see one particular brick because it was lying on the rim of the Grand Canyon, or being picked up at that very moment by Harvey Butchart, who suddenly smelled that old familiar smoke.

I didn't usually go near Coffeyville, Kansas, but now I was curious to see what stories its bricks might hold. After all, Kansas was the home of Dorothy, who followed the yellow brick road to adventure. Why had Oz needed fire-bricks? I imagined that if John Hance's Coffeyville brick could speak, then when it landed on the rim of the Grand Canyon, it would have said, "Something tells me I'm not in Kansas anymore."

The majority of downtown Coffeyville's buildings were brick, but most remained covered with 1950s steel sheeting. And most were abandoned. Whole rows of stores were empty, and as I peered inside through dirty windows, I saw peeling walls and old shelves covered with dirt. Coffeyville made quite a contrast with its neighboring town of Independence, which had a vibrant downtown full of shops and cafes and people. Independence had long ago removed its steel disguise and restored its original brick architecture.

Now the only reason visitors visited downtown Coffeyville was for a brief glimpse of Wild West greed and violence. On October 5, 1892, the Dalton gang rode into town and tried to rob two banks at once, leading to a shoot-out in which four of the five gang members died. Four town defenders also died. Today the town's biggest annual event is the "Dalton Defenders Days," with a reenactment of the shoot-out, all-day musical entertainment, chuckwagon feasts, crafts, games, a cake walk, and a 5k run.

I walked up the narrow Death Alley, where the shoot-out took place, and where the outlines of four bodies were painted on the ground. The alley also held the stone jail—bricks weren't sturdy enough—that had been here in 1892. I put fifty cents into a bulky old metal tape player, and it played a song and told me the story of the Dalton raid, to which a light went on inside the jail, showing me dummies of the four dead Daltons, a scene copied from a famous photograph.

If history had twisted differently, then the Coffeyville brick that had landed on the rim of the Grand Canyon could have ended up in Death Alley, pooling with blood and fame. Perhaps it was only a whim of chance, only a random pick or a fifteen-second difference, that sent one pallet of bricks into a local alley and the adjacent pallet onto a train heading west. John Hance's brick went on its own Wild West adventure, not untouched by a lust for wealth, but whereas the Dalton gang sought instant wealth, Hance undertook labors so long and extravagant and unrewarding that it's hard to avoid the conclusion that he was motivated more by the wealth of his Grand Canyon experiences, including the deep peace and beauty of living in a forest on the canyon rim, far from the hustle and gunfire of rough towns.

I checked out one of the banks the Daltons had robbed and then visited the Dalton Defenders Museum, which held the Daltons' guns and saddles. It also served as the town history museum and included displays on Coffeyville bricks. One display case held thirty-one designs of local bricks, half of them bearing the name "Coffeyville," usually as part of the name of one of the five brick companies in town. Together those companies produced 765,000 bricks a day in 1900. Some designs were geometric, and others pictorial, such as sunflowers, stars, or an oxen yoke. Coffeyville was famous for its red paving bricks, not firebricks. The most famous Coffeyville brick said simply, "DON'T SPIT ON SIDEWALK," which in the age when tuberculosis killed one in every five hundred Americans was often public law. Coffeyville's anti-spit bricks have been seen in sidewalks all over America, and from Paris to China.

John Hance's brick was made at the Coffeyville Vitrified Brick and Tile Company, started in 1894, the largest factory in town. I found an aerial photo of their massive plant in 1925, with two large shale pits, one already abandoned and filled with water. Since the edge of this photo showed the downtown, I now knew where to find the pit from which John Hance's brick had started its journey.

The pit was still there, still a lake with ducks paddling about, fringed by large chaotic piles of bricks. The factory building was still there, now serving as some sort of foundry. The bricks along the lake shore must have been there for decades, soaking up water and cold and summer sun, and they had slowly cracked open and shed dust, dissolving back into the earth from which they'd come. Their clay had remained underground for 200 million years, vibrating with the footsteps of dinosaurs and the impacts of asteroids, and then one day it was peeled to the sunlight, lifted up by strange limbs, and shaped to serve human ends. At least one chunk of the clay journeyed to a distant deep canyon where the rocks told tales about time, erosion, transformation, and uplift—tall tales as unlikely as any John Hance ever told. Inspired by the canyon's talent at erosion, the brick now sat cracking open and shedding dust, dust that flowed into a drainage, over the canyon rim, and down—down through layer after layer of rock, down through the Supai layer that had been laid down at the same time this clay was being formed in the future Kansas, down into Hance Creek, down into the Colorado River, down river to help erode the canyon deeper. A journey stranger than Dorothy's through Oz.

When I had first contacted the Coffeyville museum about their brick history, they'd put me in touch with a local expert, Norm Roller. Norm told me that if I ever came to town, he'd show me his brick collection. Now I gave him a call, and he gave me directions to his house a few miles out of town. After I'd seen the display of bricks in the museum, I expected that Norm would show me a similar collection, so I wasn't sure if the visit would be worthwhile.

Norm greeted me and led me to a small barn in his backyard where he kept his bricks. I started thinking that his collection must not be very important to him if he kept it stashed away in a barn, behind some rusty tractor. Then Norm unlocked a padlock, opened the door, and turned on the lights. I was staring at thousands of bricks, row after row of tall shelves full of bricks, a whole barn packed with bricks.

Norm started pointing out the geographical arrangement of the bricks, by state and by country. He had bricks from all over the world. Almost all of them were imprinted with their place or company of origin, or with decorative symbols like stars or animals. Some held company logos, such as bricks the Santa Fe Railway had used for its station platforms. There were commemorative bricks for town centennials or sports victories. There were bricks bearing the faces of Abraham Lincoln and Daffy Duck.

At the large section of Kansas bricks, both red and yellow, Norm pointed out the bricks from Buffalo, Kansas, and said they were the best bricks in America, the best clay fired very hard. The Buffalo brick factory, fifty miles from here, had closed only a few years ago. The bricks made in Coffeyville varied from top quality to too crumbly, made with too much sand. When the age of automobiles began, thousands of towns started paving their dirt streets with bricks, extra-thick ones laid two deep. But with time, and with heavier cars, brick streets buckled and crumbled, making them harder to maintain than asphalt or concrete streets. Even in Coffeyville the brick streets were paved over. Many towns still had a Redwall stratum of Coffeyville bricks hidden under layers of asphalt strata.

Were Coffeyville bricks ever used on the streets and sidewalks of the South Rim? Perhaps John Hance found his there. Or perhaps he found them in the town of Williams, Arizona, which I later learned still has some Coffeyville bricks visible around town today. The Coffeyville bricks could have hitched a ride on the Santa Fe Railway, which does run through Kansas, although a hundred miles from Coffeyville (and through Missouri, seventy-five miles from Fulton). Williams was on the Santa Fe mainline. But why didn't Hance have a brick from Buffalo, Kansas? As Norm's brick collection showed, it remained against the odds that Hance would have the bricks he did.

It seemed that Norm belonged to a subculture of devoted brick lovers and collectors; he had traveled to brick collector fairs all over the country. He had also been a construction contractor in town, so he appreciated bricks for their practical uses as well as their historical and artistic interest. Norm's barn was famous in the world of brick collectors, who visited him from all over.

Yet even Norm could only guess how bricks from Coffeyville and Fulton (of course, he had some bricks from Fulton) had ended up at a remote cabin on the rim of the Grand Canyon.

The mysterious bricks were a good symbol of the mystery of John Hance himself, for there had been plenty of mystery about how he'd ended up living on the rim of the Grand Canyon. Even after I'd traced his biographical story, there was still plenty of mystery in why one person follows the course he or she does, the mystery of how one life blends with the currents of a nation's history. Hance had become a character in a much larger story, which helped to create him.

Like the Fulton brick, John Hance had migrated to the canyon from Missouri. It was his Missouri roots that had made me curious about his origins. I had followed his path until it became the gravel road to his old family homestead near Rolla. But then I ran into a locked gate, for this was now private pasture land. The homestead was still hidden, around further bends. It would remain a mystery. Some miles away I found a cemetery that held a dozen Hance graves, but it was a mystery to me how they might be related to John. It was a mystery how the plentiful Hances in Missouri could have completely forgotten about John Hance, a Grand Canyon legend.

It was all a mystery to clay, which was content to sit underground for 200 million years. Supai Formation clay was content never to wonder if it had been unearthed by rain or by the shovel of John Hance building a trail, a trail that was the farthest tentacle of a restless searching that had filled the continent with trails. Clay couldn't grasp the dreams of men or nations, the vision of a beckoning frontier—of land and gold, of freedom, adventure, and natural beauty. But clay joined into the dream and the adventure, journeying with it, mapping it out, sheltering it, cooking for it, warming it, adding to its energy, adding to the national story that required heroes like John Hance to tell tales as tall as the Rockies and the canyon cliffs.

NOTES

ABBREVIATIONS

BL   Bancroft Library, University of California, Berkeley
GCNPMC   Grand Canyon National Park Museum Collection
GCNPRL   Grand Canyon National Park Research Library
LO   Lowell Observatory, Flagstaff, AZ

CHAPTER I

1. John F. Kennedy, "Special Message to Congress on Urgent National Needs," May 25, 1961.
2. Elbert King, *Moon Trip: A Personal Account of the Apollo Program and Its Science* (Houston: University of Houston Press, 1989), 28.
3. "Shepard, Carpenter Join Astronaut Canyon Hike," *Arizona Daily Sun,* Mar. 5, 1964.
4. "Astronauts Hike into Canyon," *Arizona Republic,* Mar. 6, 1964.
5. Quoted in "Astronauts Ride Mules Out of Grand Canyon," *Arizona Daily Sun,* Mar. 6, 1964.
6. Buzz Aldrin, *Return to Earth* (New York: Random House, 1973), 193, 195.
7. Michael Collins, *Carrying the Fire: An Astronaut's Journey* (New York: Farrar, Straus, Giroux, 1974), 77–79.
8. Andrew Chaikin, *A Man on the Moon: The Voyages of the Apollo Astronauts* (New York: Viking, 1994), 390–391.
9. Neil Armstrong, personal communication, 2010.

10. Quoted in Don E. Wilhelms, *To a Rocky Moon: A Geologist's History of Lunar Exploration* (Tucson: University of Arizona Press, 1993), 202.

11. Eugene Cernan, personal communication, 2010.

12. Alan Bean with Andrew Chaikin, *Apollo: An Eyewitness Account by Astronaut/ Explorer/Artist/Moonwalker Alan Bean* (Shelton, CT: Greenwich Workshop Press, 1998), 59.

13. Chaikin, *A Man on the Moon*, 399.

14. "Canyon is Beneficial," *Arizona Daily Sun*, Mar. 7, 1964.

15. "Cooper Joins Astronauts in Canyon Jaunt," *Arizona Republic*, Mar. 13, 1964.

16. "Alan Shepard Says Space Only Career," *Arizona Republic*, Mar. 7, 1964.

17. Walter Cunningham, *The All-American Boys* (New York: Macmillan, 1977), 32–33.

18. King, *Moon Trip*, 29.

19. Ibid., 29–30.

20. "Canyon is Beneficial," *Arizona Daily Sun*, Mar. 7, 1964.

21. "Cooper, Schirra, Grissom on Astronaut Canyon Hike," *Arizona Daily Sun*, Mar. 12, 1964.

22. "Astronauts in 'Wet Walk,'" *Arizona Daily Sun*, Mar. 13, 1964.

23. "Astronauts Await Gemini," *Arizona Daily Sun*, Mar. 14, 1964.

24. "U.S. Long Way From Landing on Moon," *Arizona Republic*, Mar. 14, 1964.

25. "Astronauts Await Gemini," *Arizona Daily Sun*, Mar. 14, 1964.

26. Frank Borman, *Countdown: An Autobiography* (New York: William Morrow, 1988), 101.

27. *National Geographic* (Jan. 1965): 144.

28. Charlie and Dotty Duke, *Moonwalker* (Nashville: Thomas Nelson, 1990), 91–92.

29. Al Worden, *Falling to Earth: An Apollo 15 Astronaut's Journey to the Moon* (Washington, D.C.: Smithsonian Books, 2011), 117, 120.

30. Jack Lousma, personal communication, 2010.

31. Bill Pogue, personal communication, 2010.

32. Gerald Carr, personal communication, 2010.

CHAPTER 2

1. J. B. Priestley, *Midnight on the Desert: Being an Excursion into Autobiography During a Winter in America, 1935–36* (New York: Harper and Brothers, 1937), 286.

2. Quoted in Donald E. Osterbrock, *Pauper and Prince: Ritchey, Hale, and Big American Telescopes* (Tucson: University of Arizona Press, 1993), 38.

3. Ritchey to H. H. Smith, July 31, 1907, GCNPRL, file GRCA 14958.

4. Osterbrock, *Pauper and Prince*, 96.

5. National Archives and Records Administration, Pacific Region, record group 79, National Park Service (NPS), folder D6215, Museum and exhibit activities planning and preparation, maintenance, and preservation, 1924-1929, box 101.

6. Ibid.

7. Edwin Hubble to V. M. Slipher, Oct. 5, 1928, Slipher Papers, Archives, LO.

8. Hubble to V. M. Slipher, Nov. 2, 1928, Slipher Papers, LO.

9. V. M. Slipher to W. A. Cogshall, Dec. 11, 1928, Slipher Papers, LO.
10. V. M. Slipher to Roger Lowell Putnam, Jan. 12, 1929, Slipher Papers, LO.
11. V. M. Slipher to W. A. Cogshall, Slipher Papers, LO.
12. V. M. Slipher to Roger Lowell Putnam, Slipher papers, LO.
13. Mary Colter, *Manual for Drivers and Guides Descriptive of the Indian Watch Tower at Desert View and its Relation, Architecturally, to the Prehistoric Ruins of the Southwest* (Grand Canyon: Fred Harvey Co., 1933), 5.
14. Ibid., 5–6.
15. Ibid., 7.
16. Ibid., 35–36.
17. Virginia L. Grattan, *Mary Colter: Builder Upon the Red Earth* (Grand Canyon: Grand Canyon Natural History Association, 1992), 25.

CHAPTER 3

1. David Hatcher Childress, *Lost Cities of North and Central America* (Kempton, IL: Adventures Unlimited, 1992), 324.
2. Ibid., 320–321.
3. *Hoaxipedia*, the website of the Museum of Hoaxes: www.museumofhoaxes.com.
4. *American Antiquarian and Oriental Journal* (1883): 342.
5. Thomas W. Herringshaw, *Biographical Review of Prominent Men and Women of the Day* (Chicago: A. B. Gehman and Co., 1888).
6. Joseph Miller, editor, *The Arizona Story* (New York: Hastings House, 1952), 320. No specific date given for articles.
7. *Hoaxipedia*, Museum of Hoaxes.
8. Quoted in an unpublished biography by Keven McQueen.
9. Miller, *Arizona Story*, 321–322.
10. Ibid., 323.
11. Ibid, 316–319.
12. *Hoaxapedia*, Museum of Hoaxes.
13. Quoted in the article "Avatars of the Almighty," by Harold Bulle, *Cosmopolitan* 47 (1909): 201.
14. David Starr Jordan, "The Land of Patience," *The Grand Canyon of Arizona* (Chicago: Passenger Department of the Santa Fe, 1906), 88.
15. Quoted, without further reference, in Curtis MacDougall, *Hoaxes* (New York: Dover, 1958), 44–45.
16. McQueen, unpublished biography.
17. Childress, *Lost Cities*, 322.

CHAPTER 4

1. Joseph Needham, *Science and Civilisation in China,* vol. 4: *Physics and Physical Technology, Part 3: Civil Engineering and Nautics* (Cambridge: Cambridge University Press, 1971), 540.

2.   Joseph de Guignes, *Investigation of the Navigations of the Chinese to the Coast of America, and as to some Tribes situated at the Eastern Extremity of Asia,* cited in Edward P. Vining, *An Inglorious Columbus; or Evidence that Hwui Shan and a Party of Buddhist Monks from Afghanistan Discovered America in the Fifth Century AD* (New York: D. Appleton and Company, 1885), 31–32.

3.   *The Classic of Mountains and Seas,* translated by Anne Birrell (London: Penguin Books, 1999), 159.

4.   Needham, *Science and Civilisation in China,* 542.

5.   Charles Godfrey Leland, *Fusang: The Discovery of America by Chinese Buddhist Monks in the Fifth Century* (London: Trubner, 1875), 101 (in the Forgotten Books reprint).

6.   Ibid., 34.

7.   Ibid., 35.

8.   Ibid., 110.

9.   Ibid., 36.

10. Ibid., 122.

11. Ibid., 3.

12. Ibid., 109–110.

13. S. Wells Williams, *Notices of Fu-sang and Other Countries Lying East of China* (New Haven: Tuttle, Morehouse, and Taylor, 1881), quoted in Vining, *An Inglorious Columbus,* 230.

14. Ibid., 233.

15. Ibid., 240.

16. Vining, *An Inglorious Columbus,* 532.

17. Ibid., 510.

18. Alexander McAllan, *America's Place in Mythology: Disclosing the Nature of Hindoo and Buddhist Beliefs* (Brooklyn, NY, 1910), preface in Nabu reprint edition.

19. Ibid., 113.

20. Ibid., 86.

21. Ibid., 81.

22. Ibid., 100.

23. Alexander McAllan, *Ancient Chinese Account of the Grand Canyon; or, Course of the Colorado* (Brooklyn, NY, 1913), 5.

24. Ibid., 9.

25. Ibid., 11.

26. Ibid., 28.

27. Ibid., 43.

28. J. O. Kinnaman, "America's Place in Mythology," *American Antiquarian and Oriental Journal,* vol. 36 (1914): 48.

29. J. O. Kinnaman, *The Theosophical Path,* vol. 2 (February 1919), 152.

30. Henriette Mertz, *Gods from the Far East: How the Chinese Discovered America* (New York: Ballantine Books, 1975), 68 (in Forgotten Books reprint).

31. Ibid., 131–132.

32. Frank Waters, *The Book of the Hopi* (New York: Viking Penguin, 1963), 116 (paperback edition).

CHAPTER 5

1. Eugene P. Trani and David L. Wilson, *The Presidency of Warren G. Harding* (Lawrence: Regents Press of Kansas, 1977), 44–45.

2. Quoted in Laton McCartney, *The Teapot Dome Scandal: How Big Oil Bought the Harding White House and Tried to Steal the Country* (New York: Random House, 2008), 44.

3. Quoted in David H. Stratton, *Tempest Over Teapot Dome: The Story of Albert B. Fall* (Norman: University of Oklahoma Press, 1998), 197.

4. Quoted in Stratton, *Tempest Over Teapot Dome*, 28; however, this same quote appears in another book, *The Two Alberts: Fountain and Fall*, by Gordon Owen, and is attributed to another source, a Santa Fe *New Mexican* article from Feb. 22, 1892. Because David Stratton is an academic historian, he receives the benefit of the doubt for the source of this quote.

5. Quoted in Francis Russell, *The Shadow of Blooming Grove: Warren G. Harding in His Times* (New York: McGraw-Hill, 1968), 96.

6. Quoted in Joe Mitchell Chapple, *The Life and Times of Warren G. Harding: Our After-War President* (Boston: Chapple Publishing, 1924), 142.

7. Quoted in Stratton, *Tempest Over Teapot Dome*, 214.

8. Ibid., 110.

9. Ibid., 112.

10. Ibid., 211.

11. Horace M. Albright, *The Birth of the National Park Service: The Founding Years, 1913–1933* (Salt Lake City: Howe Brothers, 1985), 125.

12. Ibid., 127.

13. Ibid.

14. Ibid., 131.

15. Ibid., 135.

16. Quoted in Stratton, *Tempest Over Teapot Dome*, 95–96.

17. Ralph Cameron Papers, box 4, Special Collections, University of Arizona Library.

18. Taped interview with Horace Albright, tape 2, side 1, Grand Canyon National Park Museum Collection (GCNPMC).

19. Superintendent Minor Tillotson to Director of National Park Service, Dec. 17, 1927, Post Office file 75981, GCNPMC.

20. Bill Suran, "Will the Real Mrs. Cameron Please Stand Up?" *Ol' Pioneer*, vol. 6, no. 7 (July 1995).

21. Letter from W. W. Crosby to Postmaster General, Sept. 1, 1922, Post Office file 75981, GCNPMC.

22. W. W. Crosby to Director of National Park Service, Dec. 1, 1922, Post Office file 75981, GCNPMC.

23. Quoted in letter from W. W. Crosby to Director of National Park Service, Dec. 6, 1922, Post Office file 75981, GCNPMC.

24. W. W. Crosby to Director of National Park Service, Dec. 6, 1922, Post Office file 75981, GCNPMC.

25. Quoted in Stratton, *Tempest Over Teapot Dome*, 332.

26. Evalyn Walsh McLean, *Queen of Diamonds: The Fabled Legacy of Evalyn Walsh McLean* (Franklin, TN: Hillsboro Press, 2000), 276.

27. *Rules and Regulations* (Grand Canyon National Park, 1932), 37.

CHAPTER 6

1. *Arizona Republican*, Oct. 18, 1903: "State Maker: William R. Hearst and Party Warmly Welcomed."

2. Pete Berry to Ralph Cameron, Jan. 9, 1914, Cameron Papers, Special Collections, University of Arizona Library.

3. *Coconino Sun*, Dec. 19, 1913: "William Randolph Hearst Buys Grandview Hotel of P. D. Berry: Famous Newspaper Owner Invests in Hotel and Homestead. Is it New Railroad, Big Hotel Project, or What?"

4. *New York Times*, Feb. 10, 1914: "Hearst Seeks Senate? Said to be After Arizona Nomination—Buys Land for Hotel."

5. *Coconino Sun*, Mar. 13, 1914: "Magnificent New Tourist Hotel for Grand Canyon."

6. Julia Morgan's papers are in Special Collections at the Robert E. Kennedy Library, California Polytechnic State University at San Luis Obispo. Her papers do not contain any architectural plans for a cottage, simply drawings.

7. Frank Kittredge, memo to NPS Director, Aug. 31, 1938, file L3023, Grand Canyon National Park Research Library (GCNPRL).

8. Kittredge, memo to NPS Director, June 19, 1939, file L3023, GCNPRL.

9. J. R. Eakin to Stephen Mather, Feb. 26, 1926, file L3023, GCNPRL.

10. J. V. Lloyd, memo to NPS Director, May 29, 1940, file L3023, GCNPRL.

11. Harold G. Davidson, *Jimmy Swinnerton: The Artist and His Work* (New York: Hearst Books, 1985), 71.

12. Ibid., 72.

13. Eakin to Mather, Feb. 26, 1926, file L3023, GCNPRL.

14. Ibid.

15. Clark M. Carrell, Report on the Hearst Properties in Grand Canyon National Park, Mar. 29, 1939, file L3023, GCNPRL.

16. Howard Stricklin interview with Julie Russell, Aug. 26, 1981, GCRA 40195, GCNPMC.

17. Horace Albright interview with Julie Russell, Apr. 7, 1981, GCRA 35965, GCNPMC.

18. Enabling bill for Grand Canyon National Park, Feb. 26, 1919.

19. Horace Albright interview.

20. Stephen Mather to William Randolph Hearst, Apr. 8, 1922, file L3023, GCNPRL.

21. J. R. Eakin to Stephen Mather, June 17, 1924, file L3023, GCNPRL.

22. Stephen Mather to J. R. Eakin, June 29, 1924, file L3023, GCNPRL.

23. Albright interview.

24. Horace Albright, *The Birth of the National Park Service*, 233.

25. Horace M. Albright to John D. Costello, Feb. 23, 1929, file L3023, GCNPRL.

26. John Francis Neylan to William Randolph Hearst, John Francis Neylan Papers, box 192, folder: "Grand Canyon Property," Bancroft Library (BL), University of California, Berkeley.

27. David Nasaw, *The Chief: The Life of William Randolph Hearst* (Boston: Houghton Mifflin, 2000), 147.

28. Ibid., 208; Theodore Roosevelt to James Sherman.

29. Ibid., 210: Theodore Roosevelt to John St. Loe Stratchey.

30. Ibid., 211.

31. Ibid., 480, editorial in *New York American*, Oct. 31, 1933.

32. Quoted in Arthur Schlesinger Jr., *The Coming of the New Deal* (Boston: Houghton Mifflin, 1958), 565.

33. Harold Ickes, *The Secret Diaries of Harold Ickes*, vol. 1: *The First Thousand Days, 1933–1936* (New York: Simon and Schuster, 1953), 383–384.

34. Harold Ickes, *The New Democracy* (New York: W. W. Norton, 1934), 19–20.

35. Ibid., 38–39.

36. Ibid., 72–73.

37. Ickes's speech of Nov. 19, 1934, quoted in T. H. Watkins, *Righteous Pilgrim: The Life and Times of Harold L. Ickes, 1874–1952* (New York: Henry Holt and Company, 1990), 550.

38. Ibid., 550.

39. Ibid., 550.

40. Ickes's speech of 1938, quoted in Watkins, *Righteous Pilgrim*, 581.

41. Albright, *Birth of the National Park Service*, 307–308.

42. Ickes, *Diaries*, vol. 1, 472.

43. Ibid., Dec. 22, 1935, 492.

44. Ibid., Jan. 18, 1936, 519.

45. Ibid., Feb. 4, 1936, 533.

46. Ibid., July 7, 1936, 633.

47. Watkins, *Righteous Pilgrim*, 438.

48. Ickes, *Diaries*, vol. 1, Aug. 25, 1936, 669–670.

49. Ibid.

50. Ickes, *Diaries*, vol. 1, Aug. 30, 1936, 671.

51. Ibid., Sept. 26, 1936, 685.

52. Quoted in Nasaw, *The Chief*, 523.

53. Ickes, *The Secret Diaries of Harold Ickes*, vol. 2: *The Inside Struggle, 1936–1939* (New York: Simon and Schuster, 1954), Nov. 14, 1936, 5.

54. Horace Albright interview.

55. Dick Gilliland to A. T. Sokolow, William Randolph Hearst Papers, carton 9, folder 29, BL.

56. Quoted in Taylor Coffman, *Building for Hearst and Morgan: Voices from the George Loorz Papers* (Berkeley, CA: Berkeley Hills Books, 2003), 266.

57. Quoted in Nasaw, *The Chief*, 529.

58. Quoted in Taylor Coffman, *Building for Hearst and Morgan*, 310.

59. *Time,* Mar. 13, 1939.
60. Frank Kittredge to Miner Tillotson, Sept. 22, 1938, file L3023, GCNPRL.
61. Frank Kittredge to Miner Tillotson, Nov. 18, 1938, file L3023, GCNPRL.
62. Harold Ickes, *America's House of Lords* (New York: Harcourt, Brace, 1939), 182.
63. Hearst to Martin F. Huberth, Dec. 5, 1941, William Randolph Hearst Papers, carton 10, folder 44, BL.
64. Memorandum from Frederic L. Kirgis, Acting Solicitor, Department of the Interior, Feb. 28, 1938, file L3023, GCNPRL.
65. H. C. Bryant to Director of NPS, July 9, 1939, file L3023, GCNPRL.
66. Harold Ickes to W. C. Mendenhall and Others, July 10, 1939, file L3023, GCNPRL.
67. Frank Lathrop to Frank Kittredge, July 31, 1939, file L3023, GCNPRL.
68. Declaration of Taking, Sept. 16, 1939, file L3023, GCNPRL.
69. Ickes, *The Secret Diaries of Harold Ickes,* vol. 3: *The Lowering Clouds, 1939–1941* (New York: Simon and Schuster, 1954), Oct. 17, 1939, 41.
70. Ibid., 63.
71. Telegram from A. E. Demaray to H. C. Bryant, Nov. 30, 1939, file L3023, GCNPRL.
72. Senator Carl Hayden to Harold Ickes, Dec. 22, 1939, William Randolph Hearst Papers, carton 42, folder 1, BL.
73. Harold Ickes to Senator Carl Hayden, Jan. 4, 1940, William Randolph Hearst Papers, carton 42, folder 1, BL.
74. Ibid.
75. John Francis Neylan to Senator Hiram Johnson, Oct. 16, 1939, Neylan Papers, box 192, file: "Grand Canyon Property," BL.
76. Memorandum, Frank Kittredge, Oct. 25, 1939, file L3023, GCNPRL.
77. Frank Kittredge to A. E. Demaray, Dec. 9, 1939, file L3023, GCNPRL.
78. *Coconino Sun,* Mar. 1, 1940: "Arizona Senator Charges Heady Wine of Power Endangered Private Lands: Deplores Condemnation Suit Against Hearst Property at Grand Canyon as Example of Disregard of Promises."
79. *Coconino Sun,* Feb. 9, 1940: "Grand Canyon Official Can't Pacify County: J. V. Lloyd Admits Park Promises Are Scraps of Paper."
80. Harold Ickes to R. P. Gilliland, Feb. 26, 1940, file L3023, GCNPRL.
81. *Coconino Sun,* Mar. 8, 1940. "Stinky Brink."
82. J. V. Lloyd to A. E. Demaray, Mar. 15, 1940, file L3023, GCNPRL.
83. Arizona Hotel Association newsletter, Christmas 1939, file L3023, GCNPRL.
84. Resolution, Williams–Grand Canyon Chamber of Commerce, Dec. 21, 1939, file L3023, GCNPRL.
85. H. C. Bryant to Foster Rockwell, Dec. 27, 1939, file L3023, GCNPRL.
86. H. C. Bryant to Mary Stevenson, Dec. 27, 1939, file L3023, GCNPRL.
87. Arno Cammerer to Andy Matson, Dec. ?, 1939, file L3023, GCNPRL.
88. Resolution, Coconino County Board of Supervisors, Dec. 20, 1939, file L3023, GCNPRL.

89. Harold Ickes to Governor R. T. Jones, Feb. 6, 1940, file L3023, GCNPRL.

90. H. C. Bryant to A. E. Demaray, Jan. 4, 1940, file L3023, GCNPRL.

91. J. V. Lloyd to A. E. Demaray, Feb. 1, 1940, file L3023, GCNPRL.

92. A. E. Demaray to Harold Ickes, June 4, 1940, file L3023, GCNPRL.

93. Frank Kittredge to A. E. Demaray, June 18, 1940, file L3023, GCNPRL.

94. Memorandum, Frank Kittredge, Aug. 12, 1940, file L3023, GCNPRL.

95. Henry S. MacKay Jr. to William Randolph Hearst, Oct. 3, 1941, Hearst Papers, box 8, folder 17, BL.

96. William Randolph Hearst to Martin F. Huberth, Dec. 5, 1941, Hearst papers, carton 10, folder 44, BL.

CHAPTER 7

1. Louise Hinchliffe to Danny Cushing, Dec. 30, 1971, file 62441, GCNPMC.

2. This account is problematic because, between two rough drafts and the *Sunset* article, McKee gave significant variations of events. The version presented here generally follows the *Sunset* article and adds the most plausible details from the more-detailed rough drafts. All these sources are found in file GRCA 62441, GCNPMC.

3. Owens's name is sometimes mistaken as "Owen," including by Marguerite Henry in her novel, and the movie repeated her mistake.

4. Marguerite Henry, *Brighty of the Grand Canyon* (Chicago: Rand McNally, 1953), 64 (in the Aladdin paperback edition).

5. Robert W. McKee, Recollections, 1987, file GCRA 65570, GCNPMC.

6. Thomas McKee to Marguerite Henry, Jan. 19, 1954, file GCRA 62441, GCNPMC.

7. Thomas McKee, "Brighty, Free Citizen: How the Sagacious Hermit Donkey of the Grand Canyon Maintained His Liberty for Thirty Years," *Sunset* (August 1922).

8. Ibid.

9. Thomas McKee, "The Passing of Bright Angel: A Saga of the Grand Canyon," file GCRA 62441, GCNPMC.

10. Ibid.

11. Diaries of Thomas McKee, file GCRA 65570, GCNPMC.

12. Marguerite Henry, *Dear Readers and Riders* (Chicago: Rand McNally, 1969), 80.

13. Ibid., 81.

14. Quoted in "Norman Foster's Brighty of the Grand Canyon," *Arizona Highways* (May 1966): 3.

15. Henry, *Brighty*, 13.

16. Ibid., 49.

17. Ibid., 187–188.

18. Ibid., 222.

19. Theodore Roosevelt, *A Book Lover's Holiday in the Open* (New York: Charles Scribner's Sons, 1919), 18.

20. Robert McKee, Recollections, 1987, file GCRA 65570, GCNPMC.
21. Thomas McKee to Marguerite Henry, Mar. 12, 1954, file GCRA 62441, GCNPMC.
22. Quoted in Marguerite Henry, "The Story Behind Brighty," file GCRA 75971, GCNPMC.
23. Many years later, in an interview with a Park Service historian, the head of the construction company that was building the transcanyon pipeline at that time, Elling Halvorsen, claimed that it was his helicopter that filmed the aerial scenes in the movie, and his work crew that built the river cable car for hauling their supplies. Both claims seem to be incorrect.
24. U.S. District Court document, file GCRA 75830, GCNPMC.
25. Henry, *Brighty*, 52.
26. Robert McKee to Peter and Martha Kruger, file GCRA 62441, GCNPMC.
27. Marguerite Henry to Merrill D. Beal, Dec. 14, 1968, file GCRA 99889, GCNPMC.
28. Press release, Wild Burro Protection Association, April 20, 1978, file GCRA 99889, GCNPMC.
29. Ibid.
30. Scotty Kolb, Secretary-Treasurer of the Southwestern Donkey and Mule Society, to U.S. Department of the Interior, June 26, 1978, file GCRA 99889, GCNPMC.
31. Memo, drafted by James E. Walters, Resource Management Specialist, Grand Canyon National Park, May 12, 1978, file GCRA 99889, GCNPMC.
32. Marguerite Henry to Carmine Cardamone, Nov. 25, 1978, file GCRA 99889, GCNPMC.

CHAPTER 8

1. Interview with Jack and Betty Verkamp, transcript in GRCA file 65555, GCNPMC.
2. Verkamp family recollections, personal communications, 2009.
3. Al Richmond, personal communication, 2009.
4. Mike Anderson, personal communication, 2009.
5. Lyle E. Style, *Ain't Got No Cigarettes: Memories of Music Legend Roger Miller* (Winnipeg, Canada; Great Plains Publications, 2005), 229.
6. Lyle Style, personal communication, 2009.

CHAPTER 9

1. The El Tovar *Impressions* books are in Special Collections, Cline Library, Northern Arizona University, Flagstaff.

CHAPTER 10

1. John C. Van Dyke, *The Grand Canyon of the Colorado* (New York: Charles Scribner's Sons, 1927), 1–2.

2. Ibid., 4.
3. John Muir, "The Grand Canyon of the Colorado," *Century Illustrated Monthly Magazine* (Nov. 1902): 107–116.
4. Mary Austin, *The Land of Journey's Ending* (New York: AMS Press, 1969), 421.
5. Van Dyke, *Grand Canyon of the Colorado*, 15.
6. Charles Dudley Warner, *Our Italy* (New York: Harper and Brothers, 1891), 177–200.
7. Ibid.
8. Hamlin Garland, "The Grand Canyon at Night," *Grand Canyon of Arizona* (Chicago: Santa Fe Railway, 1906), 61–62.
9. Willa Cather, *The Song of the Lark* (New York: Penguin Books, 1999), 103.
10. Ellsworth Kolb, *Through the Grand Canyon from Wyoming to Mexico* (New York: Macmillan, 1914), ix.
11. Harriet Monroe, *A Poet's Life: Seventy Years in a Changing World* (New York: Macmillan, 1938), 164.
12. Ibid., 165–166.
13. Ibid., 166.
14. Harriet Monroe, "The Grand Canyon of the Colorado," *Atlantic Monthly* (Dec. 1899): 816–821.
15. Monroe, *A Poet's Life*.
16. Monroe, "The Grand Canyon of the Colorado."
17. Monroe, *A Poet's Life*, 168.
18. Carl Sandburg, "Many Hats," *The Complete Poems of Carl Sandburg* (New York: Harcourt Brace Jovanovich, 1970), 432.
19. Harriet Monroe, "The Poetry of George Sterling," *Poetry* (Mar. 1916): 308–309.
20. Quoted in Monroe, *A Poet's Life*.
21. George Sterling, "At the Grand Canyon," *Sonnets to Craig* (New York: Viking Press, 1928).
22. Quoted in Ben F. Johnson III, *Fierce Solitude: A Life of John Gould Fletcher* (Fayetteville: University of Arkansas Press, 1994), 21.
23. Ibid., 29.
24. John Gould Fletcher, "The Grand Canyon of the Colorado," *Breakers and Granite* (New York: Macmillan, 1921), 95.
25. William Drake, *Sara Teasdale: Woman and Poet* (New York: Harper and Row, 1979), 195.
26. Ibid., 204.
27. Ibid., 222.
28. Carl Sandburg, review of *The Vanishing American* (1926), in *The Movies Are: Carl Sandburg's Film Reviews and Essays, 1920–1928*, edited by Arne Bernstein (Chicago: Lake Claremont Press, 2000), 301.
29. Carl Sandburg, "Slabs of the Sunburnt West," *Collected Poems*, 310.
30. Ibid., 311.
31. Ibid., 312.

32. Ibid., 314.
33. Carl Sandburg, "Many Hats," *Collected Poems*, 430.
34. Ibid., 432.
35. Ibid., 430.
36. Ibid., 434.
37. Ibid., 435.
38. Edgar Lee Masters, letter to Edwina Babcock, Jan. 7, 1925, Masters Papers, Princeton University Library.
39. Edgar Lee Masters, *Across Spoon River* (New York: Holt, Rinehart, and Winston, 1936), 414–416.
40. Edgar Lee Masters, *Invisible Landscapes* (New York: Macmillan Company, 1935), 96.
41. Ibid., 97.
42. Alfred Noyes, *The Book of Earth* (New York: Frederick A. Stokes Company, 1925), 2.
43. Ibid., 11.
44. Ibid., 328.
45. Quoted in Harriet Monroe, *A Poet's Life*, 265.
46. Henry Van Dyke, *The Grand Canyon and Other Poems* (New York: Charles Scribner's Sons, 1914), 5.
47. Ibid., 6.
48. Ibid., 7–8.
49. Quoted in Donald Worster, *A Passion for Nature: The Life of John Muir* (New York: Oxford University Press, 2008), 376.
50. This and following Muir quotes are from Muir, "Grand Canyon of the Colorado," 107–116.
51. This and following Burroughs quotes are from John Burroughs, "The Grand Canyon of the Colorado," *Century Illustrated Monthly Magazine* (Jan. 1911): 425–438.
52. Van Dyke, *Grand Canyon of the Colorado*, 60.
53. Ibid., 81–82.
54. Ibid., 72, 73, 132.
55. Austin, *Land of Journeys' Ending*, 425.
56. Mary Austin, *The Children Sing in the Far West* (Boston: Houghton Mifflin, 1928), 70.
57. Austin, *Land of Journeys' Ending*, 425.
58. Van Dyke, *Grand Canyon of the Colorado*, 216–217.
59. Carl Sandburg, "Many Hats," *Complete Poems*, 434.

CHAPTER II

1. Quoted in H. V. Marrot, *The Life and Letters of John Galsworthy* (New York: Charles Scribner's Sons, 1936), 336.
2. John Galsworthy to Margaret Morris, March 26, 1912, in Morris, *My Galsworthy Story* (London: Peter Owen, 1967), 82–83.

3. Catherine Dupré, *John Galsworthy: A Biography* (New York: Coward, McCann and Geoghegan, 1976), 188–189.

4. John Galsworthy, "Meditation on Finality," in *The Inn of Tranquility* (New York: Charles Scribner's Sons, 1912).

5. Ibid.

6. Rudolf Sauter, *Galsworthy the Man: An Intimate Portrait* (London: Peter Owen, 1967), 72.

7. Ibid., 73–74.

8. Ibid., 74–75.

9. J. B. Priestley, *Rain Upon Godshill: A Further Chapter in Autobiography* (New York: Harper and Brothers, 1939), 12.

10. J. B. Priestley, *Midnight on the Desert: Being an Excursion into Autobiography During a Winter in America, 1935–36* (New York: Harper and Brothers, 1937), 2–3.

11. J. B. Priestley, *Bright Day* (London: William Heinnemann, 1946), 86.

12. Priestley, *Midnight on the Desert*, 298–299.

13. J. B. Priestley, *Man and Time* (New York: Dell, Laurel Edition, 1968), 212–213.

14. Priestley, *Midnight on the Desert*, 286–287.

15. Ibid., 286.

16. Ibid.

17. Priestley, *They Walk in the City* (New York: Harper and Brothers, 1936), 131–132.

18. Priestley, *Midnight on the Desert*, 282.

19. Ibid., 283–285.

20. J. B. Priestley, *Margin Released* (London: Heron Books, 1962), 166.

21. J. B. Priestley, *Essays of Five Decades* (Boston: Little, Brown and Company, 1968), 231.

22. George Bernard Shaw, "Why I Won't Go to America," *The (London) Observer*, Feb. 15, 1920.

23. "Shaw Sees Grand Canyon; Reminds Him of Religion," *New York Times*, March 7, 1936.

24. Priestley, *Midnight on the Desert*, 293.

25. Ibid., 295.

26. Ibid., 101.

27. Ibid., 285.

28. Sackville-West to Woolf, Mar. 28, 1933, in *The Letters of Vita Sackville-West and Virginia Woolf*, edited by Louise DeSalvo and Mitchell Leaska (San Francisco: Cleis Press, 1984), 366.

29. Ibid.

30. Unpublished entry in diary of Harold Nicolson, Mar. 1933, quoted in Victoria Glendinning, *Vita: A Biography of Vita Sackville-West* (New York: Alfred A. Knopf, 1983), 259.

31. Harold Nicolson, *Letters and Diaries, 1930–1939* (New York: Atheneum, 1966), 145.

32. Ibid., 146.

33. Ibid.

34. Sackville-West to Woolf, April 9, 1933, in *Letters of Vita Sackville-West and Virginia Woolf*, 369.

35. Ibid., letter of June 11, 1933, 376.

36. Ibid., letter of April 24, 1940, 431.

37. Michael Stevens, *V. Sackville-West: A Critical Biography* (New York: Charles Scribner's Sons, 1974), 113.

38. Vita Sackville-West diaries, Feb. 24, 1942, quoted in Glendinning, *Vita,* 317.

39. Quoted in Victoria Glendinning, *Leonard Woolf: A Biography* (New York: Free Press, 2006), 337.

40. Ibid.

41. Quoted in J. H. Willis, Jr., *Leonard and Virginia Woolf as Publishers: The Hogarth Press, 1917–41* (Charlottesville: University Press of Virginia, 1992), 359.

42. Quoted in Glendinning, *Vita*, 318.

43. Vita Sackville-West, *Grand Canyon* (New York: Doubleday, Doran, and Company, 1942), 22.

44. Ibid., 8.

45. Ibid., 38.

46. Ibid., 53.

47. Ibid., 106.

48. Ibid., 167.

49. Ibid., 149.

50. Ibid., 283–284.

51. Ibid., 282.

52. Ibid., 299.

53. Ibid., 304.

54. David Ellis, *D. H. Lawrence: Dying Game, 1922–1930* (Cambridge: Cambridge University Press, 1998), 57.

55. Aldous Huxley to Mary Hutchinson, May 10, 1926, quoted in Nicholas Murray, *Aldous Huxley: A Biography* (New York: Macmillan, 2003), 182.

56. Aldous Huxley to Robert Nichols, May 13, 1926, in *Letters of Aldous Huxley*, edited by Grover Smith (New York: Harper and Row: 1969), 268–269.

57. Aldous Huxley, *Brave New World* (New York: HarperCollins, 2010), 110.

CHAPTER 12

1. Henry Miller, *The Air-Conditioned Nightmare* (New York: New Directions, 1945), 10.

2. Ibid.

3. Ibid., 14.

4. Miller, *Tropic of Capricorn* (New York: Grove Press, 1961), 151.

5. Ibid., 152.

6. From a proposal for an American travel book, quoted in Jay Martin, *Always Merry and Bright: The Life of Henry Miller* (Santa Barbara, CA: Capra Press, 1978), 372.

7. Miller, *Air-Conditioned Nightmare*, 240.
8. Ibid., 19–20.
9. Ibid., 28–29.
10. Ibid., 239.
11. Ibid., 238.
12. Henry Miller, *Letters to Anaïs Nin*, edited and introduced by Gunther Stuhlmann (New York: George Putnam's Sons, 1965), 257.
13. Ibid., 255.
14. Ibid., 258.
15. Miller, *Air-Conditioned Nightmare*, 240.
16. Miller, *Letters to Anaïs Nin*, 258.
17. Ibid., 260.
18. Ibid., 261.
19. Miller, *Air-Conditioned Nightmare*, 227.
20. Ibid., 219.
21. Ibid., 221–222.
22. Ibid., 223.
23. Miller, *Letters to Anaïs Nin*, 260.
24. Ibid., 259.
25. Ibid., 265.
26. Ibid., 266.
27. Anaïs Nin, *The Diary of Anaïs Nin*, vol. 3: *1939-1944* (New York: Harcourt, Brace and World, 1969), 55. Copyright renewed 1997 by Rupert Pole and Gunther Stuhlmann.
28. Lawrence Clark Powell, in *Conversations with Henry Miller*, edited by Frank Kersnowski and Alice Hughes (Jackson: University Press of Mississippi, 1994), 11.
29. Jonathan Cott, in Kersnowski and Hughes, *Conversations with Henry Miller*, 182.

CHAPTER 13

1. Hamlin Garland, "John Hance: A Study," *The Grand Canyon of Arizona* (Chicago: Santa Fe Railway, 1902), 108.
2. Ruth Hance Thayer, "Fact or Fiction: The Hance Brothers of Yavapai and Coconino Counties, Arizona," a paper written for an English class at Northern Arizona University in 1963, and in the archives of Grand Canyon National Park and the Camp Verde Historical Society, 2.
3. Eathan Allen Pinnell, *The Diary of Captain Eathan Allen Pinnell*, edited by Michael E. Banasik (Iowa City: Camp Pope Bookshop, 1999).
4. A. J. Hamilton, *A Fort Delaware Journal: The Diary of a Yankee Private, A. J. Hamilton, 1862–65*, edited by W. Emerson Wilson (Wilmington, DE: Fort Delaware Society, 1981), 50.
5. Ibid., 66.
6. Ibid., 34.

7. Joseph G. Rosa, *Wild Bill Hickok: The Man and his Myth* (Lawrence: University Press of Kansas, 1996).
8. Thayer, *Fact or Fiction*, 2.

CHAPTER 14

1. Henry Bellamann, *Kings Row* (New York: Simon and Schuster, 1940), 4.
2. Ibid.
3. Ibid., 108.

BIBLIOGRAPHY

Albright, Horace M. *The Birth of the National Park Service: The Founding Years, 1913–1933.* Salt Lake City: Howe Brothers, 1985.

Aldrin, Edwin "Buzz." *Return to Earth.* New York: Random House, 1973.

Anderson, Michael F. *Living at the Edge: Explorers, Exploiters and Settlers of the Grand Canyon Region.* Grand Canyon: Grand Canyon Association, 1998.

———. *Polishing the Jewel: An Administrative History of Grand Canyon National Park.* Grand Canyon: Grand Canyon Association, 2000.

Anthony, Carl Sferrazza. *Florence Harding: The First Lady, the Jazz Age, and the Death of America's Most Scandalous President.* New York: William Morrow and Co., 1998.

Austin, Mary. *The Children Sing in the Far West.* Boston: Houghton Mifflin, 1928.

———. *The Land of Journeys' Ending.* New York: Century Company, 1924.

———. *The Land of Little Rain.* Boston: Houghton Mifflin, 1903.

Babbitt, Bruce, editor. *Grand Canyon: An Anthology.* Flagstaff, AZ: Northland Press, 1978.

Bair, Deirdre. *Anaïs Nin: A Biography.* New York: Putnam's, 1995.

Bartusiak, Marcia. *The Day We Found the Universe.* New York: Pantheon, 2009.

Baum, L. Frank. *Dorothy and the Wizard in Oz.* Chicago: Reilly and Britton, 1908.

Bean, Alan, with Andrew Chaikin. *Apollo: An Eyewitness Account by Astronaut/Explorer/Artist/Moonwalker Alan Bean.* Shelton: Greenwich Workshop Press, 1998.

Beattie, Donald A. *Taking Science to the Moon: Lunar Experiments and the Apollo Program.* Baltimore: Johns Hopkins University Press, 2001.

Bedford, Sybille. *Aldous Huxley: A Biography.* Chicago: Ivan R. Dee, 1973.

Bellamann, Henry. *Kings Row.* New York: Simon and Schuster, 1940.

Berger, Todd, editor. *Reflections of Grand Canyon Historians: Ideas, Arguments, and First-Person Accounts.* Grand Canyon: Grand Canyon Association, 2008.

Berke, Arnold. *Mary Colter: Architect of the Southwest.* New York: Princeton Architectural Press, 2002.

Billingsley, George H., Earle E. Spamer, and Dove Menkes. *Quest for the Pillar of Gold: The Mines and Miners of the Grand Canyon.* Grand Canyon: Grand Canyon Association, 1997.

Birrell, Anne, translator. *The Classic of Mountains and Seas.* London: Penguin Books, 1999.

Borman, Frank. *Countdown: An Autobiography.* New York: William Morrow, 1988.

Braine, John. *J. B. Priestley.* New York: Barnes and Noble, 1978.

Cahill, Daniel J. *Harriet Monroe.* New York: Twayne, 1973.

Cather, Willa. *The Song of the Lark.* New York: Penguin Books, 1999.

Chaikin, Andrew. *A Man on the Moon: The Voyages of the Apollo Astronauts.* New York: Viking, 1994.

Chapple, Joe Mitchell. *The Life and Times of Warren G. Harding: Our After-War President.* Boston: Chapple, 1924.

Childress, David Hatcher. *Lost Cities of North and Central America.* Kempton: Adventures Unlimited, 1992.

Christianson, Gale E. *Edwin Hubble: Mariner of the Nebulae.* New York: Farrar, Straus, and Giroux, 1995.

Coffman, Taylor. *Building for Hearst and Morgan: Voices from the George Loorz Papers.* Berkeley: Berkeley Hills Books, 2003.

Cole, Michael. *Secrets of El Tovar Canyon.* Cedarburg, WI: Foremost Press, 2009.

Collins, Michael. *Carrying the Fire: An Astronaut's Journey.* New York: Random House, 1973.

Colter, Mary. *Manual for Drivers and Guides Descriptive of the Indian Watch Tower at Desert View and its Relation, Architecturally, to the Prehistoric Ruins of the Southwest.* Grand Canyon: Fred Harvey Co., 1933.

Corle, Edwin. *Listen, Bright Angel.* New York: Duell, Sloan, and Pearce, 1946.

Cunningham, Walter. *The All-American Boys.* New York: Macmillan, 1977.

Cusic, Don. *Roger Miller: Dang Me!* Nashville: Brackish, 2012.

Davidson, Harold G. *Jimmy Swinnerton: The Artist and His Work.* New York: Hearst Books, 1985.

Davis, Kenneth S. *FDR: The New Deal Years 1933–1937: A History.* New York: Random House, 1986.

De Guignes, Joseph. *Investigation of the Navigations of the Chinese to the Coast of America, and as to Some Tribes Situated at the Eastern Extremity of Asia.* Paris, 1761.

DeSalvo, Louise, and Mitchell Leaska, editors. *The Letters of Vita Sackville-West and Virginia Woolf.* San Francisco: Cleis Press, 1984.

Downes, Randolph C. *The Rise of Warren Gamaliel Harding, 1865–1920.* Columbus: Ohio State University Press, 1970.

Drake, William. *Sara Teasdale: Woman and Poet.* New York: Harper and Row, 1979.

Duke, Charlie, and Dotty Duke. *Moonwalker.* Nashville: Thomas Nelson, 1990.

Dupré, Catherine. *John Galsworthy: A Biography.* New York: Coward, McCann, and Geoghegan, 1976.

Dutton, Clarence E. *Tertiary History of the Grand Cañon District.* Tucson: University of Arizona Press, 2001.

Ellis, David. *D. H. Lawrence: Dying Game, 1922–1930.* Cambridge: Cambridge University Press, 1998.

Emerson, Willis George. *The Smoky God, or A Voyage to the Inner World.* Chicago: Forbes and Company, 1908.

Evans, Edna. *Tales From the Grand Canyon: Some True, Some Tall.* Flagstaff, AZ: Northland Press, 1985.

Ferguson, Robert. *Henry Miller: A Life.* New York: W. W. Norton, 1991.

Fink, Augusta. *I-Mary: A Biography of Mary Austin.* Tucson: University of Arizona Press, 1983.

Fletcher, John Gould. *Breakers and Granite.* New York: Macmillan, 1921.

Florence, Ronald. *The Perfect Machine: Building the Palomar Telescope.* New York: HarperCollins, 1994.

Galsworthy, John. *The Inn of Tranquility.* New York: Charles Scribner's Sons, 1912.

Garis, Howard Roger. *Five Thousand Miles Underground.* New York: Stratemeyer Syndicate, 1908.

Gindin, James. *The English Climate: An Excursion into a Biography of John Galsworthy.* Ann Arbor: University of Michigan Press, 1979.

———. *John Galsworthy's Life and Art: An Alien's Fortress.* Ann Arbor: University of Michigan Press, 1987.

Glendinning, Victoria. *Leonard Woolf: A Biography.* New York: Free Press, 2006.

———. *Vita: A Biography of Vita Sackville-West.* New York: Alfred A. Knopf, 1983.

Goodman, Susan, and Carl Dowson. *Mary Austin and the American West.* Berkeley: University of California Press, 2009.

Grattan, Virginia L. *Mary Colter: Builder Upon the Red Earth.* Grand Canyon: Grand Canyon Natural History Association, 1992.

Gutman, Dan. *The Return of the Homework Machine.* New York: Simon and Schuster, 2009.

Hamilton, A. J. *A Fort Delaware Journal: The Diary of a Yankee Private.* Wilmington, DE: Fort Delaware Society, 1981.

Hansen, James R. *First Man: The Life of Neil A. Armstrong.* New York: Simon and Schuster, 2005.

Harris, Hendon M. *The Asiatic Fathers of America.* Taipei: Wen Ho Printing, 1973.

Healy, Paul. *Cissy: The Biography of Eleanor M. "Cissy" Patterson.* Garden City, NY: Doubleday, 1966.

Henry, Marguerite. *Brighty of the Grand Canyon.* Chicago: Rand McNally, 1953.

———. *Dear Readers and Riders.* Chicago: Rand McNally, 1969.

Herringshaw, Thomas W. *Biographical Review of Prominent Men and Women of the Day.* Chicago: A. B. Gehman and Co., 1888.

Hoge, Alice Albright. *Cissy Patterson.* New York: Random House, 1966.

Holroyd, Michael. *Bernard Shaw,* vol. 3: *1918–1950: The Lure of Fantasy.* New York: Random House, 1991.

Hughes, Donald J. *In the House of Stone and Light: A Human History of the Grand Canyon.* Grand Canyon: Grand Canyon Natural History Association, 1978.

Huxley, Aldous. *After Many a Summer Dies the Swan.* New York: Harper and Brothers, 1939.

———. *Brave New World.* New York: HarperCollins, 2010.

———. *Letters of Aldous Huxley.* Edited by Grover Smith. New York: Harper and Row, 1969.

Ickes, Harold. *America's House of Lords.* New York: Harcourt, Brace, 1939.

———. *The New Democracy.* New York: W. W. Norton, 1934.

———. *The Secret Diaries of Harold Ickes,* vol. 1: *The First Thousand Days, 1933–1936.* New York: Simon and Schuster, 1953.

———. *The Secret Diaries of Harold Ickes,* vol. 2: *The Inside Struggle, 1936–1939.* New York: Simon and Schuster, 1954.

———. *The Secret Diaries of Harold Ickes,* vol. 3: *The Lowering Clouds, 1939–1941.* New York: Simon and Schuster, 1954.

Johnson, Ben F., III. *Fierce Solitude: A Life of John Gould Fletcher.* Fayetteville: University of Arkansas Press, 1994.

Kelly, James Paul. *Prince Izon: A Romance of the Grand Canyon.* Chicago: A. C. McClurg Co., 1910.

Kersnowski, Frank, and Alice Hughes. *Conversations with Henry Miller.* Jackson: University Press of Mississippi, 1994.

King, Elbert. *Moon Trip: A Personal Account of the Apollo Program and Its Science.* Houston: University of Houston Press, 1989.

Kinsey, Joni Louise. *Thomas Moran and the Surveying of the American West.* Washington, D.C.: Smithsonian Institution Press, 1992.

Kolb, Ellsworth. *Through the Grand Canyon From Wyoming to Mexico.* New York: Macmillan, 1914.

Leavengood, Betty. *Grand Canyon Women: Lives Shaped by Landscape.* Grand Canyon: Grand Canyon Association, 2004.

Leland, Charles Godfrey. *Fusang: The Discovery of America by Chinese Buddhist Monks in the Fifth Century.* London: Trubner, 1875.

Levy, David H. *Shoemaker by Levy: The Man Who Made an Impact.* Princeton, NJ: Princeton University Press, 2000.

MacDougall, Curtis. *Hoaxes.* New York: Dover, 1958.

McAllan, Alexander. *America's Place in Mythology: Disclosing the Nature of Hindoo and Buddhist Beliefs.* Brooklyn, 1910.

———. *Ancient Chinese Account of the Grand Canyon, or, Course of the Colorado.* Brooklyn, 1913.

McCartney, Laton. *The Teapot Dome Scandal: How Big Oil Bought the Harding White House and Tried to Steal the Country.* New York: Random House, 2008.

McFarland, Elizabeth. *Grand Canyon Viewpoints*. Phoenix: W. A. Krueger Co., 1978.

———. *This Is the Grand Canyon*. Phoenix: W. A. Krueger Co., 1970.

McLean, Evalyn Walsh. *Queen of Diamonds: The Fabled Legacy of Evalyn Walsh McLean*. Franklin, TN: Hillsboro, 2000.

Mangum, Richard, and Sherry Mangum. *Grand Canyon–Flagstaff Stage Coach Line: A History and Exploration Guide*. Flagstaff, AZ: Hexagon, 1999.

Marrot, H. V. *The Life and Letters of John Galsworthy*. New York: Charles Scribner's Sons, 1936.

Martin, Jay. *Always Merry and Bright: The Life of Henry Miller*. Santa Barbara, CA: Capra Press, 1978.

Masters, Edgar Lee. *Across Spoon River*. New York: Holt, Rinehart, and Winston, 1936.

———. *Invisible Landscapes*. New York: Macmillan, 1935.

Mertz, Henriette. *Gods from the Far East: How the Chinese Discovered America*. New York: Ballantine Books, 1975.

Miller, Henry. *The Air-Conditioned Nightmare*. New York: New Directions, 1945.

———. *Letters to Anaïs Nin*. Edited by Gunther Stuhlmann. New York: George Putnam's Sons, 1965.

———. *Tropic of Capricorn*. New York: Grove Press, 1961.

Miller, Joseph, editor. *The Arizona Story*. New York: Hastings House, 1952.

———. *The Arizona Cavalcade: The Turbulent Times*. New York: Hastings House, 1962.

Monroe, Harriet. *A Poet's Life: Seventy Years in a Changing World*. New York: Macmillan, 1938.

Morehouse, Barbara J. *A Place Called Grand Canyon: Contested Geographies*. Tucson: University of Arizona Press, 1996.

Morris, Edmund. *The Rise of Theodore Roosevelt*. New York: Coward, McCann and Geoghegan, 1979.

———. *Theodore Rex*. New York: Random House, 2001.

Morris, Margaret. *My Galsworthy Story*. London: Peter Owen, 1967.

Murray, Nicholas. *Aldous Huxley: A Biography*. New York: Macmillan, 2003.

Nasaw, David. *The Chief: The Life of William Randolph Hearst*. Boston: Houghton Mifflin, 2000.

Needham, Joseph. *Science and Civilisation in China*, vol. 4: *Physics and Physical Technology, Part 3: Civil Engineering and Nautics*. Cambridge: Cambridge University Press, 1971.

Nicolson, Harold. *Letters and Diaries, 1930-1939*. New York: Atheneum, 1966.

Nicolson, Nigel. *Portrait of a Marriage*. New York: Atheneum, 1973.

———, editor. *Vita and Harold: The Letters of Vita Sackville-West and Harold Nicholson*. New York: G. P. Putnam's Sons, 1992.

Nin, Anaïs. *The Diaries of Anaïs Nin*, vol. 3: *1939–1944*. New York: Harcourt, Brace and World, 1969.

Niven, Penelope. *Carl Sandburg: A Biography*. New York: Charles Scribner's Sons, 1991.

Noyes, Alfred. *The Book of Earth*. New York: Frederick A. Stokes, 1925.

———. *Watchers of the Sky*. New York: Frederick A. Stokes, 1922.

Osterbrock, Donald E. *Pauper and Prince: Ritchey, Hale, and Big American Telescopes*. Tucson: University of Arizona Press, 1993.

Owen, Gordon R. *The Two Alberts: Fountain and Fall*. Las Cruces, NM: Yucca Tree Press, 2006.

Pinnell, Eathan Allen. *The Diary of Captain Eathan Allen Pinnell*. Edited by Michael E. Banasik. Iowa City: Camp Pope Bookshop, 1999.

Powell, John Wesley. *The Exploration of the Colorado River and Its Canyons*. New York: Viking Penguin, 1987.

Priestley, J. B. *Bright Day*. London: William Heinnemann, 1946.

———. *Essays of Five Decades*. Boston: Little, Brown and Company, 1968.

———. *Man and Time*. New York: Dell, 1968.

———. *Margin Released*. London: Heron Books, 1962.

———. *Midnight on the Desert: Being an Excursion into Autobiography During a Winter in America, 1935–36*. New York: Harper and Brothers, 1937.

———. *Rain Upon Godshill: A Further Chapter in Autobiography*. New York: Harper and Brothers, 1939.

———. *They Walk in the City*. New York: Harper and Brothers, 1936.

Primeau, Ronald. *Beyond Spoon River: The Legacy of Edgar Lee Masters*. Austin: University of Texas Press, 1981.

Procter, Ben H. *William Randolph Hearst: The Early Years, 1863–1910*. New York: Oxford University Press, 1998.

———. *William Randolph Hearst: The Later Years, 1911–1951*. New York: Oxford University Press, 2007.

Raitt, Suzanne. *Vita and Virginia: The Work and Friendship of V. Sackville-West and Virginia Woolf*. Oxford: Clarendon, 1993.

Renehan, Edward. *John Burroughs: An American Naturalist*. Hensonville, NY: Black Dome Press, 1998.

Roosevelt, Theodore. *A Book Lover's Holiday in the Open*. New York: Charles Scribner's Sons, 1919.

Rosa, Joseph G. *Wild Bill Hickok: The Man and His Myth*. Lawrence: University Press of Kansas, 1996.

Russell, Francis. *The Shadow of Blooming Grove: Warren G. Harding in His Times*. New York: McGraw Hill, 1968.

Russell, Herbert K. *Edgar Lee Masters: A Biography*. Urbana: University of Illinois Press, 2001.

Sackville-West, Vita. *Grand Canyon*. New York: Doubleday, Doran, and Company, 1942.

Sandburg, Carl. *The Complete Poems of Carl Sandburg*. New York: Harcourt Brace Jovanovich, 1970.

———. *The Movies Are: Carl Sandburg's Film Reviews and Essays, 1920-1928*. Edited by Arne Bernstein. Chicago: Lake Claremont, 2000.

Santa Fe Railway. *The Grand Canyon of Arizona*. Chicago: Santa Fe Railway, 1902.

Sauter, Rudolf. *Galsworthy the Man: An Intimate Portrait*. London: Peter Owen, 1967.

Schlesinger, Arthur, Jr. *The Coming of the New Deal.* Boston: Houghton Mifflin, 1958.

Schullery, Paul. *The Grand Canyon: Early Impressions.* Boulder: Pruett, 1989.

Shanklin, Robert. *Steve Mather of the National Parks.* New York: Alfred A. Knopf, 1951.

Standish, David. *The Hollow Earth: The Long and Curious History of Imagining Lands, Fantastic Creatures, Advanced Civilizations, and Marvelous Machines Below Earth's Surface.* Cambridge: Da Capo Press, 2007.

Stegner, Wallace. *Beyond the Hundredth Meridian: John Wesley Powell and the Second Opening of the West.* Boston: Houghton Mifflin, 1953.

Steinbeck, Thomas. *In the Shadow of the Cypress.* New York: Gallery Books, 2010.

Sterling, George. *Sonnets to Craig.* New York: Viking Press, 1928.

Stevens, Michael. *V. Sackville-West: A Critical Biography.* New York: Charles Scribner's Sons, 1974.

Stratton, David H. *Tempest Over Teapot Dome: The Story of Albert B. Fall.* Norman: University of Oklahoma Press, 1998.

Style, Lyle E. *Ain't Got No Cigarettes: Memories of Music Legend Roger Miller.* Winnipeg: Great Plains, 2005.

Swain, Donald C. *Wilderness Defender: Horace M. Albright and Conservation.* Chicago: University of Chicago Press, 1970.

Swanberg, W. A. *Citizen Hearst: A Biography of William Randolph Hearst.* New York: Charles Scribner's Sons, 1961.

Trani, Eugene P., and David L. Wilson. *The Presidency of Warren G. Harding.* Lawrence: Regents Press of Kansas, 1977.

Trimble, Marshall. *In Old Arizona: True Tales of the Wild Frontier!* Phoenix: Golden West, 1986.

Van Dyke, Henry. *The Grand Canyon and Other Poems.* New York: Charles Scribner's Sons, 1914.

Van Dyke, John C. *The Desert: Further Studies in Natural Appearances.* Baltimore: Johns Hopkins University Press, 1999.

———. *The Grand Canyon of the Colorado.* New York: Charles Scribner's Sons, 1927.

Verkamp, Margaret M. *History of Grand Canyon National Park.* Flagstaff, AZ: Grand Canyon Pioneers Society, 1993.

Vining, Edward P. *An Inglorious Columbus: or Evidence that Hwui Shan and a Party of Buddhist Monks from Afghanistan Discovered America in the Fifth Century AD.* New York: D. Appleton and Co., 1885.

Warner, Charles Dudley. *Our Italy.* New York: Harper and Brothers, 1891.

Waters, Frank. *The Book of the Hopi.* New York: Viking Penguin, 1963.

Watkins, T. H. *Righteous Pilgrim: The Life and Times of Harold L. Ickes, 1874–1952.* New York: Henry Holt and Co., 1990.

Watson, Sara Ruth. *V. Sackville-West.* New York: Twayne, 1972.

Wilhelms, Don E. *To a Rocky Moon: A Geologist's History of Lunar Exploration.* Tucson: University of Arizona Press, 1993.

Williams, Ellen. *Harriet Monroe and the Poetry Renaissance: The First Ten Years of Poetry 1912–1922.* Urbana: University of Illinois Press, 1977.

Williams, S. Wells. *Notices of Fu-sang and Other Countries Lying East of China*. New Haven: Tuttle, Morehouse, and Taylor, 1881.

Willis, J. H., Jr. *Leonard and Virginia Woolf as Publishers: The Hogarth Press, 1917–41*. Charlottesville: University Press of Virginia, 1992.

Winslow, Kathryn. *Henry Miller: Full of Life*. Los Angeles: Jeremy P. Tarcher, 1986.

Worden, Al. *Falling to Earth: An Apollo 15 Astronaut's Journey to the Moon*. Washington, D.C.: Smithsonian Books, 2011.

Worster, Donald. *A Passion for Nature: The Life of John Muir*. New York: Oxford University Press, 2008.

Wright, Helen. *Explorer of the Universe: A Biography of George Ellery Hale*. Melville: American Institute of Physics, 1994.

Zarley, Joel. *The Shadow of Isis*. Columbus: Purple Palm Press, 2011.

PERMISSIONS

Excerpt from *Carrying the Fire: An Astronaut's Journey* by Michael Collins. Copyright © 1974 by Michael Collins. Reprinted by permission of Farrar, Straus and Giroux, LLC.

Excerpts from *Across Spoon River* by Edgar Lee Masters. Copyright © 1936, published by Holt, Rinehart, and Winston. Reprinted courtesy of Hillary Masters.

Excerpts from *Invisible Landscapes* by Edgar Lee Masters. Copyright © 1935, published by Macmillan. Reprinted courtesy of Hillary Masters.

Excerpt from *The Air-Conditioned Nightmare* by Henry Miller. Copyright © 1945 by New Directions Publishing Corp. Reprinted by permission of New Directions Publishing Corp.

Excerpt from *Tropic of Cancer* by Henry Miller. Copyright © 1961 by Grove Press, Inc. Used by permission of Grove/Atlantic, Inc.

Excerpt from *The Chief: The Life of William Randolph Hearst* by David Nasaw. Reprinted by permission of Houghton Mifflin Harcourt Publishing Company. All rights reserved.

Excerpt from *The Diary of Anaïs Nin, Volume Three: 1939<n>1944*. Copyright © 1969 by Anaïs Nin and renewed Rupert Pole and Gunther Stuhlmann. Reprinted by permission of Houghton Mifflin Harcourt Publishing Company. All rights reserved.

Excerpts from *Grand Canyon* by Vita Sackville-West. Copyright © 1942 by Vita Sackville-West. Reproduced with permission of Curtis Brown Group Ltd, London, on behalf of the Estate of Vita Sackville-West.

Excerpts from "Many Hats" from *The Complete Poems of Carl Sandburg*, revised and expanded edition. Copyright © 1969, 1970 by Lilian Steichen Sandburg, trustee. Reprinted by permission of Houghton Mifflin Harcourt Publishing Company. All rights reserved.

INDEX

Numbers in *italics* refer to photographs